Christian Ambivalence
Toward Its Old Testament

# Christian Ambivalence Toward Its Old Testament

*Interactive Creativity* versus *Static Obedience*

ALEXANDER BLAIR

WIPF & STOCK • Eugene, Oregon

CHRISTIAN AMBIVALENCE TOWARD ITS OLD TESTAMENT
Interactive Creativity versus Static Obedience

Copyright © 2011 Alexander Blair. All rights reserved. Except for brief quotations in critical publications or reviews, no part of this book may be reproduced in any manner without prior written permission from the publisher. Write: Permissions, Wipf and Stock Publishers, 199 W. 8th Ave., Suite 3, Eugene, OR 97401.

Wipf & Stock
An Imprint of Wipf and Stock Publishers
199 W. 8th Ave., Suite 3
Eugene, OR 97401
www.wipfandstock.com

ISBN 13: 978-1-60899-106-8

Manufactured in the U.S.A.

*If they do not listen to Moses and the prophets,*
*neither will they be convinced even if someone rises from the dead.*
*Luke 16:31*

# Contents

*Preface* ix

*Acknowledgements* xv

*Abbreviations* xvi

1  The Source of the Ambivalence: Three Abstract Orientations; Three Historical Movements  1

2  The New Testament I: Continuity with the Old Testament  73

3  The New Testament II: Discontinuity with the Old Testament  114

4  A Millennium of Neo-Platonic Theology: Allegorizing Interpretation of Both Testaments  161

5  Forty Years of Corporate Orientation in New England: A New Society Requires an Old Testament  206

6  The Modern Perspective: Explicit Rejection of the Old Testament  223

7  The Communal Orientation: First Western Corporate Understanding of Scripture  257

8  Contemporary Perennial Theological Systems  301

9  Contemporary Modern Theological Systems  322

10  Contemporary Communal Theological Systems  349

*Bibliography* 387

# Preface

THE TORAH AND PROPHETS, Israel's tradition, *presuppose* that human community survival requires human interaction among its members and with nature; that is, survival requires a culture, a civilization. The Torah and Prophets then *call, invite,* that human community to generate its culture through mutually creative multi-way interactions, so that each individual's individuality contributes to the continuous, joint, complementary, *interactive creation* of a common communal life. Such a delegation of joint responsibility for creating cultural order, for creating "truth," is inconceivable within the classical Graeco-Roman cultural world, for which truth is fixed, and each person is separately responsible for carrying out that person's pre-assigned social role.

When the Graeco-Roman European world took colonial control of the Middle East in the third century BCE, it set about "civilizing" its new empire; that is, imposing its western orientation of control "from above." Judea found itself torn between its continuing Israelite cultural orientation among its common people and a Hellenistic-leaning reinterpretation of that tradition by a Judean establishment serving at the pleasure of the occupying European power. Jesus of Nazareth was a leader working "from below" among the common people to maintain the tradition of Torah and Prophets against the leaders' collaboration with the occupiers' cultural Europeanization program. His disciples produced a body of tradition (eventually called "New Testament" after Jeremiah 31:31, which in its own age was a call for reform from top-down monarchic control back to interactively created social order) using the Hebrew Scriptures, the Torah, Prophets, and Writings, to urge maintenance of Israel's tradition of distributed creative interactive control against corroding influence from both self-interest and the imposed European ideology of a pre-determined right and wrong.

Following the traditional emphasis of Israel as Servant to the nations as, for example, the success of Moses and the Exodus returnees to Canaan in bringing much of the existing Canaanite population into inclusion in Israel, this new reform movement worked from the now large Jewish dispersion to bring the Mediterranean world into inclusion (unfortunately, thus widening their isolation from Israel's colonial leadership). By the fourth century, this separated Christian movement grew to acquire official status in Europe under the emperor Constantine. Its Hebrew Scriptures, without which the Christian movement's New Testament program to reform European culture according to the Hebrew tradition would be unintelligible, acquired canonical status in the European world under the name "Old Testament."

How would the Western world react to this counter invasion from below by what, especially for its leaders, was an inconvenient call for community-wide responsibility for creating truth? How would the European world handle an invasion of a canonically authoritative Scripture that calls to a way of life that is nearly diametrically opposed to its commitment scheme, its metaphysics, ontology, ethics, social institutions, and individual psyches? Could this cultural invasion even express in Indo-European languages a call too culturally foreign to have a name? Or would the call be reinterpreted to fit reality as the West already understood it? This issue is the subject of the present book.

The biblical and western positions cannot be compared unless the comparer can characterize each of them. The Western world has had two thousand years experience not recognizing the difference between the two orientations. Is it possible, in a spirit of academic neutrality, to "compare and contrast" Christianity's non-Western canonical scriptures with their European interpretation, or does the word "academic" limit us to Western ontology, to Scripture's Western interpretation, and not its intended program as expressed within its own culture?

Chapter 1 attempts to characterize the difference between the two orientations without using biblical material whose figurative language would first require interpretation. This chapter endeavors to describe both orientations with the most literal language possible. And, since writer and readers are Western, the task is attempted in chapter 1 in the strictest Western manner: first *abstractly*; then by narrating two *historical examples*; then with two present-day secular Western philosophies. The modern philosophies are of two varieties: a current Western modification of classical Greek essentialism and an emerging Western secular anti-essentialist philosophy of interactive human relations that is philosophically similar to the biblical cultural orientation. Substantial justification as to this similarity will be presented in chapter 2.

Displaying two alternative perspectives is, of course, not the same as insisting on one of them. Rather, the academic claim here will be that the two are irreconcilably contradictory, that one cannot consistently assert both. Ironically, the philosophy that does *not* ask for "fundamentalist" automatic acceptance is the anti-essentialist biblical perspective. It does not describe reality as an unchanging *a priori* truth to be *learned* but, rather, *invites* the community to interact *jointly* and *continuously* to *construct* an interacting, hence constantly changing, community structure, tradition, and truth.

The introduction of these two alternative possibilities into human culture, clarified in chapter 1, is key for the history of Western interpretation of the Bible offered in the remaining chapters. The study of this history will be attempted independently of presuppositions peculiar to either alternative, relying only on methods compatible with both, such as the analysis of language.

Chapter 2 begins the history of Christian interpretation of the Old Testament with the interpretation made by the earliest Christian document, the New Testament. Comparison of the results from studies in 1953 by biblical scholars C. H. Dodd and Rudolf Bultmann on the relation between the testaments reveals a continuous use by the New of the Old to interpret its described new events in a way visible to Dodd's interactive orientation. It is, however, structurally masked from view by Bultmann's modern-existentialist orientation.

Chapter 3 analyzes the Jewish apocalyptic literary tradition flourishing in those parts of the Bible that defend against Western cultural influence, the third division of the Old Testament and the whole of the New. The apocalyptic tradition looked toward a future salvation from individualistic Western cultural oppression in an effort to renew Israel's interactive community responsibility for creating its culture, and to the extension of this responsibility as a "light to the nations" (Isa 42:6 = Luke 2:32) by spreading this creative interactive tradition through which "all the families of the earth shall be blessed" (Gen 12:3 = Gal 3:8), a tradition then being directed to the Mediterranean world through the Jewish dispersion.

Chapters 4 and 8 describe a conversion not of the West by the biblical tradition but of a masking of biblical meanings by a cultural limitation in Western conceptuality. Western theologians interpreted that figurative socially interactive biblical language not metonymically, interactively, as intended, but rather allegorically, abstractly, to make it fit the continuing non-interactive classical Western middle-Platonic and neo-Platonic philosophical positions, inaugurally in the programs of Origen, Augustine, Aquinas, and Luther, and continuing in those of twentieth-century Rahner and Tillich.

Chapter 5 describes a brief forty years of interactive community solidarity in early puritan New England necessary for this small isolated community's physical survival, evidenced by a brief shift in preaching emphasis from that described in chapter 4 to metonymic use of Old Testament calls for responsible creative internal interaction by all.

Chapters 6 and 9 trace the continuation of the West's domesticated Christianity into the even more literal-minded Enlightenment period. This period replaced allegorical interpretation of both testaments with rejection of the Old and interpretation of the New as empirical psychological order in Schleiermacher, or existentialist absence of order in Bultmann, each replacing pre-Enlightenment *a priori* order. Both explicitly reject the Old Testament, thus making explicit the earlier tacit Western assumption that Christianity is a new religion conforming sensibly to the Western understanding of truth as independent of culture.

Chapters 7 and 10 recount a post-Enlightenment theological rediscovery of the community-created order so central in Scripture and still persisting below systematic theology's line of sight until recently in pre-urban small towns hearing scriptural narrative and participating in liturgy. This discovery was enabled for theologians by the new anti-essentialist Western philosophy of internal relations distinguished in chapter 1. Pioneers were church historians Möhler and Newman in the nineteenth century, and biblical scholars Dodd and Eichrodt and theologians Metz, Gutiérrez, and Chauvet in the twentieth.

This book thus offers an outline history of Western Christian theology over its two millennia, but one not undertaken within the European cultural tradition but from a neutral position aware of the difference between the biblical and European cultural orientations.

The Old Testament itself is never treated systematically (except for the one systematic passage, Genesis 1), as systematic treatment misses its meaning. The Old Testament was written as a history of its own community life as tool for subsequent metonymic "learning by one's mistakes." The present book's subtitle implies the question, "Can Christianity understand its New Testament?" The answer is: before 1832 peasants could, theologians couldn't; after 1832 some theologians can, middle-class consumers can't, politicians don't want to, Africans and *mestizo* Latin-Americans implicitly always did.

# Acknowledgements

THE AUTHOR WISHES TO acknowledge three communities outside Indo-European culture: Navaho, *mestizo* Latin American, and African West Indian, to which he was sent as "missionary" only to find each of them already several times more "Christian" than he. He also thanks three North-American minority communities where he served as pastor, and four decades of students who eagerly argued philosophical, sociological, or theological issues coming out of their various class and ethnic backgrounds.

This work would not exist without academic associates who read and challenged early parts of it during its slow academic construction: Doug Adams, Julian Boyd, Norman Gottwald, Edward Hobbs, John Mbishibishi, James McClendon, Don Morgan, Ted Peters, Andrew Porter, David Stagaman. Those who disagreed with it helped most.

In 1968 I quizzed an introduction-to-philosophy class, "Pick and describe one of the three historical solutions to the mind-body problem." When I pointed out to a very protected young student that she had melded all three solutions into one jumble, a look of amazement began to come into her eyes and she said, "You mean there's more than one answer to the same question?"

# Abbreviations

| | |
|---|---|
| AAR | American Academy of Religion |
| AJT | *American Journal of Theology* |
| BA | *Biblical Archaeologist* |
| CBQ | *Catholic Biblical Quarterly* |
| CHB | *Cambridge History of the Bible* |
| FOTC | *The Fathers of the Church* |
| HTR | *Harvard Theological Review* |
| JAAR | *Journal of the American Academy of Religion* |
| JSOT | *Journal for the Study of the Old Testament* |
| JTC | *Journal for Theology and the Church* |
| LXX | Septuagint version of the Old Testament |
| NPNF | Schaff, Philip. *The Nicene and Post-Nicene Fathers* |
| NRSV | New Revised Standard Version |
| PG | Migne, J. P. *Patrologiae Cursus Completus, Series Graeca* |
| SBL | Society of Biblical Literature |
| ThLZ | *Theologische Literaturzeitung* |
| WA | Luther, Martin. *D. Martin Luthers Werke. Kritische Gesammtausgabe* |
| ZAW | *Zeitschrift für die alttestamentliche Wissenschaft* |
| ZThK | *Zeitschrift für Theologie und Kirche* |

1

# The Source of the Ambivalence

*Three Abstract Orientations; Three Historical Movements*

THE CHRISTIAN MOVEMENT IN the Indo-European West has viewed its Old Testament in two ways. At times it appears as central to the faith, the larger part of the written word of God, a recounting of half the history of God's people, and the delineation of the incarnation of Christ before the event. At other times it appears as the history of an ancient ethnic tribal alliance, riddled with violence, confusing church and state, insufficiently universal, and without comfort for individuals now emancipated from oppressive primitive cultures.

The *basic thesis* of this book is that such Christian ambivalence toward the Old Testament, characteristic of the Christian movement since its introduction into the West in the first century, reflects two interacting basic ambivalences at the core of Western civilization itself: an ambivalence between concern for self and interest in others and an ambivalence between wanting to be in control and wanting to be told what to do. The Old Testament asks for interest in others and for interactive shared control. Western culture has been more interested in self, and that self has moved through time from an earlier acceptance of being told what to do to a more recent manipulation into it.

In this first chapter these historical orientations are laid out, first abstractly so as to be available for analyzing any historical period, and then concretely through examples of their incarnations in secular Western history. This method provides the foundation for the nine remaining chapters to trace the history of the West's struggle with biblical positions introduced into it by the Jewish dispersion through its soon to be separated component, the Christian movement.

## I ABSTRACT CLASSIFICATION OF SOCIAL STRUCTURES INTO THREE TYPES

How do the human individual and the human community relate? Often the two are seen as in tension when it comes to their relative importance. But the concept of the individual, the indivisible one, the smallest unit in the analysis of humanity, implies a larger divisible unit to which it belongs. And conversely, the concept of community, "com-unity," a gathering into unity of smaller components, implies that smaller units are brought together. The concepts of individual and community are not opposed to each other; each requires the other for its meaning. Individuals belong to communities, and communities are made up of individuals.

How human individuals belong to human communities involves two issues: (1) how the individuals are related to one another and (2) who or what determines these relations.

(1) The first issue: how the members *relate* (the structure relating the individual members as a community), is normally a mixture in various proportions of two ideal types, called *generic* and *organic*.

To relate *generically* is to relate as similars—doing similar things—such as: a community using the same language, or farm workers hoeing in parallel rows, or teachers teaching separate first grade classes using the same teaching method. Some similarities are independent of the interactors' choice, such as several persons having the same eye color. Examples in philosophical literature of advocation of generic relation include Immanuel Kant's "categorical imperative": "So act that the maxim of your will could always hold at the same time as a principle establishing universal law"[1] and from Jean-Paul Sartre: "To choose to be this or that is to affirm at the same time the value of what we choose . . . . The image is valid for everybody . . . . In choosing myself, I choose man."[2]

To relate *organically*, on the other hand, is to relate by performing complementary, thus different, tasks that are part of the same project: a kitchen crew preparing dinner for the field workers coming in at dusk, or a teacher having a class learn by interacting with teacher and one another. Distinct individuals or groups interact with one another with complementary roles; they are not alike and do not do the same things as, for example, in the complementary roles of voter, legislator, police

---

1. Kant, *Critique of Practical Reason*, 30.
2. Sartre, *Existentialism*, 20–21.

officer, prisoner, prosecuting attorney, defense attorney, judge, and jury member. Most communities are not purely generic or organic but have mixed generic and organic relations as, for example, twelve jurors listening together generically during testimony, then retiring to reach a verdict through organic interaction among themselves. Plato (427–347 BCE) in *The Republic* proposes three social classes: philosopher-rulers, soldiers, and productive workers, in complementary organic relation with one another. Each class makes a different contribution to the whole; the community relies on useful differences among the classes. But the members within each class relate generically; each member performs the functions pre-assigned to its class.

(2) *The source* of the community structure is the other issue. A structure, be it generic or organic, is called cosmological if it is *imposed from outside* the whole human community and its physical environment. A chief example is the mixed organic-generic class structure in Plato's *Republic* in which the community has, or "participates in," a timeless *a priori* "cosmic" order. Individuals, separately or together, cannot modify their social class assignments. Membership in the philosopher, soldier, or worker class is an intrinsic part of what the philosopher, soldier, or worker *is*—part of its cosmically imposed essence. The member can vary only in how well it conforms to this assigned fixed essence. Cosmological order is eternal. It does not change over time.

A community structure is called anthropological if it is determined, within physical environmental limits, by voluntary choices of some human agency within it, be it a single despot, an oligarchy, or the interacting intentional individual choices of all its members, with possible interaction with nature or voluntary interaction with some intelligent agency outside the community. Since control is an organic relation between controllers and those controlled, an anthropologically controlled community possesses at least the organic relation of control (unlike cosmological communities, organic or not, which are controlled from outside).

Among anthropologically controlled communities, I call *corporate* those whose anthropological control is distributed so as to give *every member* a significant intentional interactive part in the control. The continuing contributions each member chooses to make to community interaction permit and invite responding complementary contributions from others—for example, asking someone a question or putting something up for sale. Each member acts, initiating or responding, by choice among the possibilities offered at that point by the total context, communal and inanimate. Such choices change the context within which others can act in turn, thus limiting some possibilities and opening others. These changes, however, do not dominate any others by removing all future choice for creative intentional contribution. Thus the relational structure of the corporate community develops continuously, created by and consisting of the members' interaction. A member can increase the space for others' interaction only by actively entering the field, thus also closing off some of the other's choices. But the other is thus further enabled to *inter*act, learning to accept the limitations of contexts that also offer opportunity for creative participation. The group has authority and sufficient freedom to create, within natural limits, its own structure and goals, to create its *world*. The structure thus created may include some predominantly generic elements, such as a common language that facilitates the group's corporate interaction, but every individual retains an organic relation with the others as co-creator of community order. As said, influence from outside the community, such as from a god, another community, or a larger including community, is not excluded.

The corporate orientation thus contradicts the cosmological one as to *fact*, recognizing no total *a priori* control. It also differs as to *goal*, building significant intentional interactive participation by every member in the creation of its structure with many possible optimum outcomes rather than just one cosmically assigned one. It gives all its members more responsibility, more independence, more interdependence, and more significance.

In any community, the *essence* of each member—what the member *is*—is determined by the community's source of order. Assigned essences are fixed, like emperor, soldier, or farmer in Plato's *Republic*. But essences change in communities with changing control. In corporate communities the essence of a member is constantly created and changed by the continuous intentional interaction between that member and others who are also interacting with still others and thus changing. Examples include being proposed to as *spouse*, offered admission as college *student*, or interacted with by some as a *friend*. Thus, a member's essence develops as it interacts within the social structure: its essence *is* its constantly changing collection of current roles, along with skills and motivations from earlier roles, in community interaction. Yet each individual retains continuity as the same person.

An *intrinsic* or *internal* relation with another is a relation that affects one's essence, who one is. A *bilaterally* internal relation is a relation that changes the essences of both interactors: marriage changes two singles into a wife and a husband. In a cosmologically structured community, generic or organic, there is only monolateral intrinsic relation with cosmic order. No other internal relation exists. In a corporately interacting community, each member is directly bilaterally internally related with some others and they with others so that all members are indirectly multilaterally internally related with all. None are totally dominated.

Thus, in this study the term "corporate" describes a *community interacting under distributed control by its members through intentional multilaterally internal, essence-creating relations among all members acting as principals*. There is no word in English, or Western languages generally, for precisely this concept. We use "corporate" for it, chosen from candidates that require the smallest modification of their common English meaning. In this context, "corporate" distinguishes *creative complementary interaction* from other more legalistically- or more individually-controlled relations.

The Old Testament, and the non-Western Semitic culture within which it was produced, were corporately oriented—as much of the third world has been since pre-history. Most of the Old Testament took the corporate position for granted, urging a shared human control against those trying to control unilaterally. But the Priestly school, the last contributors to the Torah and Prophets, faced the rising threat of Indo-European cosmologically oriented cultures by inserting an explicit literal claim for the corporate orientation at the epic's beginning, the creation of humanity, Gen 1:27–28:

> God created humankind/*adam* [this choice of English words is offered by this New Revised Standard Version (NRSV) translation; I would prefer not "human*kind*," a generic collection of similars but the internally interacting one human community אדם, *adam*] in his image, in the image of God he created them/*him* [this English pronoun should be *it* to agree with its singular antecedent *adam*, a Hebrew common noun with no plural]; male and female he created them [here *them*, the community *adam*'s members, contrasts correctly with our earlier singular *it*]. . . .

And God said to them, "Be fruitful and multiply . . . and have dominion . . . over every living thing."

Thus, the human community *adam* is "in his image" and is given "dominion"; that is, *adam* is given both ability and authority to interact with him, one another, and nature. And this "image of God," attributed to the community rather than its separate members, has *diversity*, *complementarity*, and *creativity*. Male and female provide a paradigmatic case in that progeny-dependent economy for *dissimilar* but *complementary* partners who are able to *create* what *similar* partners could not. Each individual participates creatively in its interactive social world. "Salvation" is not of individuals separately, it is of the community through the creative interaction of its members. Salvation is *of the community*; individuals participate in it precisely as *interactive participants* in their community's ongoing interactive creation.

The epic continues with the half-millennium earlier and less literal, but equally metonymy-relating, Jahwist source: "for Adam there was not found a helper as his partner" (Gen 2:20); with *adam*, מרא, human community, in whole-for-part metonymy (specifically, synecdoche, an interactively relating figurative meaning) for *ish* (איש, male person) to prepare for figurative use of *ish* and *ishshah*, the equally interacting "first family," as part-for-whole metonymy for the human community in dramatic creative interaction, moving from dysfunction to reconciliation among its members and thus also with its God.

The non-corporately oriented West, weak on internal interaction, misreads Scripture's continuously used *interacting metonymy* as *static metaphor*. The West readily understands the *metaphor* "the ship plows the sea" as a static analogy between a ship figuratively "plowing" the sea and a plow literally plowing the ground, a B as to D relation is *abstractly analogous* to an A as to C relation. Stating the analogy does not seek to *change* anything. The bumper sticker "No Viet Nam war in Central America" shortly after the end of the Viet Nam war sought to *change something*, the mining of the Nicaraguan harbor by the United States. It was a metonymy: B *relates* with C as A does. The metonymy seeks to use a past bad choice to *change* a pending one—an essence-changing thus *intrinsic* relation.

So the community, not the individual, is in God's image. Individuals who try "to be like gods" (Gen 3:5) by seeking individual propitiation for unilaterally bestowed offerings as with the Palestinian agricultural gods, will retreat to "dust," to isolation from community interaction as they were before birth: "you are dust and to dust you shall return" (Gen 3:19c), a metonym for the fall of humanity from multilaterally internal interaction. Lastly, God explicitly delegates "dominion"—community responsibility for creating a *social structure*, tradition, *torah*, "law" within which creative human multilaterally internal interaction can take place. Throughout this study we will see this Old Testament fourfold-claim that God shares creativity and control with humanity, a sharing directly disallowed in the West by several variations on Platonic control, and later by empirical control by nature.

Sustaining all but the most trivial interaction among members of a community, whether imposed or self-created, requires a structure—an order, tradition, law, civilization, culture—as vehicle for its interaction. The cosmological view holds that such a structure, the *logos*, is unchanging and provided in advance. By contrast, a corporate community builds its interactive structure continuously using the structure thus far established. A corporate structure changes as it develops; but to remain corporate, the rate of change must respect a need for sufficient stability to be continuously learned, accepted, and creatively participated in by the members. For example, there could be no conveying of information without a continuing minimal community commitment to truth-telling and a reasonably stable community language to tell it in. Platonism holds that each member is born with a microcosmic mental copy of unchanging cosmic order, including all concepts and truths ready to be expressed in words and statements and then obeyed. In contrast, a corporate community's language and other symbolic structures so necessary for its creative interaction are created by, reflect, assist, and are part of that interaction. Such an origin of community structure is obvious in a corporately oriented culture; it was stated three millennia ago by Israel in language-for-culture metonymy at Gen 2:19: "whatever the man [האדם, *ha adam*, the human *community*] called every living creature, that was its name."

Corporately interacting communities also need *presiding* roles, roles not as rulers but as delegated interactive coordinators of ongoing community construction of its social structures.

In any community the amount of order can vary from total compulsion to total disorder. One extreme features a blind obedience of slaves; a middle range features a communally created structure sufficient for corporate creative interaction; and the other extreme features complete autonomy for each self, in which case there would no longer be any community. The nominal form of government does not denote the featured type of community. An absolute monarch could choose to preside in a way that makes a community corporate—the Genesis passage above suggests this for its God. And a democracy wherein everyone votes in self interest (as with the philosopher Thomas Hobbes, page 18 below) would quickly become an oligarchy of the few who have the most effective "sales spin."

Because there are indefinitely many possible social structures created by and then dependent on continuing creative interaction, the goal of improving interaction can be realized in many only vaguely comparable ways. And one cannot predict precisely the overall effect of an act since in each of the resulting series of successive reactions spreading in the community, each successive reacting individual has a choice how to react. Hence the exact comparison of the effectiveness of several proposals for increasing creative interaction is multiply impossible. There is no "perfect" behavior. But a corporate community recognizing no *a priori* Forms incompatible with essence-changing internal relations has chosen instead a "meta-Form," a goal of maintaining and developing an interactive structure that encourages creative essence-changing participation by everyone. This goal will be reached with varying degrees of success.

Ethics in a corporate context differs from ethics in cosmological and non-corporate anthropological contexts. Ethical systems assign responsibility to individuals for choosing among possible *acts*. In a cosmological orientation one's choice is predetermined by or, less strictly, prescribed by one's cosmological Form. The *end* of an act (what is to be accomplished) and the *means* (the way to accomplish it) are identical, conformity to the norm. But in corporate interaction one acts strategically to encourage continuing unfolding multilaterally creative interactive response from all those involved, present and future. The end is distinct from the means. Such an end involves considering all consequences of an act, including those beyond the originally presented issue.

Non-indigenous sub-communities may relate to the whole more or less corporately; that is, may have roles either creatively interactive, antagonistic, or non-relational with the community as a whole. If some sub-communities contribute less interactively, then the overall community is less corporate. A corporate society is pluralistic; it looks forward to distinctive creative interactive contributions not only from individuals but from subgroups.

Both naturally and socially constructed worlds need some minimal generic similarity as platform for creative interaction. Natural sexual procreation requires members of the *same* species but *different* sex. Similarly, social interaction requires a *common* language for interaction of *distinct* speaker and hearer. Noam Chomsky (below, page 55) analyzes the grammatical *structure* of language while Ludwig Wittgenstein (page 47) analyzes its *use*.

Communities persist through time, and present members are related to past and future members as well as current ones—a community has a *diachronic* dimension as well as a *synchronic* one. A corporate community acts within an interaction among its inherited past structures, current circumstances, and its own intentions for the future. In contrast, Enlightenment *critical history* describes past events objectively and empirically, intentionally ignoring any interactive relation with either that past or the historian's present cultural context. But a history taking a community's past actions as a source helpful in deciding how to act in the present to further future goals, accepts a corporate, interactive relation among the three. This issue is developed on page 30 below.

Epistemology, the study of knowing, comes in generic and corporate versions. In the generic view, facts are objective; they are independent of their being known. But, in the corporate view, "knowing" may include interacting creatively with the thing known in order to accomplish a corporately realizable result. This does not require the knower and known to "know" the same thing theoretically or apply the same principles practically. For example, my cat and I recognize and *know* each other, we interact creatively even though we do not speak, think, or act in the same way. We enjoy a *corporate intersubjectivity* but very little *generic intersubjectivity*. My cat and I know some things about each other, but this is only a small contributing part of knowing each other. Knowing, as interacting, is basically a doing (practical reason), with knowing about (theoretical reason) an abstraction useful in the doing.[3] Gen 4:1 explicitly expresses corporate knowing, "Now the man knew his wife Eve, and she conceived and bore Cain." The generic view separates

---

3. Some sympathetic with the corporate orientation refuse this extension of meaning, e.g., Rorty, *Philosophy and the Mirror of Nature*, 356. Yet Rorty, and Kant (page 16), concede that knowing is a relation of the object to the subject.

theoretical and practical reason; the corporate view treats the first as a component of the second.

In addition to the cosmological and anthropological orientations, two other orientations have appeared—both isolating the individual from relation with community. The first orientation strives to merge the individual so completely with the cosmos, the "all," that individual identity is lost in mysticism. The second urges the single human being to be free of all outside control from cosmos or other human beings, thus enabling the individual to act without need for, or obligation to, anything other than self. This second view will be considered here, and I call it the *self-as-such* orientation. An example is the existentialism of Søren Kierkegaard and his followers. Whereas corporately or generically oriented individuals may choose spouses for complementary or, respectively, similar human relation, individuals who make the *self-as-such* choice strive to become as unrelated as Kierkegaard himself did—he dramatized his existentialist orientation by breaking his high social engagement to Regina Olsen. Some use the English term "individual" to mean "unrelated" as with the translation of Kierkegaard's "hiin Enkelte," the single one, into "the Individual."[4]

Of the three anthropological orientations (generic, corporate, and *self-as-such*), each two share something in common against the third. The self-as-such and generic views agree in seeing one person's individuality as independent of all other persons; whereas, the corporate view finds that person's individuality in its interaction with the other members of its community. The self-as-such and corporate views agree in that they reject cosmological control; whereas the generic view is open to control from outside the community. The generic and corporate views agree in that they are ways of explaining the relation between the individual and the community; whereas, the self-as-such view treats the person independently of any community.

The three anthropological orientations impose different limitations. From the self-as-such view, influencing one's neighbors is in poor taste and is discouraged. The generic view allows one to influence others unilaterally but without change in either's essence. The corporate view encourages creative interaction that changes essences, including those of the interacting ones, such as a parent allowing a child to help in some task. In all of these relations, the two parties offer *different* contributions,

---

4. The original of Kierkegaard's "'The Individual,'" in *Point of View*.

hence the relations are non-symmetrical. For each contribution the relation is "hierarchical" in the sense that the one making the contribution leads with *that* contribution; for example, an expert's role is balanced by the presiding role of the person hiring the expert. A teacher's active attempt to teach is only accomplished if the students respond with active learning.

What is "education" in each orientation? From the generic view, education is the process by which a culture reproduces copies of its more erudite, skillful, or insightful members. From the corporate view, education is the creative interactive practice in applying the corporate cultural tradition to contemporary issues. From the enduring cosmological view, education is bringing to mind already known and unchanging facts and rules. And for the existentialist, education is the provision of a protected environment in which the young can learn to express themselves without being accountable to the constraints of community.

The self-as-such orientation has a practical difficulty maintaining its distinction from the wider generic one because a public philosophical insistence on one person's freedom from social constraints implicitly invites others to imitate, and appropriation by imitation is a generic relation among persons. Kierkegaard himself tried, unsuccessfully, to dodge his paradoxical urging of others not to allow themselves to be urged by offering his position anonymously under the pseudonym Johannes Climacus. He also ate food prepared by others and used the Danish language. Living as a self-as-such outside all community relation denies one the possibility of influencing others. Subsequent chapters describe existentialists like Mary Daly (below, chapter 9.1) who claim their position as cosmological truth, as God's will, and thus find themselves within the cosmological perspective.

In summary, the term "corporate" as used in this study *names a concept substantially missing* until recently in Western academic culture. It refers to a community that allows each member an original intentional active complementary part in the ongoing creation of its culture, thus differing from its ordinary English sense, which is closer to our "organic." The term "individual" is used in this study for a member of *any* community, be it cosmological, generic or corporate. In our terminology, individual and community are not opposed, rather, being an innovative contributor to communal creativity gives the *individual wider importance in the corporate orientation* than in the others. The contrasting terms to "corporate" are "cosmological" or "merely organic" or "generic" or "self-as-such," but not "individual."

Among the social structures abstractly characterized thus far, three (the *cosmological, non-corporate anthropological,* and *corporate anthropological*) will serve as a skeletal philosophical grid for this study's analysis of the history of Western biblical interpretation.

## II THE PERENNIAL HISTORICAL MOVEMENT

The three *abstract orientations* defined above, cosmological, non-corporate anthropological, and corporate anthropological, have been active in the West respectively in *three historical philosophical movements*: the *perennial* throughout Western history, the *modern* over the last four centuries, and the *communal* challenging the West during the last two centuries.

The *perennial philosophy,* the European philosophical system inherited from classical Greece, has the cosmological orientation. In its most characteristic form, Platonism, there is a cosmic order of perfect immaterial unchanging Forms that provide the structure for all imperfect, material, and changeable objects, including human beings. "There is such a thing as Beauty itself, and Goodness, and Greatness. All beautiful things become beautiful through Beauty" (Plato, *Phaedo*, 100). Physical circles drawn by pencil, which can be lopsided and capable of being erased, are only imperfect reflections of the perfectly circular and inerasable Form of Circularity. Human beings are born innately knowing circles because each individual human mind is a microcosm reflecting the order (the structure) of the cosmos. Plato's *Meno* 82–85 describes extracting a proof of the Pythagorean Theorem for isosceles right triangles from an untutored slave. Aristotle (384–322 BCE) moves slightly away: we learn Forms *transcendentally* by seeing things that exhibit them like circular objects in nature, rather than knowing them innately.

Because we begin the history of Christian interpretation of the Old Testament with its earliest instance, that made by the New Testament—with that interpretation in turn to be made by comparing the contrasting results of twentieth century modern and communal scholarly analyses of the New Testament—we delay further treatment of perennial philosophy until chapter 4. There we begin an account of European interpretation of the New Testament, a treatment in terms of the perennially based theologians Augustine, Aquinas, and Luther, who *are* simultaneously also the major Western philosophers between Plotinus' death in 270 and the end of perennial hegemony in the West with Descartes' *Discourse* in 1637.

### III THE MODERN HISTORICAL MOVEMENT

The medieval lord was born into a cosmologically dictated responsibility for managing the well-being of his estate as an organic community. His complement, the serf, was born into working the land for the same purpose. By the Renaissance, the land-holder was responsible only for individual success; he had reduced himself from responsible local sovereign to private owner. A new class of entrepreneurs had arisen, committed to acting in first-person self interest, hence independently of both cosmic order and traditional organic structure. A new philosophy was thus required, an *anthropologically* oriented one eliminating the cosmological control that had held both lord and serf accountable to an organic structure. In its place was an empirical generic analysis of society, a change legitimizing the self-serving interests of the owner. The peasants, with their dependence on a stable organic relation, were now below the line-of-sight of the philosophers, whose privilege as part of the controlling class continued during this change.

I call *modern* this anthropologically oriented generic-leaning philosophy of the Enlightenment, first formalized publicly by Descartes in 1637 and still dominant in the West. It understands knowledge as a property of the individual, as found in the rationalism of Descartes, the empiricism of Hobbes and Hume, the transcendentalism of Kant, the existentialism of Kierkegaard, and the empiricism and logical positivism of the twentieth century.

Resistance to the new perspective by the church, institutionally committed to the perennial perspective, resulted in separation of philosophy from theology at the Enlightenment. Philosophy continued as abstract representation of the basic social commitments of an increasingly secular European culture, while theology now did the same but only for the increasingly disestablished church. The church maintained overall loyalty to the perennial perspective until the appearance in the nineteenth century of explicitly modern theology with Schleiermacher and explicitly communal theology with Möhler (chapters 6, 7 below).

The new epistemology of René Descartes in his *Discourse on the Method of Rightly Conducting the Reason and Seeking Truth in the*

*Sciences* (1637) and his *Meditations on the First Philosophy in which the Existence of God, and the Real Distinction of Mind and Body, are Demonstrated* (1641) is generally taken as the beginning of the modern period in philosophy. Descartes begins his first Meditation with the sentence: "Several years have now elapsed since I first became aware that I had accepted, even from my youth, many false opinions for true, and that consequently what I afterwards based on such principles was highly doubtful; and from that time I was convinced of the necessity of undertaking once in my life to rid myself of all the opinions I had adopted, and of commencing anew the work of building from the foundation, if I desired to establish a firm and abiding superstructure in the sciences." In fact, Descartes called in question all opinion, all he has "received either from or through the senses"[5]—that is, learned directly from the senses or received through them from tradition, and replaced this knowledge, or rather replaced the two methods of observation and dependence on tradition used to obtain it, with a new method, the method of establishing one fact by rational introspection and then giving an "exact demonstration . . . similar to that in use among the geometers"[6] of the other principles of his system. The one fact was *cogito*, "I think," and the principles deduced from it were the existence of the self, the distinction of mind from body, the immortality of the soul, and the existence of God. This position, technically called *rationalism*, asserts that human reason in the individual acting alone is sufficient without reference to sense data, the accumulated cultural tradition, or revelation. It generalizes the method used, since Euclid, in geometry, Descartes's specialty. Descartes, avoiding church censorship with scholastic philosophical terms and honorary inclusion of a merely theoretically existing God, managed to publish a philosophical system not based on cosmological control or organic relations. For this he is recognized as inaugurator of Enlightenment philosophy.

Contemporaneous and subsequent *empiricists*, Thomas Hobbes, John Locke, George Berkeley, and David Hume, working in a less censored English environment, rejected such a rationalist source for knowledge and claimed instead that all knowledge was based on experience through the senses. Hobbes wrote, "For there is no conception in a mans mind, which hath not first, totally, or by parts, been begotten upon the

---

5. Descartes, *Meditations*, 112, 113.
6. Descartes, *Meditations*, "Synopsis of the Six Following Meditations," 108.

organs of Sense,"[7] and this view, stated with increasing sophistication, was basic for the other three empiricists.

Both rationalists and empiricists, despite their differences, were primarily interested in epistemological method (how we know), and the epistemologies of both were based on *first-person* mental processes in the individual. Both positions skirted solipsism.

Descartes's rather formal existence of God was the only one of his principles derived from the *cogito* that moved beyond the first-person. For Berkeley, the existence of God was his sole defense against solipsism. Hume's system did not include the existence of God. Thus, the rationalists and empiricists broke with the medieval cosmological mixed organic-generic perspective and took a strong *anthropological* stand ambiguously situated between the *generic* and *self-as-such* perspectives, generally assuming it to conform to the former. None of them found a use for the organic perspective.

Immanuel Kant's *Critique of Pure Reason* (1781–1787) combined the empiricist observation of sense data with a rationalist disposition to interpret it *transcendentally*; that is, with a pre-existing human cognitive structure having two stages: a *sensibility* organizing individual sense intuitions within two sensory modes of intuition (space and time) and an *understanding* synthesizing the thus intuited representations *transcendentally* into judgments under one of twelve abstract *categories* such as, "*a* has the property *b*" or "*a* causes *b*." The concepts "having a property" and "causing" are in the understanding, not in the observed object. Such judgments are called *synthetic a priori*; that is, true neither rationally nor empirically but in the sense of just being the inborn way the generic human individual senses and cognizes objects. What is known is not the external object-in-itself but what appears after its input has been synthesized by the senses and then processed transcendentally by the mind, the *phenomenal* object. The phenomenal object is "only the relation of the object to the subject, and not that which is internal to the object in itself."[8] Although we do not know the object in itself, we do know our relation with it—the object is not an illusion. Whereas Descartes still claimed an epistemological method reaching a truth independent of the method, Kant offers a knowledge consisting of empirical data molded by the sensory modes and fitted into blank forms of judgment from the

---

7. Hobbes, *Leviathan*, 1.1 (p. 3).
8. Kant, *Critique of Pure Reason*, B67.

understanding's twelve categories. The boundary between ontology, the study of reality, and epistemology, the study of knowing, has weakened. Knowing is no longer objective but is a *transcendental* relation between subject and physical object. The move from Descartes to Kant repeats a two millennia-earlier move from Plato's *Republic* to Aristotle's *de Anima*.

Kant's synthesizing of representations into the concept of the object, the *transcendental unity of apperception*, sees the representations as unified in one consciousness that is presumed to be identical through time. The subject knows generically; different individuals know the same things not by consultation but separately through their identical transcendental structures. Kant is generic. Two centuries later, experimental scientists *will consult* (below, page 59), thus gaining a corporately constructed understanding of the physical world.

Kant limits cognition to judgments based on sensation, rejecting *dialectical judgments*—those judgments made independently of sense representations—as *illusion*. The rejection of dialectical judgments outlaws metaphysics and the cosmological perspective. Three traditional areas of dialectical judgment (morality, the existence of God, and immortality of the soul) survive in Kant as practical choices of the will rather than theoretical judgments. In contrast, for the communal orientation, which does not separate theoretical and practical reason, such a demotion is neither possible nor, as we will see, needed.

In *Critique of Practical Reason* (1788) Kant looks for a purely rational basis for practical reason. He finds it by insisting on a generic and universal practical principle equally applicable to everyone. Kant says practical principles "are subjective, or maxims, when the condition is regarded by the subject as valid only for his own will. They are objective, or practical laws, when the condition is recognized as objective, i.e. as valid for the will of every rational being" (§1, p. 17). It must apply equally to everyone: "the rule is objectively and universally valid only when it holds without any contingent subjective conditions which differentiate one rational being from another" (§1, p. 19). The resulting *categorical imperative*, "So act that the maxim of your will could always hold at the same time as a principle establishing universal law" (§7, p. 30) is given the same shaping function in practical reason—reason used in ethics or value judgments—as the categories have in theoretical reason. Kant is looking for ethical rules for the community, but it is a generic community, needing generic rules. There is neither provision for complementary rules for complementary contributors, nor is there provision for an interactive establishing of rules when any of several alternatives might resolve the same dysfunctional problem, as there is in corporate orientations.

A significant partial move away from the modern movement is the existentialism of Søren Kierkegaard. In his *Concluding Unscientific Postscript* (1846), the most systematic account of his anti-systematic ("unscientific") program, he condemns all philosophical system from perennial to corporate, finding each useless for the passionate, inwardly turned existing self. Against all system: "Speculative philosophy is objective, and objectively there is no truth for existing individuals, but only approximations; for the existing individual is precluded from becoming altogether objective by the fact that he exists" (p. 201). Against generic or organic system: "Only in subjectivity is there decisiveness, to seek objectivity is to be in error" (p. 181). "The scribbling modern philosophy holds passion in contempt; and yet passion is the culmination of existence for an existing individual" (p. 176). Kierkegaard is against corporate system. Spirit, passion, decisiveness, truth are private, first person, cannot be shared between human beings. "A direct relationship between one spiritual being and another, with respect to the essential truth, is unthinkable. If such a relationship is assumed, it means that one of the parties has ceased to be spirit" (p. 221). And "The knower is essentially *integer* [whole, complete], and . . . with respect to the knowledge of the eternal truth he is confronted with no other difficulty than the circumstance that he exists, which . . . means that existing, the process of transformation to inwardness in and by existing, is the truth" (p. 184). Truth belongs ultimately only to the self as "existing," as making independent choices, as passionate rather than passive, as self-as-such.

Existentialism accomplished the unimaginable: the rejection of Western theoretical reason, the bulwark of both the perennial and modern movements. Attacking theoretical reason opened the way for the soon-emerging communal movement's reduction of theoretical reason to merely a useful but truncated form of practical reason. After the First World War, existentialism was one jumping-off point for passing from the modern perspective toward, but not reaching, the communal perspective in Martin Heidegger's essence-changing relation of worker with his tools (treated later in this chapter).

In conclusion, we have found a historical movement, the *modern movement*, beginning with Descartes's *cogito*, a movement (a) formally epistemological, hence anthropological, (b) with a first-person epistemology, and (c) lying along a range of positions from a universalizing and therefore generic pole (Kant), to a self-as-such pole (Kierkegaard), with Descartes and Hume at undefined points between these generic and self-as-such poles.

## IV THE COMMUNAL HISTORICAL MOVEMENT

The philosophical freeing of community from cosmological control at the Enlightenment encouraged the German romantic movement additional freedom from non-creative similarity or passive organic relation; and a vast increase in historical knowledge in the nineteenth century challenged the previous Western merely empirical understanding of the relation with the past. These three influences led to the *communal* historical movement with corporate anthropological basis, always lurking as practice in the lower classes, and now challenging the perennial and modern movements for the first time in the West (excepting the fourth-century, near-east leaning Antiochian Fathers, chapter 4.II.2 below).

The communal movement is presented here in six overlapping manifestations: Hegel's theoretical recognition of an internally interactive structure for all reality; early Marx's first Western advocacy of the corporate perspective; Gadamer's extension of an early Heidegger insight into a corporate philosophy of history; corporate language philosophy in late Wittgenstein; and corporate philosophy of natural science in Charles S. Peirce and Lakatos. Finally we note Alasdair MacIntyre's attempt to hold the line against these developments with an Aristotelian perennial moral philosophy.

### *1 An Inside-Out Philosophical View of the World: Georg W. F. Hegel*

Political philosophy contained the seeds of a corporate perspective even during its modern phase. In *Leviathan* (1651) Thomas Hobbes presented an early version of the social contract theory later to appear in Locke and Rousseau. As a modern thinker, Hobbes had a problem with the obviously social nature of justice. "Justice, and Injustice are none of the Faculties neither of the Body, nor Mind. If they were, they might be in a man that were alone in the world, as well as his Senses, and Passions.

They are Qualities, that relate to men in Society, not in Solitude."[9] As an empiricist, Hobbes wished to base this social concept somehow on a characteristic of the generic human self, the "man that were alone in the world." He did so by claiming that self-preservation is an empirical characteristic of the self and then somewhat preemptively taking this characteristic as a right. He argued that since the unbridled use of this right may be counter-productive, the same empirical laws of nature also permit "that a man be willing, when others are so too, as farre-forth, as for Peace, and defense of himself he shall think it necessary, to lay down this right to all things; and be contented with so much liberty against other men, as he would allow other men against himself."[10] Such a covenant is sufficient to define justice: "For where no covenant hath preceded, there hath no Right been transferred, and every man has right to every thing; and consequently, no action can be Unjust. But when a Covenant is made, then to break it is Unjust."[11] Thus, social justice is given its origin in the voluntary contracting by selves among themselves to redistribute and thus limit the natural rights they already possessed singly (logically) prior to membership in society, in exchange for other advantages. For Hobbes, humanity is not intrinsically social; rather the existing interacting community is created by agreement among intrinsically independent selves for self-serving purposes. The social contract creates the possibility of social justice, but it is founded on the generic interests of selves taken as rights.

Hobbes new position is given further expression by John Locke in his *Two Treatises of Government* (1689–1690) and in Jean-Jacques Rousseau's *Social Contract* (1762). Rousseau puts it this way: "In place of the individual person of each contracting party, this act of association creates an artificial and collective body, . . . and by this same act that body acquires its unity, its common ego, its life and its will. The public person thus formed by the union of all other persons . . . is now known as the . . . body politic."[12] This body politic then subjects its members to a radical socialization, as Rousseau tells us fulsomely:

---

9. Hobbes, *Leviathan*, 1.13 (p. 63). In contrast, Emmanuel Levinas surprisingly places the origin of social justice precisely in the single self-as-such (chapter 7 below).

10. Hobbes, *Leviathan*, 1.14 (pp. 64–65).

11. Ibid., 1.15 (p. 71).

12. Rousseau, *Social Contract*, 1.6, p. 61.

> The passing from the state of nature to the civil society produces a remarkable change in man; it puts justice as a rule of conduct in the place of instinct, and gives his actions the moral quality they previously lacked. It is only then, when the voice of duty has taken the place of physical impulse and right that of desire, that man, who has hitherto thought only of himself, finds himself compelled to act on other principles, and to consult his reason rather than study his inclinations . . . . His faculties are so exercised and developed, his mind is so enlarged, his sentiments so ennobled, and his whole spirit so elevated that . . . he should constantly bless the happy hour that lifted him for ever from the state of nature and from a narrow, stupid animal made a creature of intelligence and a man.[13]

While Rousseau formally maintains the Enlightenment position that community justice originates in natural rights of its separate members, such passages on the unity, ego, life, and will of the body politic amount to a communal orientation. Georg Wilhelm Friedrich Hegel kept the body politic and left out the Enlightenment-based prior natural rights of the individual. His seminal *Phenomenology of Spirit*[14] (1807) is an abstract study(*-logy*) of the *phenomenon* of ongoing creation of the world—*physical, cultural,* and *divine*—by ever-evolving essence-creating multilaterally internal interaction among the *forces of nature*, the *members of the human community*, and the European-held three *persons of God*, within each and among the three; this interaction is called *Geist*, or spirit, as in "team spirit."

For Hegel, to know anything is to interact with it directly or through others indirectly. Hence the *Begriff* (concept, notion, idea) of a material object (a member, or subgroup of a human community, or a deity) *is the set*, the *collection*, of its *roles in the overall interaction*.

The most inclusive concept (participatory role in interaction) is *Being* (having roles), a concept which interacts with its negative *Nothing* (without roles) to produce *Becoming* (acquiring roles). "The truth of Being and of Nothing is accordingly the unity of the two and this unity is Becoming . . . . The whole progress of philosophizing . . . merely renders explicit what is implicit in a notion [*Begriff*, concept, interactive role]."[15]

---

13. Ibid., 1.8, p. 64–65.

14. Hegel, *Phenomenology of Spirit*. References for quotations of Hegel are to paragraph numbers in Miller translation.

15. Hegel, *Logic*, 128–29.

In the human cultural world, the concepts are roles in social interactions, all but the most trivial of which require a pre-existing social institution (language, custom, law, etc.). One cannot *be* a first grade teacher without a class of first-grade students. A man and a woman *become*, take on the roles of, husband and wife in the social institution of family. Husband and wife become parents by interacting to produce and nurture a child, whose being or essence is the developing sum of the *natural* interactions between the parents' genetic structures and the *social* interactive formation of the child after birth. "The relationship of husband and wife is . . . one in which one consciousness immediately recognizes itself in another. . . . [But] this relationship . . . has its actual existence not in itself but in the child—an 'other' in whose coming into existence is the relationship" (§456).

As the individual acquires interactive skills through interactive induction into its social world, it acquires awareness of others *and* self-awareness (*Selbstbewußtsein*) as intentional creative fellow-interactor with others. That is, the individual is an intentional contributor to the essences of others, and accepts essential change from the intending others. Self-awareness "has its own self-certainty in the other free self-consciousness [self-awareness], and possesses its truth precisely in that 'other'" (§349). It recognizes itself thus because, as said above, it *is* its essence-changing roles in its internal relation with the similarly counter-relating others. "The deed . . . is the actual self" (§464). A lord unilaterally controlling a bondsman does not find his self-awareness in an interaction with the self-awareness of the other, "for what the bondsman does is really the action of the lord. The latter's essential nature is to exist only for himself" (§191). The effect of the interaction on the lord's self-awareness is no greater than that from pulling the cord that summons the bondsman.

*God*, also, is characterized by Hegel as part of the net of interactors. The Father reaches self-awareness as free creator through interaction with the Son: "The first is the Absolute Being, Spirit that is in and for itself . . . . But in the actualization of its notion [*Begriff*, concept, interactive role] . . . it passes over into *being-for-another*, its self-identity becomes an *actual*, *self-sacrificing* absolute Being . . . . [T]he third moment is the return of [the two, now united] into their original simplicity . . . . [and] the externalization of this . . . Spirit . . . makes itself a participant in the self-[awareness] of the believer" (§§ 532–533).

*Nature*, also, is claimed by Hegel as a network of interactions. Twentieth-century natural science confirms both eighteenth century science and Hegel with its understanding of the physical world as an interaction of gravitational, electro-magnetic, "strong," and "weak" interactive forces (more recently reduced to two). Thus, Hegel claims the "what I am" of nature, or "who I am" of human persons, or "who God is" of eighteenth-century Europe's established triune God *is* the set of interacting roles held by parts or members within and among the three.

Hegel's phenomenology of spirit, describing the world by its interactions rather than its objects, diverges fundamentally from all previous Western philosophy. Platonism offers a *logos* of Forms, telling each separate individual what it ought to do not only as idea but also as ethical perfection. Modern philosophy describes a world to be observed rather than erected interactively. With Hegel there is no sanction against proscribed acts (as in Platonism), but there is one against failing to *inter*act—one becomes less of a person.

Hegel's characterization of the world could be represented as a fishing net of interactive relations, with each cord-segment a microscopic interaction, each knot a microscopic *interactor* able to vary the direction of pull on each of its attached cord segments, and with its essence represented by its physical position resulting from the combination of its elastic attachment to its own position together with all the pushes *and* pulls through its attached cord-segments to neighboring knots, which in turn are dependent on their attachments and interactions with the first-mentioned and still other knots. One could then mark off a large section of the net as a "thing," this stomach, this mother, this oil company, with its relations with the others represented by the net-segments that cross its boundary. One could demark as many "things" as one wished, some included inside others, some partly overlapping others (as for example the mother who is also oil company treasurer), some distinct, either with some common boundary or distant from one another. This net would also need to be multi-dimensional and with a time dimension.

This "*inverted* [*verkehrte*, inside-out]" view of the world as relations (§157) is of the *same* world Western philosophy previously knew, only viewed from outside as a world of things, whether relating or not. In the inside-out view of a world in which things *are* their interactions, one does not need to define "internal relation"—every interaction is bilaterally intrinsic and changes what both things *are*. Such a three-fold world need not look for outside control; it has "retained *for itself the principle of change and alteration*" (§157).

Has Hegel reached the corporate orientation? He offers a world of intentional internal human relations interactively created by the human community supported by a non-intentional physical interaction of nature and a non-physical intentional (spiritual) interaction with a god. This description of the world disallows both perennial and modern philosophies but does not explicitly call for a communal commitment to interact strategically to invite creative interactive response from all community members. Yet his suggestive portrayal of the sterility of the lord's role in the lord-bondsman relation raised a stir in Europe. Hegel's establishment-supported role in 1807 as top Western philosopher was necessarily as explainer, not as reformer. Forty years later, Marx understood Hegel and became reformer, and was promptly banished from the continent.

Hegel turned the Enlightenment social contract, based on individual self-interest, inside-out. The individual autonomy needed to engage in a social contract is a *result* of acculturation into an interacting community, not a prerequisite. Self-interest metamorphoses to become equivalent to community interest. Freedom comes not from isolation but from belonging to a social context and thus gaining both opportunity and competence to join in creative activity: "Absolute freedom has thus removed the antithesis between the universal and the individual will" (§595).

Hegel's radical reorientation of Western philosophy was not understood. Perennial philosophers claimed Hegel as their own with the Hegelian *logos* of interacting concepts controlling the world from above rather than as he did, as that *same* world seen inside-out as roles and interactions. Paul Tillich speaks of "the classical tradition from Parmenides to Hegel" (below, page 302). Modern philosophers do the same, seeing the Hegelian *logos* as physical laws controlling the physical and psychological world.

The Hegelian *logos* of interacting roles, the Platonic *logos* of Forms, and the Kantian synthetic *a priori* categories all offer explanation of the peculiar fact that many human beings find themselves living in the same "world"; that is, participating in a common social structure with common meanings. But, unlike the Platonic Forms and their successors (the neo-Platonic mind-of-God, modern philosophy's natural causes, and the Kantian categories), all of which see individual human choice as within an *already existing* common "world," the Hegelian logos takes human choice as *creative part* of the world interactive structure. When one interacts in the social world, one changes that world not only for oneself but for those in direct or indirect interaction with one. Platonism sees individual essence as who that individual ought to be. Kant sees it as the individual's ability to unify its representations (above, page 16). But Hegel sees it as its set of community-creating roles in internal interaction with other persons, nature, and its community's god or spirit.

## 2 Political Philosophy: Karl Marx

Karl Marx (1818–1883), a reform-minded political activist outside the university and the elite class, agreed with Hegel, but chose the role of reformer and challenged the rising industrial world to allow the working class a larger share of creative interactive input into their work. Hegel described the human community's interactively created world objectively; Marx agitated for a broader distribution of that creativity among its members.

In the first section by Marx alone of his and Friedrich Engels' *The German Ideology* (1845–1846) Marx says, "The philosophers have only interpreted the world, in various ways; the point, however, is to change it."[16] This reform is practical, not theoretical: "the 'liberation' of 'man' is not advanced a single step by reducing philosophy, theology, substance and all the trash to 'self-consciousness [Selbstbewustsein, self-awareness]' . . . . it is only possible to achieve real liberation in the real world and by employing real means, . . . slavery cannot be abolished without the steam engine and the mule and spinning-jenny, serfdom cannot be abolished without improved agriculture" (p. 133). Liberation of workers to a more creative role requires a change from top-down management toward worker initiative rather than blind obedience.

Such a reform project requires a detailed analysis of community interaction. Marx says, "This conception of history depends on our ability to expound the real process of production, . . . and to comprehend the form of intercourse . . . created by this mode of production, . . . to show it in its action as State, to explain all the different theoretical products and forms of consciousness, religion, philosophy, ethics, etc., . . . by which

---

16. Marx, "Feuerbach," 11 [Tucker, *Reader*, 109].

means ... the whole thing can be depicted in its totality (and therefore, too, the reciprocal action of these various sides on one another)" (p. 128). This passage, like many others, follows its mention of influence in one direction, from production to social intercourse, with reminders not to forget the Hegel-emphasized interactive influence in *both* directions that Marx always finds. He condemns Ludwig Feuerbach's non-interactive modern empiricism explicitly: "The materialist doctrine that men are products of circumstances ... forgets that it is men who change circumstances,"[17] and, thus, are in two-way interaction.

Marx calls Hegel's human internal interactions and roles "material" in the sense of being in the human world, unlike cosmological Forms or empirical laws that control the human world from the outside. Human concepts, decisions, and social structures are as "material" as mules and spinning-jennies, and all of them are in multilateral interaction with one another. Marx says:

> In direct contrast to German philosophy which descends from heaven to earth, here we ascend from earth to heaven. . . . Morality, religion, metaphysics, all the rest of ideology and their corresponding forms of consciousness thus no longer retain the semblance of independence. They have no history, no development. Rather, as human communities develop their material production and their material intercourse, their real existence, they change along with these their thinking and the products of their thinking. . . . As soon as this active life-process is described, history ceases to be a collection of dead facts as it is with the *themselves still abstract empiricists*, or an imagined activity of imagined subjects, as with the idealists.[18]

Marx claims human thinking is part of doing, making explicit his disagreement with the "from heaven" of perennial philosophy and with "the empiricists" and "the idealists" of modern philosophy.

In Hegel and Marx's world of internal interaction, any portion of the world can be conceived as a "thing," or taken together with other things as components of a larger thing, or subdivided into smaller component things as a system of things. Marx says, "production is . . . at the same time consumption, and consumption is at the same time

---

17. Ibid., 3 [Tucker, *Reader*, 108].
18. Marx, *Die Deutsche Ideologie*, 26–27 [Tucker, *Reader*, 118–19].

production."[19] Production and consumption can be conceived separately but are interactively bound with each other, and are also part of a larger unit ("relations of production") that also includes distribution, exchange, and division of labor. In such a world, things in intrinsic relation have no absolute boundaries separating them. Each enjoys an identity as interacting part of the whole, while at the same time the essence of each is determined by the total of all interactions among them and their interaction with still others.[20]

Such interrelatedness exists not just between objects but also between subject and object. Knowing something is an internal relation with it. "The premises from which we begin are not arbitrary ones, not dogmas, but real premises . . . . They are the real individuals, their activity and the material conditions under which they live . . . . These premises can thus be verified in a purely empirical [*empirisch*] way" (p. 113); that is, through internal relation as participating member of the social world, as just quoted, not "with the themselves still abstract empiricists" nor the idealists or perennialists (as in second paragraph, above). Here Marx typically keeps the word "empirical" *but adjusts its meaning to fit a corporately understood world structure*, unlike abstract "empiricists," who do not.

Marx says, "The human essence is no abstraction inherent in each single individual. In its reality it is the ensemble of the social relations."[21] Thus, he states Hegel's central point and, for once, in Hegel's "inside-out" terms. "Only in community with others has each individual the means of cultivating his gifts in all directions; only in the community, therefore, is personal freedom possible" (p. 161). Such a freedom to contribute *creatively* to the community has a cost; it requires the individual to engage in it with others rather than attempt to control unilaterally or to withdraw into isolation.

For Marx, *production* is basic to human life in two ways, "life involves before everything else eating and drinking, a habitation, clothing, and many other things. The first historical act is thus the production of the means to satisfy these needs, the production of material life itself"

---

19. Marx, *Critique of Political Economy*, "Introduction," 278.

20. This "philosophy of internal relations" as basic to Marx's system is treated extensively in Ollman, *Alienation*, 26–40, 256–76.

21. Marx, "Feuerbach," 6, against Feuerbach's non-dialectical empiricism, outlined clearly, for example, at the start of Feuerbach's 1841 *The Essence of Christianity*.

(p. 120). "This mode of production . . . . is . . . a definite form of expressing their life . . . . What they are, therefore, coincides with their production, both with *what* they produce and with *how* they produce" (p. 114). At each of the tribal, feudal, and industrial stages in history, the "how they produce" limits the worker's creative input in the work, reducing responsible creative interaction toward passive conformity. "These various conditions, which appear first as conditions of self-activity [*Selbstbetätigung*, self-doing, creative activity by the self], later as fetters upon it, form in the whole evolution of history a coherent series of forms of intercourse, the coherence of which consists in this: in the place of an earlier form of intercourse, which has become a fetter, a new one is put, corresponding to the more developed productive forces and, hence, to the advanced mode of the self-activity of individuals—a form which in its turn becomes a fetter and is then replaced by another" (pp. 158–59). The present alienating fetter is a division of labor in which the class of workers "was determined by their common interests over against a third party, was always a community to which these individuals belonged only as average individuals [*Durchschnittsindividuen*, cross-sectional, typical, generically related individuals] . . . in which they participated not as individuals but as members of a class" (p. 161). The fetter here is the non-creative relation of workers with owner, with its consequent generic relation among the workers—precisely the ideal in Plato's *Republic*.

In the capitalist period this loss of reciprocal creativity in relations, this *alienation*, emerges thus: the worker performs routine tasks specified by the owner. Raw materials and machines are the property of the owner. The worker does not interact creatively with the owner, other workers, or the consumer, and has no creative part in the product's design, the manner of its production, or its suitability for the consumer. The worker works only for his own physical subsistence in generic relation with the other workers. The owner is not interested in the worker or the consumer as human beings but only in selling the finished product at a profit to add to his own power and subsistence. The consumer is often manipulated into buying the product for reasons not related to its actual use; thus, the market hides, sometimes omits, use value of the product. The resulting alienation of worker, owner, and consumer from one another has eliminated the creative aspect of the interaction for all three. Marx says, "The division of labour implies the contradiction between the interest of the separate individual . . . and the communal interest of all individuals who have intercourse with one another.... As long as a cleavage exists between the particular and the common interest... man's own deed becomes an alien power opposed to him, which enslaves him instead of being controlled by him" (p. 124). This complaint is not about the worker's physical deprivation, the worker's "particular interest" as it would be in the competitive twenty-first century; it is about the worker deprived of creative contribution to a "common interest."

This alienation infects every other area of society as well. "The State is the form in which the individuals of a ruling class assert their common interests" (p. 151). "Religion, family, state, law, morality, science, art, etc., are only particular modes of production, and fall under its general law."[22] In other words, all aspects of society share in the alienating organic, but not corporate, treatment of the community as a whole by the exploitive elites of these social structures.

Marx says:

> In the previous substitutes for the community, in the State, etc. personal freedom has existed only for the individuals who developed within the relationships of the ruling class, and only in so far as they were individuals of this class. The illusory community, in which individuals have up till now combined, always took on an independent existence in relation to them, and was at the same time, since it was the combination of one class over against another, not only a completely illusory community, but a new fetter as well. In the real community the individuals obtain their freedom in and through their association.... This contradiction between the productive forces and the form of intercourse, which, as we saw has occurred several times in past history,... necessarily on each occasion burst out in a revolution (pp. 160–61).

But the proletarian revolution will be different: "With the community of revolutionary proletarians, on the other hand, who take their conditions of existence and those of all members of society under their control, it is just the reverse; it is as individuals that the individuals participate in it" (pp. 161–62). As above, "individuals" are "real individuals" whose essences include unfettered corporate interaction with the *whole* community, not just within one class opposing the others.

If Marx's advocacy of destruction of all alienating social structures—be they private property, family, class, state, law, science, art, or

---

22. Marx, *Economic and Philosophic Manuscripts*, 136.

religion—is *misunderstood* as to be done first, as it often is, to clear a way for construction of a corporately interacting society, this would eliminate any interactive aspect of the old structures the community might use to begin the time-consuming interactive creation of sufficient replacement structures even to maintain the previous level of creative interaction, much less exceed it. Historically, many revolutions have only made things worse. The French revolution eliminated five partially interacting structures (monarchy, nobility, church, provinces, and guilds) to produce a single state authority in unilateral control from Gibraltar to the gates of Moscow.

In Western society, the social classes at the bottom have always maintained some underground corporate life unrecognized by the dominant class. This class has even produced reformers from time to time. But, as said, starting from scratch is not the answer. The Old Testament recognizes such spiral descents from corporate relation toward a complete loss of human dignity in a morass of economic and military exploitation, but it places this continuing historical conflict not between humanity and alienating structures but between two natural gregarious and defensive tendencies within humanity to build respectively corporate and alienating structures. Lacking a controlling *logos*, or a controlling nature, it was necessary to "choose this day whom you will serve" (Josh 24:15), to choose between a god of creative interaction and a god of self-serving exploitation. The Old Testament takes for granted what today is considered empirical fact, that the same human powers needed for corporate relations (the power to discriminate, to choose, to offer, to accept) can also be used to dominate. The Joshua passage and the whole Old Testament is written as a tool for community learning by its own past mistakes, not for voiding its past and starting over. It calls for continuous human creation of its multilaterally internal interaction within an ever-developing, community-created social structure (tradition, Torah, "law"), within which it can interact creatively. Marx shares the Old Testament goal of human solidarity: both ask for continuous improvement, not for sudden unpracticed revolutionary perfection.

Political followers of Marx, like philosophical followers of Hegel, did not recognize their leader's interactive base. Marxism moved in 1848 from early Marx's shared creative internal relations, "historical materialism," to Engel's ambiguous "dialectical materialism," and finally to *economic determinism* which misunderstands Marx's multilaterally internal relation as rather a one-way causal relation from a controlling empirically understood economic base to an ideational superstructure as epiphenomenon of it. It wants the cotton gin but rejects worker-manager interaction. Such economic determinism, and the modern movement as a whole, "invert" not Hegel but Platonism (thus revealing its origin) by claiming an upward controlling "material" base rather than a downward controlling ideational base, both independent of human choice. The communal perspective's call for human community-created multilaterally internal relation, only implicit in Hegel and weakened by unilateral revolution in Marxism, is totally contradicted by economic determinism.

Marx has been as impossible for scholars with perennial or modern orientations to understand as has Hegel, and for similar reasons. Both groups understand Hegel as offering a perennial *logos* of Forms, and Marx as offering an empiricist exposition of economics; whereas, in fact, both Hegel and Marx agree that the *human community* "*retained for itself the principle of change and alteration*" (Hegel, page 23 above).

Later in this chapter we find Jürgen Habermas reducing Marxist political interaction all the way down to Kantian empiricist emancipation. And in chapter 9, Norman Gottwald applies Marxist economic determinism to biblical studies. But in chapter 10, German political theology and Latin-American liberation theology compete with current Marxism's economic determinism by offering biblical human solidarity compatible with Hegel and early Marx.

### 3 Philosophy of Culture: Martin Heidegger, Hans-Georg Gadamer

One of the modern period's achievements was its development of *critical history*, a neutral, objective, uninterpreted literal account of past events on analogy with the period's empirical natural science, and equally independent of any non-empirical part of an investigator's cultural orientation. Methods used included the discovery and comparison of sources with a factual accuracy similarly empirically estimated, as classically described in David Hume's *An Enquiry Concerning Human Understanding* (1748).[23] With this method, modern historians have managed an immense amount of historical investigation and discovery, giving the West a never previously existing empirical historical perspective.

---

23. Hume, *Human Understanding*, section 10, middle third.

But this intense interest in history itself belied the assumed disinterested historian, and a recognition of the necessary presuppositions and interests of the historian led gradually to awareness that history is an interpretation of the past by those writing it in the present. We have already seen Hegel and Marx move beyond critical history. Two pioneers in the post-critical philosophy of history were Wilhelm Dilthey and Ernst Troeltsch.

Wilhelm Dilthey (1833–1911) looked for a way to understand the historical past in a more sophisticated manner than critical history, one that would include its meaning as a community way of life. In his *Der Aufbau der Geschichtlichen Welt in den Geisteswissenschaften* he holds that the past can be understood in the same way as one understands the life world of one's own age; both can be understood through *cultural objectifications*, which are "the manifold forms in which the things that individuals hold in common have objectified themselves in the world of the senses" (p. 209)—things that can be heard or seen, like speech or books or architectural structures. "Its realm extends from the style of life and the forms of social intercourse, to the system of purposes which society has created for itself, to custom, law, state, religion, art, science and philosophy" (p. 208). One learns one's own *present culture* through such cultural objectifications (pp. 208–9):

> From this world of cultural objectifications the self receives sustenance from earliest childhood. It is also the medium in which the understanding of other persons and their life expressions is accomplished. For each thing in which the culture has objectified itself contains something of oneself and the other together. Every plaza with trees planted, every living room with seating arranged, is understandable to us from infancy because human planning, arranging, and valuing done together have allotted plaza and furniture its place. The child . . . . can only learn to understand the gestures and facial expressions, movements and exclamations, words and sentences because it always encounters them as the same and in the same relation to what they mean and express. Thus the individual becomes oriented in the world of cultural objectifications.

*Past cultures* also can be so understood. "Past ages, in which the great total forces of history have taken shape, are present in the cultural objectifications. The individual, as bearer and representative of the common features interwoven in him, enjoys and comprehends the history in which they arise. The individual understands history by being a historical being" (p. 151).

Dilthey moves beyond critical history by recognizing that cultural objectifications have relational cultural meanings. But he remains within the critical orientation in two respects. He does not recognize that individuals may learn relational meanings as participants as well as by observation. And he does not take account of differences between the meaning of a past cultural objectification within its own culture and what it may appear to objectify in the later observer's different culture. Over a period of six centuries, a cathedral's cultural meaning may have changed from center for high liturgical celebration of community solidarity to empty high-Gothic tourist attraction, and over two centuries the purpose of the American public school system may have changed from education for a responsible citizenry to individual child care and employment certification.

The circular *hermeneutic* relation between the meanings of part and whole, of word and sentence containing it, of event and its cultural context, has been recognized in the West from antiquity. But while both perennial and Enlightenment critical orientations presuppose a fixed cultural context, the communal orientation's recognition of a continuously changing cultural context requires taking account of such change to recover an artifact's earlier meaning. Dilthey misses the possible changes in cultures, both earlier meanings outside present culture and additional meaning for earlier events given by their effect on later culture. In the words of Hans-Georg Gadamer, "Dilthey ultimately conceives inquiring into the historical past as *deciphering and not as historical experience*."[24]

Ernst Troeltsch (1865–1923) was under the three-fold influence of neo-Kantian philosophy, of Dilthey, and of Max Weber, who himself was partly influenced by Marx. Troeltsch wrestled with the nature of history in Der Historismus und seine Probleme (1922). He found history differing from the natural sciences of his day by its dealing with "life unities." "History has generally no simple basic element analogous to the element, taken indifferently as atom or as energy, in natural science, but rather has before it from the beginning nothing but composite objects, in which an abundance of psychological elementary events along with certain natural conditions is always already bound up into a life unity or totality" (pp. 32–33).

---

24. Gadamer, *Truth and Method*, 241.

Troeltsch's goal was a "philosophical mastering of historicism" (p. 113), to be realized somehow through "the fundamental historicizing of all our thought about humanity, its culture, and its values" (p. 102). How can historicism be mastered by submitting oneself completely to history? This question, turned into a defining statement, characterizes Troeltsch's program. Troeltsch says the historicism to be mastered is the old critical history of facts, separated from the values to be drawn from them as in the neo-Kantian-influenced history of Adolph von Harnack.[25] In the emerging historicizing of everything, history—although influenced by "certain natural conditions"—is to be understood from within itself, and the necessity and the possibility of such an understanding derive from the recognition that, for us, history (all of our recoverable socializing structure laid out before us) is all there is; there is no absolute method for obtaining truth nor is there a standard for measuring it from outside history. Not everything in a particular culture is true, but each culture contains within it its own standard of truth.

Martin Heidegger (1889–1976) made explicit a bilateral internal relation between a single human worker and the worker's tools, which Gadamer was to extend to multilateral internal human relations, an extension impossible within Heidegger's first-person phenomenological approach limiting him to considering only one person at a time, and which led to his being incorrectly taken as theoretician of the non-communal existentialist movement.

What does it mean to say that things are, that things have 'Being'? In *Being and Time* (1927) Heidegger begins his investigation of Being by saying that Being is "that which determines entities as entities, that on the basis of which entities are already understood" (pp. 25–26). So if "Being means the Being of entities, then entities themselves turn out to be what is investigated" (p. 26). To investigate entities, Heidegger chooses an adaptation of the phenomenological method of Edmund Husserl, a starting point squarely in the first-person perspective and so precluding any communal method or result. Phenomenology "uncovers" the thing being investigated and allows it to show itself directly with no separate image in the investigator (like sense-datum in empiricism or idea in idealism), distinct from the thing being investigated. Investigator and investigated are in direct relation; there is no subject-object separation. The motto of phenomenology is, "To the things themselves!" (pp.

---

25. So Troeltsch in his "The Dogmatics of the 'Religionsgeschichtliche Schule,'" 12.

58–59). "Only as phenomenology, is ontology [the study of Being] possible" (p. 60).

From this first-person starting point, early Heidegger argues that the fundamental relation between such a first-person and anything except another person can be internal. He rejects the cosmological perspective as incorrect and the empirical perspective as undesirable. This first-person starting point precludes reaching a corporate perspective, so that Heidegger's starting with the self was often mistaken as implying that he was an existentialist.

Which entities should be studied first? Since phenomenology studies things through their relation to the investigator, Heidegger starts with study of the investigator. "Looking at something, understanding and conceiving it, choosing access to it—all these ways of behaving are constitutive for our inquiry, and therefore are modes of Being for those particular entities which we, the inquirers, are ourselves. Thus to work out the question of Being adequately, we must make an entity—the enquirer—transparent in his own Being. . . . This entity which each of us is himself and which includes inquiring as one of the possibilities of its Being, we shall denote by the term '*Dasein*'" (pp. 26–27). Dasein, literally "be there," a person in a "world," is thus a human being not as biological whole but as enquirer in, as capable of understanding entities there, thus in a *one-way internal* relation with it. But knowing the world does not make one become part of it; knowing the world does not place a Dasein in direct relation with another Dasein.

The Being of Dasein includes its being an enquirer; Dasein is *in-a-world*, in an environment (pp. 78–80). "Dasein" is literally "being there,"; Dasein's existence includes a *there*, a "world"; we do not need to prove its existence any more than that of Dasein itself. "The question of whether there is a world at all and whether its Being can be proved, makes no sense if it is raised by *Dasein* as Being-in-the-world; and who else would raise it?" (pp. 246–47) "'The scandal of philosophy' is not that this proof has yet to be given, but that such proofs are expected and attempted again and again" (p. 249).

The elements of Dasein's world relate to it in three ways: as *present-at-hand* objects appearing to be independent of Dasein, as *ready-to-hand* equipment understood not as mere objects but as transparent to Dasein's use of them in carrying out its activities in the world, and as *Dasein-with*, in which each Dasein has its own world.

The *ready-to-hand* relation is phenomenologically the closest with Dasein. A hammer, for example, presents itself primordially as a tool for driving nails, not as an odd shaped physical body with steel and wood parts—"the less we just stare at the hammer-Thing, and the more we seize hold of it and use it, the more primordial does our relationship to it become, and the more unveiledly is it encountered as that which it is—as equipment" (p. 98). The relation between user and hammer is internal—what each one *is* depends on the other. The hammer *is* a hammer because the Dasein can use it for hammering, and some Daseins *are* hammer users because they so use hammers. There is not "subject" and "object"; the hammer is an extension of Dasein as Dasein builds the house. But the hammer, not being a Dasein, does not have a world, and the interpretations "hammer" and "user" are only in Dasein's world. Non-manufactured items, like food and beautiful sunsets, are also *ready-to-hand* (p. 100).

A carpenter happens on a tool in the hardware store and thinks, "Ha! This is just what I need for the job I am doing today." The carpenter, being in the world of carpentering, interprets the tool by seeing how it fits in the world in which he is already involved. His world provides a *fore-structure* for the interpretation. Similarly, an interpretation of a document, or of a historical event, is the recognition of a relation between the document or event and elements in the interpreter's world context; it gives a *meaning* to the document or event. "In interpreting, we do not, so to speak, throw a 'signification' over some naked thing which is present-at-hand, we do not stick a value on it; but when something within-the-world is encountered as such, the thing in question already has an involvement which is disclosed in our understanding of the world, and this involvement is one which gets laid out by the interpretation" (pp. 190–91).

Interpreting a tool, text, or event adds to our world of understanding; this modifies the fore-structure and so also our interpretation. When the carpenter starts to use the new tool and finds that it doesn't quite fit the job, he has to modify the tool, its use, the job, or all three. In the same way, as one continues to examine a document, the understanding of both the document and one's world may be changed. There is, thus, an ongoing intrinsic bilateral or *circular aspect to understanding*, an aspect which is an abomination to all essentialists (Platonic, Aristotelian, and modern) who wish for a fixed "objective" signification they can reach without the object changing in the process. As Plato puts it, "So how could that which is never in the same state be anything? . . . No indeed, nor could it be known by anyone. For at the very moment when the one who is going to know it approaches, it would become something else and different" (*Cratylus* 439C–440A). This *hermeneutic circle*, implied in Hegel, visible in Troeltsch, and made explicit here in Heidegger, claims an unavoidable *internal* character for the relation between interpreter and interpreted. "The 'circle' in understanding belongs to the structure of meaning, and the latter phenomenon is rooted in the existential constitution of Dasein" (p. 195).

The circular part-whole relation between hammer head and hammer, between the meaning of a part and the whole of a document, between a historical event and its own historical context, has always been recognized in the West, but recognized as *static*, unchanging. This wider hermeneutic circle adds to such a past interpretation the event's bilaterally internal relation with *subsequent* contexts, giving it additional meanings. This adds to the event's essence, and so violates the event's unchanging Platonic Form, or the modern ability to classify it into its proper genus. Below we find Gadamer further extending the circle to relations with other Daseins, something Heidegger cannot do from his first-person phenomenological starting point—he does not allow any shared world among Daseins.

Things become related to Dasein as *present-at-hand* when they are perceived theoretically rather than practically, when they are seen as objective and not internally related to Dasein. Heidegger holds that Sophocles and the pre-Socratic philosophers Heraclitus and Parmenides still perceived Dasein's *Da*, Dasein's world, to be internally related to Dasein, and he attributes to Plato the shift to the present Western understanding of ordinary things like hammers as *present-at-hand*.[26] Once a thing is given an unchangeable Platonic Form, then what it is, its "whatness," is fixed and independent of Dasein. Breaking its relation with Dasein allows a questioning of its "thatness," of whether it exists. But Heidegger replaces Platonic essence with *existence*, understood as *what* a thing is *to Dasein* (not *whether* it is) as *what* the *there* is that is al-

---

26. Heidegger's forerunner Kierkegaard also found this division: "Socrates infinite merit is to have been an *existing* thinker, not a speculative philosopher who forgets what it means to exist." *Concluding Unscientific Postscript*, 184.

ready part of Being-there. Platonism obscures, covers up, the previously uncovered direct internal relation of Dasein with its world:

> It was in the Sophists and in Plato that appearance was declared to be mere appearance and thus degraded. At the same time being, as *idea* [Form], was exalted to a supersensory realm. A chasm, *chörismos*, was created between the merely apparent here below and the real being somewhere on high. In that chasm Christianity settled down, at the same time reinterpreting the lower as the created and the higher as the creator. These refashioned weapons it turned against antiquity (as paganism) [i.e. against the pre-Socratic view of relation with reality as internal] and so disfigured it. Nietzsche was right in saying that Christianity is Platonism for the people.[27]

But even Heidegger's *ready-to-hand* relation itself does not extend to relations between Daseins; it puts a reader in bilaterally internal relation with an old document but not with the deceased *Dasein-with* who wrote it, nor with his "world." Heidegger's substantial early theological education could not reveal to him that Scripture agreed with him on his *ready-to-hand* relation, and surpassed him in also broadening his *Dasein-with* relation, thus also extending his *ready-to-hand* relation.

The third kind of relation, with another Dasein as *Dasein-with*, is phenomenologically distinct from the other two. Clothing made by a garment worker to fit another Dasein appears in the worker's world as *ready-to-hand*, but the Dasein for which it is made appears in the worker's world as more than *present-at-hand* or *ready-to-hand*; it appears as "a distinct entity that not only differs from equipment and things, but, itself a Dasein, is 'in' the world [the garment worker's world] in the form of being-in-the-world [its own distinct world]. . . . The characterizing of an encounter with another is still yet by one's own Dasein."[28] There is no phenomenal world common to both Daseins within whose shared changing interpretation the two could act jointly and intentionally in complementary creative cooperation. Nevertheless, since the other Dasein is in the worker's world (having its own world), mere manipulation of it as *ready-to-hand*, or knowing it only theoretically as *present-at-hand*, ignores part of its phenomenal relation with the worker. "By

---

27. The quotation, p. 90, the whole paragraph, pp. 79–172, of Heidegger's *An Introduction to Metaphysics*.

28. Heidegger, *Sein und Zeit*, 118 [*Being and Time*, 154].

reason of this *clinging-to-like* being-in-the-world, the world is always something that I share with others. The world of Dasein is a *with-world*, Being-in is *Being-with* others. Their being visible within Dasein's world is *Dasein-with*."[29]

*Being-with* is as intrinsic to Dasein as is *ready-to-hand-ness*; both are part of Dasein's being-there. "Being-with is an existential characteristic of Dasein even when factically no Other is present-at-hand . . . . Being-alone is a deficient mode of Being-with; its very possibility is the proof of this" (pp. 156–57).

Dasein can be *authentic* or *inauthentic*. It is commonly *inauthentic*, fallen into submission to "everydayness," "averageness," the "leveling down" of all possibilities. "In utilizing public means of transport and in making use of information services such as the newspaper, every Other is like the next. This Being-with-one-another dissolves one's own Dasein completely into the kind of Being of 'the Others,' in such a way, indeed, that the Others, as distinguishable and explicit, vanish more and more. In this inconspicuousness and unascertainability, the real dictatorship of the 'they' [*das Man*, the generic person] is unfolded" (p. 164). One's world has lapsed into the "lowest common denominator" of all the others' worlds.

*Authentic* Dasein, on the other hand, is "the Self that has been taken hold of in its own way" (p. 167), a self that has found itself, that is *resolute*. Authentic Dasein calls itself out of generic personhood so as to be "individualized down to itself in its uncanniness, . . . something that simply cannot be mistaken for anything else" (p. 322). Heidegger's authentic self, grown out of German romanticism, offers a basic ingredient that will be needed in the communal perspective, the distinctness of the self from others required for any bilaterally creative relation with them. But Heidegger's phenomenalist base prevents recognition of a community world distinct from the two phenomenal worlds and within which a bilaterally intrinsic interaction of Daseins could take place.

A paradigmatic way Heidegger sees Dasein called to authenticity is by anticipation of its own death: "in anticipating death it understands itself unambiguously in terms of its ownmost distinctive possibility" (p. 435). This death is non-relational: "By its very essence, death is in every case mine. . . . This ownmost non-relational possibility is at the same time the uttermost one" (pp. 284, 294). Such centrality of indi-

29. Ibid., 118 [*Being and Time*, 154–55].

vidual death is a result of the radical first-person orientation of the phenomenological standpoint's rejection of the generic and merely-organic bringing together of multiple "first-persons" from Plato to Kant, and its unawareness of the corporate option of death as *most relational possibility*; for example, the biblical Isa 53:5 "by his bruises we are healed" and Rom 6:4 "we have been buried with him by baptism into death" or the rabbinic Emmanuel Levinas "to be for death in order to be for that which is after me."[30]

If the authentic self's mode of being in the world is not the generic mode of the "they," then, we want to ask, what mode is it: self-as-such, or corporate? Heidegger answers that phenomenological analysis is neutral; there are several modes of being an authentic self.

The attitude which expresses Dasein's being-in-a-world is called *care (Sorge)*. *Care* toward the *ready-to-hand* is called *concern (Besorgen)*, and *care* toward *Dasein-with* is called *solicitude (Fürsorge)*. Heidegger distinguishes three modes of solicitude. Solicitude is in a deficient mode when persons "who are with one another do not 'matter' to one another" (p. 158). In its positive modes solicitude "has two extreme possibilities. It can . . . take away 'care' from the Other and put itself in his position in concern . . . . In such solicitude the Other can become one who is dominated and a dependent" (p. 158). At the other extreme, solicitude acts toward the other "not in order to take away his 'care' but rather to give it back to him authentically . . . . This kind of solicitude pertains essentially . . . to the existence of the Other, not to a '*what*' with which he is concerned; it helps the Other to become transparent to himself *in* his care and to become *free for* it" (p. 159). Thus, Dasein's solicitude is deficient if it ignores others and positive both when it dominates another (taking away the other's authenticity) and when it acts to free another to be authentic. Heidegger calls the third kind of bond *authentic*: "when [two] devote themselves to the same affair in common, their doing so is determined by the manner in which their Dasein, each in its own way, has been taken hold of. They thus become *authentically* bound together" (p. 159). "Only by authentically Being-their-Selves in resoluteness can people authentically be with one another" (p. 344). Heidegger allows a relation in which people work together with such solicitude for one another's authenticity that they take up no project with complementary roles, thus making either party dependent on what is done by the

---

30. Levinas, "Meaning and Sense," 50.

other.[31] They can work together only in parallel, not in interaction—the phenomenalist movement allows no internal, essence-changing relation between persons.

Heidegger's intellectual predecessor Kierkegaard similarly looked for a completely non-coercive relation between selves: "Inwardness [authenticity] cannot be directly communicated, for its direct expression is precisely externality. . . . the reproduction of inwardness in the recipient constitutes the resonance by reason of which the thing said remains absent. . . . To communicate in this manner constitutes the most beautiful triumph of the resigned inwardness."[32]

Advocacy of inwardness (Kierkegaard) or authenticity (Heidegger) is a historically significant protest against cosmological control or generic conformity. But both disallow sharing with others of contributions and of control in what would then be a jointly created common "world." Platonism did provide a common world; each mind possessing a microcosmic copy of *a priori* cosmic order enabling persons to communicate using one same preexisting semantic (if not phonetic) language. The Enlightenment replaced this common world with a common natural human cognitive ability to apprehend an *a priori* natural world. But first-person phenomenalism eliminated both common worlds. This void will be filled by Gadamer, next, with an extension of Heidegger's workman-tool *ready-to-hand* relation into a members-to-members multilaterally interactive community structure.

Early Heidegger was taken as theoretician of the existentialist movement because anti-essentialism and authenticity of the self are basic to that movement. But in 1930 he wrote, "It was never my idea to preach an 'existential philosophy.' Rather, I have been concerned with renewing the question of *ontology*."[33] But Gadamer's extension of the *ready-to-hand* relation to the being-with-others relation, to be taken up after the next four paragraphs, inaugurates the philosophy-of-history manifestation of the communal movement.

---

31. So also Martin Buber describes Heidegger: "In *mere* solicitude man remains essentially with himself, even if he is moved with extreme pity; . . . the barriers of his own being are not thereby breached," in "The Doctrine of Heidegger" 5 in Buber, "What is Man?", 170.

32. Kierkegaard, *Concluding Unscientific Postscript*, 232.

33. Heidegger, *Hegel's Phenomenology of Spirit*, 13.

But first we sketch Heidegger's later development, in which he makes language a social connection prior to thought, to prepare for its use by Louis-Marie Chauvet in chapter 10, below.

The later Heidegger maintains his search for a non-Platonic Being but no longer through analysis of particular Dasein's first-person world. In *What is Metaphysics* (1929) he interprets Kierkegaard's "dread" as fear of nothingness and raises the question, "Why are there beings at all and not rather Nothing?"[34] leading to marvel that there is anything at all. The earlier "existence" as "whatness" of a thing to Dasein (above, page 36) is no longer the path to "Being." In "Postscript" (1943) to *What is Metaphysics* he adds, "Nothing, as the Other to beings, is the veil of Being."[35] In *Letter on Humanism* (1947) Heidegger says that what he earlier called authenticity of the self is "an 'ecstatic' relation of the self's essence to the truth of Being." The initiative has shifted—Dasein's search for Being has now changed into Being's approach toward Dasein. "Thought brings the relation of Being to the self's essence. It does not create or cause this relation; it brings it from Being only as that which was delivered to it by Being. This offering consists in the fact that in thinking Being comes to language. Language is the house of Being. In this lodging the self dwells."[36] In *Identity and Difference* (1957) he says, "At stake is simply experiencing this owning in which self and Being are delivered over to each other."[37] In *On the Way to Language*[38] (1959) he adds, "If the self dwells within the claim of Being through its language, then we Europeans . . . dwell in a completely different house than do East Asians." Language has replaced Dasein as the path to Being—"the word itself is the relation, in that it holds each thing into being and sustains it there. Without this maintenance, the whole of things, the 'world,' would sink away into obscurity, including the 'I.'" Language is prior to the individual: "Language is in its essence neither expression nor activity of human beings. Language speaks." Being has the initiative; language is

---

34. Heidegger, "Was ist Metaphysik?", 19 ["What is Metaphysics?", 112].

35. Heidegger, "Nachwort zu: 'Was ist Metaphysik?'", 107 [*Existence and Being*, 192].

36. Heidegger, "Brief über den Humanismus" (1967) 163, 145 ["Letter on Humanism", 212, 193].

37. Heidegger, *Identität und Differenz*, 100 [*Identity and Difference*, 36].

38. Heidegger, *Unterwegs zur Sprache*, 90; 176f; and 19 [*On the Way to Language*, 5; 73; and *Poetry, Language, Thought*, 197].

its means of speaking its truth to individuals. Heidegger lets language express and stabilize the community's culture.

The later Heidegger's exalting of language as *a priori* call from Being is a significant move away from the Western perennial, modern, and *self-as-such* views of language as a mere *a posteriori* expression of individual thought. French philosophy adapted Heidegger's exalting of language to support a communal perspective. In 1964 Emmanuel Levinas wrote: "There never was a moment in which *meaning first came to birth out of a meaningless being*, outside of a historical position where language is spoken. And that was doubtless what was meant when we were taught that language is the house of being."[39] In 1987 the French theologian Louis-Marie Chauvet simply names later Heidegger's *a priori* origin of language (that never identified "Being)" as interactive human community (below, page 385).

Back to our story. Hans-Georg Gadamer (1900–2002) in *Truth and Method* (1960) extends early Heidegger's *fore-structure* of meaning of a *ready-to-hand* tool (e.g., a hammer) for its single Dasein user to a *fore-structure* of meaning of a community's past corporate interactive experience as a "tool," for a human community in making present choices. Thus, Gadamer introduces his corporate philosophy of history as extension of Heidegger's phenomenally limited internal *ready-to-hand* relation. A decade later Gadamer, in his "Hegel's 'Inverted World'"[40] (1971), also brings forward Hegel's *verkehrte* (inside-out, "inverted") view of the world (above, page 22) in which a person *is* the collection of that person's interactive roles in community.

Gadamer begins in *Truth and Method* by saying the "truth" he looks for in history is not empirical "facts" about the past (as with a police interrogator's "Just the facts, ma'am!"). Rather, the "truth" Gadamer looks for is past community insight that throws some light on a current community issue—a "truth" belonging to the common world of this community yet still intrinsically related with that past world. Such a search differs from the modern period's attempt to study the past objectively; it is not bound by an exclusive authority of "classical" choices from past historical periods (classical Greece, Renaissance painting, classical music, and the like), but it interacts with the past, it is internally related with it.

---

39. Levinas, "Meaning and Sense," 38.
40. Gadamer, *Hegel's Dialectic*, chapter 2.

A case where the authority of the past *is* still recognized as useful in structuring the community's present is the judge's application of a law promulgated in the community's past to a new situation in that community arising since the law was adopted, thus adding to the meanings of both the original law and of the present situation. Here, past and present are bilaterally internally relating. Similarly, the findings of the historian add to the meaning of both past and present situations. And understanding a non-binding law from a different culture involves interpreting its meaning in its own context then translating it into contexts in the historian's culture, seeing what it would say in such contexts. It is the same for religious texts: the secular historian no less than the theologian can understand them only by perceiving not their apparent literal meaning today but what their intended effect in their own cultural context would be in the interpreter's context. A similar relation exists for all historical study (pp. 324–41).

This cultural context, this tradition from within which we interpret, is a fore-structure of meaning for interpreting *present* community relations. It is an extension of Heidegger's fore-structure of meaning from single Dasein's *ready-to-hand* past experience with tools to experience with one's whole human community. "History does not belong to us; we belong to it. Long before we understand ourselves through the process of self-examination, we understand ourselves in a self-evident way in the family, society and state in which we live. The focus of subjectivity is a distorting mirror. The self-awareness of the individual is only a flickering in the closed circuits of historical life" (p. 276). In Gadamer's open advocacy of the corporate view, Hegel's inaugural "inside-out" description of internal interaction to a modern West becomes "outside-in." Both are "*verkehrte*" in German.

Thus, the fore-structure for interpreting history is also a product of history, a product of a long process of making history by applying the past to the present over and over. We understand the past in terms of the present, the present in terms of the past. Past and present are *bilaterally internally* related; they form a hermeneutic circle. Gadamer says:

> The circle, then, is not formal in nature. It is neither subjective nor objective but describes understanding as the interplay of the movement of tradition and the movement of the interpreter. The anticipation of meaning that governs our understanding of a text is not an act of subjectivity but proceeds from the commonality

that binds us to the tradition. But this commonality is constantly being formed in our relation to tradition. Tradition is not simply a permanent precondition, rather we produce it ourselves inasmuch as we understand, participate in the evolution of tradition, and hence further determine it ourselves. Thus, the circle of understanding is not a "methodological" circle, but describes an element in the ontological structure of understanding (p. 293).

One inherits one's fore-structure from a long development of the tradition within which one lives; one also sees it modified before one's eyes as it is used by oneself and others to interpret something new—one must "be aware of one's own bias, so that the text can present itself in all its otherness and thus assert its own truth against one's own fore-meanings" (p. 269).

The interplay of the tradition and the interpreters' horizon takes place through time; understanding is intrinsically a temporal process. In interpreting the past the passage of time is not an impediment to be overcome; rather, it provides a continuing array of new standpoints from which more comprehensive understandings of the past can be reached. We can understand it in some ways not possible in its own time, because we can see both historical consequences and new applications to later situations, including our own. This contrasts with critical history, which ignores the temporal distance and tries to understand the past in itself independently of relations with its future (p. 298). More generally, it contrasts with both Platonism and critical empirical science: "classical metaphysics as a whole is an ontology of the present-at-hand, and modern science is, unbeknownst to itself, its heir" (p. 455). Human beings, having free will, can influence their relations with others, thus changing their own essences, which thus are not totally controlled empirically or cosmologically. Gadamer says, "The overcoming of all prejudices, this global demand of the Enlightenment, will itself prove to be a prejudice" (p. 276). Gadamer is not asking that we interpret social relations in such a relational way. Rather, Gadamer is claiming that we always do so, that knowledge is intrinsically a relation, an interpretation.

Gadamer assumes a much sharper style when he contrasts his corporate position with opposing schools of thought. In the "Afterword" of *Truth and Method* Gadamer says, for example:

> What is remarkable is that, for the sake of rationality [theoretical reason], theory of science here abandons itself to complete

> irrationality and considers philosophical reflection on certain aspects of practical cognition to be illegitimate; it even charges the philosophy that does so with immunizing its contentions against experience. It fails to recognize that it is itself complicit with a much more fatal immunization against experience—for example, against that of common sense and the experience one gains in living. It always does so when it promotes the uncritical expansion of scientific management beyond specific contexts—for example, when it assigns responsibility for political decisions to experts (p. 554).

Gadamer agrees with Hegel, saying, "Fortunately, there can be agreement about the fact that there is only one 'logic of scientific investigation'—but also that it is not sufficient, since at any given time the viewpoints that select the relevant topics of enquiry and foreground them as subjects of research cannot themselves be derived from the logic of investigation" (pp. 554–55). A broader and clearer elaboration of forces, past, current, and future, is open. There is no absolute world to compare it with as in perennial and modern perspectives—no teleological movement, Platonic or empirical, in history. Each particular cultural world is different, yet capable of extending its horizon to include additional human interactive experiences, and so to include some common ground with other particular cultural worlds with which it comes in historical contact (p. 447).

### 4 Language Philosophy: Ludwig Wittgenstein

Language philosophy, like the three philosophical developments already treated in this division, developed the seeds of a communal perspective while still practiced in a modern mode. In the 1890s the logician Gottlob Frege took logic, which serves as core of both perennial and modern philosophies, to be based not on cosmological order or on Kant's twelve synthetic *a priori* categories but on *language*. Then Ludwig Wittgenstein claimed that language is constructed by the community, thus implying that logic, hence perennial, modern, and communal philosophies are also socially constructed.

Frege held three specific positions later to be built on by Wittgenstein. The first is the priority given to *judgments over concepts*, that is, to whole propositions over components (Kant's categories are skeletal judgments, not concepts). "Instead of putting a judgment together out of an individual as subject and an already previously formed concept as predicate, we do the opposite and arrive at a concept by splitting up the content of possible judgement."[41] One of Frege's several illustrations is the way the same proposition can be split up into subject and predicate (that is, name and concept) in three ways in the three sentences: "Mary gave the document to John," "The document was given to John by Mary," and "John was given the document by Mary."[42]

Frege's second significant position is his introduction of *force* to separate assertive force of a statement from its propositional content. He does so in order to distinguish propositions, which are either true or false, from component parts of propositions, which are neither. Working within the objective orientation of the cosmological and modern perspectives, Frege sees assertions properly made only after some propositional content, "a thought," (for example, "everyone dies,") has been judged objectively true. "We may distinguish: (1) the apprehension of a thought—thinking, (2) the recognition of the truth of a thought—judgement, (3) the manifestation of this judgement—assertion."[43] An assertion conveys abstract information to another. "How does a thought act: By being apprehended and taken to be true. . . . The influence of one person on another is brought about for the most part by thoughts."[44] Communal language philosophy does not ask us to believe everything we are told; rather, assertive force will just be the *speaker's claim to the hearer* that his statement is true.

Frege's third contribution to language philosophy of communal interest is his upholding of the public, intersubjective nature of what is said in language. In Frege, however, the public still knows, and discusses, the same things known through the same Kantian transcendental process. Frege distinguishes two parts of meaning, *sense* and *reference*. The reference of an expression is the object designated, while the sense is the mode of presentation of the object through the senses. For example, "morning star" and "evening star" have the same reference (the planet Venus) but not the same sense.[45] Frege introduced the distinction to show how the sense and reference of an assertive sentence are related to

---

41. Frege, "Boole's Logical Calculus and the Concept-script," 17.
42. Frege, "Logic," 141.
43. Frege, "The Thought," 294.
44. Ibid., 310.
45. Frege, "On Sense and Reference," 57.

the senses and references of its component parts. In his system the sense of an assertive sentence is its propositional content and its reference is its objective truth or falsity—positions both necessarily abandoned in communal language philosophy. The communal interest is in Frege's claim that both sense and reference are *public*, not private, as ideas are: "The idea is subjective: one man's idea is not that of another. . . . This constitutes an essential distinction between the idea and the sign's sense, which may be the common property of many, and therefore is not a part or a mode of the individual mind."[46] The reference of an expression is also public. "The regular connection between a sign, its sense, and its reference is of such a kind that to the sign there corresponds a definite sense and to that in turn a definite reference."[47]

Although Frege's position remains modern, by *starting with language* he has avoided the first-person position of rationalism and empiricism based on the thinking processes or empirical experience of individuals. His results fit with language taken as social institution.

Ludwig Wittgenstein (1889–1951) at the end of his academic life produced a thoroughly communal philosophy of language built on Frege's three new positions. His positions, developed here, are taken from part 1 of his *Philosophical Investigations*[48] (translation 1953).

Wittgenstein begins his critique with a critique of Augustine's account of learning language by hearing one's elders name objects as they approach them (*Confessions* 1.8). Wittgenstein says for Augustine, "the individual words in language name objects—sentences are combinations of such names" (§ 1). For Wittgenstein, by contrast, the meaning of language is its *use as tool in social interaction*, and that use requires *whole sentences*, not separate components. Language use is *Sprachspiele* (*play of speech* or, more conventionally translated, *language-game*) as part of community interaction. Wittgenstein says, "the term 'language-game [Sprach*spiele*]' is meant to bring into prominence the fact that the *speaking* of language is part of an activity, or of a form of life" (§ 23). A "form of life" is a community structure, a social institution, that enables social interaction. Wittgenstein offers vivid examples of elementary language games, such as a stonemason calling out the whole sentences

---

46. Ibid., 58.

47. Ibid., 56.

48. References are to the numbered *remarks* in part 1, or, for *notes,* to page numbers.

"Block!" or "Slab!" to let his assistant know which of the two to pass up next (§ 2). Wittgenstein adds, "I shall also call the whole, consisting of language and the actions into which it is woven, the play of language, or 'language-game'" (§ 7). The meaning (sense) of an expression is not its mode of presentation (as in Frege) but what it does in the language game being played: "But doesn't the fact that sentences have the same sense consist in their having the same *use*?" (§ 20). Learning a language is learning not just its structure but how to use it—and this includes learning the cultural interactions themselves in which it is used. The young Augustine learned more than the words for objects his elders talked about, he learned there were such objects and their significance in the cultural world of his elders. More than learning the syntax for asking a question, he learned the social move of doing so.

Wittgenstein appropriates Frege's distinction between force and propositional content but says the two should not be separated; the propositional content alone "is not a *move* in the language-game" (§ 22). Whereas in Frege, a logician, the meaning of a sentence (its sense) is just its propositional content; in Wittgenstein the meaning, its use, includes its force. Whereas Frege relates assertive force to reference, hence to truth, Wittgenstein relates it to sense, hence to use, in accord with his communal orientation lacking the systematizable "truth" of the perennial or modern orientations.

Assertions are not the only moves in language. Wittgenstein gives equal significance to other kinds of force, offering an indefinitely large list of kinds of sentences, or language games—including ordering, obeying orders, describing, reporting, hypothesizing, joking, asking, thanking, cursing, greeting, praying (§ 23), recounting, chatting (§ 25), exclaiming (§ 27). These are all active, intentional, potentially creative moves by individuals using their community's language "form of life" interaction-structure. This structure has been created by the community itself through time: "Our language can be seen as an ancient city: a maze of little streets and squares, of old and new houses, and of houses with additions from various periods; and this surrounded by a multitude of new boroughs with straight regular streets and uniform houses" (§ 18).

Such a conception of language as social institution disallows taking language as mere expression of individual human thought based on introspection, observation, or microcosmic copy of *a priori* world structure (as in modern or cosmologically oriented philosophies).

Wittgenstein concedes he is asking us to abandon cosmological and modern ways of understanding to clear the way for a communal one. "Where does our investigation get its importance from, since it seems only to destroy everything interesting, that is, all that is great and important? . . . What we are destroying is nothing but houses of cards and we are clearing up the ground of language on which they stand" (§ 118). Philosophy is based on language, but also, he says, the cosmological and modern philosophies have been misled by it. "These are, of course, not empirical problems; they are solved, rather, by looking into the workings of our language, and that in such a way as to make us recognize those workings: *in despite of* an urge to misunderstand them. The problems are solved, not by giving new information but by arranging what we have always known. Philosophy is a battle against the bewitchment of our intelligence by means of language" (§ 109).

The bewitchment is spread by means of language, but its origin is the search by Western societies, cosmological or modern, for short-cuts around a responsibility of all to be both creative and receptive in maintaining a participatory social structure. Systemization is the bewitching short-cut to which Platonism succumbs with its Forms, and generic perspectives with their *genera* or common characteristics. Wittgenstein says:

> Consider for example the proceedings that we call "games." . . . What is common to them all?—Don't say: "There *must* be something common, or they would not be called 'games'—but *look and see* whether there is anything common to all. For if you look at them you will not see something that is common to *all*, but similarities, relationships, and a whole series of them at that. To repeat: don't think, but look! . . . I can think of no better expression to characterize these similarities than "family resemblances"; for the various resemblances between members of a family: build, features, colour of eyes, gait, temperament, etc. etc. overlap and criss-cross in the same way (§§ 66–67).

And it is the same with language. "For someone might object against me: '. . . You talk about all sorts of language-games, but have nowhere said what the essence of a language-game, and hence of language, is: what is common to all these activities. . . .' And this is true—Instead of producing something common to all that we call language, I am saying that these phenomena have no one thing in common which makes us use the same word for all—but that they are *related* to one another in many different ways" (§ 65). The warning is not against the discovery of a structure (a grammar, some rules) for games or for language but against a *generic or cosmological characterization* of this structure that misses its complexity and open-endedness.

Structural rules are *constitutive of the structure*, not *prescriptive*. Without, for example, the constitutive rules for baseball defining "strike," "run," and "out" there would not *be* a game of baseball. Constitutive rules for language do not tell us what to say, rather they give words meaning: "Without these rules the word has as yet no meaning, and if we change the rules, it now has another meaning" (p. 147 note (b)). The rules are customs, uses, institutions, techniques, practices: "To obey a rule, to make a report, to give an order, . . . are *customs* (uses, institutions). . . . To understand a language means to be master of a technique" (§ 199). The rules correspond to the fact that language is public rather than private. "'Obeying a rule' is a practice. . . . It is not possible to obey a rule 'privately': otherwise thinking one was obeying a rule would be the same thing as obeying it" (§ 202).

To help those still bewitched by a non-relational view of the world, Wittgenstein mounts a refutation of the first-person empiricist position on its own terms, and does so by arguing against *private language*. By a private language Wittgenstein means a language having words that "refer to what can only be known to the person speaking; to his immediate private sensations" (§ 243), that is, a language with words with a *private reference*. The Enlightenment position that knowledge comes from first-person experience (and once recognized can then be expressed in language independently of the external world or other minds) implies that our ordinary language, even though used by more than one person, is such a private language. Wittgenstein's claim that a private language is impossible thus amounts to a rejection of Enlightenment first-person epistemology, a rejection of first-person rationalism and empiricism.

Two fundamental errors are made, according to Wittgenstein, in holding that there is a private language, (a) that a sensation-word can have a private sense, and (b) that a sensation-word can have a private reference.

(a) According to Wittgenstein, no word can be given a purely ostensive definition (a definition of its sense) merely by indicating its reference. Wittgenstein says if one points to two nuts and says this is called *two*, the other may:

> suppose that "two" is the name given to *this* group of nuts! ... Perhaps you say ... "This *number* is called 'two.'" For the word "number" here shows what place in language, in grammar, we assign to the word. But this means that the word "number" must be explained before the ostensive definition can be understood .... Defining, then, by means of other words! And what about the last definition in this chain? ... The ostensive definition explains the use—the meaning—of the word [only] when the overall role of the word in language is clear (§§ 28–30).

The original definition cannot be made entirely by ostention. Every definition of the sense (i.e., the use) of a word depends on the sense of other words, requires a context of use.

In particular, the attempt of an individual to make a private definition for words referring to allegedly private sensations (such as "pain" or "the color blue") requires a prior context of sense. To assign a word privately to refer to some sensation of my own, with no communication with anyone else, I would also have to decide privately on a sense for the word before I could apply it to a subsequent sensation. But then I could not justify my memory of this sense independently but only by comparing it with my memory of this sense; that is, with itself (§§ 258–69). "One would like to say: whatever is going to seem right to me is right" (§ 258). "As if someone were to buy several copies of the morning paper to assure himself that what it said was true" (§ 265). Rather, assigning a sense to the word requires a public context of sense: "When we speak of someone's having given a name to pain, what is presupposed is the existence of the grammar of the word "pain"; it shews the post where the new word is stationed" (§ 257). A word for a sensation cannot be given a sense in a purely first-person or private manner. A sensation-word's *sense* is public.

(b) Neither is the sensation itself (the reference of the word) a purely first-person or private matter. My sensation of pain is personal in the sense that only I *have* it, but it is not private in the sense that only I know it because other people often know when I am in pain through my natural pain-behavior (such as wincing, or attending to the injured part) (§ 246). Nor is it private in the sense that I know it better than others because "I know that I am in pain" ordinarily means either that I am in pain, or that it makes no sense to say that I doubt that I am in pain (§ 246). The sensations we talk about are not private but public; that is, the public context needed for defining the reference of words referring to them does exist. A sensation-word's *reference* is public.[49]

If individuals could associate a word with a sensation (or with any referent) independently of any social context, the references of the word among different individuals would be unrelated to one another; and if the word had a sense—a use in society—that sense would have no relation to the references:

> Suppose everyone had a box with something in it: we call it a "beetle." No one can look into anyone else's box, and everyone says he knows what a beetle is only by looking at *his* beetle.— Here it would be quite possible for everyone to have something different in his box. One might even imagine such a thing constantly changing.—But suppose the word "beetle" had a use in these people's language?—If so it would not be used as the name of a thing. The thing in the box has no place in the language-game at all; not even as a *something*: for the box might even be empty (§ 293).

Wittgenstein is saying that individuals can talk with one another only about things that have both a public sense and a public reference, which each individual has learned as part of learning the community's language. It is not sufficient to learn the words, or even the sense, from the community; individuals must also learn what they refer to from the community. The word "pain" has a *public* reference by means of its *public* sense. "A child has hurt himself and he cries; then adults talk to him and teach him exclamations and, later, sentences. They teach the child new pain-behavior" (§ 244). "I recognize that there is something there (in me) which I can call 'pain' without getting into conflict with the way other people use this word" (§ 283). "You learned the *concept* 'pain' when you learned language" (§ 384). Similarly, for color words (§§ 273–79): "Look at the blue of the sky and say to yourself 'How blue the sky is!'—... the idea never crosses your mind that this impression of color belongs only to *you*. And you have no hesitation in exclaiming that to someone else. And if you point at anything as you say the words you point at the sky. I am saying: you have not the feeling of pointing-into-yourself, which

---

49. Part of this systematization of Wittgenstein's argument against private language is treated in Kenny, *Wittgenstein*, 156–58, 178–202.

often accompanies 'naming the sensation' when one is thinking about 'private language'" (§ 275). "How do I know that this color is red?—It could be an answer to say: 'I have learnt English'" (§ 381).

Wittgenstein's argument against private language thus has two stages, (a) separating the sense from the reference of sensation-words and showing that it is public, and (b) then showing that the reference of sensation-words is also public. Language and meaning belong to the community, not the generic individual. The argument, if accepted, decimates Enlightenment first-person epistemology—the basis of modern philosophy.

Wittgenstein also rejects the cosmological perspective when he says, in effect, "don't think, but look!" With the cosmological perspective, *forms* are real and material things are derivative; with the modern perspective, *things* are real and ideas of them are derivative. Each position is the reverse of the other, yet both hold their respective realities as objective and independent of the knowing subject. By contrast, for Wittgenstein reality is to be found not in cosmological forms nor in the material world nor in the individual self but in the form of the life of a humanity having the diversity, creativity, and authority to create its form of life within its natural environment—exactly the humanity depicted in Gen 1:27–28 and shown naming the domestic and wild animals in Gen 2:19b–20a. Language, a primary element in humanity's interactive creation of reality, is *a priori* to a participating member but *a posteriori* to the community that is its ongoing creator.

Wittgenstein does not speak in biblical terms, but he *does* lay a corporate anthropological foundation needed for the West to recognize the intended meaning of the biblical epic. Speaking in interacting metonymy, *not* static allegory, one could say Wittgenstein places humanity in a garden, in the east, naming the animals, embracing one another, deciding whether to eat the apple of communal dysfunction. Such a humanity could be bewitched by a systematic perennial or modern god, but would interact communally with a corporate god walking in the cool of the evening and challenging it with "Why are you hiding behind those trees?"

The complementary relation between the constitutive rules of language and the rule-constituted behavior they make possible is filled out for the schematic-minded academic world in the speech-act theory of, among others, John Austin and early John Searle.

Austin claims in *How to Do Things with Words* that the making of an assertion is as much doing something as is the making of a promise, the issuing of an order, or the asking of a question. He gives the name *illocutionary force* to the aspect of the utterance that indicates the social function—such as assertive force, interrogative force, and the others.

Searle, in *Speech Acts* (1969), classifies such illocutionary acts into five types: *assertives,* which commit the speaker to the truth of the propositional content of the utterance; *directives* (commands, requests, questions), attempts by the speaker to get the hearer to do something; *commissives* (promises, bets, threats), which commit the speaker to some future course of action; *expressives* (apologies, thanks, congratulations), expressions of psychological states about presumed states of affairs; and *declaratives,* which create a correspondence between the propositional content and the wider social institutional world by means of the speech act itself ("I resign," "I take you as husband," "I confer the degree of . . .").[50] This classification reveals a taxonomic predilection in Searle that is intentionally avoided by Wittgenstein but which helps show that language exists as a means for community interaction.

Searle also analyzes the constitutive rules for each of the five types of illocutionary acts. His constitutive rules for promises, for example, are: if a speaker is to promise to a hearer that he will do something, then (1) the propositional content of the utterance must be that he will do the something (propositional rule), (2) a promise is uttered only if the hearer would prefer that the speaker do it, and the speaker believes that the hearer would prefer it (otherwise it is not a promise but an assertion or a threat), (3) a promise is uttered only if it is not obvious to both speaker and hearer that the speaker will do it anyway (2 and 3 are preparatory rules), (4) a promise is uttered only if the speaker intends to do it (sincerity rule), and (5) the utterance of a promise counts as the undertaking of an obligation to do it (the essential rule) (p. 63).

Searle displays a taxonomic predilection avoided by Wittgenstein who says "don't think, but look" but necessary in further academic analysis of the use of language. Yet Austin and Searle maintain Wittgenstein's basic point that meaning is conveyed by saying something to someone else for a purpose—that is, with both propositional content and illocutionary force. An assertion, for example, is not merely a linguistic representation of a thought of the speaker; rather through it the speaker

---

50. Searle, "A Classification of Illocutionary Acts."

makes a public commitment to the truth of the propositional content by *telling the hearer* that it *is* a fact. This conception of speaking as *social act*, not just neutral expression of fact or idea, transcends the first-person perspective of the perennial orientation and of modern rationalism and empiricism.

According to Searle, language creates *institutional facts*. He says, "Any newspaper records facts of the following sorts: Mr Smith married Miss Jones; the Dodgers beat the Giants three to two in eleven innings; Green was convicted of larceny; and Congress passed the Appropriations Bill.... Such facts ... I propose to call *institutional facts*. They are indeed facts; but their existence, unlike the existence of brute facts, presupposes the existence of certain human institutions.... These 'institutions' are systems of constitutive rules" (p. 51). Searle skirts the question whether all facts are institutional, which post-critical philosophy of science, below, holds. Language—like marriage, baseball, and law—is itself an institution. The obligation created by asserting or promising is as much an institutional fact as being married or having won a ball game. This claim relativizes the distinction between commissives and declaratives, and ultimately among all Searle's five types of illocutionary act. It restates Wittgenstein's core point: The meaning of an expression is its use in communal interaction; language *is* a community form-of-life.

Searle engaged in a published exchange with Noam Chomsky, whose work in linguistics is within the modern perspective. Searle began the interchange by saying, "The purpose of language is communication in much the same sense that the purpose of the heart is to pump blood. In both cases it is possible to study the structure independently of function but pointless and perverse to do so, since structure and function so obviously interact."[51] This "failure to see the essential connection between language and communication, between meaning and speech acts" is the greatest "defect of the Chomskyan theory."[52]

Chomsky's answer treats the issue as "the object of inquiry" in the chapter so entitled in *Reflections on Language*.[53] He counters with two arguments: (a) The structure of neither the language organ nor the heart is determined by its use; although if either had been too dysfunctional, its evolutionary development might have been aborted (pp. 57–58). Hence,

51. Searle, "Chomsky's Revolution in Linguistics," III.
52. Ibid., V.
53. Chomsky, *Reflections on Language*, chapter 2.

our primary concern should be the study of their structure, not their use. And (b) language is essentially a system for expression of thought (pp. 60–64). From these two arguments Chomsky concludes that there is not the essential connection Searle claims between language and communication, between meaning and speech acts.

Chomsky's claim (b) is a normal position for an empiricist investigating language ability cross-culturally to avoid the effects of cultural influence. His argument (a) so concedes by its concession to natural selection. The Searle-Chomsky disagreement merely reflects their differing communal and empirical interests.

After this exchange, the two scholars effectively reversed positions. Searle abandoned Wittgenstein by 1974,[54] limiting the term "meaning" to representation and using "communication." Previously, Searle used "meaning" to include both representation and the speaker's intention that the hearer recognize the speaker's meaning intention. Searle also renamed his school of language philosophy from "institutional" to "intentional."[55] His subsequent work was within the modern perspective. Meanwhile, Chomsky became prominent as a communally oriented speaker on political issues.

Peter Winch, in *The Idea of a Social Science and its Relation to Philosophy* (1958), begins the extension of the philosophy of language (itself a most basic social institution) to social institutions as a whole—extending the analysis of speech acts as components in the net of multilateral interactions to all social acts—thus enlarging Wittgenstein's "I shall also call the whole, consisting of language and actions into which it is woven, the . . . 'language-game'" (§ 7). Winch finds the sociologist Max Weber[56] already claiming that the social sciences must include the meanings of human actions, not just their empirical causal description: "Weber considers the hypothetical case of two 'non-social' beings, meeting and, in a purely physical sense, 'exchanging' objects. This occurrence, he says, is conceivable as an act of *economic* exchange only if it has a sense. The present actions of the two men must carry with them,

---

54. Searle, "Meaning, Communication, and Representation."

55. "Institutional" in Searle, *Speech Acts*, 71, "intentional," in Searle, "Meaning, Communication, and Representation," 25.

56. Weber, "R. Stammlers 'Ueberwindung' der materialistischen Geschichtsauffassung." Winch, belonging to the language-philosophy manifestation of the communal movement, draws on the political-philosophy manifestation through Weber, as Troeltsch, belonging to the cultural studies manifestation, does (page 32 above).

or represent, a regulation of their future behavior. Action with a sense is symbolic: it goes together with certain other actions in the sense that it *commits* the agent to behaving in one way rather than another in the future" (pp. 49–50).

Generalizing Wittgenstein's argument against private language, Winch says, "I can only be committed in the future by what I do now if my present act is the *application of a rule*" (p. 50). "It is only in a situation in which it makes sense to suppose that somebody else could in principle discover the rule which I am following that I can intelligibly be said to follow a rule at all" (p. 30). "Establishing a standard is not an activity which it makes sense to ascribe to any individual in complete isolation from other individuals" (p. 32).

In *Ethics and Action* Winch adds, "There are important formal analogies between language and other social institutions; for to act in the context of a social institution is always to commit oneself in some way for the future.... To lack [such] integrity is to act with the appearance of fulfilling a certain role but without the intention of shouldering the responsibilities to which the role commits one. If that, *per absurdum*, were to become the rule, the whole concept of a social role would thereby collapse."[57]

A more recent shift toward a communal orientation in sociology and economics is celebrated in Walter Powell and Paul DiMaggio's collection of articles in *The New Institutionalism in Organizational Analysis* (1991). Contributors Roger Friedland and Robert R. Alford preface their contribution "Bringing Society Back In: Symbols, Practices, and Institutional Contradictions" with this summary (p. 232):

> The social sciences are in the midst of a theoretical retreat from society. The retreat has taken two paths, one toward the utilitarian individual and the other toward the power-oriented organization. In this chapter we argue to the contrary, that it is not possible to understand individual or organizational behavior without locating it in a societal context. But to posit the exteriority of society in a nonfunctionalist, nondeterminist manner requires an alternative conception of society as an interinstitutional system. We conceive of institutions as both supraorganizational patterns of activity through which humans conduct their material life in time and space, and symbolic systems through which they categorize that activity and infuse it with meaning.

---

57. Winch, *Ethics and Action*, 70.

> The central institutions of the contemporary capitalist West—capitalist market, bureaucratic state, democracy, nuclear family, and Christian religion—shape individual preferences and organizational interests as well as the repertoire of behaviors by which they may attain them. These institutions are potentially contradictory and hence make multiple logics available to individuals and organizations. Individuals and organizations transform the institutional relations of society by exploiting these contradictions.

Subsequent chapters of this book examine the interaction between the Christian movement and other institutions with contradictory logics—and the resulting contradictory logics within the Christian movement itself—theoretically, for example, among perennial, modern, and corporate theologies and between modern and hermeneutically oriented biblical studies and church history, and practically between power-oriented and empowering pastoral methods for interacting within the church and with the other institutions.

### 5 Post-Critical Philosophy of Natural Science: Charles S. Peirce, Imre Lakatos

A communal understanding of natural science as a social institution appeared earlier than it did for history and for language.

In 1869 the natural scientist Charles Sanders Peirce leveled a devastating communal attack on Descartes, "the father of modern philosophy," in four points (5.264):[58]

(1) "We cannot begin with complete doubt. We must begin with all the prejudices which we actually have when we enter upon the study of philosophy" (5.265).

(2) "To make single individuals absolute judges of truth is most pernicious. . . . We individually cannot reasonably hope to attain the ultimate philosophy which we pursue; we can only seek it, therefore, for the *community* of philosophers" (5.265).

(3) Against Descartes' single deductive chain "in the mode of the geometers" he says, "Philosophy ought . . . to trust rather to the multitude and variety of its arguments than to the conclusiveness of any one. Its reasoning should not form a chain which is no stronger than its weakest link but a cable whose fibres may

---

58. References are to volume and paragraph numbers in Peirce, *Collected Papers*.

be ever so slender, provided they are sufficiently numerous and intimately connected" (5.265).

(4) "Scholasticism . . . undertook to explain all created things. But there are many facts which Cartesianism not only does not explain, but renders absolutely inexplicable" (5.264).

These claims attack not only Cartesian rationalism but Kantian transcendental epistemology as well. Whereas Kant claimed that different individuals learn the same things through their similar modes of perception and categories of thought, Peirce claims that knowledge belongs to the community—that community knowledge builds on previous community knowledge through the interaction of scholars who do *not* all know the same thing. "In storming the stronghold of truth one mounts upon the shoulders of another who has to ordinary apprehension failed, but has in truth succeeded by virtue of the lessons of his failure" (7.51). Scientific investigation is communal; scientific knowledge is the ongoing result of continuous multilaterally internal relation among scientists.

Peirce founded the *American pragmatic school*, defining pragmatism thus: "Consider what effects, that might conceivably have practical bearings, we conceive the object of our conception to have. Then, our conception of these effects is the whole of our conception of the object" (5.402). Like Hegel, Peirce is saying that things are their actions on the world. Peirce's definition eliminates theoretical meaning in the perennial and modern senses; it eliminates the distinction between theoretical and practical reason. Peirce says, "The whole function of thought is to produce habits of action. . . . There is no distinction of meaning so fine as to consist in anything but a possible difference of practice" (5.400).

American communal pragmatists, including Peirce, William James, John Dewey, and George Herbert Mead, provide a foundation for subsequent post-critical philosophers of education—and of natural science with Karl Popper, Thomas Kuhn, and Imre Lakatos.

In "Falsification and the Methodology of Scientific Research Programmes"[59] (1970), Imre Lakatos traces the history of the philosophy of science from the pre-Enlightenment view that science proves facts, through to Popper's view of science as a series of generalizing conjectures corrected by discovery of counterexamples, and to Kuhn's as a series of revolutionary new scientific paradigms, and to his own view of

---

59. Lakatos, *The Methodology of Scientific Research Programmes*, 8–101.

science as a *collection* of research programs—each program consisting of cooperative contributions over many years from many scientists. Such a research program begins with the construction of a *theory* that agrees with as many observed facts as can be managed, in full knowledge that this first version will have many counterexamples. The counterexamples do not refute the theory; they spur on the search for adjustments that will make for a wider fit between theory and observation. The successful programs are those that not only continue to improve the fit with observed data but also predict previously unimagined facts (pp. 47–52). Two examples: the theory of gravitation when first worked out for several moving objects in space disagreed with the orbits of the known planets, thus predicting the location of another previously unobserved planet. The theory of relativity successfully predicted a previously unimagined change in apparent positions of distant stars nearly behind the sun during its eclipse by the moon (p. 39). Successful programs discover new facts, not merely explain old ones.

There is no sharp boundary between *observation* and *theory*. Both are part of socially constructed reality. Galileo "observed" mountains on the moon with his telescope, but the *theory* of lenses was too new to win against Aristotle's *theory* that the moon was a faultless crystal ball (p. 14). More recently, some have questioned the theory of radio telescopes used to locate astronomical bodies. In 1815, W. Prout claimed that the atomic weights of all pure elements are whole numbers. He did so knowing full well that anomalies existed, such as chlorine's atomic weight of 35.5. When the *theory* of pure samples was changed a century later to include centrifugal as well as chemical separation, two isotopes of chlorine appeared: chlorine 35 and chlorine 36 (pp. 43, 53–54). Community creation of language includes *creating the concepts* as well as assigning names for them.

Lakatos differentiates between *passivist, conservative activist,* and *revolutionary activist* theories of knowledge:

> "Passivists" hold that true knowledge is Nature's imprint on a perfectly inert mind: mental *activity* can only result in bias and distortion. The most influential passivist school is classical empiricism. Now *conservative "activists"* hold that we are born with our basic expectations; with them we turn the world into "our world" but must then live for ever in the prison of our world. The idea that we live and die in the prison of our "conceptual frame-

work" was developed primarily by Kant: pessimistic Kantians thought that the real world is for ever unknowable because of this prison, while optimistic Kantians thought that God created our conceptual framework to fit the world. But *revolutionary activists* believe that the conceptual frameworks can be developed and also replaced by new *better* ones; it is *we* who create our "prisons" and we can also, critically, demolish them (p. 20).

Lakatos is claiming that our community's scientific understanding of the physical world we live in is active as well as passive, is always moving forward through a creative internal circular relation between our conceptual frameworks and that understanding, with each constantly changing the other.

## 6 Remodernizing Communal Political Philosophy: Jürgen Habermas

Two current non-communally oriented philosophers, empiricist Jürgen Habermas and perennialist Alasdair MacIntyre, display, under pressure from communal philosophy, some communal components (interpretation and interaction in Habermas and development of tradition and social imputation of identity in MacIntyre) but do not recognize multilaterally internal interaction as their foundation. Habermas's attempt to absorb the mentioned communal features into a still continuing modern orientation is treated in this section; MacIntyre's attempt to absorb the other mentioned communal features into a continuing perennial orientation is taken up in the next.

Political philosopher Jürgen Habermas inherited a *critical theory* tradition, starting with the corporate breakthrough of Hegel and Marx, corrupted backwards toward Kant's *Critique of Pure Reason* by Engels and others, and renewed in the years from 1923 to 1973 by Frankfurt Marxist scholars Max Horkheimer, Theodor Adorno, and Herbert Marcuse, who sought to reform a corrupt Marxism and fit it to twentieth century circumstances. It will emerge that Habermas, like Marxism itself, moved progressively backwards from early Marx's own communal base.

*Critical theory* is a theory on the way the human community reflects on its own formation in order to further that formation. Habermas presents his first version of critical theory in *Knowledge and Human Interests* (1968).

There, Habermas says, critical theory offers a particular epistemology, or basis for knowledge: We never know anything disinterestedly, merely theoretically. Rather, what we know is related internally to three communal *interests*. (1) The *instrumental interest* in technically exploitable knowledge is pursued through *empirical-analytic* inquiry. (2) The *practical interest* is pursued through *historical-hermeneutic* inquiry aiming at maintaining action-orienting communicatively accomplished synchronic and diachronic mutual understanding. (3) The *emancipatory interest* is pursued through *critical* inquiry seeking liberation from systematic communicative distortion, ideology, illusion, false consciousness, and whatever else blocks a society's coming of age, a maturity of "autonomy and responsibility," *Mündigkeit* (being of age), "enlightenment," as in Kant's essay "What is Enlightenment?" in which the members interact without domination by others. The emancipatory interest is basic; the instrumental and historical-hermeneutic interests emerge as necessary specifications of it when the community interacts respectively with the material world or internally with itself (pp. 191–98).

The instrumental and hermeneutic interests are drawn out of C. S. Peirce and Dilthey. From Peirce (above, page 58), Habermas draws out technical interest as the epistemological basis for instrumental inquiry, and also the intersubjective character of empirical science requiring both historical-hermeneutic and instrumental action. From Dilthey (above, page 31), he draws out the mutual understanding mediated by language as basis for the historical-hermeneutic inquiry.

From Hegel, Habermas draws out the corporate nature of critical self-reflection. He rejects a supposed Hegelian convergence to an *a priori* absolute truth as being inconsistent with its corporate circular nature (p. 10), holding rather to Hegel's actual, more flexible, goal of an emancipation that can take many different forms. From Marx he takes the concretizing of the instrumental and practical interests in cooperative labor. For Habermas, as for Marx, technical progress may open the possibility of reducing technically necessary social limitations; thus the instrumental interest serves the emancipatory interest. He also takes from Marx the concretization of the blockages to autonomy-and-responsibility as false consciousness imposed by forces of exploitation, hence the need for a critical social theory to reveal them and thus raise the consciousness of society.

From Freud, Habermas takes psychoanalytic repression as analogue of distorted communication caused by institutionalized power blocking resolution of conflicts and coming of age. He also takes from Freud the view that civilization consists not solely in maintaining technical means for survival but also coercive and ideological means for enforcing cooperation.

How communal is Habermas? Marx's basic interest could be called emancipation, but it would be not Habermas's emancipation of the individual but rather, unlike subsequent Marxism, emancipation of the community from dysfunction toward intentional internal interaction, so that an emancipated individual would be one who participates constructively in that community's community interaction. When the slaves in the southern United States were "emancipated" in 1865, their freedom as separate selves and as a class lasted only until the next meal, whereupon they returned to their quarters on their plantations and resumed their work. A century later the descendents of the former owners *and* of former slaves were *less* emancipated to intentional internal interaction. The emancipations of both Marx and Habermas exploit empirical-analytic and historical-hermeneutic interests. But Marx's empirical-analytic interest is based on a communal internal relation, while Habermas's is based on a modern freedom from restraint by others. From the historical-hermeneutic interest, Marx exploits communal history and Habermas exploits critical history. Habermas will later have to yield to critics on his confusing generic Kantian and corporate Hegelian-Marxian conceptions of emancipation.

In a public exchange with Gadamer,[60] Habermas objects to Gadamer's giving the hermeneutic interest primacy over his critical interest. Habermas says if a society understands itself in the context of a systematically communicatively distorted tradition (an ideology), then the distortion will be continued indefinitely unless there is some critical emancipatory interest to direct the hermeneutic enterprise toward Kant's autonomy-and-responsibility.

Gadamer responds to Habermas's critique in "On the Scope and Function of Hermeneutical Reflection."[61] Gadamer acknowledges com-

---

60. Habermas, "Summation and Response" to Gadamer's "On the Scope and Function of Hermeneutical Reflection"; also "A Review of Gadamer's *Truth and Method*.

61. Pagination is for reprinted version in Gadamer, *Philosophical Hermeneutics*.

mon ground with Habermas but nevertheless makes the following points, as detailed in the following subsections (a)–(g). (a) The interpretation of the present, which is available through the application of the tradition, is the only absolute in the sense that the community cannot get outside of it. The instrumental and emancipatory interests are human interests and hence, cannot have an *a priori* status outside this hermeneutic whole. (b) Interpretation itself leads to emancipation from rigidified prejudices, since the fore-structures that make understanding possible are always modified by the fusion of horizons during the understanding. "This is something that *hermeneutical reflection* teaches us: that social community, with all its tensions and disruptions, ever and ever again leads back to a common area of social understanding through which it exists" (p. 42). (c) Because of the finitude of human existence and the particularity of reflection, a society cannot base *every* understanding on explicit reflection and consensus (p. 34). (d) Explicit consensus does not guarantee shared meaning "precisely because meaning can be expressed even where it is not actually intended" (p. 30). Together, (c) and (d) imply that the merging of horizons is not the same thing as an understanding defined by explicit consensus; rather, it is a communally effective working relation of the two sides (as exemplified on page 9, above, by my relation with my cat). Consensus is a generic rather than communal concept.

(e) The analogy drawn by Habermas between emancipation of society and psychoanalytic emancipation of the individual is improper because the analyst, acting as a professional, influences the patient from outside the mutual interpretive relationship between them. "But what happens when he uses the same kind of reflection . . . [when] he is not the doctor but a partner in a game?" The psychoanalytic power "must be given its boundaries through the societal context and consciousness, within which the analyst and also his patient are on even terms with everybody else. . . . Most fundamentally: Over against what self-interpretation of the social consciousness (and all morality is such) is it in place to inquire *behind* that consciousness—and when is it not?" (pp. 41–42). (f) An *a priori* emancipatory reflection, independent of the existing social relationships of understanding, is anti-authoritarian and ultimately anarchistic, rejecting authority as well as power. "The basically emancipatory consciousness must have in mind the dissolution of all authority, all obedience" (p. 42). "I cannot accept . . . that reason and authority are abstract antitheses, as the emancipatory Enlightenment did. Rather . . . they stand in a basically ambivalent relation, a relation I think should be explored" hermeneutically (p. 33). (g) If the scientific method associated with the instrumental interest, and the *a priori* critical reflection associated with the emancipatory interest, fall outside of interpretation and the merging of horizons then they themselves become "a hermeneutically false consciousness, the antidote for which can only be a more universal hermeneutical reflection" (p. 42).

In 1970, critics forced Habermas to revise his system to make its generic base more explicit. They complained that Enlightenment Kantian transcendental critical reflection and Marxian (or Freudian) critical self-reflection, which appear to be synthesized in *Knowledge and Human Interests*, are too distinct to be unified.[62] The first is a theoretical reflection on the conditions for generic human knowledge, whereas the second is a self-reflection by a particular corporate (or single) body in the effort to eliminate particular communal (or single) self-deceptions. Habermas admitted this confusion in 1975,[63] abandoned the latter, and declared himself to be for the less communal former in the modified form of *rational reconstruction of pragmatics*, presented in "What is Universal Pragmatics?" (1976).

*Pragmatics* is the study of the *use of language*. In the speech-act theory of Wittgenstein, Austin, and early Searle this would be understood as the use of language for communication, with constitutive rules corporately created by the community as described by Searle, and originally claimed by Wittgenstein: "Disputes do not break out . . . over the question whether a rule has been obeyed or not. That is part of the framework on which the working of our language is based" (*Philosophical Investigations* §§ 240–41). Habermas, however, regains his generic base by defining rational reconstructive sciences as *"sciences that systematically reconstruct the intuitive knowledge of competent subjects"* (p. 9), thus making rational reconstruction of pragmatics be a systemization of individual competence to *express* meaning rather than community competence to *communicate* meaning. This projects Wittgenstein's community use of language to interact onto individual competence to express oneself, thus losing its original communal dimension. Pragmatic competence in the

---

62. Apel, "Wissenschaft als Emanzipation?"; Dietrich Böhler, "Zum problem des emanzipatorischen Interesses"; McCarthy, *The Critical Theory of Jürgen Habermas*.

63. Habermas, "A Postscript to *Knowledge and Human Interests*," 182; also Habermas, *Theory and Practice*, 22.

individual is the generic base for Habermas's new critical theory: it fits better with a critical theory originating with Kant's three "critiques."

Habermas adapts Searle's constitutive rules for *communicating* within a community into individual pragmatic competence to *express* meaning. To free himself further from communally defined meaning, Habermas systematizes, as Chomsky did, to a general cross-cultural level—*universal* pragmatics—to get a pragmatic competence holding across all languages. Habermas also considers only *institutionally unbound* speech acts—that is, speech acts whose force is not dependent on some specific social institution such as marriage but is the original creation of language itself, like promising (pp. 38–39) (Wittgenstein would say promising is also a social institution). This last pruning eliminates Searle's declarative category of illocutionary acts, the category Searle calls paradigmatic for all speech, showing language as a whole to be a social institution for interacting with others (above, page 55).

Habermas also groups Searle's directives and commissives together, with a resulting taxonomy of three kinds of illocutionary acts: constatives (Searle's assertives), regulatives (Searle's directives and commissives), and expressives. These three acts thematize respectively the cognitive, interactive, and expressive communicative attitudes of the speaker, used respectively in relations with the external, social, and inner worlds (pp. 67–68). For Habermas, each illocutionary act not only thematizes one of these attitudes but is "the medium of interrelating three worlds; for every successful communicative action there exists a threefold relation between the utterance and (a) 'the external world' as the totality of existing states of affairs, (b) 'our social world' as the totality of all normatively regulated interpersonal relations that count as legitimate in a given society, and (c) 'a particular inner world' (of the speaker) as the totality of his intentional experiences" (p. 67). The first two ways of relating with the world through language reproduce, respectively, the earlier version's technical and hermeneutic knowledge-constitutive interests. Moreover, the now properly universalized emancipatory interest appears in the revised critical theory as *language* itself. Habermas says, "What raises us out of nature is the only thing whose nature we can know: *language*. Through its structure, [emancipation is] posited for us. Our first sentence expresses unequivocally the intention of universal and unconstrained consensus."[64] Habermas's emancipating language competence is generic and universalizing.

Habermas concedes that "the model of transcendental philosophy undeniably suggests itself," but he distinguishes universal pragmatics from Kantian transcendental philosophy in two ways. (a) In the present system utterances are generated; whereas, in the Kantian system experiences are constituted ('how one speaks' in place of 'how one knows'). (b) In the present system the reconstruction in systematic form of the *a priori* rule-consciousness of competent speakers is *a posteriori*, rather than being justified by a transcendental critical reflection ('rational reconstruction of how one speaks' in place of 'rational reconstruction of how one knows') (pp. 23–25).

Habermas, starting with Enlightenment emancipation, sidesteps Kant's generic *a priori* transcendental understanding by substituting an *a posteriori* study of generic pragmatic competence. He does so in order to reach an *a posteriori* emancipatory interest outside the historical-hermeneutic whole (seen by Marx, Gadamer, and Wittgenstein as inclusive of all interest, and found language-wise by the latter two in communal language use rather than generic language competence). The disagreement reflects the difference between the Enlightenment emancipatory goal, *freedom from restraint*, and the communal emancipatory goal, promotion of ties of multilaterally internal *interdependent interaction* among community members.

### 7 A Communally Decorated Perennial Moral Philosophy: Alasdair MacIntyre

Alasdair MacIntyre, like Habermas, includes features from the communal movement in a system that is fundamentally not communal. His moral philosophy includes cosmologically based narrative from Homer's epics and virtues from Aristotle's *Ethics*, yet allows for tradition and social imputation of identity. He does not use Sophocles's drama, which is built on corporately suggestive unawares violation of social roles, itself a potential dramatic challenge to the perennial perspective. MacIntyre remains within the perennial orientation.

In his *After Virtue* (1981), MacIntyre says current Western moral philosophy is an incoherent shell of the classical Western cosmological

---

64. Habermas, *Knowledge and Human Interests*, 314.

moral perspective lost at the Enlightenment. "What we possess . . . are the fragments of a conceptual scheme, parts which now lack those contexts from which their significance derived" (p. 2). He recounts a series of unsuccessful attempts to provide coherent generic rational justifications of morality, passions, and desires (Hume), reason (Kant), utility (Benjamin Franklin and John Stuart Mill), and bureaucratic utility (as disclosed by Max Weber)—attempts only to be abandoned by the existentialist reduction of morality to individual choice (Kierkegaard) or will (Nietzsche), and by the emotivist view that ethical statements are expressions of attitudes that are used to produce similar attitudes in others. Yet, MacIntyre claims, ordinary ethical language today still reveals a persistent assumption that ethical matters are matters of fact.

How might moral philosophy be reconnected to its pre-Enlightenment moral tradition? MacIntyre sketches that lost tradition. Homer in the eighth century BCE portrays a heroic society that includes "a conception of what is required by the social role which each individual inhabits; a conception of excellences or virtues as those qualities which enable an individual to do what his or her role requires; and a conception of the human condition as . . . vulnerable to destiny" (p. 116)—all unified by means of epic narrative. The *virtues* needed include justice, courage, and honesty. Thus, for MacIntyre: in the heroic tradition one inhabits an assigned social role as part of one's essence, with virtues being capacities to fill that role. Particular individuals have particular roles, so *narrative* is the appropriate rationality for understanding community. But "all questions of choice arise within the framework; the framework itself therefore cannot be chosen" (p. 118). The community has no responsibility for the frame. Homer's heroic community is cosmologically controlled.

MacIntyre's historical sketch continues: In a more complex society a tragic conflict of roles can arise, say, between family and citizen roles—and the *dramatic* rationality of Sophocles (c.495–c.406) reveals this conflict, implying an inadequacy in Homer's perspective. But Plato and Aristotle do not give up Homer's cosmological base; instead they suppress the conflict of roles by abandoning the particularity of narrative and dramatic rationalizations for *universalizing* ones. Plato's *Republic* searches abstractly for the ideal polity. Aristotle's *Politics* rejects the ideal approach and systematizes practical, existing polities; and his *Ethics* avoids the conflict of roles by replacing the end or *telos* for each individual based on that individual's social role with a general biological-political *telos* for the universal individual: "Human beings, like the members of all other species, have a specific nature, and that nature is such that they . . . move by nature towards a specific *telos*. The good is defined in terms of their specific characteristics" (p. 139). Applying the one good to specific cases is not routine but requires the additional virtue of good judgment: "The exercise of such judgment is not a routinizable application of rules. Hence . . . there is relatively little mention of rules anywhere in the *Ethics*" (p. 141). MacIntyre considers Aristotle's making the individual responsible for applying the good to be an improvement over Plato. Nevertheless, he says for Plato and for Aristotle that "there exists a cosmic order which dictates the place of each virtue in a total harmonious scheme of human life" (p. 133).

But MacIntyre sees Aristotle as still needing supplementation with narrative rationality from Homer, and with recognition of a development of tradition. MacIntyre says Aristotle himself builds on previous tradition, writing "we say," not "I say" (p. 138); but the absence of any historical sense not only "debars Aristotle from recognizing his own thought as part of a tradition, it also severely limits what he can say about narrative. Hence . . . the relationship between virtues and forms of narratives . . . present in epic and tragic writers has to wait—a very long wait—for successors to Aristotle whose biblical culture has educated them to think historically" (p. 138)—and thus to add Homer's narrative rationality and MacIntyre's development of rationality to the pre-Enlightenment Aristotelian tradition's universalizing cosmological rationality.

MacIntyre does this. He says an individual life has its unity as a *character* in an enacted narrative, a narrative centered on that individual (but including other characters as well) and included in a larger narrative for a larger community over a longer time. Thus, personal identity for the individual is not based on psychological continuity but on social imputation of identity:

> What is crucial to human beings as characters in enacted narratives is that, possessing only the resources of psychological continuity, we have to be able to respond to the imputation of strict identity. I am forever whatever I have been at any time for others—and I may at any time be called upon to answer for it—no matter how changed I may be now. There is no way of *founding* my identity—or lack of it—on the psychological continuity or

> discontinuity of the self. The self inhabits a character whose unity is given as the unity of a character.... The characters in a history are not a collection of persons, but the concept of a person is that of a character abstracted from a history (p. 202).

Thus, a second additional virtue is needed, namely, "having an adequate sense of the traditions to which one belongs or which confront one.... Living traditions... continue a not-yet-completed narrative" (p. 207).

MacIntyre's moral philosophy remains perennial. In the communal perspective one is not forever what one has been to others. Rather, who one is is constantly changing through constant choices by oneself and by the others; one is the collection of one's roles in both *past* and *current* community internal interaction—interaction that constantly modifies who one is and what one's internally relating community is. One's past interactions show up in the present as being a changed member in a changed community, and thus continue to be significant along with more recent interactions. Narrative does not have an ontological status independent of continuing interaction, but is a tool created by the community for communal remembering of its past for use as a present influence, requiring it to be interpreted hermeneutically to preserve it for further extension in meaning interactively with the ever new present. Virtues are tools more systematic than narrative for stability in community interaction, but still need modification through time. MacIntyre's sources are all Greek, and the one Greek insight he does not incorporate into his system is Sophocles' dramatic conflict of social roles, an issue the corporate perspective exists to resolve.

MacIntyre closes his book by saying, "exhaustion is shared by every... political tradition within our culture" (p. 244), so that, as at the decline of the Roman empire, we need "new forms of community within which... moral life can be sustained through the new dark ages. We are waiting... for another... St. Benedict" (p. 245). We will find MacIntyre's conception of human relation and sectarian solution echoed (below, page 368) in his look-alike twentieth century theologian Stanley Hauerwas.

Viewed from the corporate perspective, MacIntyre offers a sectarian solution, a waiting by a select group for better times (which, when they came after the medieval period as Renaissance, actually moved Western culture even further away from creative interactive contribution by all parts of the community). What are needed are prophets, not a holding operation. (Medieval religious orders were actually more proactive than MacIntyre allows, and the underclasses more corporately oriented.) The corporate perspective, in contrast, would ask for a *new creative* virtue (still practiced in the peasant class and in third-world cultures not yet under European colonization), a virtue to risk a *multilaterally internal interaction* with and within the "exhausted" society that would change members from consumers to sharers of creativity with one another—cultures which, like ancient Israel, could be "a light to the gentiles."

After the Enlightenment, Renaissance entrepreneurial pressure broke the hegemony of classical Western philosophy of cosmological control with a modern philosophy, soon itself to become torn between a romantic search for social relation and a competing existentialist independence for the self. The romantic movement initiated another revolt, this time against this culturally flat Enlightenment, a revolt that moved a succession of early innovators (Hobbes, Rousseau, Dilthey, Troeltsch, Heidegger, Frege) to build a philosophy leading toward but not reaching a communal orientation. Hegel did reach it, claiming that each individual is multilaterally internally related with the others—in fact is the collection of all that individual's roles in these interactions. Marx worked for more even distribution of creativity between management and workers in such internal interactions. Kierkegaard rejected all control: cosmological, modern, or interactive. Heidegger rejected cosmological and social control but recognized an internal relation of a single human being with its tools, thus beginning the reduction of Kant's theoretical reason to being a part of practical reason. Gadamer extended that relation with tools to multilaterally intrinsic relation with other human beings. He initially, and late Wittgenstein definitively, revealed language as paradigmatic example of the social institutions needed for multilaterally internal community interaction. Post-critical natural science recognized understanding of nature (that is, the study of natural science itself) as being interactively constructed by the internally relating scientific community.

Where did this new movement come from? All of these philosophers understood their work as steps in the continuing development of European philosophy. None of them claimed any source outside the Western tradition, and all of them ignored the corporately oriented Old and New Testaments still enjoying formal canonical status in Europe, and though Hegel, Heidegger, Gadamer, Kierkegaard, MacIntyre, and others had had academic theological training). Marx, Kierkegaard, and Heidegger went so far as to imply that the church suppressed the possibility of even an approach toward the reforms they favored, implying that only with the loss of Christian cultural hegemony could these reforms find acceptance. Most European progressives today think the same. The emerging communal perspective's development as a counter force not just to the Enlightenment but also to a Western Christianity separated from its base in corporate Scripture, implies that Scripture's corporate perspective could not until now be expressed in translation into Indo-European languages as yet lacking the vocabulary and interactive literary conventions to describe internal social relation. But, was an implicit corporate tradition in fact surviving below the academic world's line-of-sight in Western non-elite classes and in dispersion Judaism in their corporate participation in liturgy and metonymic (rather than allegorical) application of biblical narrative to current community life? Could these factors account for the recent emergence of a communal perspective? If so, that was not recognized by the scholars.

But there is an obvious influence in the opposite direction. The rest of the present book is an account of how the communal turn, once accomplished within secular Western philosophy, opened the way for the first ever explicit recognition by Western Christian theologians of the Old Testament as a thoroughly corporate document, and the equally corporate New Testament as applying that same tradition to the life of its "new" community—a recognition pioneered by communally oriented biblical scholars in the last two and a half centuries (including Johannes Weiss, Walther Eichrodt, and C. H. Dodd (chapter 2, next)) who, in turn, opened the way for theologians like Johann Adam Möhler, Johann Baptist Metz, Gustavo Gutiérrez, and Louis-Marie Chauvet (chapters 8 and 10, below) to reconstruct a corresponding biblically-based communal theology.

2

## The New Testament I

*Continuity with the Old Testament*

THE STUDY OF CHRISTIAN ambivalence toward the Old Testament properly begins with consideration of the Christian movement's earliest available source, the New Testament.

Is the New Testament itself ambivalent toward the Old Testament? If not, does it confront the West with a Christianity continuing the *corporate* tradition of the Old Testament, or does it promulgate a new religion within the West's then *cosmological* perspective?

The Old Testament's editors schematized it into three parts—Torah, Prophets, and Writings—as accounts of the handling of three crises in Israel's history: its beginning after humanity fell into total dysfunction at Babel; its institution, under threat from outside, of a monarchy balanced by prophets; and its return, powerless from the Babylonian captivity. Was the New Testament intended as a fourth part of Israel's tradition and, if so, was it to meet the crisis of a European occupation that imposed an incompatible cultural tradition, or the crisis of moving into dispersion, or of a mission to the West thus made practicable? Or was it intended not as a next stage for Israel but as foundation for a new religion? This latter is what happened, but was that its purpose or was it intended for that fourth stage?

Word-for-word literal translation from Semitic to Indo-European language is impossible because Western culture and its languages cannot recognize or express community internal interaction well. Ezek 37 "valley of dry bones" is not literal but a figure for corporately dysfunctional community. And the same for Paul's epistles, even though in Greek: his "power" of "death" (Rom 7:5) means "contagious influence" of "community dysfunction."

This chapter analyzes the New Testament's relation to the Old at three progressively more abstract levels: (I) recognizing an intimate New Testament literary dependence on the Old Testament, (II) devising a taxonomy of New Testament applications of Old Testament passages, and (III) analyzing the thus indicated New Testament theological dependence on the Old Testament. Chapter 3 analyzes the interactive apocalyptic idiom within which the New Testament is written, also necessarily missed by modern scholars.

## I THE EXISTENCE OF AN INTIMATE LITERARY RELATION TO THE OLD TESTAMENT

The Nestle-Aland *Novum Testamentum Graece* indicates 480 direct quotations of the Old Testament, and some 3840 allusions to specific Old Testament texts, for a total of 4320 short, "atomic" references to the Old Testament.[1] These references average one reference to the Old Testament every 1.87 New Testament verses. This standard work seeks to represent a consensus, and some individual scholars find more Old Testament allusions. For example, Howard Clark Kee finds 257 Old Testament quotations, allusions, or influences in the 231 verses of Mark 11–16, for an average of one "atomic" relation to the Old Testament per 0.93 verse,[2] more than twice the frequency of the Nestle-Aland listings for the same part of Mark, even though Kee intentionally omits a number of the Nestle-Aland instances.

There are also large-scale literary similarities with the Old Testament, such as correspondence of the five parts of Matthew beginning with chapters 1, 8, 11, 19, and 26 with the five books of the Torah, and use of the apocalyptic literary form, as in Daniel, by the writer of Revelation. There are also intermediate-scale similarities, such as between the seven bowls of wrath in Revelation 16 and the plagues in Exod 7–10, and between Jesus' Sermon on the Mount in Matt 5–7 and the giving of the Law to Moses on Mount Sinai.[3]

Often the relation of larger units is signaled by atomic allusions. The words "six days" in Mark 9:2 alluding to the words "six days" in

---

1. *Novum Testamentum Graece*, Appendix III, "Loci citate vel allegati."

2. Kee, "The Function of Scriptural Quotations and Allusions in Mark 11–16," 165–88.

3. Some larger-scale similarities are collected in Sahlin, "The New Exodus of Salvation according to St. Paul."

Exod 24:16, for example, call attention to the similarity between the transfiguration and the giving of the Law to Moses, including going to the top of the mountain, being accompanied by three close companions two of whom are brothers, God speaking out of a cloud, having a shining face or garments, and finding faithless disciples on return.[4] Another example is Matt 2:15 = Hos 11:1 "Out of Egypt have I called my son," which calls attention to a more extended correspondence between the "Son" Jesus and the "son" Israel whom God called out of Egypt, baptized in the Red Sea, and tempted in the wilderness.

These two larger-scale examples support the widely held position that New Testament quotations of short Old Testament passages do not lift them out of their Old Testament context but refer the reader to the whole historical account containing the quotation.[5] What is of greater interest for this study is that such quotations, including these two examples, *also* serve to interpret the *wider New Testament context* into which a quotation is introduced. The New Testament has a literary relation to the Old because its writers wished *to interpret their own situation* by examples from their own past community experience, much of which was enshrined in the Old Testament.

## II NEW TESTAMENT APPLICATION OF OLD TESTAMENT PASSAGES

Some intimate literary connection between the Testaments is generally accepted, although some scholars manage to ignore it. But scholars differ on its purpose, on what the New Testament writers intended by using it. I will show that communal presuppositions can distinguish two possible uses of an Old Testament passage: *typology*, a giving of meaning to new events through a bilaterally internal relation within the *same* continuing history with the earlier referred to events, and *allegory*, a universalizing use of the abstract structure of the earlier event to make visible an analogous, but *not* interacting, structure in a present *different* history. Modern presuppositions see all use of the past as universalizing. Thus, communal presuppositions provide a finer distinction than can

---

4. Hobbs, "Norman Perrin on Methodology," 86–87.

5. So Rendall, "Quotation in Scripture," 214–21; Dodd, *According to the Scriptures*, 61; Lindars, *New Testament Apologetic*, 15; Childs, *Biblical Theology in Crisis*, 116; etc. But disagreeing are Sundberg, "On Testimonies," 278; Barr, *Old and New in Interpretation*, 142–43.

be reached with non-communal ones that are not able to recognize the historical relation here called typology, and instead tend to call typology any relation between two passages, one in each Testament. Under the communally understood typology-allegory distinction, we will find that the New Testament never uses the Old Testament allegorically, as its use of the Old Testament is history-extending, and that the New Testament is as corporate in its perspective as is the Old—all in contrast to the findings under modern presuppositions.

The distinction between typology and allegory will be made in the course of constructing a taxonomy of New Testament applications of Old Testament passages. Organizing the totality of New Testament usages of the Old Testament into taxonomies has been attempted by several scholars. C. K. Barrett, G. W. H. Lampe, and K. J. Woollcombe break ground with a classification of New Testament use of the Old Testament under the three heads: (a) fulfillment of prophecy, (b) typology, and (c) allegory.[6] Walther Eichrodt's classification includes (a) typology, (b) allegory, (c) paraenesis (i.e., moralizing use of the Old Testament), and (d) prophecy and fulfillment.[7] Barnabas Lindars distinguishes (a) legal citation, (b) the rewritten Bible, (c) typology, (d) moral apophthegms, and (e) apocalyptic eschatology.[8] James Barr lists seven kinds of New Testament use of the Old Testament: (a) typology, (b) allegory, (c) use of Old Testament examples in paraenesis, (d) fulfillment of prophecy, (e) proofs from linguistic details, (f) situation similarities in literary style and language, and (g) situation similarities in action.[9] These several taxonomies come from various perspectives and are not all at the same level of abstraction.

I attempt the construction of a taxonomy of New Testament applications of Old Testament passages, taking communal distinctions into account, and choosing a single level of abstraction. My categories are:

1. Fulfillment of prophecy
2. Typology
3. Allegory

---

6. Barrett, "The Interpretation of the Old Testament in the New," 410; Lampe, "The Reasonableness of Typology," 14; Woollcombe, "The Biblical Origins and Patristic Development of Typology," 42.

7. Eichrodt, "Is Typological Exegesis an Appropriate Method?", 227–29.

8. Lindars, *New Testament Apologetic*, 272–83.

9. Barr, *Old and New in Interpretation*, 113–15.

4. Legal citation
5. Proverbial citation

The third category, allegory, will turn out to be empty.

Such a categorization of New Testament applications of Old Testament passages has a generic cast, but is undertaken here as a subsidiary part of the generic-corporate inclusive project of showing that the New Testament writers applied their community experience recorded in Old Testament passages to make present choices understandable by relating them with past events within the one corporately relating history of Israel. The construction of this taxonomy is built on a critique of the existing taxonomies, and will demonstrate that unyielding differences among them reflect the modern or communal presuppositions of their authors.

## 1 Fulfillment of Prophecy

The fulfillment of prophecy category is defined as the class of those New Testament uses of the Old Testament in which the New Testament treats an Old Testament passage as predicting–asking for, urging—an eschatologically significant change, and claims that an event in its current period fits that prediction (a fulfillment of that eschatological promise). Examples where such a literal fulfillment of prophecy appears to be implied are: Matt 1:22 "All this took place to fulfill what had been spoken by the Lord through the prophet, 'Look, the virgin shall conceive . . .'" (where the quotation of Isa 7:14 is explicit[10]); Matt 2:2 "Where is the child who has been born king of the Jews?", where there is a reference to some expectation; as in Jer 23:5 and Zech 9:9, where the expectation is implied; Matt 2:11 "They offered him gifts of gold, frankincense and myrrh," a fulfillment of Isa 60:6 that would pass unnoticed by one who did not recognize the Old Testament allusion; and the whole passion narrative, a fulfillment of the servant passages of Isaiah and the psalms of lament.

The category "fulfillment of prophecy" described here corresponds to "fulfillment of prophecy" in the taxonomies of Barrett, Lampe, Woollcombe, Eichrodt, and Barr,[11] and "apocalyptic eschatology" (the

---

10. For the discrepancy between Matthew's "virgin, παρθενος" from the Greek Septuagint translation of the Old Testament and Isaiah's Hebrew "young woman, עלמה," see chapter 4.I.1.

11. Barr, *Old and New in Interpretation*, 118–26; the eschatological aspect is treated on pp. 124–25.

final triumph of corporate human interaction) in Lindars, who names this category—a category that emphasizes the eschatological element in the present application rather than the problematic ascription of literal prediction of a specific event to the prophet's original intention. The term category here also includes the category "promise and fulfillment" of Walther Zimmerli.[12] "Prophecy" [noun] refers to the prophet who transmits the promise, while "promise" refers to God who originates the promise. God promises directly to Abraham: Rom 4:18 = Gen 15:5 "So numerous shall your descendants be"; whereas, on another occasion the prophet Joel transmits God's promise: Acts 2:16–17 = Joel 2:28 "This is what was spoken through the prophet Joel: 'In the last days it will be, God declares, that I will pour out my spirit upon all flesh.'" Both of these fit the category "fulfillment of prophecy." The terms "apocalyptic eschatology" of Lindars and "promise and fulfillment" of Zimmerli are each in its own way theologically more sophisticated than "fulfillment of prophecy," but I retain the latter in the present taxonomy as being closer to the surface of New Testament use of the Old Testament. The category fulfillment of prophecy will be further developed in the next section when I show its intimate relation to typology, and it will truly become "apocalyptic eschatology" in the part of this chapter on New Testament theological use of the Old Testament.

## 2 Typology

Typological interpretation is here defined as a community's use of one of its *own past historical choices*, including its objective facticity and its internal interactive meaning—to interpret a *present* pending community choice. Such typology puts past community interactive successes and failures in internal interaction with pending community interactive choices; it is learning by one's own past mistakes and successes.

I explicate this definition with an example, 1 Cor 10:1–11:

> I do not want you to be unaware, brothers and sisters, that our ancestors were all under the cloud, and all passed through the sea, and all were baptized into Moses in the cloud and in the sea, and all ate the same spiritual food and all drank the same spiritual drink. For they drank from the spiritual rock which followed them, and the rock was Christ. Nevertheless God was not

---

12. Zimmerli, "Promise and Fulfillment," 89–122.

> pleased with most of them; and they were struck down in the wilderness.
>
> Now these things occurred as examples [τυποι, *types*] for us, so that we might not desire evil as they did. Do not become idolaters as some of them did; as it is written, "The people sat down to eat and drink and they rose up to play." We must not indulge in sexual immorality as some of them did, and twenty three thousand fell in a single day. We must not put Christ to the test, as some of them did, and were destroyed by serpents. And do not complain as some of them did, and were destroyed by the destroyer. These things happened to them to serve as an example [τύπικως, *as a type, typically*], and they were written down to instruct us, on whom the ends of the ages have come.

Paul uses Exodus-Corinth typology in this passage to influence the fractious behavior of the church in Corinth. In the Red Sea–Christian baptism typology that introduces the passage, the two events are the saving of Israel at the Red Sea by God-inspired corporate interaction; and the saving of the Corinthian congregation, which is inaugurated at the baptism of its membership. The typological relation of these two community salvations is signaled by the *formal similarity* of both groups passing through water, used typologically to say that as God created and saved Israel for responsible community interaction through water in the Exodus, so he creates and saves this *same* Israel (descendents of "our ancestors" (1 Cor 10:1)) from destructive community interaction through water in baptism at Corinth.[13] The regaining of commitment as people-of-God, by means of the Red Sea exodus, now calls for the same among those brought into the same community by baptism in Corinth. Note the two levels in typology: the level of formal similarity and the level of intentional historical continuity interaction, which enables the typological embedding of the new event in the (thus extended) community tradition, thus giving that event the same communal significance. This meaning, responsible membership in the same people of God, is, of course, extended through the second-level *historical intentional interac-*

---

13. This typological relationship, widely accepted by communally oriented scholars, is explicitly rejected by Sanders, *Paul and Palestinian Judaism*, 512–13, 547, because he cannot see a relation between membership in Israel and participation in the body of Christ, for reasons indicated in chapter 3 (page 144, note 37).

*tive relation* with the earlier event, not through the *formal similarity* used as identifying flag of that relation.

The relation between type and antitype may be *antithetic*, as in the Fall-Resurrection typology of 1 Cor 15:22: "For as all die in Adam, so all will be made alive in Christ." The identifying flag is the antithesis of competitive residents in Babel and resurrected Christ; the second level historical relation, the typological relation, is the reversing of the dysfunctional human community *adam* to shared creative internal interaction through the servant ministry of the people of God led by its anointed leader or *messiah*.

Thus, typology is an interactive use by a present community of a remembered past experience of that community, a type, to inform a present pending choice, an antitype. Its use by the community is a diachronic internal interaction in the community between past and present choices. In this example, some of Paul's details come not from Exodus but are antitypes from previously used typology, thus already in the tradition before Paul added his use. The "rock that followed them" and which "was Christ," was a very stationary physical rock at Meribah in Exod 17:6 and appeared to follow them in Isa 48:21 (and was said to do so in the Tosephta[14]) and, non-typologically, to be Wisdom or *logos* in Philo.[15]

The purpose of typology is not to interpret the tradition but to interpret the new event.[16] Paul's whole passage quoted above intends a point about the communal life of the church at Corinth: "Now these things occurred as types for us, not to desire evil as they did . . ." It also effects the adding of the thus interpreted Corinthian conflict to the tradition.

Such an enlargement of the tradition by incorporating a new event into it does, of course, reflect back on the significance of the old event; "all were baptized into Moses" is a description of the Exodus in New Testament categories when looking backwards through a Red Sea–baptismal font typology.[17] As with Gadamer, the two events are

14. Tosephta, Tractate Sukka 3:11. Compare Isa 48:21 "Those he led through the desert never went thirsty; he made water spring for them from the rock."

15. Wisdom in Philo, *Legum allegoria*, 2.21.86; Logos in Philo, *Quod deterius potiori insidiari soleat*, 31.118.

16. So also the 22 biblical scholars in this chapter note 26, and Lindbeck, *The Nature of Doctrine*, 118–19, all in agreement with Gadamer, page 43 above.

17. In the Talmud, proselyte baptism is related typologically to the immersion of the Exodus people implied in the washing of clothes in Exod 19:10 and the sprinkling

in bilaterally intrinsic relation. Reinterpretation of old events does not contradict but rather interactively extends their original old-tradition meaning; it is a reasonable addition to the meaning of the old events based on their subsequent influence.[18] But the center of interest is in the new events. The New Testament is not a commentary on the Old—it is not a retelling of the old story. Rather, it makes a place for a new story within the continuing tradition, just as, for example, the Old Testament prophets are not a commentary on earlier Old Testament events but a continuing Scripture that interprets new events in terms of Israel's already established relation with its God: Isa 42:9 "See, the former things have come to pass, and new things I now declare, before they spring forth, I tell you of them."

Different cultures understand their historical continuity through time differently. The New Testament community understands the history it is recounting as the story of the continuing support from a God who delegated to it responsibility for continuously developing an ever-new creatively internally interacting life together and with other communities. And so the continuity between type and antitype is of the same kind; it is always a continuity in this continuous yet ever new saving relation with its God. This claim is transparently illustrated by the examples given. Accordingly, in New Testament typology the relation is *not* based on generalization, or on participation in the same abstract essence, or on cyclic repetition, or on sequential continuity, or on empirical historical causation. A brief look at these five kinds of historical continuity not used in New Testament typology will make clearer the one kind that is used.

With New Testament typology, the relation between type and antitype is not a generalization or constant working out of some rule of behavior as it is, for example, in the early Christian letter 1 Clement 4–6, where a list of six cases of evil flowing from jealousy (stretching from Cain and Abel to Saul and David) is related to another list of evils in the present, to Peter, to Paul, to "a great multitude of the chosen," to two specific female martyrs, to wives, and to cities and nations. Such a relation, based on inductive reasoning, is foreign to the New Testament

---

with blood in Exod 24:8 (Yebamot 46b, Keritot 9a), pointed out by Jeremias, "Paulus als Hillelit," 91.

18. So also Amsler, *L'Ancien Testament dans l'Église*, 220f, as well as Gadamer, page 42 above.

conception of history. Rather, New Testament typology is always a relation between two specific potentially mutually interacting past and present historical situations. The warnings in the second part of the quotation above from 1 Corinthians 10 or in Stephen's speech in Acts 7 are not generalizations. Rather, they present a complex tissue of typological relation between the past interacting community Israel and the same community Israel in the present. Even Hebrews 11 on faith, which appears to generalize (as in Heb 11:39 "Yet all these, though they were commended for their faith, did not receive what was promised . . ."), goes on to unify us with all these past worthies whose work for the future is justified by the present fulfillment: Heb 11:40 ". . . since God had provided something better so that they would not, apart from us, be made perfect."

The typological relation in the New Testament is also not based on participation in a common Platonic essence. The word *túpos* is used, to be sure, in Acts 7:44 = Heb 8:5 = Exod 25:40 LXX to refer to the heavenly pattern shown Moses on the mountain by which the Jerusalem temple was to be made, but here it has the non-historical meaning *pattern*. Stephen's speech in Acts 7 uses this *analogical* relation between the Jerusalem temple and its heavenly pattern, already in the post-exilic Exodus passage, to connect up a different antithetic *typological* relation between God's absence from the Jerusalem temple as prophets had been killed and his presence in Jesus.[19] Two temples also show up in Heb 9:1–28: While the high priest offers the blood of goats and calves "that cannot perfect the conscience" in the old temple, "a mere copy [ἀντίτυπα, *antitype*] of the true one" (v. 24), Christ offers his own blood in the true temple. That is, old temple sacrifice has become antithetic type of the crucifixion. Both are historical sacrificial events made in the name of the same community within the same tradition.[20]

New Testament typological correspondence does not base itself on a repetition of events within a cyclic view of history.[21] The two events are always distinct particular instances of God's saving action. In one of the most fully developed typological relations within the Old Testament, Isaiah's use in 40–55 of both the creation and the Exodus are shown as

---

19. Hanson recognizes this double relationship, *Allegory and Event*, 95.

20. *Contra* Bultmann, "Ursprung," 210. For Bultmann the gospel is an escape from history (page 110 below).

21. As Bultmann claims, "Ursprung" 205.

types of the return from captivity, and we read both 43:1 "But now thus says the Lord, he who created you, O Jacob, he who formed you, O Israel: ...," and 43:18–19 "... Do not remember the former things, or consider the things of old. I am about to do a new thing; now it springs forth, do you not perceive it?" The two passages together say God's concern for Israel is the same in both the related events, but the events are radically different.

New Testament typological correspondence is never based on a sequential continuity in history. The two typologically related events are generally separated by a long history and they stand out from it as related to each other because the antitype is a vivid past community choice solving a crisis similar to the present one.

And finally, the New Testament does not take the type–antitype relation in a modern sense (as empirical cause of the antitype). Rather, it sees God calling humanity to use its past interactive experience to help make current interactive choices.

New Testament typology, based on neither generalization nor natural causation, presupposes a structure and meaning for history quite distinct from that of modern critical history (above, chapter 1.III). Also, not participating in a single universal essence distinguishes it from perennial perspectives. Hence, New Testament typology as defined by Paul has generally been unrecognized in the Western world, and the reintroduction in 1939 of typology so defined by Leonhard Goppelt in *Typos: The Typological Interpretation of the Old Testament in the New* has been widely rejected by modern scholars. Its rejecters include Bultmann, who refuses to recognize typology as a communal historical relation and reduces it to allegory: "the distinction can ... be ignored between allegory (the art of finding prediction or deeper truths of any sort in the wording of scripture) and typology (the interpretation of persons, events, or institutions of the past as foreshadowing prototypes)."[22] Another objector, Friedrich Baumgärtel, complains that typology is not literal enough for the critical-historical perspective, and at the same time too objectified for the existentialist perspective. For the critical-historical objection: typological interpretation is "no longer possible for us today, because our contemporary historical thinking demands of us ... that the literal meaning of the Old Testament witness be 'understood'";[23] and for

---

22. Bultmann, *Theology of the New Testament*, 1.117.
23. Baumgärtel, "The Hermeneutical Problem of the Old Testament," 143.

the existentialist objection: "The information that events of the New Testament are foreshadowed in the Old Testament has no impact on my existence; rather, it forces me into the role of intellectual spectator."[24] The critical-historical objection will be further explored with James Barr in the next section, and the existentialist objection with Bultmann in this chapter's final section.

The literal meaning of both Greek *túpos* and English *type*, is *example* or *model*, and is well within the static relations common to these two Indo-European cultures. The Alexandrian Septuagint translators and New Testament writers were confined to the Greek language in use by the international readership they were serving; so that when translating a Hebrew concept new to Hellenistic culture, they could only extend the meaning of the nearest available Greek word, just as most new concepts in any culture are named with new extensions of meaning for existing words, thus enlarging the reach of the existing language (for example, from "they cast their nets" to "going on the net"). The word *túpos* (type), or its adverbial form *túpikos* (as a type, typically), occurs 12 times in the New Testament: three in the literal Greek sense of *example* or *model* (Acts 7:44, 23:25, Hebrews 8:5), three as typology in the communal sense (Rom 6:17, 1 Cor 10:6 and 11), and six as paraenetic typology—that is, examples for individual rather than community behavior, in 1 Tim 4:12, Phil 3:17, 1 Thes 1:7, 2 Thes 3:9, Titus 2:7, and 1 Peter 5:3. Leonhard Goppelt introduced the Western scholarly word *typology* in his 1939 dissertation[25] to distinguish from allegory the thousands of New Testament communal interpretations of contemporaneous events using Old Testament types, as biblical Paul did, and John Henry Newman recovered in 1845.

In New Testament typology the move from type to antitype normally involves *intensification*; that is, the new event is presented as greater than the corresponding old one. The intensification is frequently explicit, as in the Jonah-Christ typology of Matt 12:41 "See, something greater than Jonah is here," and in the Adam-Christ typology of Rom 5:15 "For if the many died through the one man's trespass, much more

---

24. Baumgärtel, *Verheissung*, 138. Several more objectors to typology are listed in Amsler, *L'Ancien Testament dans l'Église*, 220–27, and in Rendtorff, "Hermeneutik des Alten Testaments als Frage nach der Geschichte," 33.

25. Goppelt, *Typos*; the dissertation, chapters 1–9; the explicit distinction, pp.42–58.

surely have the grace of God and the free gift in the grace of the one man, Jesus Christ, abounded for many." The center of interest, of importance, in typological interpretation is normally the second event, the antitype being interpreted and given a place in the already existing tradition. Hence, although not required by the definition of typology, there is normally an intensification in moving from type to antitype, and this is always the case in New Testament typology except when used paraenetically—that is, as ethical example (see 7 Paraenetic Typology) rather than a radical historical change. Paul's passage 1 Cor 10:1–11 has no intensification at the point where a series of paraenetic applications are made, "Do not become idolaters, as some of them did . . . ." Instead, it is at the end of this series that the jolt of absolute intensification comes: "they were written down to instruct us, on whom the ends of the ages have come." Such a jolt is strongest when a major historical discontinuity is impending, as in Isaiah 40–55 on the eve of return from captivity, or in Daniel and other apocalyptic writings in the face of possible complete loss of Israelite cultural identity under Hellenistic rule. In such crises the ultimate fulfillment of the promise, implicit or explicit, in God's saving relation with his people seems to draw closer—the figurative characterization of the intensification comes in language literally more absolute.

Typological use of Old Testament material is a major method used in virtually every book of the New Testament in writing a meaningful history of Jesus and the primitive church. For example, the Moses-Jesus typological system is the basis of Matthew 2 (infancy), 4 (temptation), 5–7 (Sermon on the Mount), Mark 9 (transfiguration), Luke 10 (appointment of the seventy), Acts 7 (Stephen's speech), 1 Corinthians 10, 2 Corinthians 3, Hebrews 3, 8, 12:18–29, Rev 15:1–4, and is a factor in many other passages, such as Mark 14:12–25 (last supper), John 1:17, Acts 3, Heb 11:23–28. Also, the Moses-Jesus typology is only one constituent (along with typological relations with many other representative leaders in Israel including Abraham, David, and the prophets) of the Israel-Church typology and the basic New Testament message—interpreting the new events it reports as Israel's return to and continuation of its historical tradition.

Contemporaneous scholars using the term typology in the sense given it here include Samuel Amsler, Bernhard Anderson, Ray Brown, Joseph Cahill, Oscar Cullmann, Walther Eichrodt, E. Earle Ellis, Northrup Frye, Leonhard Goppelt, R. P. C. Hanson, A. G. Hebert, J. N.

D. Kelly, G. W. H. Lampe, Barnabas Lindars, George Lindbeck, Gerhard von Rad, Alan Richardson, Harald Sahlin, Brooke Foss Westcott, Hans Walter Wolff, K. J. Woollcombe, and G. Ernest Wright.[26] These scholars all emphasize the historical continuity maintained by typology, and most make explicit the intensification of antitype over type. These twenty-two scholars thus reveal a communal understanding of history. Necessarily disagreeing with this definition are those scholars who do not hold a communal view of history, including the cosmologically oriented tradition from Origen, Augustine, and Thomas Aquinas to the present (chapters 4 and 8, below); the modern scholars Rudolf Bultmann[27] and James Barr;[28] and the semi-communal Wolfhart Pannenberg, who wants a salvation-historical relation but does not think the formal similarity in typology is adequate to convey it.[29]

Typological use of the Old Testament and prophetic fulfillment use are not sharply distinguished in the New Testament.[30] The use of an atomic allusion to the Old Testament to signal a relation between larger units (above, page 74) is often a use of a fulfillment of prophecy relation to call attention to a larger-scale typological relation; for example, Matthew's use of Matt 2:15 = Hos 11:1 "Out of Egypt have I called my

---

26. Amsler, *L'Ancien Testament dans l'Église*, 141–47, 215–17; Anderson, "Exodus Typology in Second Isaiah," 178–80; Brown, *The Gospel according to John, (i-xii)* CXI; Cahill, "Hermeneutical Implications of Typology," 267, 273; Cullmann, *Christ and Time*, 134; Eichrodt, "Is Typological Exegesis an Appropriate Method?", 226–27, 234, and 242; Ellis, *Paul's Use of the Old Testament*, 52, 127–28; Frye, *Creation and Recreation*, 60; Goppelt, *Typos*, 17–18, 198–205, and 218–23; R. Hanson, *Allegory and Event*, 7; Hebert, "Introduction," vi; Kelly, *Early Christian Doctrines*, 71; Lampe, "Typological Exegesis," 202, also "The Reasonableness of Typology," 29; Lindars, *New Testament Apologetic*, 205; Lindbeck, *The Nature of Doctrine*, 117–18; von Rad, "Typological Interpretation of the Old Testament," 20–21; Richardson, *History, Sacred and Profane*, 222; Sahlin, "The New Exodus of Salvation according to St. Paul"; Westcott, *The Epistle to the Hebrews* (1889!), 200; Wolff, "The Understanding of History," 334; Woollcombe, "The Biblical Origins," 40; G. Ernest Wright, *God Who Acts*, 61–65.

27. In two different ways, one in Bultmann, "Ursprung," 205, the other in Bultmann, *Theology of the New Testament*, 1.117.

28. Barr, *Old and New in Interpretation*, 104–11. Barr will be analyzed in section 4, Lack of New Testament Allegorical Use of the Old Testament.

29. Pannenberg, "Redemptive Event and History," 1.28–31 (= Westermann, ed., *Hermeneutics*, 326–29). Similarly, Rendtorff, a member of the "Pannenberg Circle," in "Hermeneutik des Alten Testaments als Frage nach der Geschichte," 33.

30. This is discussed for example in Eichrodt, "Is Typological Exegesis an Appropriate Method?", 229, and in Goppelt, *Typos*, 209–37.

son" is a prophecy signaling the son-Son typology, which is developed at some length, including baptism and temptation in the wilderness. In the passage Acts 3:22 = Deut 18:15 "Moses said 'the Lord your God will raise up for you from your own people a prophet like me...'"; the New Testament writer appears to separate prophecy, "Moses said," from typology, "a prophet like me," but actually this "prophecy" is a typological creation of the Deuteronomist, writing in 621 BCE—after the fact—who has, in turn, interpreted typologically, or "prophesied," the accession of King Josiah in 640 BCE.

Although typology and fulfillment of prophecy overlap, they are not identical categories. One difference already noted is that fulfillment of prophecy by its nature requires an intensification, whereas some typology, that used in paraenesis, has none.

Another difference is that fulfillment of prophecy taken literalistically implies a verbalization of the prophecy or promise at the earlier time, whereas typology only requires that the additional meaning for the type first comes into evidence when the second event occurs. Also for the modern critical historian, the additional meaning can only arise for fulfillment of prophecy uses of the Old Testament when the fulfillment occurs, since the prophet is taken to be speaking to his own time rather than to ours.[31] But this distinction did not limit the biblical writers. When the earlier text makes it clear that the material refers to its own time, the later writer can merely claim, as in 1 Cor 10:11, "Now these things happened to them to serve as types, and they were written down to instruct us." In other words, the original event is a type and the original writing down of it was an as-yet unapplied prophecy for future guidance—a reasonable claim in a culture consciously living within the framework of its own tradition and expecting the process to continue, so that what it adds to the tradition now can reasonably be expected to be used typologically, or "prophetically," in the future. Thus, "fulfillment of prophecy" is *typology in disguise*. Prophecy does not preempt an outcome as it would if intended literally; rather, as *typology in disguise* it clarifies a predicament and challenges human initiative to meet it.

Goppelt, C. H. Dodd, and E. Earle Ellis all take prophecy as *typology in disguise*. Goppelt, in analyzing Romans 9–11, says, "This typology is not to be distinguished from prophecy; rather it is a principle that

---

31. For example in section I of Bultmann's "Prophecy and Fulfillment," 182–87 (= Westermann, ed., *Hermeneutics*, 50–55).

forms and upholds it."[32] Dodd did not yet know in England the term "typology" proposed by Goppelt in Germany just before the war, but in *According to the Scriptures* Dodd characterizes promise and fulfillment as typology as characterized here. On the passage Acts 13:32–33 "We bring you the good news [tidings] that what God promised to our ancestors he has fulfilled for us, their children, by raising Jesus" Dodd comments: "The 'good tidings' consist primarily in the news of what has happened; to understand how they are 'good tidings,' they must be related to what has gone on before." And a little later, "the Christian gospel could not be adequately or convincingly set forth unless the communication of facts about Jesus was supported by reference to the Old Testament which gave significance to the facts."[33] And Ellis says, "New Testament typology did not involve merely a catalogue of 'types'; it penetrated into the spirit of New Testament exegesis [of the Old Testament] in all its forms."[34]

Such a New Testament dependence on prophecy and typology was unsettling to the modern mind, and one of the achievements of nineteenth century critical-historical study was to break the connection between Old Testament prophecy and its contemporary situation by claiming that the prophets "actually" spoke to their own time. But twentieth century critical study of the New Testament itself indicates that its writers were not nineteenth century critical historians and did not break the connection between the prophets and their own age. Rather, they used their Old Testament tradition as corporate framework within which to interpret the events of their own day, working within the assumed diachronic bilateral internal relation between their community's past and present, precisely as characterized by Gadamer (page 43, above). If the constant New Testament references to the Old are ignored, the New Testament's interpretation of its own contemporaneous events is lost, leaving only an empty shell that can be interpreted to mean almost anything.

The analysis of typology will be further sharpened by contrasting it with allegory.

32. Goppelt, *Typos*, 228.
33. Dodd, *According to the Scriptures*, 14, 16.
34. Ellis, *Paul's Use of the Old Testament*, 134.

## 3 Allegory, as Contrasted with Metonymy

Allegory is representation of a meaning structure in a given context by an *abstractly analogous* meaning structure in another *otherwise unrelated* context. Either context may be literal or figurative. The allegory serves only to clarify, to explain, to portray aesthetically the first context's abstract structure. Neither structure is changed: unlike typology, it does not find or propose any *internal interaction* in or between the two meaning structures.

### Example of Allegorical Interpretation

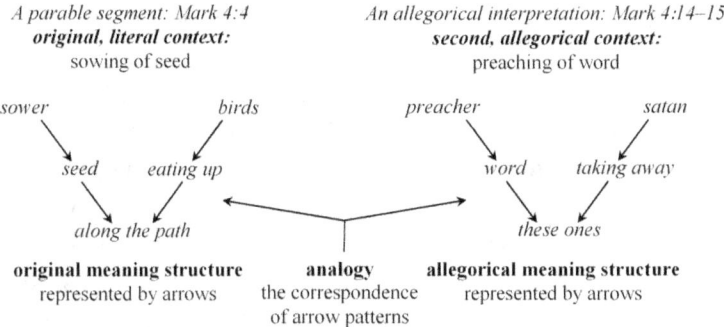

"A sower went out to sow. And as he sowed, some seed fell on the path, and birds came and ate it up . . ." is interpreted to mean: "The sower sows the word. These are the ones on the path where the word is sown: when they hear, Satan immediately comes and takes away the word that is sown in them . . ." The *original context* is the sowing of seed and the *original meaning structure* is the relation among sower, seed, along the path, birds, and eating up (represented by the arrows on the left side of the chart above). The *second context* is the preaching of the word. The *second meaning structure* (arrows on the right side) is an analogous relation among preacher, word, these ones, satan, and taking away—built on an abstract pairing of sower with preacher, seed with word, etc., to present an abstract *analogy* between them (*outside both contexts*); thus, not implying any interactive relation between them. Similar analyses hold for the parable's other three kinds of soil.

This middle-Platonic interpretation takes the parable to say that salvation for each individual is conformity with an unchanging Word or *logos*, the Western occupiers' basic conception of reality, the conception from which Jesus was working to rescue Judea. It found its way into

Mark's Gospel during the forty years of its assembly. But a *parable*, like a joke, has failed if it has to be explained—an issue treated extensively below on page 329.

The original parable was told to and understood by Judean *sowers and reapers* still maintaining their pre-conquest creative interactive community life in spite of three centuries of middle-Platonic European colonial control. Jesus could expect his hearers to extend their described non-dominating *mutually creative interaction* with soil, seed, birds, and path-users to their interactive relations with family and neighbors— wives converting the grain into family bread, daughters nursing the grandchildren, grandparents giving sage advice, neighbors using the path to work, visit, share, and support a *creative interactive* community life incompatible with passive obedience to an *unchangeable* "truth."

The earlier first interpretation of the parable, Mark 4:9 "Let anyone with ears to hear listen" means: let anyone attuned to the Judean metonymic style, do so. The second, Mark 4:10–12 = Isa 6:9–10, from Isaiah's call as prophet, reminds members to expect non-uniform application of non-directive prophetic input, as with the response of soil, seed, and birds. The third very late middle-Platonic *allegorical* interpretation Mark 4:13–20 diagrammed above necessarily misses the interactive *metonymic* meaning of the parable and its two earlier interpretations. This allegorical interpretation found its way into the account toward the end of forty years of Gospel assembly by Greek-speaking education committees in congregations outside Judea. These committees selected from a mass of individual orally-transmitted accounts, arranged the selections, and reduced the whole to writing. There is clinical evidence that metonymy and metaphor are based on different mental processes. Roman Jakobson reports[35] two kinds of aphasia, which he calls similarity-disorder and contiguity-disorder; that is, abstract analogy disorder and interactive metonymy disorder. In similarity-disorder, the similarity aspect of language is blocked, but the contiguity aspect is preserved. The patient cannot understand the meaning of single words or give synonyms but can use words in verbal contexts. In contiguity-disorder the grammar is lost and sentences degenerate into word heaps, while words and their meanings remain. Similarity-disorder patients are unable to use metaphor, which is based on similarity, but maintain the ability to use metonymy, which is based on interaction. And contiguity-disorder patients can-

---

35. Jakobson, "Two Aspects of Language," 77–89.

not use metonymy but can use metaphor. Western non-recognition of metonymy is, of course, a cultural disability, not an individual mental disability.

At a larger social level, using typology to promote creative interaction between two parts of one social context, and using allegory to explicate a single structure by abstract analogy with a similar structure in another non-interacting context, are fundamentally different projects. The impossibility of internal interaction under one-directional control, cosmological or empirical, disallows the concept of typological relation—a Western cultural "continuity-disorder" masking Scripture's core call to internally interactive relation.

The scholars Amsler, Anderson, Cahill, Cullmann, Eichrodt, Ellis, Frye, Goppelt, R. P. C. Hanson, Hebert, Kelly, Lampe, Lindars, Lindbeck, von Rad, Richardson, Wolff, Woollcombe, and Wright, who concur on the definition of typology (above, page 85), also concur on the definition of allegory and its distinction from typology, mostly in conjunction with their characterization of typology (their definition of typology emerges for the West only when it is differentiated from allegory). Western scholars not accepting such a typology also concur on this definition of allegory, for example, John Dominic Crossan, who calls on Goethe, Yeats, Coleridge, Eliot, and Paul Ricoeur for support.[36]

The modern scholar James Barr strongly rejects any distinction between typology and allegory. In his *Old and New in Interpretation* (1966) he summarizes his understanding of the position of Lampe, R. P. C Hanson, and von Rad as follows: "The distinction generally made is that typology is based on historical correspondences and thus related to the Bible's own historical emphasis; while, judged by that same emphasis, allegory is non-historical and anti-historical" (p. 104). He rejects this distinction, saying that allegory is not anti-historical because the second allegorical context may be a historical one, as in the traditional exegesis of the Song of Songs[37] as characterizing God's relation to Israel or Christ's relation to the church and Augustine's allegorical interpretation of the parable of the Good Samaritan (p. 106). He allows that these examples are more typical of Christian use of allegory than Philo's, whose interest is non-historical (p. 107). But, Barr says, in a case where Paul dealt with

---

36. Crossan, *In Parables*, 9–11.

37. Song of Songs is a tissue of passages such as Song 7:7 "You are stately as a palm tree, and your breasts are like its clusters. I say I will climb the palm tree . . ."

a legal-economic issue (the pay of apostles), he allegorizes a legal text: "You shall not muzzle an ox while it is treading out the grain" (1 Cor 9:9 = Deut 25:4). He says "Allegory cannot be described categorically as anti-historical in character, and we cannot make this into an ultimate distinction from typology" (p. 107). The difference "never was a method difference at all, but rather a difference in the subject matter" (p. 110).

Barr's opponents, of course, do not distinguish typology from allegory by calling it "historical" in Barr's sense, which is the modern critical-historical view of history defined by Hume and subsumed into Kant's theoretical reason. Such critical history views events in the past, with context in some culture in the past, as only properly knowable by an impartial, objective historian—one who does not belong to that history, one whose interest in that past is not bound up in participation in the present continuing life of that same community, one who does not bring the two historical contexts together; hence, for whom every relation between the two events can at most amount to allegory. Barr, consistently with his own orientation, has imposed that modern horizon on the New Testament writers' typological interpretation, reducing useful past experience to mere past empirical "facts."

Barr says typology understood as a relation between historical entities also raises the issue, "whether the 'historical' meaning of the text as used in the typology could be fitted with the contextual meaning of the text in its own environment and historical setting" (p. 111)—in other words, whether the interpreted meanings fit the original meanings. This question points to the core of the communal position: that typology is not a method of pruning meanings to make them fit as allegory is but of *creating additional meaning* for both contexts. A change in present behavior resulting from past experience adds to the meaning, the essence, of both past and present historical events; it is a corporate, essence-changing relation.

The communal school fully recognizes that it violates fundamental positions of both perennial and modern philosophy by taking the term "history" to include interactive influence as well as static facts, and "typology" to refer to diachronic bilateral essence-changing relations between past community events and contemporaneous issues. Furthermore, it claims Paul uses "type" in this sense. Unlike Barr's usual attribution in other issues of some value to both sides he considers, Barr never takes up the meaning of the term "history." His *Old and New in*

*Interpretation* defends "Old" modern critical-historical interpretation of Scripture against the "New" method proposed by communal scholars without recognizing or countering the substance of that "new" position. Barr's modern orientation, inherited from the perennial "So how could that which is never in the same state be anything? ... For at the very moment when the one who is going to know it approaches, it would become something else" (Plato, *Cratylus* 439C-440A), necessarily prohibits him from recognizing the issue raised by the communal scholars.

### 4 Lack of New Testament Allegorical Use of the Old Testament

Having distinguished allegory and typology from one another, let us evaluate the extent of New Testament allegorical use of the Old Testament. Very few instances have been suggested in the literature discussed; those that have are analyzed here:

1. Gal 4:30 = Gen 21:10–11 "... the child of the slave will not share the inheritance with the child of the free woman."
2. 1 Cor 9:9 = Deut 25:4 "You shall not muzzle an ox while it is treading out the grain."
3. Matt 12:40 = Jonah 1:17 "Jonah was three days and three nights in the belly of the sea monster . . . ."
4. 1 Cor 10:1–11 using Exod 13–32 and Num 11–25 "Our ancestors were all under the cloud, and all passed through the sea . . . ."
5. 1 Cor 5:6–8 "the unleavened bread of sincerity and truth" = Deut 16:3 "unleavened bread . . . the bread of affliction."

Paul calls one of his Old Testament usages (1) allegory. Augustine, *De utilitate credendi* 8 gives three instances, (1), (3), and (4). Barr in *Old and New in Interpretation* 110 produces only two examples, (1) and (2). Woollcombe[38] gives (1), (2), and (5). C. K. Barrett[39] gives (1). R. P. C. Hanson[40] gives (1) and (2). I have excluded (a) cases where a scholar claims an allegorical detail within an overall typological interpretation of an Old Testament text (this would merely be part of the first-level formal similarity used to call attention to the second-level historical continuity), and (b) cases where New Testament allegorization is not of an Old Testament text. The five examples given are all those directly proposed

---

38. Lampe and Woollcombe, *Essays on Typology*, 55.
39. Barrett, "The Interpretation of the Old Testament in the New," I 391.
40. R. Hanson, "Biblical Exegesis in the Early Church," I 412.

in the literature referred to in this chapter (some indirect suggestions will appear below with Barr's category "paraenetic use of Old Testament examples"). The five direct examples can be evaluated as follows:

(1) Although Paul calls his use of the Old Testament "allegory" in Gal 4:24 "Now this is an allegory: these women are two covenants . . . ," his use of the Old Testament in this passage is typological (as the term is defined in this study). The two women and their two lines of offspring actually participate in the two covenants Paul is contrasting in their continuing existence in Paul's own day.[41] Thus Paul does not intend "allegory" in its classical Greek rhetorical meaning. The word "allegory" occurs only this once in the New Testament, and it will emerge in (2) that Paul never interprets the Old Testament allegorically.

(2) Deut 25:4 "You shall not muzzle an ox . . ." is a legal text rather than a narrative one but, as such, is even more likely to be taken as internally interacting application by a later community holding itself to be in historical continuity with its earlier self. Subsequent application of a law to a new situation not anticipated when it was adopted requires a judgment, an *interpretation*, bringing the new context into internal relation with the original community intention, and this adds to the meaning of both the original law and the subsequent tradition rather than merely providing an abstract literal analogy between them. We found Gadamer (above, page 43) in 1960 using legal interpretation as one kind of typological interpretation already in use in the Western world. Paul's application of this text appears to be intended as a legitimate legal citation. It is a typological relation but is classified separately here as "legal citation." The Mishnah provides that an employee's consumption of vegetable foodstuffs already detached from the soil on which he is working is tax-exempt income on the basis of Deut 23:24–25 "If you go into your neighbor's vineyard, you may eat . . . "[42]; and the Talmud provides an additional derivation of this principle based on Deut 25:4, ascribed to Rabina (5th century): ". . . it is written 'You shall not muzzle an ox when it treads out the grain.' . . . Why write 'ox'? To assimilate the muzzler to the muzzled. . . . Just as the muzzled may eat of what is

---

41. So also Goppelt, *Typos*, 5, note; Lampe, "The Reasonableness of Typology," 35; Ellis, *Paul's Use of the Old Testament*, 53; and Diodore of Tarsus, *In Psalmum*, praef., wherein Diodore indirectly excuses Paul's poor Greek (quoted in chapter 4, page 175).

42. Mishnah, tractate Baba Meṣiʿa, 7:2.

detached, so the muzzler may eat of what is detached."[43] The step from muzzled to muzzler is metonymy, seeing both in the same context of live workers processing food, and Paul's later application to church workers is *typology*. Although the derivation specifically from Deut 25:4 is late, both the resulting legal principle and the general method of derivation are in the Mishnah and are already established in the rabbinic tradition by the third or second century.

(3) Matt 12:40 "Jonah . . ." This use of the Old Testament is typological: as earlier, after three days in the belly of the sea monster, Jonah saved Nineveh with his preaching; even so, now after three days "in the heart of the earth," the Son of man—"something greater than Jonah"—will save *this* evil and adulterous generation. "[T]*his* . . . generation" makes it clear the two events belong to the same history. The equality of the three-day periods is not merely a coincidence. Three days, a primitive proof of death, later became a conventional time to remain dead, as "forty" was a conventional time to remain in the wilderness, and such conventions amount to a stock of formal analogies ready for use to signal typological relations. (If Paul's age took Jonah as fiction rather than as an account for metonymic use, then his usage would be proverbial citation, treated below.)

(4) 1 Cor 10:1–11 "Our ancestors were all under the cloud . . ." This passage has already been analyzed earlier as typology. The Exodus people are referred to as "our ancestors," making it explicit that the present trials in the Corinthian church are part of the same particular history as the Exodus trials.

(5) 1 Cor 5:6–8 "The unleavened bread of sincerity and truth." This passage relates past and present; Passover and Eucharist; the Exodus and the Jesus-led move away from European cultural domination; self-serving social behavior; and "sincerity and truth." All these relations are typologically related—they grow out of experiencing "affliction."

Thus, we are left with no New Testament allegorical application of the Old Testament according to the definition of allegory as abstract analogy. Barnabas Lindars's omission of allegory from his taxonomy agrees with this result. Since there are thousands of typological and fulfillment of prophecy uses of the Old Testament, it appears that the New Testament was interpreting its own current events as a continuing part

---

43. Talmud, tractate Baba Meṣi'a, 88b-89a, translation from *The Babilonian Talmud*, vol. *Baba Mezia*, 511–12.

of its own interacting history preserved in its Old Testament, not illustrating them with themes or examples from someone else's culture.

The generic perspective endemic today finds meaning in generalizations, not particulars, and so is scandalized by the particularity of Old Testament history, and happy to think the New Testament escapes the particularity of Israel by generalizing its truths to every individual in the world. But as we have seen, the New Testament does not do this. The Old Testament does have the whole human race in its purview, but it is a human race understood differently, not as generalizable individuals but as complementarily interacting communities with *different* functions as, for example, the complementary savior-saved relation between Israel and the nations in Gen 12:3 "in you all the families of the earth shall be blessed"; and Isa 49:6 "I will give you as a light to the nations"; or the different callings of Israel and Persia in Isa 44:1, 28, "Jacob my servant" and "Cyrus . . . my shepherd"—both nations elected but not for the same function. New Testament typology preserves this complementary difference in function between communities; allegory would universalize abstract facts from Israel's history, freeze them, and serve them to every individual.

## 5 Legal Citation; Proverbial Citation

The fourth category of New Testament use of the Old Testament is *legal citation*. Legal citation is one of Lindars's categories. Examples of legal citation are Mark 10:7–8 = Gen 2:24 "a man shall leave his father and mother and be joined to his wife, and the two shall become one flesh," and Mark 10:19 = Rom 13:9 = Exod 20:12–16 "You know the commandments: 'You shall not murder; You shall not . . . .'" That legal citation is a form of typology that has just been noted in item (2), above. The corporate perspective views law as part of the tradition created historically by the human community, for example, as delegated by God in Gen 1:27–28. Legal citation relates the past to the present without leaving the internally interactive historical context. The law in question held in Israel before, and the same law, reinterpreted, holds in the same Israel, also reinterpreted, in the present. The Western translation of "Torah" as "Law" reduces typology to mere literal citation.

*Proverbial citation* is the fifth and last category of New Testament use of the Old Testament. In this category the New Testament simply quotes or alludes to proverbial material in the tradition. Examples are

Heb 12:5 = Prov 3:11–12 "My child, do not regard lightly the discipline of the Lord . . . ," and 1 Pet 3:10 = Ps 34:12–16 "Those who desire life and desire to see good days, let them keep their tongues from evil . . . ." This category is Lindars's "moral apophthegms" category. A proverb in the Old Testament is a universal principle applicable within the overall historical context, not a historical event. Because proverbial material is already universal in the Old Testament, its use in the New does not involve an additional abstracting of Old Testament material. Rather, its use is a mere extension to the new situation of the universalization already accomplished in the Old Testament and already subordinate to interactive history. Proverbial citation keeps the cited proverbial material in the same history; it does not transfer it as good example to a different history.

## 6 The Remaining Proposed Categories

The five categories (fulfillment of prophecy, typology, allegory, legal citation, and proverbial citation) include all the methods—excepting allegory, which is empty—of New Testament application of Old Testament passages that will appear at the level of abstraction selected for this analysis. The remaining proposed categories fit into one or another of these five, as will be shown in this and the following section.

Lindars's category "the rewritten Bible" consists of New Testament interpretations of substantial pieces of Old Testament history, such as Stephen's speech in Acts 7. These passages are typological. For example, in Stephen's speech the past disobedience of Israel reaches its climax in the crucifixion of Jesus.

Barr's categories "situation similarities in style and language" and "situation similarities in action" are most easily characterized ostensively by giving his examples: *Magnificat* (Luke 1:46–55) is similar in style and language to the Song of Hannah (1 Sam 2:1–10), and the Sermon on the Mount (Matthew 5–7) is similar in action to the giving of the Law through Moses in Exodus. *Magnificat* and the Song of Hannah are presented in the tradition as sung by particular persons in particular crisis situations; that is, as actions. Thus, for the New Testament both the *Magnificat* and the Sermon on the Mount are events similar to Old Testament events. This similarity in each case is the formal similarity used in typology to call attention to a typological relation between the two events. In the first, Mary thanks God for her election to bear in her time the chosen representative of that one people whose corporate life so radically reflects acceptance of God's delegation of creative interactive responsibility, just as Hannah had done for the same people some seventeen hundred years earlier. Jesus on the mount calls for continued responsible interaction within the community-created internally relating social structure, tradition, and Law (Gen 1:28, page 5, above), as Moses did nineteen hundred years earlier. Barr's placing these examples in a separate category is closer to the surface than the analysis in this study.

For his category "proofs from linguistic details" Barr gives two examples: the argument in Gal 3:16 = Gen 12:7 that God's promise to Abraham (and his singular seed) refers to Christ and the argument in Mark 12:36 that David in Ps 110:1 calls his son Lord. In both cases, Barr cannot recognize the use of the singular as metonym for the whole. With this recognition, the examples appear as fulfillment of prophecy use of the Old Testament.

### 7 Paraenetic Typology

Barr's category "use of Old Testament examples in paraenesis" is more substantial from the perspective of the taxonomy being developed in this study, and out of it will emerge a subcategory for this taxonomy: *paraenetic typology*. Barr's examples are 2 Peter 2:15 "following the road of Balaam," and similar passages in Jude 11 and Rev 2:14, and 1 Peter 3:1–6 "Wives, . . . accept the authority of your husbands . . . . Thus Sarah obeyed Abraham." Bultmann extends the first two of these to 2 Peter 2:4–16 and Jude 5–11 and adds five more similar cases of the use of Old Testament narrative as paraenetic warning: Heb 11, 12:16, James 5:11, 17, and Rev 2:20.[44] Eichrodt gives no examples but refers to Bultmann.[45]

How should such paraenetic use of Old Testament narrative be classified? Is it typology or allegory? This depends, of course, on how one perceives the relation between the Old Testament example and the behavior advocated by the paraenesis, and there appear to be two possible ways of construing this relation. For example, in the case of 1 Peter 3:1–6 "Wives, . . . accept the authority of your husbands . . . . Thus Sarah obeyed Abraham," if Sarah is taken as mother of the people, making her

---

44. Bultmann, "Ursprung und Sinn der Typologie als hermeneutischer Methode," 212.

45. Eichrodt, "Is Typological Exegesis an Appropriate Method?", 228.

complementary role to the father of the people to be normative (traditional) behavior in the nation, so that subordination by all to shared responsibility in all social relations in Israel is historically related to it; then we have typology. If on the other hand Sarah is taken as an unrelated individual, or as a wife in some history unrelated to the reader's own, then her behavior is at most an example the author of 1 Peter wishes the reader's wife to follow; and then we have allegory. But 1 Peter does take Sarah as a responsible interacting mother of the people, as verse 6 indicates, "you have become her daughters . . . ," thus the passage is paraenetic typology.

As for the other examples before us, "Jezebel" in Rev 2:20 is a pseudonym, hence implies a regular, not paraenetic, typological relation. Hebrews 11 on faith has already been treated as paraenetic typology. The other passages also all appear to be paraenetic exhortation to their readers as participants in a People of God continuous with the Old Testament community from which the types are taken, and so are paraenetic typology.

With these examples of paraenetic typology before us, the following differences from other typology can be noted. (a) With paraenetic typology the formal similarity of type and antitype consists in both being ethical behavior, and ethical behavior has a more intrinsic relation to salvation than do the events used for constructing the formal similarity in ordinary typology—for example, passing through water, which is instrumentally related to salvation in the case of the Red Sea and related as a sign in the case of baptism. (b) In paraenetic typology the antitype is always something still to be done by the human community rather than already in progress. Hence (c) the type—the model for the action being advocated—becomes more important, and there is no intensification in passing from type to antitype. Hence (d) paraenetic typology does not correspond naturally to fulfillment of prophecy, which is intensifying. In earlier New Testament passages like 1 Corinthians 10 paraenetic typology occurs within a context of intensifying typology, and the transition from paraenesis to intensification (from imperative to eschatological) is abrupt: "[but] they were written down to instruct us, on whom the ends of the ages have come." In late uses of paraenetic typology in the pastoral epistles, eschatological concerns and intensification virtually disappear. (e) In the pastoral epistles there is a tendency to group several types together, a slightly generic move; for example, Jude 11 "they go the way of Cain, and abandon themselves to Balaam's error for the sake of gain, and perish in Koran's rebellion." (f) The paraenetic emphasis tends to be on the work of the individual member as contribution to the corporate antitypical event. We have here the door through which non-typological generic ethical generalization, as in the long list in 1 Clement 4–6 (above page 81), can later enter in—a universalizing interpretation characteristic of perennial and modern theology throughout the centuries, as will be shown.

Typology used paraenetically thus differs significantly from other typology, and the definitions made above could have been formed to make it appear as a separate category, as in Eichrodt, Bultmann, and Barr. Nevertheless, paraenetic typology, like other typology, is a relation within history that takes the two events as belonging to the same particular history and so fits the definition of typology with which this study started.

This study has found all New Testament use of the Old Testament, averaging more than one of every two New Testament verses, to belong to one of the four categories: fulfillment of prophecy, typology, legal citation, and proverbial citation. Thus, the New Testament understands itself as *new* only in *extending* to the Judean dispersion and Western world the same Old Testament tradition already calling for creative social interaction in Israel and in mission to the whole world. The New Testament community thus does understand itself as acting in a fourth stage in Israel's history—dealing with the three issues outlined in this chapter's introduction: resisting the Western cosmological orientation in Judea; the same in the dispersion; and pursuing the mission to the gentiles thus made practicable.

This conclusion is based on a comparison of the *results* of communally oriented and modern scholars, rather than on the *presuppositions* of either of their perspectives. Without postulating either perspective, it has been shown that the communal perspective provides a more comprehensive interpretation of the New Testament. The communal perspective cannot claim any *a priori* superiority over the modern perspective, as it does not admit any basis outside both perspectives for such a claim. What has been shown, rather, is that *for this particular document, the New Testament,* use of the communal perspective reveals a major pervasive and coherent structure masked by the presuppositions of the modern perspective. This result calls in question whether the New

Testament message can be recognized without some accommodation to the corporate perspective.

This result has been obtained at the level of New Testament application of Old Testament passages. Next, this result will be checked at the level of New Testament theology.

## III NEW TESTAMENT THEOLOGICAL DEPENDENCE ON THE OLD TESTAMENT: TWO VIEWS

To what extent does New Testament theology depend on the Old Testament? This issue is related to, and is as disputed as, the application of Old Testament passages just treated. It will be handled in this study in a characteristic manner—the presentation of three different scholarly positions—followed by an attempt to reach some conclusions by comparing them. The first position is that "the substructure of New Testament theology" comes from the Old Testament, formulated by C. H. Dodd in 1953 in *According to the Scriptures: The Substructure of New Testament Theology*, and elaborated by Barnabas Lindars and Howard Clark Kee. The second position is that New Testament theology is essentially independent of any relation to the Old Testament, as implied in Rudolf Bultmann's *Theology of the New Testament* (1948–1953). And the third, to be presented in the next chapter, is that the New Testament is written within the Palestinian apocalyptic spirit of its own age, claimed by Johannes Weiss and Albert Schweitzer at the turn to the 20th century, and revived since 1960 by Ernst Käsemann and scholars following him who further claim that the New Testament represents a movement selectively extracting precisely the corporate Old Testament position (as identified by Dodd) from an apocalyptic mix of corporate Israelitic and perennial Indo-European perspectives.

The Dodd and Bultmann positions will be contrasted at a theological level in the remainder of the present chapter, showing their opposing positions to depend on their respective communal or modern presuppositions. Early in the next chapter we show that the perennial-philosophy component in first-century apocalyptic provides an additional rationale for modern theology to miss the New Testament corporate base found by Dodd and Käsemann.

## 1 New Testament Theology Based on Old Testament Theology: Continuity with Corporate Israel; Equivalence of Christology and Ecclesiology

In *According to the Scriptures* C. H. Dodd claims that the Christian movement arose directly at Jesus' resurrection as a renewed "Israel of God" in continuity with the Old Testament Israel as People of God. Specifically, it developed and proclaimed the New Testament doctrines of ecclesiology, Christology, and atonement by interpreting its life through typological application of Israel's history as narrated in the Old Testament.

The new community's very use of Israel-church typology made clear a New Testament *ecclesiology* integral with the covenant people Israel. Dodd says the early Christians, disgraced and discredited "until the risen Christ raised them up" (p. 113), "were aware that they belonged to the new 'Israel of God,' which had emerged, as the prophets had always said it would, out of judgment and disaster," and as in Mark 12:11 = Ps 118:23 "This was the Lord's doing, and it is amazing in our eyes," and 1 Cor 1:27–28 "God chose what is foolish . . . weak . . . low and despised in the world, things that are not, to reduce to nothing things that are." This renewal ecclesiology was already present in the prophecies of Joel, Zechariah, and Second Isaiah (p. 112).

In the same way, Dodd claims New Testament *Christology* is built on the way this victorious renewal of Israel comes out of disaster and judgment in the death and resurrection of Jesus Christ (pp. 114–23). These events were understood in the earliest period, according to Dodd, as the application of the "messianic titles" *Son of Man* (Ps 8, Ps 80, Dan 7), *Servant* (Isa 40–55), *King* (Ps 2, Zech 9:9), and *Lord* (Ps 110) from the Old Testament. According to Dodd, the term "Son of Man" in the Old Testament is "Israel, under the similitude of a human figure" (p. 117), and "Servant" in Second Isaiah "is either a pure personification of Israel . . . or else he is an individual whose experience in humiliation and in glory is vicarious; or in other words, who fulfils representatively the destiny of Israel" (p. 118). The application of the titles "Son of Man" and "Servant" to Jesus made him their "inclusive representative"; that is, an individual who represented in his person the whole corporate life of the community, so that in him the prophecies for Israel were fulfilled, and in him the people of God were judged, died, and rose to new life. The other two messianic titles, "King" and "Lord," set Jesus over against the people of God as sovereign Lord. The church as body of Christ (1 Cor

12:12 and Rom 12:15) derives from the messianic role for Jesus, while the church as body with Christ as head (Eph 1:22) derives from the role as sovereign. The two roles are combined in the doctrine of Christ as high priest in Hebrews and the exaltation of the servant through his suffering in John. Thus, Dodd unites New Testament ecclesiology and New Testament Christology; they are two aspects of the same doctrine—two ways of formulating the same corporate relation between God and his people.

Dodd holds that the New Testament doctrine of *atonement* results from applying to the crucifixion a combination of the vicarious or representative nature of the suffering of the Servant in Second Isaiah, the expiatory nature of this same suffering, the relation between the Servant and the covenant in Isa 42:6, 49:8 "I have given you as a covenant to the people," the relation between the king and the blood of the covenant in Zech 9:9–11 = John 12:15 "Lo, your king comes to you; . . . humble and riding on a donkey . . . . because of the blood of my covenant with you, I will set your prisoners free," and the new covenant in Jer 31:31–34 "they shall all know me." This complexity of ideas provides the basis, Dodd asserts, for the variously developed doctrines of atonement in Paul, Hebrews, and John. Thus, the New Testament doctrine of atonement is corporate and continuous with the saving relation of God to his corporate people in the Old Testament (pp. 123–25).

Dodd proposes a thoroughly corporate orientation for the New Testament writers, including a salvation-historical continuity with the people of the Old Testament. Dodd's pioneering effort has been refined by subsequent communally oriented New Testament scholars, and results are presented from two of these: Barnabas Lindars and Howard Clark Kee.

Barnabas Lindars, in *New Testament Apologetic: The Doctrinal Significance of the Old Testament Quotations* (1961), reconstructs the historical stages in which New Testament doctrine was formed from the Old Testament during the early period (from which no finished written documents are available) up to the earliest extant New Testament writing, that of Paul. He does this by observing the progressive shifts in the use by the Christian community of the same Old Testament texts to interpret new situations. His analysis is a *tour de force* showing in high detail a pervasive dependence of New Testament doctrine on the Old Testament.

Lindars finds five stages in the development of New Testament doctrine in the period from its beginning to Paul. Old Testament quotations were first used to interpret the *resurrection* of Jesus. Then the same quotes, and some new ones, were successively used to explain his *passion*, then the *whole ministry* of Jesus, then his *birth and preexistence*—all before Paul used them in his letters, the earliest New Testament books, to deal with the problems he faced in his work. Lindars's communally oriented results are sketched here for subsequent comparison with Bultmann's modern results.

Lindars says the Christian movement first used passages from the prophets and the psalms to interpret Jesus' ministry as being a critical point in the Judean apocalyptic expectation of the coming of the new age. Examples are 1 Cor 15:4 = Hos 6:2 "he was raised on the third day," Acts 2:25–28 = Ps 16:8–11 "For you will not . . . let your Holy One experience corruption," Acts 2:34 = Ps 110:1 "Sit at my right hand," and Acts 2:17–21 = Joel 2:28:32 "I will pour out my spirit," which interpret the resurrection as the conquest of death, the raising of the Messiah to God's right hand, and the manifestation of the Spirit (pp. 36–55).

The second stage in the development of Christian doctrine, according to Lindars, was the explaining of the *suffering and death* of this Messiah Jesus, so different from the conventional first-century conception of the Messiah. This "passion apologetic" was accomplished by quotations and allusions to Isaiah 53 (the chief Servant poem) by all of the principal writers of the New Testament, thus leading to an early doctrine of the atonement as reflected, for example, in 1 Cor 15:3 "For I handed on to you as of first importance what I in turn had received: that Christ died for our sins in accordance with the scriptures" (pp. 75–679). Passion apologetic also relied on Psalms 22, 31, 34, 41, 69, and 109; and Zech 9–13 (pp. 88–134).

The third stage was the extension of passion apologetic to the *whole life* of Jesus. For example, Ps 2:7 "You are my son; today I have begotten you," originally used as a prediction of the resurrection as in Acts 13:13 and Heb 1:5, and in this third stage is used with Isa 42:1 in the baptism story Mark 1:11, "You are my beloved Son; with you I am well pleased," to push the revelation of Jesus' messiahship back from the resurrection to the baptism (pp. 139–42). Another example is Isa 42:1–4 "Here is my servant, whom I uphold . . ." which, quoted in full in Matt 12:18–21, shows traces in its modified text of four successive stages of application:

recognition at resurrection ("Here is"); at baptism (as in Mark 1:11); the non-violent ministry of Jesus ("not wrangle" replaces "not cry"); and the gentile mission ("gentiles" replaces "coastlands," the Jewish dispersion)—all before its use by Matthew to explain the Markan doctrine that persecuted, crucified Jesus—messiah from the start—first became publicly known as Messiah at the resurrection (pp. 144–51).

Isaiah 6:9–10 "Keep listening, but do not comprehend . . ." is first used to explain the lack of response to the church's preaching. John 12:40 was next used to explain the rejection of Jesus by some during his ministry. Mark 4:11–12, implying a doctrine of an elite that was to develop into a doctrine of election, was still later used by Paul in 2 Cor 3:14 to argue against the necessity of becoming a Jew in order to be a Christian (because under the letter of the law, taken as static rule rather than pre-colonial creative interaction, comprehension is impossible) and was used further by Paul in Rom 11:7 to show that part of Israel is hardened until the gentiles come in (pp. 159–66). "When Mark opens his Gospel with the words 'The beginning of the gospel of Jesus Christ,' he is not setting out to draw a picture of the figure expected in late Judaism. He is describing the life of an historical Person which has come to be understood messianically" (p. 186). The typologically applied Old Testament passages ensure this understanding.

The fourth stage in the development of Christian doctrine was acceptance of the Davidic nature of the Messiah, with *birth* in Bethlehem, Matt 2:6 = Mic 5:2 "And you, Bethlehem . . . are by no means least . . . from you shall come a ruler . . . ." This pushed the moment of messianic manifestation back from the baptism to the birth, a step reflected in the infancy narratives in Matthew and Luke and crucially important in the later development of Christology along metaphysical lines more accommodating to Hellenistic thought (p. 190). The Son of man designation for Jesus, Matt 26:64 = Dan 7:13–14 "Son of man . . . coming on the clouds of heaven," led to the doctrine of Christ pre-existing in heaven (pp. 210–14).

When we reach the time of Paul's writing, we find *Paul* applying doctrines that have already been worked out (the superseding of the law, the spiritual temple of the Body of Christ, and the preaching to the gentiles) to the specific problems he encounters in his own work (p. 222). He uses the Old Testament passage Isa 49:1 = Gal 1:15 "God . . . set me apart before I was born" to justify the gentile mission, corresponding to its use in Isa 49:1–6 "The Lord called me before I was born . . . I will give you as a light to the nations." The passage is also so used in Acts 13:47 and in the *Nunc Dimittis* Luke 2:32 (p. 223). Paul uses Gal 3:13f = Deut 21:23 "Cursed is everyone who hangs on a tree" (which, earlier, was part of the passion apologetic in Acts 5:30: God raised while the Sanhedrin condemned) to show "Christ redeemed us from the curse of the law by becoming a curse for us . . . in order that . . . the blessing of Abraham might come to the gentiles" (pp. 232–35).

Paul combines Gal 3:6 = Rom 4:3 = James 2:23 = Gen 15:6 "Abraham believed God, and it was reckoned to him as righteousness" with Gal 3:8 = Acts 3:25 = Gen 12:3 and Gen 22:18 "In you all the families of the earth shall be blessed" and "By your offspring shall all the nations of the earth gain blessing for themselves" to serve his work with the gentiles to whom he wrote. Whereas the first of these passages is used in James in its usual Jewish and primitive Christian way to mean that faith leads to good works and the second is applied in Acts to mean that the Jews will continue to be the means of blessing if they follow Jesus, Paul combines the two to mean that the gentiles, too, if they have faith, can be descendants of Abraham (Gal 3:7, Rom 4:16). And by applying the collective word "offspring" to Christ in the singular (Gal 3:16), he makes Christ the inclusive representative of the true Israel: Gal 3:29 "And if you belong to Christ, then you are Abraham's offspring, heirs according to the promise" (compare with Rom 4:24). Thus, Christ has the same inclusive representative role for Israel as Abraham does, and Israel is now those who are "in Christ," who are "baptized into Christ," who have "clothed themselves with Christ," who are "one in Christ" (Gal 3:26–28), (pp. 225–27). Paul also supports this redefinition of Israel with a quotation from the universalistic second Isaiah—for example, Rom 15:21 = Isa 52:15 "Those who have never been told of him shall see . . ." (pp. 240–48). Jesus' crucifixion indirectly by Rome was the price paid for the renewal of Israel's original call to be a light to the nations.

Lindars's analysis is a *tour de force* that shows New Testament theology to have been created in successive stages over two decades. He does so by applying the Old Testament theological structure to the new situation; that is, by using the Old Testament narrative typologically. This procedure created a New Testament theology based on both a historical continuity between Israel and the church and an intrinsic relation between Christology and ecclesiology. Lindars's work is an elaboration of Dodd's work, the new element being the attempt to trace through five stages the successive application and extension of the tradition to new events in the fledgling Christian movement's rapidly changing circumstances. One more scholar who has refined Dodd's work will be considered.

Howard Clark Kee's sociologically oriented study of Mark in his *Community of the New Age: Studies in Mark's Gospel* 1977 exhibits the same perspective as Dodd's *According to the Scriptures*. Kee says, ". . . in every case the images employed in Mark to represent Christian existence are corporate" (p. 107). The New Testament community represents itself in Mark as continuous with the Israel of the Old Testament. For example, in the feeding story (Mark 6:30–35) Jesus has compassion on the crowd because they are like sheep without a shepherd (Zech 13:7); here Jesus shows the same concern as did Moses when Joshua was commissioned as leader "that the congregation of the Lord may not be like sheep without a shepherd" (Num 27:17). The feeding in the "deserted place" (Mark 6:32, 35) corresponds to the manna for Israel in the desert. Kee says, "The overall significance of the feeding story cannot be mistaken: as once God called his people out of Egypt and sustained them miraculously until they could enter the land of promise, so God is calling together a new people, who likewise will be preserved in their time of difficulty until they enter the New Age" (pp. 111–12).

The image of covenant occurs in Mark 14:24 "This is my blood of the covenant." Its world wide scope is proclaimed in Mark 13:27 "gather his elect from the four winds [= Zech 2:6], from the ends of the earth to the ends of heaven [= Deut 31:4]" and in Mark 11:17 = Isa 56:7 "My house shall be called a house of prayer for all the nations."

Kee's sociological approach brings into prominence Jesus' representative leadership function in the community. Kee analyzes the many titles of Jesus (pp. 116–44), showing how the primitive church redefined the concept of messiah, as in Mark 12:10–11 = Ps 118:22–23 "The stone that the builders rejected has become the cornerstone."

Thus, according to Kee, Mark presents its community as being historically continuous with Israel and does so largely through typological application of images from the Old Testament. In particular, Kee agrees with Dodd (page 103, above) in seeing New Testament Christology and New Testament ecclesiology as two ways of formulating the same continuing relation between God and his people. Kee says, "Neither conceptually nor in literary ways is it possible, therefore, to draw an absolute distinction in Mark between Jesus and his followers, or in theological terms, between Christology and ecclesiology" (p. 143).

Thus, the communally oriented New Testament scholars Dodd, Lindars, and Kee hold that New Testament theology is a continuation of Old Testament theology, applying Old Testament events typologically to interpret the new events it reports.

## 2 A New Testament Theology Independent of Old Testament Theology: Existential Freedom from Corporate History

A quite different view of the relation of the New Testament to the Old is evident in the modern New Testament scholar Rudolf Bultmann.

Bultmann's classic *Theology of the New Testament* (1948–1953) does not disagree with the exegeses of specific New Testament texts in the material we have considered from Dodd, Lindars, or Kee. Bultmann agrees with Lindars that the first two stages in the development of Christian doctrine were attempts to interpret the resurrection and the crucifixion (1.43–47), and that a theology of the life and baptism (and of the pre-existence and birth) of Jesus were developed later (1.130–32). Bultmann's claim that the Servant of Isaiah 53 was not used to interpret Jesus in the earliest period (1.31, 47) is in formal agreement with Lindars's placing its use in the second of his five stages in the development of christological doctrine (Lindars pp. 78–81).

Yet in spite of agreement on these details, the overall impression of the relation of the two Testaments is radically different. Reading Bultmann's book, one would certainly not gain the impression that the New Testament alluded to the Old Testament for metonymic support on average once every 1.87 verses. There is no Old Testament scriptural index. Most of the New Testament passages taken as typologically related to the Old Testament by the scholars treated in the previous section are not treated, and those listed in the book's New Testament scriptural index[46] are discussed without reference to any Old Testament connection. When Bultmann does recognize an OT connection, it is generally negative. For example, Mark 12:35–37 = Ps 110:1 "... David himself calls him Lord; so how can he be his son?" is taken as a New Testament criticism

---

46. The scriptural index in the English translation is identical with the one in the German original, Bultmann, *Theologie des Neuen Testaments*.

of the title "Son of David" (1.28), and Matt 5:21–22 "You have heard .... But I say to you . . ." is said to "throw legalism and the will of God into sharp contrast" (1.13). The temptation story, the story of Jesus' entry into Jerusalem, and the passion story—all of which involve a large amount of Old Testament imagery—are characterized as legend or colored by legend (1.27). Bultmann's point that the critical-historical meaning of these passages is insufficient to demonstrate Jesus' messianic self-consciousness is correct; the scholars Dodd, Lindars, and Kee above would say they were written precisely not to describe Jesus psychologically but typologically, or "colored by legend," in order to place Jesus' dramatic interactions into bilaterally internal relation with Israel's communal past. Bultmann's tone of dismissal of such Old Testament-ridden passages is patent. Bultmann also has Jesus using the Old Testament against itself, as in Mark 10:5 "Because of your hardness of heart [Moses] wrote this commandment for you" (1.15), and in Mark 10:17–19, 12:28–34 where Jesus' quoting of the ten or two commandments is interpreted as demonstrating the impossibility of following them (1.16). Both positions interpret Jesus correctly, but both points are also intended by the Old Testament.

Bultmann emphasizes Hellenistic influence in the New Testament parallel to Old Testament influence, Stoic cosmology and natural theology, popular Hellenistic philosophy, the *via negationis*, mystery and salvation deities, and gnostic dualism (1.70–72, 79, 106–8, 172–83). Paul is characterized as a Hellenistic Jew whose Jewish background was hellenized before his conversion and who inherited an already hellenized version of Christianity (1.187–89).[47] The titles of Jesus (1.48–53) are listed and described in terms of their use in the primitive church "to indicate his significance and dignity," with bare mention of their having been "borrowed from the tradition of Jewish messianic faith; in which motifs of diverse origin were admittedly united" (1.48). When Bultmann comes to the title Son of David, which he admits "comes out of the national tradition," it is sufficiently characterized by the phrases "seems not to have played any great role," "its occurrence is relatively rare in the synoptic

---

47. Differing from Martin Hengel: "the distinction between 'Palestinian' Judaism and the 'Hellenistic' Judaism of the Greek-speaking Diaspora, which has been customary for so long, now becomes very questionable," *Judaism and Hellenism*, 311–12; and E. P. Sanders: Paul's differences from Palestinian Judaism are not based on Hellenistic Judaism, *Paul and Palestinian Judaism*, 555.

tradition," "the title is of no importance to [Paul]," and, regarding its use in Rom 1:3, "is evidently due to a handed-down formula" (1.49).

It is hard to avoid the conclusion that Bultmann avoids the Old Testament and that when he feels he must refer to it he does so with reluctance and aversion. Since the Goppelt-von Rad position had flourished in Old Testament circles in Germany for two decades when Bultmann wrote, it appears that the negative use of Old Testament material in the book reflects a conscious opposition to the Goppelt-von Rad position. The theoretical basis for such an opposition is not hard to find in Bultmann's book.

For Bultmann, the church is the "eschatological congregation," that is, "the congregation of the end of days" (1.37). Since it "does not draw a boundary between itself, as a new religion, and Judaism," the question arises "how far is 'Israel'—the subject to whom salvation happens— understood as meaning an absolutely eschatological entity, as it is by Paul, and how far as just the empirical People of history? Will the earliest church eliminate from the idea of the Chosen People whatever applies only to the historical People?" (1.53–54). "The relation of the Church to Israel's history is a peculiarly paradoxical one. . . . The eschatological Congregation is not simply the historical successor and heir of the empirical Israel of history but the heir of the ideal Israel" (1.96–97).

> [Jesus'] ministry was not understood as a decisive event for Israel's history like the call of Moses, the exodus from Egypt, the giving of the Law on Sinai, or God's raising up of kings and prophets . . . . Of course not! For Jesus' importance as Messiah-Son-of-Man lies not at all in what he did in the past, but entirely in what is expected of him for the future. And once this expectation is fulfilled by the eschatological drama, that event will never become, like the crossing of the Red Sea, a past to which one could look back thankfully, drawing confidence from it, but it will be God's last deed of all, by which he puts history to an end" (1.36).

Now it is clear what, for Bultmann, is really wrong with the Old Testament events—*they are historical*, whereas the New Testament eschatological congregation *transcends history*. Correspondence with Old Testament events is "not a paralleling of historical persons and events, but an interpretation of Old Testament history as a foreshadowing of what would happen in the eschatological period" (1.36); that is, an interpretation of history as foreshadowing a salvation outside of history. It implies a salvation unrelated to any responsibility for multilaterally creative relations in human community, an existentialist or gnostic ghost of the modern or perennial views. In contrast, typology as understood by the 22 scholars in note 26 on page 86 above implies a corporate salvation within the same continuing history. But Bultmann places salvation outside of history and says, "the distinction can . . . be ignored between allegory (the art of finding prediction or deeper truths of any sort in the wording of scripture) and typology (the interpretation of persons, events, or institutions of the past as foreshadowing prototypes)" (1.117). For Bultmann, typology is allegory, and both are irrelevant.

What is Bultmann's ideal transhistorical eschatological congregation like? What is this "end of history"? Bultmann says:

> Unlike the prophets' preaching, [Jesus'] preaching is directed not primarily to the people as a whole, but *to individuals*. The judgment comes not on nations but on individuals who must give account of themselves before God; and it is individuals whom coming salvation will bless. Judgment and salvation are eschatological events in the strict sense; i.e. events in which the present world and all history cease to be. Thus, Jesus' idea of God is dehistoricized, and man seen under this idea of God is dehistoricized, that is, the relation between God and man is released from its ties to world history (1.25).[48]

Bultmann goes on to say the relation is radically "historicized" in a different sense of "history," namely an existentialist one—"precisely that God who stands aloof from the history of nations, meets each man in his own little history. . . . Dehistoricized man (i.e. naked of his supposed security within his historical group) is guided into his concrete encounter with his neighbor, in which he finds his true history" (1.25–26).

This last passage is in coherence with both perennial and modern theological positions that justification by faith implies justification without relying on human resources (thus including community without relying on it). This is in contrast with the communal position, for which a relation (justification) is not possible without dedication of resources from both sides, and human resources always include the community that gives the self its individuality, that always includes its "supposed security" within its historical community.

---

48. Translation restored to original syntax.

Bultmann and the hegemony of the existentialist phase of modern theology have past. Biblical scholars in the sixties and seventies reacted strongly against it; several of them are quoted on pages 252–255 below. Yet the position was stated tautly and clearly by Bultmann, and it enjoyed wide acceptance for nearly half a century. The Bultmann school could not in principle see the historical relation between the Testaments as essential to the New Testament message because it held that that message was concerned with the dehistoricized self and confronted it with the possibility of an ideal, not historical or social, relation to God. The Bultmann school's understanding of the relation between the Testaments is limited not by the New Testament material but by the school's self-as-such presuppositions. The Bultmann school and the Goppelt-Dodd-von Rad school both include able scholars; the differing results are due to differing socio-philosophical presuppositions.

Which results, those of the communal Dodd school or the modern-existentialist Bultmann school, come closer to the intentions of the New Testament? Critical methods are used by both schools in reaching their differing positions, hence the critical method cannot provide the answer to this question. In fact, critical analysis is itself a particular interpretation. Performed on analogy with critical natural science (Kant, Hume), it interprets into a horizon not recognizing non-empirical meaning. Both the Dodd and Bultmann schools use the critical method as a tool in interpreting into horizons—communal and existentialist—each wider than the critical one; their results depend on those horizons as well as the critical horizon. Again we ask, are there neutral, horizon-free, criteria for judging one of these schools as a better interpreter of this text?

According to this chapter's analysis, the following conclusions can be drawn without assuming the presuppositions of either school. A communally oriented New Testament study reveals a much richer structure, for example, the interactive relation between Christology and ecclesiology and the continuity between Israel and the church. Also included is a corporate analysis of the self, different from but no less comprehensive than those proposed by the modern or existentialist programs. The presuppositions of the Barr and Bultmann schools preclude the discovering of such richer structures, both of New Testament literary use of the Old Testament (Barr) and of its theological use (Bultmann). It appears that the communal perspective is a wider-reaching platform for interpreting the New Testament than either the modern or existentialist ones.

Academically, this argument implies not that the communal perspective is true, but only that a holder of the modern or existentialist perspective misses, thus implicitly rejects, a substantial part of the intended New Testament message for the same reason Bultmann explicitly rejects the entire Old Testament message.

This tentative conclusion will be strengthened in the next chapter with two additional findings. *First:* Israel's continuing pre-exilic corporate orientation was in active conflict with the contradicting Hellenistic perennial orientation in Palestinian apocalyptic culture; and the New Testament, a record of a movement for return to the earlier orientation, was intentionally corporate, not accidentally. *Second:* whereas the corporate orientation was explicit in the Old Testament, now under occupation this politically powerless continuing corporately oriented reform party could only express itself in its New Testament via the then double-valued apocalyptic idiom. This allowed the perennially oriented controlling party to misunderstand such words as "remnant" and "resurrection" in their Hellenistic meanings and thus unwittingly interpret much apocalyptic writing, including the New Testament, in a way contrary to its reason for being.

3

## The New Testament II

*Discontinuity with the Old Testament*

WITH THE PERVASIVE New Testament allusions to an Old Testament that many twentieth century scholars have conceded to be corporate, how has it been possible for competent modern scholars like Bultmann, Barr, and many others to maintain that the New Testament has a modern or even existentialist base? For example, how can they conceive resurrection to be generic when the New Testament itself illustrates it with the very corporate resurrection of Israel in Hosea 6:2 "On the third day he will raise us up"; in Matt 16:21, Luke 9:22, Luke 24:46, John 5:21, Acts 10:40, 1 Cor 15:4, and 15 more New Testament passages; and Ezek 37:10–11 "the breath came into them and they lived . . . . these bones are the whole house of Israel"; in John 20:22 "he breathed on them"; in Matt 27:52, John 5:28, Rom 8:23, 1 Cor 12:4–11, Thess 4:8, Rev 11:7–11; and 8 more passages? Why have generically oriented biblical scholars not been forced to reject the New Testament as they do the Old? In this chapter we look for some characteristic of the New Testament sufficiently different from the Old to allow those with modern or existentialist presuppositions to interpret the New Testament generically, even while indirectly conceding the Old Testament to be corporate.

The New Testament writers did not consult the Old Testament as a book of fixed abstract truths like those offered by Western philosophical or scientific writers. Rather, these writers viewed the Old Testament as a history and critique of their *own* political and cultural life to date as People of God, a tradition passed on as a corpus of examples for future typological community use for "learning by our own mistakes." But during three centuries of Greco-Roman colonial occupation, their colonially appointed local ruling officials had the large-scale power to suppress corporately oriented prophetic challenges as earlier Israelite rulers had not, causing the emergence of an *apocalyptic style* of writing that was understandable to the still corporately oriented Judean subjects but avoided literally explicit challenges to the rulers. The New Testament is written in such an apocalyptic style. This subterfuge was further assisted by the New Testament's being written in Koiné Greek, the trade language of the Middle Eastern colonial region, an Indo-European language with few metonymic word meanings that might suggest typological relations between social contexts. No philosopher in Europe held the corporate position until Hegel in 1807 (chapter 1, above); and no Western Christian theologian did so until Johann Adam Möhler in 1825 (chapter 7, below).

## I THE NEED TO DEFINE APOCALYPTIC

In 1960 Ernst Käsemann, who had been a student of Bultmann, broke ranks with the German New Testament scholarly consensus of the time and announced that "apocalyptic was the mother of all Christian theology."[1] Earlier, the history-of-religions school had taken uncomfortable notice of apocalyptic in the New Testament at the turn to the twentieth century,[2] with Albert Schweitzer saying, "The modern spirit is here breaking in wreaths of foam upon the sharp cliffs of the rockbound eschatological world-view of Jesus."[3] But apocalyptic was not accepted as central to the New Testament until the spectacular revolt from Bultmann's influence and the rehabilitation of apocalyptic from 1960 on. Käsemann appears to except Jesus from both the apocalyptic of John the Baptist who preceded him and from the New Testament theology that followed him: "Jesus admittedly made the apocalyptically determined message of John his point of departure; his own preaching, however, did not bear a fundamentally apocalyptic stamp but proclaimed the immediacy of the God who was near at hand."[4] Ulrich Wilckens in 1961 took the same position: "The distinctions from apocalyptic thought are significant even if we acknowledge it as the native soil for the proclamation

---

1. Käsemann, "The Beginnings of Christian Theology," 102.

2. Weiss, *Jesus' Proclamation of the Kingdom of God*; Bousset, *Die Religion des Judentum*; Schweitzer, *Quest*.

3. Schweitzer, *Quest*, 252.

4. Käsemann, "The Beginnings of Christian Theology," 101, expanded in "On the Subject of Primitive Christian Apocalyptic," 111–24.

of Jesus."[5] It will appear that, for both scholars, this separation is only from the generic Indo-European component of eclectic apocalyptic, not from the preexilic corporate component, thus reversing the whole consensus in the Bultmann period.

More recent New Testament studies continue to give apocalyptic a central place. J. Christiaan Beker's book *Paul the Apostle: The Triumph of God in Life and Thought* (1980) claims an "apocalyptic" subtitle (p. ix), and says, "only a consistent apocalyptic interpretation of Paul's thought is able to demonstrate its fundamental coherence" (p. 143); and Howard Clark Kee's *Community of the New Age: Studies in Mark's Gospel* (1977) claims to show Mark's Gospel to be apocalyptic in literary genre, in theological structure, and in concrete relation to the community which produced it (pp. 65–66). The meaning of this shift to apocalyptic in German and American New Testament studies depends, however, on what apocalyptic is taken to be. What is apocalyptic?

The concept apocalyptic is derived from the literary genre apocalypse, the form of writings such as Daniel, 1 Enoch, 2 Baruch, 2 Esdras, the Apocalypse of Abraham, and Revelation. Only small portions of the New Testament are written in a sustained apocalyptic literary form, such as the synoptic apocalypse (Mark 13) and the book of Revelation. This is not the sense of the term intended in the recent renewal of interest in apocalyptic among New Testament scholars.

The recent concern is rather for a pervasive orientation in the general culture of Israel that is reflected in its literature at that time, an orientation that first flourished in the fifth century BCE and then again from the second century BCE to the first century CE, and was a means in these periods for maintaining the covenant commitments of Israel to God, and so was a successor of the prophetic movement that had flourished under the Israelite monarchy. The apocalyptic orientation is most explicitly represented by material written in an apocalyptic literary form but underlies other literature in its periods as well.

Apocalyptic, a less direct replacement for prophecy, did of course differ from it, but scholars have not agreed on the nature of this difference. Five different characterizations of apocalyptic by five post-1960 biblical scholars illustrate this disagreement.

Klaus Koch characterizes apocalyptic as a particular interpretation of history. A community present at the beginning of the end-time

5. Wilckens, "The Understanding of Revelation," 70–71.

interprets a sequence of events as a coherent pattern pointing to that end-time, for the purpose of allowing the community to participate in the final, all-encompassing coming of God.[6] For Koch, apocalyptic differs from prophecy primarily in how radical and once-for-all the change brought on by the crisis is. Even so, apocalyptic remains within the history of the corporate community. Thus, Koch understands apocalyptic to retain the corporate orientation of the preexilic tradition.

For Wolfhart Pannenberg, apocalyptic's end-time looms so large as to stand outside history. "The fulfillment was no longer (as was still the case with the prophets) expected within history and therefore seen as a goal which could be superseded, but it was expected at the end of the whole of world history; . . . the promise was bound to the law. . . . an eternal law which is the unchangeable ground of all world history," a "history moving toward a future still hidden from the world but already revealed in Jesus Christ."[7] Pannenberg's characterization reflects his own affinity with a cosmologically mis-interpreted Hegel.[8]

Paul Hanson sees the difference between the periods as a shift in the relation between the historical and the trans-historical, or cosmic. "The prophets, affirming the historical realm as a suitable context for divine activity, understood it as their task to translate the vision of divine activity from the cosmic level to the level of the politico-historical realm of everyday life. The [apocalyptic] visionaries, disillusioned with the historical realm, disclosed their vision in a manner of growing indifference to . . . the contingencies of the politico-historical realm, thereby leaving the language increasingly in the language of the cosmic realm."[9] Thus, the pre-apocalyptic Old Testament brought God's activity down to the politico-historical realm but apocalyptic discontinued this practice. Seeing the primary locus of divine activity in its cosmic form (rather than its particular historical or social form) belongs to the cosmological orientation.

Hans Dieter Betz's reading is even sharper: "To the apocalypticist 'world history' in its entirety is identical with the 'evil eon' . . . . Consequently, the quest for the meaning of history can no longer be an-

6. Koch, *The Rediscovery of Apocalyptic*, 33.

7. Pannenberg, "Redemptive Event and History," 20, 15 (= Westermann, ed., *Hermeneutics*, 319, 314).

8. Interpretations of Hegel are discussed on page 23 above.

9. P. Hanson, *The Dawn of Apocalyptic*, 12.

swered by the concept of the salvation history of Israel.... Apocalypticism does not fulfill the concept of salvation history, but replaces it.... The *eschaton* cannot bring the fulfillment, but only the abolition of history."[10] Betz's reading of apocalypticism is existentialist. Von Rad offers a fifth view of the difference between apocalyptic and the prophets:

> The decisive factor, as I see it, is the incompatibility between apocalyptic literature's view of history and that of the prophets. The prophetic message is specifically rooted in the saving history, that is to say, it is rooted in definite election traditions. But there is no way which leads from this to the apocalyptic view of history.... In the panorama of history given in Daniel's two great night-visions, the picture of the empires and the vision of the four beasts, there is absolutely no mention of Israel's history; here God deals only with the empires, and even the son of man does not come from Israel but "with the clouds of heaven."[11]

Such a universalization of history in apocalyptic appears to von Rad to be the same as in postexilic wisdom literature, and he considers apocalyptic an extension of the wisdom movement.[12] The universalism he sees in apocalyptic does not give adequate place to ethnic Israel, which is the historical medium for the transmission of tradition from the beginning of Israel down to the New Testament community. For von Rad, postexilic wisdom and apocalyptic are a cosmological side-track in the corporate Old Testament transmission of tradition, a transmission continuing into the New Testament but absent in the wisdom literature.[13]

These five contemporary understandings of apocalyptic thus include its acceptance by a communal scholar as corporate (Koch), its acceptance by a mixed corporate-cosmological scholar as cosmological (Pannenberg), its recognition by a modern scholar as cosmological (Hanson), its acceptance by an existentialist scholar as existentialist (Betz), and its rejection by a communal scholar as cosmological (von Rad). These scholars' *evaluations* of apocalyptic obviously and quite properly depend on the relation between their philosophical presuppositions and their conceptions of what apocalyptic is. But more sig-

---

10. Betz, "The Concept of Apocalyptic," 201–2.
11. Von Rad, *Old Testament Theology*, 2.303.
12. Ibid., 2.306.
13. Ibid., 2.319–429.

nificantly and less properly their *conceptions* of what apocalyptic is also depend on those presuppositions.

Further examples could be produced. We are left with the question: what is apocalyptic?[14] The answer will need to be more complex than any of these five.

## II CORPORATE-COSMOLOGICAL PLURALISM IN FIRST-CENTURY APOCALYPTIC

What is first-century apocalyptic? It appeared above that what is being characterized is a historical cultural movement rather than a literary form. The next choice is whether to describe this cultural movement according to a modern perspective in terms of characteristic abstract themes (such as cosmic emphasis or universalism), or in pedagogic terms as a collection of apocalyptic teachings such as God's ascension of his throne (Dan 7:9–10), or God's use of a mediator with royal functions (Dan 7:13–14), or in communal terms as part of the history of traditions; that is, as a partly synthesized mixture of distinct traditions with historical origins both in preexilic Israel and from outside Israel.

Because the interest here interest is in the transmission of the widely conceded corporately oriented Old Testament tradition through apocalyptic to the New Testament, the last option is chosen. This choice commits us to dealing with the whole culture of the period as a unity, with its motifs and its sociology in internal relation. This is a commitment to analysis of the transmission of Old Testament tradition, not to any *a priori* validity for the corporate orientation. Thus, this project does not allow separating "apocalyptic eschatology" as motif and "apocalypticism" as sociological *Sitz im Leben* as proposed by Paul Hanson,[15] adopted by modern scholars,[16] and rejected by communal ones.[17] The term apocalyptic characterizes a culture as a unity. It can apply to a whole culture or to a sectarian group.

Using this option, one finds that first-century apocalyptic in Israel is *eclectic* and *pluralistic*, that it is analyzable as an eclectic mixture of some

---

14. The confusion is proclaimed by Koch's title for his *The Rediscovery of Apocalyptic*, *Ratlos vor der Apokalyptik*, literally "At Wits End with Apocalyptic," and is outlined for example in the postscript of Michael E. Stone's "Lists of Revealed Things," 439–44.

15. P. Hanson, "Apocalypticism," 28–34.

16. For example Collins, "Introduction: Toward the Morphology of a Genre," 3.

17. For example Sanders, "The Genre of Palestinian Jewish Apocalypses," 450.

six contributing *historical strands of tradition*, and that the corporate-cosmological pluralism of the period cuts across these strands, emerging in each strand in the form of one or more *corporate-cosmological ranges of perspective*. The central argument of the chapter will be that in using each of the corporate-cosmological ranges in the six strands the New Testament consistently selects their corporate poles. But to show such a selectivity of the New Testament in its use of materials available in first-century apocalyptic, it is first necessary to characterize first-century apocalyptic independently of the New Testament, and that is the present project.[18]

Strands in apocalyptic that derive from the pre-apocalyptic parts of the Old Testament are (1) an *eschatological strand* from the prophets, (2) a *salvation-history strand* from the epic in the Torah and the historical books, and (3) a *wisdom strand* from the postexilic wisdom tradition. These three strands preserve for the apocalyptic period basic theological insights from each major part of the Old Testament tradition. Strands more substantially influenced by sources from outside the Old Testament are (4) the *resurrection strand*, (5) the *remnant strand*, and (6) the *powers strand*, a theory of natural and social structures personified as angels or powers.

An abstract analysis would treat the latter three of these strands of tradition as included respectively in the first three because resurrection, remnant, and powers are respectively eschatological, salvation-historical, and wisdom motifs. But the present project is rather to trace the transmission of tradition from the Old Testament through apocalyptic to the New Testament, and because resurrection, remnant, and powers in their first-century apocalyptic forms are significantly influenced by non-Old-Testament sources, these strands are here treated separately. The first three strands, also, are not to be taken as abstract motifs but as strands continuing the Old Testament prophetic, historical, and wisdom traditions.

The analysis will show that the apocalyptic tradition is not a static mixture of the various motifs included within each of these six strands

---

18. Paul Hanson in 1975 said the analysis of apocalyptic into constituent strands has not yet been carried out (*The Dawn of Apocalyptic*, 8), but the present study takes advantage of considerable work in this direction appearing in 1969 in Martin Hengel, *Judaism and Hellenism*, 1.175–254, work carried out within a history of traditions perspective.

but is an unstable combination of conflicting and even literally incompatible motifs. The strands and their ranges exist together only in mutually interacting creative tension. I isolate some of these tensions as *ranges* of possible positions between extremes within a single strand and occasionally between strands. Most ranges isolated are between corporate and cosmological emphases because the issue is the transmission of a corporate tradition through a cosmologically threatened culture. *The isolation of these ranges is the goal* of this part of the chapter. These ranges will be used later in the chapter to distinguish choices made by New Testament apocalyptic from among those available from the first-century apocalyptic tradition.

The strands and their ranges, to be developed next, are listed here. *Asterisks* identify the mentioned *key corporate-generic ranges*, which will serve later as key for the corporate-modern issue, because modern and cosmological positions share non-corporate status.

Strands and Ranges in First-Century Apocalyptic

I. Strands Continuing the Pre-Apocalyptic Old Testament Tradition
1. Eschatological Strand
    *local-definitive range* (ranging from God's triumph in a particular historical situation to God's definitive triumph once-for-all)
    * *continuous-discontinuous range* (from a new age maintaining historical continuity with the old age to a new age outside of history)
2. Salvation-Historical Strand
    *narrative-schematic range* (from salvation revealed in historical narrative to a schematized salvation history)
3. Wisdom Strand
    * *subordinate-dominant range* (from wisdom a subordinate tool to wisdom dominant over corporate history)

II. Eclectic Strands Partly Originating Outside Israel
4. Resurrection Strand
    * *corporate-generic range* (from resurrection of the community to resurrection of individuals)
5. Remnant Strand
    * *whole-individual range* (from concern with the fate of Israel as a whole to concern over which individuals belong to the remnant)

* *servant-sect range* (from the righteous as servants assisting the salvation of a larger community to the righteous as themselves the saved remnant)
6. Powers Strand
    *history-sociology range* (from historical narration to sociological analysis)

*1 The Eschatological Strand*

The eschatological strand in apocalyptic concern with the future, with God's goal or end, is a mix of two conflicting polar elements: continuing commitment to Israel's call to an active covenant-delegated prophetic servant role in building God's kingdom and passive waiting for God's imminent unilateral intervention to save a now impotent Israel.

The shift of eschatological writing from the prophetic toward the apocalyptic begins in the sixth and fifth centuries in exilic prophecy in Ezekiel and Second Isaiah [Isa.40–55] and continues in fifth and fourth century Zechariah and Malachi at a time of weakness in the face of aggressive neighboring empires. It reflects the disfranchised, alienated status of the apocalyptic seers and their constituencies as compared with the earlier prophets who from Samuel to Jeremiah had been generally successful in maintaining an institutionalized dialogical role with the monarchy.[19] A second flowering of apocalyptic, the cultural movement within which the New Testament was written, started in the second century BCE and reflects a similar disfranchisement, this time of the Hasidim, or pious ones, who opposed the hellenizing efforts of leaders serving at the pleasure of the occupying power.[20]

The disfranchised apocalyptic writers were able to continue the eschatologically oriented work of the earlier prophets through a new written style, masking their continuing prophetic work with the convention of pseudonymity—the using of the name and prophetic authority of some obscure prophet from the prophetic period. Such pseudonymity was an extension of the anonymity of second and third Isaiah, second Zechariah, and others. (Pseudonymity was also used in constructing a

---

19. Cross, *Canaanite Myth and Hebrew Epic*, 343–44; P. Hanson, *The Dawn of Apocalyptic*, disfranchised seers, p. 408, prophet's dialogical role with the monarchy, second ed. p. 490; Blenkinsopp, *Prophecy and Canon*, 110–16.

20. 1 Macc 1:11–16 and 1 and 2 Maccabees *passim*; Hengel, *Judaism and Hellenism*, 1.180, 194, 277–302, especially 287–88; P. Hanson, *The Dawn of Apocalyptic*, 408–9.

universal scheme of history, one pole of the salvation-historical strand, below.) As apocalyptic tension approached a climax, the convention of pseudonymity was dropped as in the War Scroll of the Qumran community, the synoptic apocalypse Mark 13, and the book of Revelation. The Christian community welcomed the reemergence of prophecy with John the Baptist (Matt 11:9 "a prophet? Yes, . . . and more than a prophet") and Jesus (Mark 1:22 "for he taught them as one having authority")—two new prophets once again openly opposing the rulers by calling Israel to community responsibility.

Within the eschatological strand there is a *local-definitive range* of positions on the issue of the once-for-allness of eschatologically significant events. The eschatology in the early prophets was usually a call for responsible creative interaction in some *local* historical situation without a theory about a final exhaustive change; but the later prophets and the apocalyptic writers increasingly looked forward to a *definitive crisis* in which God's will would triumph once for all. But might not that eliminate future *creative* interaction?

Apocalyptic is written from the perspective of a temporal location at the end of the old order, local or definitive, amidst events which are taken as signs of imminent change to the new. A denouement that was either already completely accomplished in the past, or would be far enough in the future to ignore in the present, would no longer be eschatological.

Related to the local-definitive range, but distinguishable from it, is a *continuous-discontinuous range* of positions on how different the new age will be from the old. The new age always differs from the old in that God's will or goal is accomplished; but there is variation in historical continuity in whether the new age continues the ethnic particularity of nations (or even the existence of human community) or whether it eliminates the physical death of individuals (or even physical existence itself). At the discontinuous pole, the coming age is so spiritualized as to be completely discontinuous with the present age, and apocalyptic merges with gnosticism. At the continuous pole, salvation history (the next strand) is emphasized.

### 2 The Salvation-History Strand

"Salvation history" is history serving as the medium for interaction between God and humanity. The salvation-history strand in apocalyptic is an extension of the understanding of history in the great epic constituting the Torah and the earlier historical books of the Old Testament. That epic began with creation and had the whole human race in its purview, although it is not described in a Western universalizing manner but metonymically. In a first period, from creation through the building of the Tower of Babel (Genesis 1–11), God deals with humanity as a whole community. In the following periods, the epic centers on God's dealings with humanity through the family of Abraham. The break between the Torah and prophetic sections coincides with another point in the periodization of the history—the entering into the promised land. The end of the prophetic division narrative coincides with the fall of the southern kingdom in 587 BCE, marking the end of another period. The Priestly period's reshuffling tends toward rationalization and schematization of this periodization, for example, dividing the periods into generations in Genesis and placing the conquest account outside the Torah.

Second Isaiah [40–55] proposed a new creation and a new exodus to inaugurate a final period, an eschatological age in which Israel would once again go out to the nations. But four centuries later, after a delay in the coming of the new age, the apocalyptic book Daniel inserted another period before the final eschatological age by changing the seventy years of captivity prophesied by Jeremiah (Jer 25:11, 29:10) to seventy weeks of years (490 years) of wrath (Dan 9:2, 24), the period of the four world kingdoms, Babylonian, Median, Persian, and Seleucid Hellenistic, which are represented by the image of four metals in Daniel 2 and four beasts in Daniel 7. At the end of this period, the final age is inaugurated with the Ancient of Days, which gives everlasting dominion over all nations to the Son of Man and to the Saints of the Most High (Dan 7:12–14, 18, 26–27). Daniel does not recount the whole scheme of periods before describing the additional one. They are, however, recounted in a contemporaneous work, 1 Enoch 85–90: the primeval period, the patriarchs, the conquest, the monarchy, the exile, the postexilic period, the judgment, and the new age—all under the guise of an elaborate allegory with bulls for patriarchs, domestic animals for Israelites, wild animals for gentiles, and so on.

Contrary to von Rad's complaint (above, page 118), this apocalyptic version of history is as much centered around Israel as is the earlier Old Testament history. To be sure, it does include four additional centuries in which Israel did not thrive in relation to the other world powers, so that the function of Israel in salvation history is seen differently. True, the Son of Man comes "with the clouds of heaven,"[21] yet is identified as Israel.[22] The basic difference between apocalyptic history and earlier Old Testament history is in its schematization, already emerging in the Priestly writings. Apocalyptic history is not so much a narrative history (out of which one can read a theory of history) as it is the mere abstract theory or theology of history itself.[23] The epic has been squeezed down to fit the universalizing wisdom framework characteristic of apocalyptic. The change is obvious, for example, when one compares the *four hundred years* of history schematized in one apocalyptic chapter, Daniel 11:

> ... Three more kings shall arise in Persia. The fourth shall be far richer than all of them, and when he has become strong through his riches, he shall stir up all against the kingdom of Greece. Then a warrior king shall arise, who shall rule with great dominion and take action as he pleases. And while still rising in power, his kingdom shall be broken and divided toward the four winds of heaven, but not to his posterity...

with the *single night* of history narrated in a chapter of the Torah, Exodus 14:

> ... As Pharaoh drew near, the Israelites looked back, and there were the Egyptians advancing on them. In great fear the Israelites cried out to the Lord. They said to Moses, "Was it because there were no graves in Egypt that you have taken us away to die in the wilderness?"...

The Daniel chapter recounts the outline of facts for identification purposes, whereas the Exodus chapter reveals the resilient yet sarcastic humanness of the Israelite community within its saving relation with God, and does so precisely by telling the story. The events of apocalyptic history are welded into a whole by means of generic schematization, whereas preexilic history is held together by such corporately oriented means as narration and typology.

---

21. Dan 7:13; von Rad on our page 118.

22. Dan 7:18, 22, 27; 1 Enoch 47:3–4, 48:9, etc.

23. Compare Koch, *The Rediscovery of Apocalyptic*, 44; Hengel, *Judaism and Hellenism*, 1.194.

Yet, narrative does occur in the literature of the apocalyptic period, as in Daniel 1–6 (Daniel's interaction with the kings, the fiery furnace, and the lion's den). And typology is used to tie the narrative events together into a coherent history in fourth century apocalyptic, and occasionally in the Qumran literature, as in the Manual of Discipline 1 QS 8:7 = Isa 28:16 "a tested stone, a precious cornerstone" and in the Damascus Document CD 7:11 = Isa 7:17, a paraenetic application of a threat to Israel. Thus, there is a *narrative-schematic range* within the salvation-history strand of apocalyptic, ranging from one pole (corporate narrative history with typology) to another pole (generic schematization of history). The schematic pole dominates first-century apocalyptic, with the exception of some Qumran literature and, as we will see below, the exception of the New Testament.

In apocalyptic, the shift from narrative toward schematization in the salvation-history strand has an impact on the shift from continuity to discontinuity in the eschatological strand (our first strand, above). A more schematized and universalized history makes the eschatological end appear to be more universal than local, more once-for-all than a continuous working out of God's will in particular historical circumstances.

Regardless of the position taken along the narrative-schematic range, the salvation-history strand in apocalyptic holds apocalyptic thought to a concern for God's triumph in the actual physical, social world in which humanity lives. It holds apocalyptic thought to continuity between the old age and the new in space, time, and social structure. It maintains a corporate perspective compared to some other strands in apocalyptic, even with the strong genericizing tendencies at the schematic pole.

### 3 The Wisdom Strand

The wisdom strand in apocalyptic is prominent. Daniel's wisdom exceeds that of the court astrologers, or wise men, in his interpretation of royal dreams or visions in Daniel 2, 4, and 5. In his own visions (Daniel 7, 8, 9, 10–12) Daniel acts out a role interpretable as either wise man or prophet—both can urge responsible behavior. Similarly, Enoch receives wisdom through dreams and visions in 1 Enoch 1:2, 13:8, 14:1, and more; and is taken by angels on a wisdom-imparting tour of the earth in 1 Enoch 17–36. The long section 1 Enoch 37–71 begins, "The second vision which he saw, the vision of wisdom . . . . Until now there has not been given by the Lord of Spirits such wisdom as I have received in accordance with my insight." This introduces 34 chapters of wisdom on the coming judgment of the wicked, the new heaven and new earth, the giving of power to the Son of Man from the throne of the Head of Days (= Ancient of Days in Dan 7), metallic symbols for the kingdoms of the world, and so on. The next section of 1 Enoch (72–82) is a treatise on astronomy and the calendar, also part of wisdom, because wisdom includes natural as well as social science. The Apocalypse of Ezra (2 Esdras 3–14) is reminiscent throughout of the wisdom book Job. The section 2 Esdras 3:1—9:25 is a theodicy: In debate with Ezra, the angel Uriel defends God's goodness and omnipotence in the face of evil.

Apocalyptic as a cultural movement includes, then, the wisdom of its period. Earlier, in the Torah and prophets, universalizing generic wisdom was subordinate to wisdom as the ability and commitment to engage effectively in multi-lateral corporate relations, revealed in decisions of wise judges and the prophets' advocacy of corporate solutions for specific social, economic, and political issues.[24] But after the exile, wisdom increasingly could be interpreted as *a priori* and independent of particular social interactions as was Hellenistic wisdom, and was equated with the law (Sirach 24:23) or the *logos* (implied in Wisdom 7:22—8:1). Universalized wisdom often became the raw material for faith, rather than narrative history or concern for specific social issues. According to Frank Moore Cross: "There is a sense in which Job brought the ancient religion of Israel to an end. History to Job was opaque. Job viewed the flux of history in despair . . . . The Lord of history failed to act. 'Ēl or Ba'l, the transcendent creator spoke . . . . Job saw him and bowed his knee."[25]

Is this the end of the corporate orientation in Israel? No, the wisdom strand does not replace the salvation-history strand in postexilic apocalyptic. Wisdom and salvation history are in tension, with a resulting *subordinate-dominant range* of relations between them. At one pole wisdom (generalized knowledge) is *subordinate* to history (particular knowledge), and at the other pole wisdom is *dominant* over history.

---

24. This is generally held, e.g. Terrien, "Amos and Wisdom," 114–15; Westermann, *Elements of Old Testament Theology*, 99.
25. Cross, *Canaanite Myth and Hebrew Epic*, 344.

### 4 The Resurrection Strand

The remaining three apocalyptic strands (resurrection, remnant, and powers) are adaptations of themes from outside Israel's early tradition and, accordingly, can more easily wander toward a Western cosmological interpretation.

The renewal of the relation between the community Israel and its God is expressed using the three-day idiom for return from dead community interaction back to interactive life (above, page 95) in Hos 5:15—6:3 "Come, let us return to the Lord; for it is he who has torn, and he will heal us. . . . After two days he will revive us; on the third day he will raise us up," and in Ezek 37:1–14 ". . . and the bones came together, bone to its bone. . . . These bones are the whole house of Israel. . . . I am going to . . . bring you up from your graves, O my people." But in Daniel and the early parts of 1 Enoch, such corporate motifs expressing the resurrection of a spiritually dead community (Israel) have shrunk to a selective resurrection of individual members of Israel, even if for a corporate purpose: Dan 12:2–3 "At that time your people shall be delivered, every one who is found written in the book. Many of those who sleep in the dust of the earth shall awake, some to everlasting life, and some to shame and everlasting contempt," and 1 Enoch 90:32–33 "And those sheep were all white, and their wool thick and pure. And all those which had been destroyed and scattered and all the wild animals . . . gathered together in that house." Scholars speculate a tradition of biological resurrection after death may have come from Iran, or from Palestinian agricultural religion. Bibliographic references for each possibility are given by Martin Hengel.[26]

In the pre-apocalyptic tradition, resurrection of the community was a renewing of corporate internal interaction among its members, not of individual members aside from their corporately sustained individuality as interactors in the community. Dysfunctionality in one community member had a dysfunctional effect on the others. But, under increased cultural influence from the West in the apocalyptic period, resurrection, still placed in the community, nevertheless shows a new potential for a generic interpretation of salvation. Not all individuals share in the salvation of Israel in the same way. Some are resurrected to life, some to shame, while others do not still need to be resurrected.

---

26. Hengel, *Judaism and Hellenism*, 1.196, notes 574 and 575.

Non-Israelites are resurrected (Dan 7:14 "all nations"; 1 Enoch 90:33 "all the wild animals") but apocalyptic resurrection is less specific than are the Torah and prophets in regard to the servant role of Israel a in the resurrection of the interactive structure of other nations.

The corporate nature of resurrection is abandoned and resurrection becomes completely generic in some apocalyptic writing, as in 2 Esdras 7:75–77 with its query and reply, "'show this also to your servant: whether after death, as soon as every one of us yields up the soul, we shall be kept in rest until those times come when you will renew the creation, or whether we shall be tormented at once?' He answered . . . 'do not be associated with those who have shown scorn, nor number yourself among those who are tormented. For you have a treasure of works laid up with the Most High.'" The fifteenth century European reformation rejected such a justification by works, which was part of rejecting the relevance of all community interaction to individual salvation.

Some generic apocalyptic is only concerned with the soul, while some keep soul and body together. The second century BCE Jubilees 23:31 says of the righteous, "their bones shall rest in the earth, and their spirits shall have much joy." First or second century CE 2 Esdras is ambivalent, saying both 7:32 "The earth shall give up those who are asleep in it," and 7:78 "as the spirit leaves the body to return again to him who gave it."

There is thus a *corporate-generic range* in apocalyptic from resurrection as entrance of the corporate community into the new age, as in Dan 12:2–3 and 1 Enoch 90:32–33, to resurrection as generic individual event, as in 2 Esdras 7:75–77.

### 5 The Remnant Strand

The apocalyptic remnant strand is an adaptation of a preexilic tradition of reduction of whole Israel to a remnant as a punishment. This preexilic tradition was concerned with the fate of Israel as a corporate whole, but in postexilic times Israel's weakness in the face of neighboring empires offered an individual Israelite a choice between continuing Israelite orthodoxy and accommodating to an occupier's foreign culture. As a result, in the apocalyptic period there is a range of emphases from concern with the fate of Israel as a whole to concern over which individuals remain sufficiently orthodox to belong in fact to the surviving remnant, and a related range of positions on whether the righteous ones simply constitute the remnant or are agents within whole Israel for welding a larger remnant.

(a) *Remnant of a nation.* In the preexilic tradition, "remnant" most literally refers to what is left of a nation after a near annihilation by an enemy in war, e.g., Josh 13:12 "the survivors [יתר, *yatar*, remnant, surviving community] of the Rephaim."

(b) *Prophetically predicted remnant.* The prophets predicted before the fact that Israel would be reduced to a remnant, as in Amos 3:12 "As the shepherd rescues from the mouth of the lion two legs, or a piece of an ear, so shall the people of Israel who live in Samaria be rescued, with the corner of a couch and part of a bed." This punishment and rescue was for Israel as a corporate body: Amos 3:2 "You only have I known of all the families of the earth; therefore I will punish you for all your iniquities." Hence, the individual members lost may not be the ones at the core of the community unrighteousness that is being punished. The prophet prophesies with the hope of effecting a change in Israel as a whole, Amos 5:15 "Hate evil and love good, and establish justice in the gate; it may be that the Lord, the God of hosts, will be gracious to the remnant of Joseph."

(c) *Noachian remnant.* In the account of the flood, Gen 7:1—9:17, the survivors are not called a "remnant," and the near annihilation is not of one nation at the hands of others but of the whole human race. However, the story provides a typological relation between the flood and subsequent punishments of Israel, implying a righteous remnant chosen on the basis of the imputed righteousness of its pre-flood representative leader Noah.

(d) *Remnant of righteous members.* From the "sound of shear silence" (1 Kgs 19:1–19), rather than of storm and earthquake, the exiled and discouraged prophet Elijah was told there were "seven thousand in Israel" still committed to God's call for corporate relations (rather than Jezebel-inspired Baal-worship's call to exploitation) and that he was to continue his work and appoint Elisha as his successor. These seven thousand are not an organized subgroup but are already integral members of Israel as a whole.[27]

(e) *Chastised remnant.* At the end of the exile Israel appears as a chastised, purified remnant: "Speak tenderly to Jerusalem, and cry to

---

27. Preexilic Old Testament uses of the term remnant are classified in Müller, *Die Vorstellung vom Rest im Alten Testament*, and Hasel, *The Remnant*.

her that she has served her term, that her penalty is paid, that she has received from the Lord's hand double for all her sins" (Isa 40:2). The purification is of Israel as a corporate unity; there is no singling out of righteous individuals to participate in the remnant. It is Israel and so resembles "prophetic remnant" (b), but it is also an after-the-fact "literal remnant" (a) because its purification comes from punishment undergone rather than from threat of punishment.

(f) *Early postexilic remnant.* After the return, the exiles still considered themselves to be the remnant of Israel: "But now for a brief moment favor has been shown by the Lord our God, who has left us a remnant" (Ezra 9:8). Ezra presents the returned remnant as the whole of Israel, thus the term remnant is ostensibly being used in the sense of the "chastised remnant" (e), but such an interpretation must be tempered in two ways.

Firstly, it depends on the returnees viewing the inhabitants they found on return, the "peoples of the lands," as "the Canaanites, the Hittites, the Perizzites, the Jebusites, the Ammonites, the Moabites, the Egyptians, and the Amorites" (Ezra 9:1), rather than as Samaritans who say, "Let us build [the temple] with you; for we worship your God as you do" (Ezra 4:2)—that is, seeing them as complete outsiders rather than now rejected members. In so far as the returned exiles maintained a sectarian exclusiveness from the Samaritans, the meaning of "remnant" moves toward a new sectarian sense (h) to be described below.

Secondly, the purified remnant also tends in postexilic prophecy to be viewed as the product of a weeding out of unrighteous individuals: "On that day . . . I will remove from your midst your proudly exultant ones" (Zeph 3:11, here taken to be a postexilic addition).

On both of these counts, postexilic Israel does not view remnant as a simple corporate whole but correlates individual membership in the remnant with the previous quality of individual performance. There is, thus, a *whole-individual range* of positions in the remnant strand, from preoccupation with the fate of Israel as a *whole* to preoccupation over which *individuals* will belong to the remnant. The conceptions "remnant of a nation" (a), "prophetic remnant" (b), "Noachian remnant" (c), and "chastised remnant" (e) are closer to the whole pole of this range, while "remnant of righteous ones" (d) and "early postexilic remnant" (f) are closer to the individual pole.[28]

28. For a useful discussion of exilic and postexilic conceptions of remnant see

After this long development of the remnant tradition, two polar conceptions of remnant emerged in Israel under European colonization in 325 BCE: (g) *servant remnant* and (h) *sect remnant*.

(g) The *servant remnant* conception was dominant at the beginning of the second outbreak of apocalyptic in the second century BCE, a product of Hasidic opposition to the Seleucid Hellenistic occupier's program that introduced a Hellenistic cosmopolitan lifestyle in Judea. Both Hasidim and hellenizers offered salvation, the first to the community as interacting whole, the other to each individual separately. The resulting divided cultural loyalties within Judaism, with one party legitimizing hellenization and the other holding as legitimate a version of the old values, put the higher class individual between two conflicting socially approved positions, rather than between socially legitimate and illegitimate loyalties as in prophetic times. Thus, the very presence of hellenization as a viable alternative, aside from its intrinsic genericizing tendencies, had the effect of forcing each individual to make constant independent (thus generic) choices between interactive and conforming contributions to its community.

In the Old Testament epic creative participation in the communal interaction of all individuals is implicit; but could only be described in its narrative style for a sample, those whose actions are narrated. Individuals emerge as persons through narration of their relations with others, and the best known are those individuals who relate as explicit representatives of Israel, namely patronymic or political leaders like Abraham, Sarah, Moses, and David. But Moses was required to decentralize his leadership among "officers over thousands, hundreds, fifties, and tens" (Exod 18:14–26). Joshua's call for each one to "choose this day whom you will serve" (Josh 24:15) was made to "the elders, the heads, the judges, and the officers of Israel" (Josh 24:1). Prophetic calls for community responsibility for creative interactive political and economic justice were directed to those whose representative role in society was made explicit through political or economic leadership. Advocacy of better treatment of debtors, orphans, and widows was directed to their oppressors. But also exiled Elijah is described explicitly as engaging the widow of Zarephath in *inter*active creativity (1 Kgs 17:8–24 = Luke 4:25–26). Prophets spoke also to the crowds so that both "public opinion" and public action thus formed would be a social force translated

---

Meyer, *The Aims of Jesus*, 225–30.

into action both by individuals and representatively by their leaders who represented Israel publicly.

Under leaders who served at the pleasure of a culturally foreign colonial power, there were no political or economic leaders implicitly understandable as metonyms for the common people. Thus, the need for creative representation of and contribution to the community's interactive covenant with God fell to underground prophets writing under a pseudonym like Daniel and to bands of disciples of underground leaders like John the Baptist and Jesus of Nazareth who with their disciples *interacted, not lectured*, to generate creative internal interaction among the Judean public—the same interaction as intended by the prophets. Every member, not just the leaders, represented and acted for Israel; every member had opportunity and responsibility for creative contribution toward a more effective Israel as interacting agent of its God.

Although the Hasidic writers say the great judgment (which is to come with the change of the age) will condemn not only the godless kingdoms of the world but also the apostate (i.e., hellenizing) Jews, as in Dan 12:2–3 and 1 Enoch 90:32–33 quoted on page 128 above, thus continuing the concern over which individuals belong to the remnant, as in the "remnant of righteous ones" (d) and the "early postexilic remnant" (f). This does not make the non-hellenizing Hasidim themselves the chosen remnant to be saved in that judgment. It is the sin of Israel as a whole for which punishment is to be meted out: "Seventy weeks [of years] are decreed for your people and your holy city, to finish the transgression, to put an end to sin, and to atone for iniquity" (Dan 9:24). The salvation of the whole must be the goal: "The wise among the people shall give understanding to many; for some days, however, they shall fall by sword and flame, and suffer captivity and plunder. . . . Some of the wise shall fall, so that they may be refined, purified, and cleansed, until the time of the end, for there is still an interval until the time appointed" (Dan 11:33, 35). The servant notion of remnant thus also includes the motif of chastisement of whole Israel from the "prophetic remnant" (b), and the "chastised remnant" (e), and hence, is close to the whole pole of the whole-individual range. Israel receives punishment as a corporate unity for corporate sin; a remnant community will survive the catastrophe; its membership is not yet specified but rather depends on the righteousness of the whole; and the Hasidim themselves are not the remnant because many others will be members at the end through the cleansing work of the Hasidim and some of the Hasidim themselves will fall. The servant concept of remnant gives the righteous the same servant function within Israel as Israel is given among the nations in preexilic and exilic Israel by Gen 12:1–3 "in you all the families of the earth shall be blessed" and Isa 49:6 "I will give you as a light to the nations."

(h) The notion of *sect remnant* (found most explicitly in the Qumran community) developed later than that of servant remnant and differs starkly from it. The Qumran community separated itself completely as the "children of light" from "false" Israel, as written in their Community Rule: "And this is the rule for the men of the community . . . . They shall separate from the congregation of the men of falsehood . . . . They shall atone . . . for those who join them to live in community and to take part in the trial and judgment and condemnation of all those who transgress the precepts."[29] Members atone only for the community. The community considers itself already to be the true remnant, the true Israel, and looks forward to taking part in the coming condemnation of the apostates.

Thus, overall within the remnant strand there is a *servant-sect range* of positions. At the servant end of this range the remnant is what will be left of whole Israel after an impending judgment. Meanwhile, the righteous, who are *not that remnant*, work within Israel to saturate it with functional community relations so that it, Israel, not the individual, will best survive the judgment. But at the sect end of the range, individually righteous members withdraw as a sect to avoid the coming judgment and destruction of the others.

Both sect and servant remnants want their members to be in relation with God, by the sect remnant individually, but by the servant remnant through creatively interacting relations within their community. The reward or salvation is the mutually interactive participation enjoyed throughout the interaction. Being able to make the contribution is half the reward; the other half is the contribution back from the other members and thus from God through the internal community interaction. One remembers Hegel's concept of the human individual *as* the collection of that individual's roles in mutual interaction in the community (above, page 20).

The servant remnant orientation is clearly corporate. The relational structure within the sect is unspecified but secondary to relation with God, while its relation to the larger community from which it separates

---

29. The Community Rule, 1 QS 5:1–7, *The Dead Sea Scrolls in English*, 78.

is specifically not corporate. But servant remnant members are called to accept capacity and authority through creative interaction with any larger community within which it finds itself in order to increase the size of the remnant.

### 6 The Powers Strand

The last strand to be identified in this analysis of apocalyptic is the *powers* strand, a characterization of interactive structures, natural and social, good and bad, personified as angels or "powers." According to the apocalyptic view, God reigns in the midst of a host of angels: 1 Enoch 61:10–11 "And he will call all of the host of the heavens, and all the holy ones above, and the host of the Lord, the Cherubim, the Seraphim and the Ophannim, and all the angels of power, and all the angels of the principalities, and the Chosen One, and the other host which is upon the dry ground and over the water, . . . and they will all say with one voice: 'Blessed is he . . . for ever and ever.'"

The *natural world* is structured and operated in a regular fashion by these angels, as in Jubilees 2:2–3:

> On the first day he created the heavens which are above and the waters and all the spirits which serve before him—the angels of the presence, and the angels of sanctification, and the angels of the spirit of fire and the angels of the spirit of the winds, and the angels of the spirit of the clouds, and of darkness, and of snow and of hail and of hoar frost, and the angels of the voices and of the thunder and of the lightning, and the angels of the spirits of cold and of heat, and of winter and of spring and of autumn and of summer, and of all the spirits of his creatures which are in the heavens and on the earth.

Also, a *socially structured community* appears to have its own life, its own principle of operation that needs to be represented in some way. In the pre-apocalyptic period, nations or communities were often represented by patronymic individuals (that is, metonyms for the ethnic groups they represent), as in the rather sophisticated genealogical table of nations in Genesis 10 (Egypt, son of Ham, etc.), or by Adam (humanity), or by political leaders, like Moses and David, who in their political office represented the community as a unity. In apocalyptic times, good leadership appeared to be scarce, and the representation of nations as corporate wholes was abstracted from human leadership (for example, giving the seventy nations of the table in Genesis 10 seventy shepherd angels) but with Israel reporting directly to God. Deuteronomy 32:8–9 LXX, NRSV, using "gods" for "angels" says, "When the Most High apportioned the nations, when he divided humankind, he fixed the boundaries of the peoples according to the number of the gods; the Lord's own portion was his people, Jacob his allotted share."[30] Poor earthly leadership of the shepherd angels is explicit in Jubilees 15:31–32: "He sanctified [Israel] and gathered it from amongst all the children of men; for there are many nations and many peoples, and all are His, and over all hath He placed spirits in authority to lead them astray from Him. But over Israel He did not appoint any angel or spirit, for He alone is their ruler, and He will preserve them and require them at the hand of His angels and His spirits, and at the hand of all His powers." In 1 Enoch 85–90 the loss of political autonomy for Israel at the exile in 587 BCE is represented by Israel's falling into the hands of the seventy angels of the nations: 1 Enoch 89:59–61 "And he called seventy shepherds and cast off those sheep that they might pasture them; and he said to the shepherds and to their companions: 'Each one of you from now on is to pasture the sheep. . . . And I will hand them over to you duly numbered, and will tell you which of them are to be destroyed, and destroy them.' . . . And He called another and said to him: 'Observe and see everything that the shepherds do against these sheep; for they will destroy from among them more than I have commanded them.'" The "another" is the archangel Michael, and the results of his recording are to be used in the final judgment against the shepherds (1 Enoch 90:22–25), who thus as fallen angels or *powers* represent the fallen *social structure* of the world. Paul will use these sociological terms in the New Testament with his four powers: flesh, law, sin, and death.

The fall of some of the angels is based on Gen 6:1–4 "When people began to multiply on the face of the ground, and daughters were born to them, the sons of God saw that they were fair; and they took wives for themselves of all that they chose." According to 1 Enoch 6:1–8:4 two hundred angels committed this great sin and the names of their leaders are given, each of which taught human beings the skills related to his name. The contentious giant offspring of these angels fought among themselves and with human beings, and contributed to the fall of hu-

---

30. Deuteronomy 32, the Song of Moses, is taken as a late addition to Deuteronomy.

manity. The two hundred angels and their offspring thus represent the many conflicting self-serving elements in fallen human culture.

The preexilic fall narrative (Genesis 3–11) portrays the fall of humanity not as a fall of individuals but of the structures of human community—as in humanity's eating of the forbidden fruit (a non-interactive condition: "being like [local] gods"); the enmity between siblings Cain and Abel (representing fallen relations between occupational groups); the flood to eliminate ubiquitous communal violence; and finally the building of the tower of Babel (loss of all ability to relate interactively due to the community's insolent attempt to excel). Apocalyptic portrays a fall of nature and a fall of corporately interacting human community, represented by the fall of the angels or powers. In the final judgment the powers will be condemned, and a renewed nature and renewed social structure will come into existence.

The use of angels and powers as personifications (better, perhaps, as "angelifications") of the structures of nature and society amounts to a schematizing or wisdom analysis of reality. The analysis of *nature* is analogous to modern natural science. The angelological analysis of *society* amounts to a first-century sociology. The substitution in the powers strand of sociology for narrative history is a systematizing move parallel with the schematization of history in the narrative-schematic range in the salvation-history strand.

But narrative history does continue in apocalyptic, so that there is a *history-sociology range* in the powers strand from narrative historical description to systematic analysis of that history. The narrative history pole tends to lean to the corporate orientation; the sociology pole is systematic and neutral, able to analyze both cosmologically and corporately oriented interaction among ethnic and occupational groups.

Both the several strands of tradition, representing the *eclecticism* of first-century apocalyptic, and the several ranges of orientation in each strand, representing its *pluralism*, begin to reveal the variety of incompatible elements in first-century apocalyptic. They help account for the diversity of contemporary characterizations sampled in this chapter's first section and proclaimed in Koch's German title "At Wits End [*Ratlos*] with Apocalyptic."

Five of the ranges, marked with asterisks in the table (page 121 above), are manifestations within their respective strands of a corporate-cosmological pluralism in first-century apocalyptic, with each of these ranges reflecting and revealing some aspect of the conflict between pre-captivity Israel's corporate orientation and the invading Hellenistic culture's cosmological orientation.

## III THE NEW TESTAMENT'S CHOICE OF CORPORATE APOCALYPTIC

This section is devoted to showing that the chronologically earliest parts of the New Testament—Paul's letters, Mark, and Q—necessarily written within the prevailing first-century apocalyptic idiom of their time (as analyzed above), unerringly take the corporate alternative in each of the five key corporate-generic ranges (marked with asterisks in the table on page 121 above), and remain within the corporate perspective in the other three ranges. Thus, this New Testament early base is *not* pluralistic on the corporate-generic issue as apocalyptic is overall but is strictly corporate. Indeed, it emerges as a manifesto for reform of Israel away from Hellenistic syncretism and back to Torah and Prophets.

C. H. Dodd and Barnabas Lindars, treated in chapter 2, were each well aware that first-century apocalyptic was the written carrier of the Old Testament tradition to the New Testament. Their work, respectively in 1953 and 1961 was a preview in England of the shift in New Testament studies in Germany and North America. We saw Lindars calling the fulfillment-of-prophecy technique for using the prophets and psalms "apocalyptic eschatology" in *New Testament Apologetic* (pp. 276–83), and concluding that the apocalyptic-eschatological interest of the age, combined with the crisis of the passion of Jesus, resulted in apocalyptic-eschatological use of the Old Testament to interpret the person and work of Jesus. We also saw Dodd using the term "apocalyptic-eschatological" in *According to the Scriptures* (pp. 62–74) to refer to apocalyptic texts used typologically from Joel, Zechariah, and Daniel to explicate the New Testament corporate eschatological perspective.

### 1 Paul's Selective Corporate Use of the Apocalyptic Idiom

The goal of this section is to locate Paul's positions along the five key corporate-generic ranges for first century apocalyptic (asterisked in the table on page 121, above). Our examination will show that Paul unerringly takes the corporate pole in each range. This understanding of Paul began to emerge in mid-nineteenth-century biblical studies in

Germany by Ferdinand C. Baur (1836), William Wrede (1904), and Albert Schweitzer (1929)[31]; but after the Bultmann period, it had to be brought back again, and this was accomplished in the nineteen-sixties by Ernst Käsemann, Krister Stendahl, and others.

With Käsemann's break with Bultmann in 1960, Paul's apocalyptic orientation began to appear to German New Testament scholars as being within the corporately oriented part of the mixed corporate-cosmological apocalyptic idiom of his time. Salvation of politically powerless occupied Israel would come not from unilateral intervention by a perennially oriented Western God but by exercising its own God's delegated responsibility for corporate community interaction at home and with other communities (Gen 12:3, Isa 49:6).

In 1963 Krister Stendahl in "The Apostle Paul and the Introspective Conscience of the West"[32] claimed that, originally, the West had radically misinterpreted Paul by moving the "power" struggle against community dysfunction to the introspective conscience of a conceived individual that did not exist in Israelite culture. He said that both Paul and *Acts* describe Paul's "conversion" as a call *as a Jew* to become a Jewish apostle to Israel and through it to the gentiles (Gal 1:15, Acts 9:15). "There is not—as we usually think—first a conversion, and then a call to apostleship." Hence, a vital interest for Paul, himself of the Jewish dispersion, was "how to define the place for Gentiles in the Church. . . . Rom. 9–11 is not an appendix to chs. 1–8 but the climax of the letter" (p. 243), as in Rom. 11:18 "do not boast over the branches, it is not you that support the root but the root that supports you." But this insight was soon lost in European Christianity. Stendahl continues, "This problem was, however, not a live one after the end of the first century, when Christianity for all practical purposes had a non-Jewish constituency" (pp. 243–44). A shift to Western cosmologically based theology was made "official" by European theologians, Origen a century later and Augustine two more centuries later (chapter 4, below).

When Paul says, Rom 7:19, "I do not do the good I want, but the evil I do not want is what I do," he does not speak of sin as a struggle within his own conscience but of sin as a *power* external to the will of the individual, as he says in the next verse: "If I do what I do not want,

---

31. Baur, "Über Zweck und Veranlassung des Römerbriefs," 59–178; Wrede, *Paul*, 123; Schweitzer, *The Mysticism of Paul the Apostle*, 219–26.

32. Stendall, pagination as reprinted in *Ecumenical Dialogue at Harvard*.

it is no longer I that do it, but sin which dwells within me." In Paul the *power* "sin" is *communal dysfunction*. An individual's attempt to improve dysfunctional community relations through interaction *requires* participation in its dysfunctionality, risking some injury for overall functional improvement. Paul's conscience was clear before his conversion: Phil 3:6 "as to righteousness under the law blameless," and after his conversion: 1 Cor 4:4 "I am not aware of anything against myself." Paul does not say this to show himself to be better than others but to show the irrelevance of a clear conscience. The individual, blameless as individual, still cannot engage in full mutual internal community interaction in the presence of sin—that is, the tradition distorted by corporate dysfunction: Rom 8:3 "the law [community structure], weakened by the flesh," and this is not a proper cause for individual introspective anguish but for working for a corporate change in Israel, now being accomplished through Israel's anointed leader, Jesus Christ: Rom 7:24–25 "Who will deliver me from this body of death: Thanks be to God through Jesus Christ our Lord!"

Sin is thus a *power*, a social force, a dysfunction in community interaction, not in the single individual: "it is no longer I that do it." There are more powers, "elemental spirits," "rules," "authorities." Paul sometimes refers to the powers in standard apocalyptic terms, as in Gal 4:3 "We were enslaved to the elemental spirits of the world," and 1 Cor 15:24 "Then comes the end, when he hands over the kingdom to God the Father after he has destroyed every rule and every authority and power," and then as in Rom 8:38–39 "For I am convinced that neither death, nor life, nor angels, nor rulers, nor things present, nor things to come, nor powers, nor height, nor depth, nor anything else in all creation, will be able to separate us from the love of God in Christ Jesus our Lord." Behind such references is Paul's conception of an alliance of four interrelated social powers active in community interaction: *death* (a reversible spiritual death of the community as with the valley of dry bones of Ezekiel 37); *sin* (corporate dysfunction as in acting in self-interest, Gen 3:5); the *flesh* (a community without God, 1 Cor 3:3–4 "you are still of the flesh . . . quarreling . . . . merely human"); and the *law* (the group's community-created social interactive structure, Torah, now "weakened by the flesh" (Rom 8:3); that is, distorted by some for unilateral control of others by identifying it with the Greek *logos*, a fixed social structure as dictated from above rather than continuously created by socially responsible community interaction). The four powers (*death*, *sin*, *flesh*, and *law*) are allied: Rom 7:13–14 "It was sin, working death in me through what is good [the law not misinterpreted], in order that sin might be shown to be sin, and through the commandment might become sinful beyond measure. For we know that the law is spiritual; but I [metonymy for the "many,"] am of the flesh, sold into slavery under sin."[33] This alliance of four powers will be overcome by the power of God through resurrection of the community: Rom 5:19–21 "For just as by the one man's [*adam's*, the human community's] disobedience many were made sinners, so by the one man's [*messiah's*] obedience many [the same 'many'] will be made righteous. But law came in, with the result that the trespass multiplied; but where sin increased, grace abounded all the more, so that, just as sin exercised dominion in death, so grace might also exercise dominion through justification [reconciliation] leading to eternal life through Jesus Christ our Lord." "Justification" here is not a translation of "judged not at fault" as in Roman law but *interactive* reconciliation with God and within the community. For two millennia, European interpreters of Paul—from perennially oriented Augustine (chapter 4, below) to modernist Bultmann (page 111 above) have taken Paul's justification through faithfulness as a generic justification of the individual through individual "faith" understood as belief distinct from interaction. But since 1960, communally oriented scholars have understood Paul's justification as *doing* one's covenant-delegated part in *working interactively* toward creation of a corporately functioning community, at home and abroad. A God-delegated creative faithfulness *is*, of course, a "work," something we *do*, not *have*.

The biblical Torah or "law," then, is not the biblical equivalent of the perennial *logos* nor of the modern period's empirical rule, either of which would be "law" as one of Paul's four dysfunctional powers. Rather, the Torah recounts the delegation to the human community of responsibility for creating its "tradition" or social structure (Gen 1:28) with none unilaterally playing God (Gen 2:17, 3:5), and narrates community creation of a basic tool, a language to facilitate interaction (Gen 2:19) as metonymy for what is called for in all humanly constructed social structure. The Old and New Testaments recount the history of interactive community-building efforts, some more functional, some less, to preserve them as a resource for future community typological learning from one's past experience.

33. Paul crams the four allied powers into one verse at Rom 7:5.

Death, separation of the community from interaction with God by community dysfunction, is the head of the alliance of four powers, the "last enemy" (1 Cor 15:24). Death, and along with it the other three powers, is defeated by the resurrection of the community, represented by that of its *messiah*, to *life*; that is, to multilaterally creative relations among members and with God: Rom 6:9 "Christ being raised from the dead will never die again; death no longer has dominion over him," and 1 Cor 15:24 "Then comes the end, when he [Christ] hands over the kingdom to God the Father, after he has destroyed every rule and every authority and power. For he must reign until he has put all his enemies under his feet. The last enemy to be destroyed is death," the dysfunction, the death, of community interaction. The crucifixion of Jesus is not a "fix" to bring each individual sinner to God but a social act that changes the internal power structure of the Israel (and other nations) that Jesus represents, enabling it to die to the self serving aspects of western acculturation through colonialization as part of this change to functionality in the social world. The apocalyptic category of powers is used by Paul to indicate the objective, historical, and corporate nature of the social world to be saved; the continuing objective, historical, and corporate nature of the redeemed world; and the socially revolutionary nature of the victory. The "dominion of death" over community will be replaced by the "dominion in life" (Rom 5:17).[34]

The discussion so far identifies Paul's position on three of the eight corporate-generic ranges in first-century apocalyptic (chart, page 121 above). Paul's eschatology is at the *definitive pole of the local-definitive range*, yet still near the *continuous history pole of the continuous-discontinuous range*. There is movement toward the *sociology pole of the history-sociology range* in the powers strand while keeping a corporate orientation.

---

34. Paul's use of the apocalyptic category of powers is treated in Sanders, *Paul and Palestinian Judaism*, 465–68; and extensively in Beker, *Paul the Apostle*, chapters 8, 10, and 11. His position on the continuous-discontinuous range in eschatology is treated extensively in Beker, *Paul the Apostle*, 136–81. Beker says "The dimensions of imminence and cosmic expectation are central to Paul, whereas that of apocalyptic dualism is tempered by the salvation-historical understanding of Israel's place in God's saving design for his creation" (p. 181), where "cosmic expectation" means the continuity of worldly (i.e., "cosmic") salvation history, and "apocalyptic dualism" means discontinuity between the ages.

In the remnant strand, Paul is at both the whole pole of the *whole-individual range* and the servant pole of the *servant-sect range*. He makes explicit in Romans 9–11 the central issue of the letter, namely the relation between Israel after the flesh and Abraham's "children of the promise." Paul himself is kinsman to the Israelites, "and to them belong the adoption, the glory, the covenants, the giving of the law, the worship, and the promises; to them belong the patriarchs, and from them, according to the flesh, comes the Christ" (Rom 9:4–5), yet Paul is "an apostle to the Gentiles" (Rom 11:13). Paul's project in Romans is to make clear the meaning of each of these two facts in the presence of the other. Paul argues that the children of the promise to Abraham are a group that only partly coincides with Israel after the flesh (9:6–13): God is ready to add to his people: "Those who were not my people I will call 'my people'" (Rom 9:25 = Hos 2:23), and lose some of his people: "Though the number of the children of Israel were like the sand of the sea, only a remnant of them will be saved" (Rom 9:27 = Isa 10:22), so that "there is no distinction between Jew and Greek.... For, 'Everyone who calls on ... the Lord shall be saved.'" (Rom 10:12–13 = Joel 2:32). Yet, this Israel with partly different members is still organically the same Israel. Speaking to the gentiles Paul says, "But if some of the branches were broken off, and you, a wild olive shoot, were grafted in their place to share the rich root of the olive tree, do not boast over the branches.... It is not you that support the root, but the root that supports you.... For if you have been cut from what is by nature a wild olive tree and grafted, contrary to nature, into a cultivated olive tree, how much more will these natural branches be grafted back into their own olive tree" (Rom 11:17–24). Eventually the rest of Israel will return: "a hardening has come upon part of Israel, until the full number of the Gentiles has come in. And so all Israel will be saved" (Rom 11:25). Stendahl, Becker, and Raymond E. Brown all see Romans 9–11 as central to the letter: Stendahl, quoted above, "Rom 9–11 is not an appendix to chs. 1–8, but the climax of the letter"; Beker, "chapters 9–11 are not an appendix but a climactic point in the letter"; and Brown, "he writes this letter explaining to the Romans the roles of Jews and Gentiles in Christ."[35]

In treating the changing membership in Israel, Paul necessarily speaks of the faithfulness or the disobedience of individual candidates for membership. But for Paul that faithfulness consists of contributing

35. Beker, *Paul the Apostle*, 87, Brown and Meier, *Antioch and Rome*, 116–17.

creatively to the corporate life of some community in corporate relation as part of God's work in the world, and the only such community Paul is in a position to invite individuals into is the one he himself belongs to (Israel), including its "hearers" or visitors. In short, individuals are important to Paul—not as generic exemplars but as actual or potential interacting members of the people of God.[36]

The Christian movement is not taken by Paul as a remnant in Judaism nor as a separate new community but as a means within Israel to restore it and strengthen its mission to the gentiles. The boundaries of the Christian movement are sharp—those who are in Christ, and thus true to God's call to Israel, but they are not fixed—the present church is not the future remnant.[37] In fact, Paul's central concern is the expansion of these boundaries to the largest remnant possible, including the gentiles. A mission to the gentiles was contemplated in apocalyptic (Dan 7:14 "that all peoples, nations, and languages should serve him," and 1 Enoch 10:21, 90:33), and was in place in first-century Judaism in the form of a large-scale inclusion by Jews in dispersion of "those who fear God"; that is, gentiles attending the synagogue (Acts 13:16). Paul is at the *whole pole of the whole-individual range* and the *servant pole of the servant-sect range* in the remnant strand.

As said, for Paul the resurrection of Christ is the resurrection of God's people to multilaterally creative internal interaction. The faithful individual is a creatively interacting member of that body of Christ, the community that Christ, messiah, represents as its anointed leader: Rom 12:4–6 "For as in one body we have many members, and not all the members have the same function, so we, who are many, are one body in Christ, and individually we are members one of another. We have gifts that differ according to the grace given to us . . . ." It would be difficult to find a better description of a corporate social body. The frequent Pauline "in Christ" is a short form for "interacting member of the body of Christ," as, for example, in Gal 3:26–28 "For in Christ Jesus you are all children of God through faith. As many of you as were baptized into Christ have clothed yourselves with Christ. . . . all of you are one in

---

36. As noted in chapter 1, page 11 above, the individual is given more creative importance in the corporate orientation than in the others.

37. *Contra* Pfeiffer, *Introduction to the Old Testament*, 437. Sanders in *Paul and Palestinian Judaism* does not recognize this flexibility in the apocalyptic movement's conception of remnant and so makes a sharp distinction between Pauline "participationist eschatology" and Palestinian Jewish "covenantal nomism" (*passim*, esp. p. 547).

Christ Jesus."[38] Participating in the body means sharing in the fate of the body: 1 Cor 12:26 "If one member suffers, all suffer together with it; if one member is honored, all rejoice together with it." Each member represents the community; the abusing or honoring of a member is the abusing or honoring of the community. The anointed one is especially representative of Israel; his abuse and honor are representative of abuse and honor for Israel. "Do you not know that all of us who have been baptized into Christ Jesus were baptized into his death? . . . We know that our old self was crucified with him so that the body of sin might be destroyed, and we might no longer be enslaved to sin" (Rom 6:3–6). Christ's death represented, shared in, and contributed essentially to the death of the community to the *power* of sin. Individuals becoming members of the community at baptism take up participation in the death of that community's self-serving communal dysfunction. One cannot be alive to self as self-serving and to self as responsible contributor to community life; that is, to the pre-occupation Israelite practice of multilaterally internal interaction. One must die to one or the other: "So you must also consider yourselves dead to sin and alive to God in Christ Jesus" (6:11). The new member's death to the power of sin is certainly individual; but just as certainly it requires a live community within which to engage as responsible essence-changing internally interacting member, precisely what baptism offered.[39]

Such participation in the death of self-serving is the underside of participation in resurrection: Rom 6:5 "For if we have been united with him in a death like his, we will certainly be united with him in a resurrection like his." Paul maintains the eschatological tension; he places this resurrection in the future: "we will certainly be . . ." The resurrection of Jesus is not an isolated individual resurrection, not a completed past event, but a "first fruits" (1 Cor 15:20–23), a representation in the community's anointed one of the continually coming resurrection of the community itself. The resurrection of the bodies of the faithful is not given to them as separate selves but as part of the corporate body in the release of the whole creation from bondage: Rom 8:21–23 "The creation itself will be set free from its bondage to decay and will obtain

---

38. So Käsemann, *Perspectives on Paul*, 106; Beker, *Paul the Apostle*, 272–75; Sanders, *Paul and Palestinian Judaism*, 456.

39. So also Käsemann, *Perspectives on Paul*, 113; Sanders, *Paul and Palestinian Judaism*, 463–68; and Beker, *Paul the Apostle*, 205.

the freedom of the glory of the children of God. We know that the whole creation has been groaning in labor pains until now; and not only the creation, but we ourselves, who have the first fruits of the Spirit, groan inwardly while we wait for adoption, the redemption of our bodies." Paul heaps sarcasm on some Corinthians for pride in an already accomplished individual "resurrection" as opposed to participating in the resurrection of shared community interaction: 1 Cor 4:8 "Already you have all you want! Already you have become rich! Quite apart from us you have become kings!" Paul is at the *corporate pole of the corporate-generic range* in the resurrection strand.

For Paul, participation in the corporate body of Christ is actualized in the Eucharist as well as in baptism: 1 Cor 10:16 "The cup of blessing which we bless, is it not a sharing in the blood of Christ? The bread which we break, is it not a sharing in the body of Christ? Because there is one bread, we who are many are one body, for we all partake of the one bread."

Paul is influenced by the *wisdom* strand of apocalyptic in his movement in the salvation-history strand toward the *schematic pole of the narrative-schematic range* and toward the sociology pole of the history-sociology range in the powers strand. Paul's schematization is refined, but schematization it is nevertheless, with the resurrection of Christ as the first fruits, to be followed by the resurrection of the whole creation, thus placing his hearers in the eschatological tension of being between these two times. Paul's analysis includes, as we have seen, the abstract sociological analysis of victory over the four social powers along with the concrete historical issue of the relation between Israel and the gentiles. Although Paul's use of postexilic wisdom is attractive to generically oriented Western theologians, Paul nevertheless uses wisdom in these two ways only as a universalizing tool subordinate to an overall corporate perspective. He remains at the *subordinate pole of the subordinate-dominant range* of the wisdom strand.

To summarize, Paul's message is fundamentally *eschatological* and fundamentally *historical*; that is, conceived within two of the three apocalyptic strands derived from the pre-apocalyptic Old Testament. Paul expounds this position through use of the fourth, fifth, and sixth apocalyptic strands of *remnant, resurrection,* and *powers.* As for the ranges, Paul takes the corporate poles of all five key corporate-generic ranges in first-century apocalyptic (asterisked in the table on page 121 above), and also keeps wisdom subordinate to salvation history in the narrative-schematic and history-sociology ranges.

Thus Paul writes within the conceptuality of first-century apocalyptic but consistently chooses corporate positions along its ranges. Since he writes in a conceptual idiom that contains both cosmological and corporate options in each range, it follows that his consistent corporate choices are not forced on him by a limitation in his cultural horizon, but are an intentional part of the tradition he wishes to transmit. In fact, his conversion was precisely from the opposing orientation. When he faces conflict over a key range in one of his congregations, he contrasts the poles *explicitly* as, for example, in his sarcastic denunciation of the generic pole of the resurrection strand in 1 Cor 10:16 "quite apart from us you have become kings!" (We will see the same explicit rejection of the sect pole of the remnant strand in Mark 10:44 "Whoever wishes to be first among you must be slave of all.") With Paul there is no presentation of abstract ranges: He did not face a modern Western taxonomic predilection. Paul not only consistently made corporate choices in the ranges but explicitly argued for those choices against their opposites. Moreover, Paul was not an independent agent but an interacting member of the early Christian community—the choices, and the awareness of them, were also a property of the community as a whole.[40]

## 2 Corporate Use of the Apocalyptic Idiom in Mark and Q

Mark also works within the first-century apocalyptic idiom, and also holds it to a strictly corporate orientation in each of the key ranges.

Mark begins with Jesus proclaiming the imminent apocalyptic expectation, "The time is fulfilled, and the kingdom of God is at hand; repent, and believe in [participate in] the good news" (1:15). Jesus forms a group of disciples who were not themselves to be the remnant but were to "fish for people" (1:17). He releases the sick from the Pauline "power" of sin: "he said to the paralytic, 'Son, your sins are forgiven [by those bringing him]'" (2:5). When necessary he confronted the powers explicitly: "Whenever the unclean spirits saw him, they fell down before him and shouted, 'You are the Son of God!'" (3:11). He conforms to the power of the law: "The sabbath was made for humankind, and not hu-

---

40. For a discussion of how choices made by individual creators of cultural artifacts are related to the communities to which they belong, see Baxandall, *Patterns of Intention*, chapter 2.

mankind for the sabbath" (2:27). He uses parables (a wisdom form) to deal with concrete historical issues—namely, the change of the age Israel is called to assist with: "With what can we compare the kingdom of God, or what parable shall we use for it? It is like . . ." (4:30–31).

The disciples are privileged: "To you has been given the secret of the kingdom of God, but for those outside everything comes in parables . . ." (4:11), but with this privilege goes the responsibility to prophesy to those who resist ". . . so that they may indeed look but not perceive, and may indeed listen but not understand" (Mark 4:12 = Isa 6:9). Jesus calls the disciples to be the means of bringing as many others as possible to reconciliation before the end comes. He sends them out two by two and gives them authority over the unclean spirits (powers) (6:7). The band of disciples is not the remnant, and membership in it is not directed toward saving the member or the band but for serving others, for enlarging the kingdom: "The cup that I drink you will drink; . . . but to sit at my right hand . . . is for those for whom it has been prepared. . . . Whoever wishes to be first among you must be slave of all" (10:39, 44), quite a reversal of western culture! That Jesus' mission, shared with the servant community of disciples he represents, extends beyond Israel is made explicit: Mark includes healings—that is, releases from powers—in the regions of Tyre, Sidon, and the Decapolis (7:24–37).

Jesus' own role is as the anointed representative leader in Israel, "You are the Christ [anointed]" (8:29), greater than David, "David himself calls him Lord" (12:37); as a leader who "came not to be served but to serve, and to give his life as a ransom for many" (10:45). That Jesus represents the anticipated corporate resurrection of Israel is implied in the hymn at the entry into Jerusalem, "Hosanna! Blessed be the one who comes in the name of the Lord! Blessed is the coming kingdom of our ancestor David!" (Luke 11:9–10 = Ps 118:26).

Jesus' last discourse before his passion (Mark 13, the "synoptic apocalypse") uses the idiom of Hasidic apocalyptic writing, Daniel and 1 Enoch, to describe the coming of the end of the age, with "the Son of man coming in clouds with great power and glory. Then he will send out the angels, and gather his elect from the four winds, from the ends of the earth to the ends of heaven" (Mark 13:26–27 = Dan 7:13–14).

Mark's narrative gospel form is nearer both the narrative pole of the narrative-schematic range in the salvation-historical strand of apocalyptic and the history pole of the history-sociology range in the powers strand than are the issue based letters of Paul. Although Paul keeps wisdom subordinate to salvation history in these two ranges, Mark is even more thoroughgoingly corporate than Paul. This is one reason why Paul has been preferred by Western theologians with cosmological leanings (such as Augustine, Luther, and Barth).

Mark's message is quite similar to Paul's, but he uses a different vocabulary: The "reign of life" becomes the "kingdom of God"; "crucifixion of the old self" becomes "repentance"; "member of the body of Christ" becomes "disciple"; "resurrection of the dead" becomes "gathering of the elect." The eschatological tension between the ages is preserved, historical continuity with Israel is maintained, and the apocalyptic strands of resurrection, remnant, and powers are called on to expound these two. Mark is at the corporate poles of the five key ranges in apocalyptic and, additionally, at the more corporate poles of the narrative-schematic and history-sociology ranges.

The same corporate alternatives in the apocalyptic idiom underlie the Q source (the non-Markan material common to Matthew and Luke). In Q, eschatological tension is paramount: "Your kingdom come" (Luke 11:2–4) and "the master of that slave will come on a day when he does not expect him" (Luke 12:39–46). Yet historical continuity with Israel is maintained: "See, something greater than Solomon is here" (Luke 11:31). The resurrection of Christ effects the resurrection of the community: "Just as Jonah became a sign to the people of Ninevah, so the Son of Man will be to this generation" (Luke 11:30). The remnant is a servant remnant: "The harvest is plentiful, but the laborers are few; therefore ask the Lord of the harvest to send out laborers into his harvest" (Luke 10:1–16). The kingdom of God is a lamp, leaven, or salt for the whole community (Luke 11:33–36, 13:20–21, 14:34–35). The remnant will only partially coincide with present Israel: "People will come from east and west . . . and will eat in the kingdom of God" (Luke 13:29); "There will be weeping and gnashing of teeth when you see Abraham and Isaac and Jacob and all the prophets in the kingdom of God and you yourselves thrown out" (Luke 13:28).

Christ's victory is a victory over the social powers of evil: "The devil . . . showed him in an instant all the kingdoms of the world. And . . . said to him, 'To you I will give their glory and all this authority, for it has been given over to me . . . . if you, then, will worship me.' . . . Jesus answered him, 'It is written, "Worship the Lord your God"'" (Luke 4:1–13);

"No slave can serve two masters" (Luke 16:13). Wisdom is subordinate to salvation history. Parable, a wisdom form, is used in Q, as in Mark, to call for the fulfillment of salvation history. In short, Q makes the same intentional corporate choices within the ranges of positions offered by first-century apocalyptic as do Paul and Mark.

The corporate apocalyptic orientation of Paul, Mark, and Q (an extension of the prophetic tension in the Torah and prophets) was transmitted to the other synoptic gospels Matthew and Luke, to John, to Acts, and to the later epistles.

Both Luke and John preserved the apocalyptic tension, yet interpreted it for later congregations outside Palestine who were less familiar with the apocalyptic literary form. Luke, with Acts, did this by going back to a mixed prophetic-narrative form as in the Old Testament (for example, adding "the times of the gentiles" (Luke 21:24) to the scheme of history in Mark 13) and by maintaining tension using a succession of prophetic speeches in crisis situations in the early Christian movement. In one of these, Stephen's speech (Acts 7) to a crowd that included Paul, the Jesus party presents its program as completely within the Tradition that the Pharisee party is also claiming to defend. This passage is preparation for Acts' later account of Paul's dramatic change of sides in the conflict between the two parties—a change from guardian of a partially objectified Tradition at home to apostle of a re-communalized same Tradition abroad. The more literal and historical interpretation in Luke-Acts interprets eschatology to those not familiar with the apocalyptic literary form.

John is structured around seven eschatological *signs* (sample metonymic acts) by Jesus evoking corporate community interaction toward local resurrection of the community. Eschatological tension between imminent and realized (future and present) eschatology is unified at John 4:23 = 5:25 = 16:32 "the hour is coming, indeed it has come...."

Eschatological tension receded in the secondary (pseudo-) Pauline letters and the pastoral epistles. This tension moved toward postponing the eschatological end in 2 Thessalonians and 2 Peter and moved toward identifying it with the resurrection in Colossians and Ephesians. Nevertheless, the New Testament as a whole, necessarily written within the prevailing first-century Palestinian mixed corporate-generic apocalyptic idiom, maintains the Old Testament corporate tradition by taking the corporate pole in each of the five key corporate-generic ranges in that idiom against the invading generic perennial Hellenistic culture—a position we can expect not to find favor with the European upper class, as we see next.

## IV FIVE OPPORTUNITIES FOR GENERICIZING THE NEW TESTAMENT

The Christian mission to Europe was spectacularly successful in the working class whose sustaining relation with their community was maintained through interactive work. The message fit the community. But the unilaterally controlling ruling class did not find distributed corporate control in their class interest, and so their cosmologically oriented philosopher-theologians developed an academic Christian theology that continued the support of ruling-class interests via cosmological control by a God identified with Plato's *logos*, thus supporting their class's interest from this invasion of a corporate gospel of distributed control as offered by both testaments. We saw an outrageous sample of this in the late allegorical third interpretation of the parable of the sower in chapter 2.II.3, above. The opposing positions of these two classes duplicated that of occupiers and natives in Judea. In 325 CE the emperor Constantine ordered the Christian bishops of the Roman Empire to Nicaea to uniformize this cosmologically oriented theological doctrine. Constantine's purpose was to make Christianity official in order to use it as a tool in controlling his empire. The resulting *perennial* theology (treated in chapter 4) was dominant in the West until eighteenth century Enlightenment modern philosophy forced it to share control with equally non-interactive *modern* theology (treated in chapters 6 and 8, below).

Modern interpreters of the apocalyptic New Testament, like perennial ones, belong to a culture that is unable to recognize a corporate interactive relation and so can find only literal or allegorical meanings (rather than the intended metonymic meanings) in the apocalyptically styled New Testament. These interpretations are here listed in the order of the asterisked entries in the table of key ranges on page 121 above.

Five Opportunities for Modernist Genericizing
of the New Testament

1. A new age maintaining some historical continuity with the old is misread as completely dehistoricized

*(in eschatological strand, a shift from continuous to discontinuous pole)*
2. Corporate "powers" sociology is misread as a generic psychological analysis of conflict within individuals
*(in wisdom strand, a shift from subordinate to dominant pole)*
3. Resurrection of Christ as first-fruits of resurrection of corporate interaction in God's community is misread as of separate resurrections of single individuals
*(in resurrection strand, a shift from corporate to generic pole)*
4. Active corporate participation in the community by a wider variety of kinds of members is misread as generic similar participation
*(in remnant strand, a shift from whole to individual pole)*
5. The church as God's agent in the world is misread as the saved end-time remnant
*(in remnant strand, a shift from servant to sect pole)*

Two other ranges, the narrative-schematic range in the salvation-history strand and the history-sociology range in the powers strand, have a mix of the two kinds of relation. Modern interpretations naturally emphasize the second, less corporate pole.

Examples of the table's five ways of genericizing the New Testament will be drawn here largely from Bultmann's *Theology of the New Testament* because that work has already been examined from the perspective of the corporate-existentialist issue in chapter 2 above—where we saw Bultmann ignoring allusions to the Old Testament and identifying typology with allegory (pages 108 and 111). Modern theologians before Bultmann's existentialist emphasis similarly misread the New Testament in the same five ways, and examples from Schleiermacher and Harnack will be exhibited in chapter 6.

(1) A first opportunity for a genericizing interpretation of the New Testament arises from its own use (as in the Old Testament) of both continuous and discontinuous eschatological change, done most spectacularly in Paul and John.

J. Christiaan Beker analyzes the way Paul applies different aspects of the continuity-discontinuity range in the Old Testament tradition to correspondingly different situations dealt with in Galatians and Romans.[41]

---

41. Beker, *Paul the Apostle*, chapter 6, "Contextual Theology in Romans and Galatians."

The situation prompting the writing of Galatians is stated clearly: Gal 1:6 "I am astonished that you are so quickly deserting the one who called you in the grace of Christ and turning to a different gospel," a gospel promoted by later missionaries from a Jerusalem congregation demanding conformity to a literally interpreted Law. Paul says, Gal 3:16 "Now the promises were made to Abraham and his singular offspring; it does not say 'And to offspring,' as of many; but . . . to one person, who is Christ." Here Abraham and Christ are both metonyms for Israel. The issue, internal to Israel, is between an Israel remaining faithful to its call given through Abraham (and renewed through Christ to be a light to the nations as corporately interacting community) and an Israel passively conforming to a fixed *logos*-like reading of its tradition as influenced by the European occupation.

The letter to the Romans does not state its issue so bluntly because Paul cannot assert a right as founder there. But this letter does treat the same issue (more precisely, Israel's call as creatively interacting community to be a "light to the nations") although, in this case, the issue is specifically whether the Roman mixed Jewish-gentile Christian congregation can belong to both Israel and Rome.[42] In Galatia there were two missions to one community; in Rome there was one mission to two communities. To the first Paul, Abraham is "the father of many nations" (Rom 4:17, 18 = Gen 17:5), the father of not only the circumcised but also the uncircumcised, as Abraham himself was at his own call (Rom 4:11-12). The issue in one case is preserving an existing corporate community (one offspring) and in the other, a mission to preserve another community (two offspring). Whereas Galatians emphasized Christ's bringing Israel back to Abraham (fulfilling the promise), in Romans the promise is not "fulfilled" but is still in effect for *all* Christian believers—those whose faith should be the same as Abraham's (Rom 4:19-25). Romans 4 does not bring in a christological reference until the very end and even then it is subordinate to God—our faith "will be reckoned to us who believe in him who raised Jesus our Lord from the dead." Romans 4 emphasizes the continuity between the ages, with its resulting continuous eschatology, and this produces a theocentric emphasis with Christ subordinate to the God who raised him and his purpose—an emphasis useful in Paul's dialogue with the discontinuous-leaning contingent in

---

42. There is an excellent nuanced treatment of the context of the letter in Brown and Meier, *Antioch and Rome*, 2-8, 109-11.

the Roman congregation. Paul uses appropriate parts of the tradition to deal with each issue he encounters. Paul says he only becomes "all things to all people" at the hermeneutic level: 1 Cor 9:22–23 "I have become all things to all people, that I might by all means save some. I do it all for the sake of the gospel."[43] There is a tissue of figures woven around these two issues in one in Romans 9–11, instances such as the wild olive and withered cultivated olive branches both grafted or re-grafted into the original olive tree with its living root.

The underlying principle is the same in both letters. There is historical *continuity* in God's call through Abraham and Christ for his people in each age to help create the *discontinuity* represented by the defeat of the four powers. But the sophistication of apocalyptic thought, especially in this example of its exploitation by Paul, as well as in the two-layered realized eschatology of John: "the hour is coming, indeed it has come" (page 150 above), is outside modern conceptuality and so invites modern single-layered interpretations that claim absolute continuity or absolute discontinuity.

Bultmann's interpretation in *Theology of the New Testament* (presented in chapter 2, page 110) claims absolute discontinuity. The church is the "eschatological congregation" (1.37). "Judgment and salvation are eschatological events in the strict sense: i.e. events in which the present world and all history cease to be" (1.25). For Bultmann the eschatological discontinuity is absolute. Eschatology swallows up history. The New Testament Christian lives in the new age, already realized, absolutely eschatological, outside corporate history and concerned only with the de-historicized individual believer. Whereas Paul emphasizes the discontinuous pole to meet a challenge in Galatia, Bultmann takes the discontinuous pole as absolute and thus completely eliminates the salvation-history strand with both its narrative and schematic poles.[44] He ignores it because his presuppositions exclude recognition of any typological, hence corporate, relation between the testaments.

(2) A second opportunity for a genericizing interpretation of the New Testament is misreading its first-century corporate sociology of

---

43. Contemporary apocalyptically oriented New Testament scholarship finds a consistent Paul, e.g., the "coherent core of Paul's gospel" in Beker, *Paul the Apostle*, 94, the "basic coherent structure of Paul's thought" in Sanders, *Paul and Palestinian Judaism*, 433.

44. Beker is well aware of his difference at this point with Bultmann, e.g., *Paul the Apostle*, 141.

conflicting social powers as generic psychology of conflict inside a self. Paul's description of the conflict, "It is no longer I that do it, but sin that dwells within me" (Rom 7:19–20, page 140 above) describes an enslaving social structure or "power" (here "sin") which inhibits the creative interaction among community members. This is characteristically reduced by modern scholars to a struggle among forces within the generic self. Such a reduction makes generic wisdom dominant over corporate history.

Bultmann so reduces it. He allows, "The estrangement between the self which is the bearer of man's real will . . . and the self which slips away from this will and falls under the sway of flesh—exactly the cleft which Rom. 7:14ff depicts—is regarded as so far-reaching that this second self seems almost a foreign one, not belonging to the same person" (1.200–1). It "seems almost foreign" because for Paul it *is* foreign. For existentialist Bultmann, a sociological characterization of religion is a mythological one:

> Paul may indeed speak in naive mythology of the battle of the spirit powers against Christ or of his battle against them (1 Cor. 2:6–8; 15:24–26). In reality, he is thereby only expressing a certain understanding of existence: The spirit powers represent the reality into which man is placed as one full of conflicts and struggle, a reality which threatens and tempts. Thus, through these mythological conceptions the insight is indirectly expressed that man does not have his life in his hand as if he were his own lord but that he is constantly confronted with the decision of choosing his lord (1.259).

That is, Bultmann takes the conflict with the powers as a mythologization of a conflict of preferences within the generic individual. He demythologizes first-century biblical sociological analysis of the community into analysis of existential authenticity in the individual. He replaces corporate salvation history with generic psychology, with generic wisdom—a shift from the subordinate to the dominant pole in the wisdom strand.

(3) A third opportunity for genericizing interpretation of the New Testament arises from not recognizing the biblical meaning of *Messiah* (*Christ* as an internally interacting leader), thus also metonymy for the community led—so that *resurrection* of Christ *is* resurrection to *corporate interaction* of the community he represents. This resurrection is also in metonymy with previous resurrections in Israel's history as seen,

for example, in Ezekiel's prophetic challenge to an Israel in Babylonian captivity, Ezek 37:10 "I prophesied [to the dry bones] as he commanded me, and the breath [interactive spirit] came into them, and they lived." So also the resurrected (that is, still interacting) Jesus says to his disciples in *Roman* captivity, John 20:21–23: "As the Father has sent me, so I send you'.... [then] he breathed on them and said to them, 'Receive the Holy Spirit [*breath* and *spirit* use the same word in Hebrew and in Greek]. If you forgive the sins [non-*inter*active behavior] of any, they are forgiven them; if you retain the sins of any, they are retained.'" Jesus charges his followers to continue what God delegated to the human community (Adam in the Covenant (Gen 1:27–28)), to practice and thus spread internally interacting, thus essence-building, community.

When the resurrection of Christ is not thus recognized as "first fruits" of resurrection of corporate world community structure, it becomes singular and generic, a vindication of the divinity of Christ as individual, the *unique* place in history where the eternal touches the temporal, not it but its effect to be imparted generically to other individuals.

Bultmann says, "Belief in the resurrection and the faith that Christ himself, yes God Himself, speaks in the proclaimed word (2 Cor. 5:20) are identical" (1.305). This ideal event, this "word," is available for appropriation by the generic self: "in the word of proclamation Christ's death-and-resurrection becomes a possibility of existence in regard to which a decision must be made" (1.302). This word "is, by nature, personal address which accosts each individual, throwing the person himself into question by rendering his self-understanding problematic, and demanding a decision of him" (1.307). For Bultmann, participation in the resurrection is generic reconsideration of the self's own self-understanding. He reads the resurrection of Christ as singular, with generic application.

Other modern interpreters who disagree with Bultmann's existentialism also relate the resurrection to the generic self taken alone, rather than as major interactive renewal of an existing corporately interacting community.

(4) A fourth opportunity for modern generic interpretation of the New Testament is offered by a shift in Israel in the apocalyptic period to a dispersed leadership among ordinary individuals because central leadership now rested with the occupying power. The danger of accepting acculturation under Seleucid Hellenistic control placed a premium

on loyalty to the tradition by all non-governing individuals (page 132 above), and such a shift under Hellenistic colonization is clear in the New Testament material treated here. The gospels emphasize Jesus' association with the common people rather than primarily with the leaders and rulers, unlike the prophets who tended to interact with Israel's elites. For Paul, not only the prominent members of the body of Christ are necessary to its proper functioning but, "on the contrary, the members of the body that seem to be weaker are indispensable" (1 Cor 12:22)—indispensable because they are equally, or more so, needed as a contributing part of the overall interacting community and *interaction* is what is to be saved. This increased emphasis on the ordinary individual as representative of corporate Israel is misread as a generic relation between the individual and God—that is, the whole pole in the remnant strand can be misread as the individual pole.

Bultmann's claim, "Unlike the prophets' preaching, [Jesus'] preaching is directed not primarily to the people as a whole, but *to individuals*" (quoted above, page 111) is based on this misreading. Actually, the prophets and Jesus addressed individuals but addressed them as interacting components of the community, asking them to interact responsibly, not asking them to find existential self-understanding as envisioned by Bultmann. The call in the New Testament to active corporate participation by a range of individual members wider than the leadership is misread by Bultmann as call for generic response of selves.

(5) A fifth opportunity for a genericizing misunderstanding of the New Testament is a reading of the servant remnant as sect remnant—that is, mistaking the reform group as being the remnant itself (rather than as servant within the larger community with the role of making the remnant be as extensive as possible, both qualitatively and quantitatively).

Bultmann recognizes neither the apocalyptic sect remnant nor servant remnant (as both have some corporate characteristics) but he comes closer to the sect remnant, interpreting the New Testament community as an already saved generic remnant. For Bultmann, the end has already been realized; the church *is* the (genericized) remnant: "The earliest Church presents itself as an eschatological sect within Judaism, distinguished from other sects and trends . . . especially by the fact that it is conscious of being already the called and chosen Congregation of the end of days" (1.42). Both his exclusive interest in the saved self as such, and his rejection of any historical process within which the remnant could be increased, place Bultmann nearest the sect pole of the servant-sect range.

A sectarian understanding of the New Testament community is also widely held today among many who do not hold Bultmann's extreme existentialist position. This position is held without awareness of any other possibility. Robert H. Pfeiffer pushes a sectarian concept of "church" back even to Isaiah: "Isaiah took constructive measures for . . . planting the seeds of the righteous 'remnant.' . . . Thus he . . . separated from the corrupt body of the people a tiny nucleus of true believers, anticipating in a vague way individual salvation, substitution of a church for the nation, and separation of the redeemed from the worldly mass of apparent believers."[45] Martin Hengel uses the word "church" in characterizing the sectarian Essene community: It "has only an external, loose connection with the national association of the people; in other words, it becomes a 'church.'"[46] Howard Clark Kee in *Community of the New Age: Studies in Mark's Gospel* recognizes the existence only of the sect theory of remnant in first-century apocalyptic: "The primary factors in apocalyptic, therefore, are the elect, esoteric community and its life-world. . . . It lives in hope of imminent vindication" (p. 107). He finds a corresponding sectarian cast to the Markan community, contrary to the findings above: "The similarities between the Markan community and the Essenes are apparent in . . . their conception of the covenant community as distinct from the main body of Jews" (p. 98). Any reform movement risks being isolated by the main body as a sect (indeed the early Christian movement became so isolated), but the New Testament itself stoutly maintains the preexilic Old Testament view of an ever-reforming Israel called to influence the world, with the Christian movement such a reform movement both in Israel and in the dispersion, claiming Israel as "a light to the nations" in both.

Modern generically oriented Western theologians implicitly recognize the Old Testament's base in a non-Western philosophy and reject it. But, needing to accept the equally corporate New Testament, they do so by genericizing it, by replacing its corporate poles that are unrecognizable to them with the generic ones on the five corporate-generic ranges in first-century apocalyptic—the only ones comprehensible in their Western tradition. Thus unable to recognize typology, they miss the

---

45. Pfeiffer, *Introduction to the Old Testament*, 437.
46. Hengel, *Judaism and Hellenism*, 1.223.

New Testament's typological use of Old Testament events to proclaim a continuing two-way internal relation with corporate ancient Israel. Such separating and genericizing of the New Testament, illustrated paradigmatically with Bultmann in chapter 2, will be further instanced in chapter 6 with Schleiermacher and Harnack and also in chapter 9 with Perrin and Terrien. Perennially oriented scholars Augustine, Thomas, and Luther (chapter 4) and Tillich and Rahner (chapter 8) reach similar results in a different way. Their neo-Platonic theology conceives any similarity between a present and a past event as a *formal*, static, non-interacting, generic, allegorical relation—the resultant of *formal* allegorical relations of each with their same Platonic *Form*.

The apocalyptic writing style in the latter parts of the Old Testament and continued in the New was not originally intended as a change from interactive to fixed meaning but as a practical defensive double-valued style for writing under Western domination. When the likes of John the Baptist and Jesus of Nazareth spoke more directly, they were promptly martyred, unlike, say, earlier Isaiah and Jeremiah, who did the same in a free Israel. When the reform movement spread with Paul and others into the already more hellenized Jewish dispersion, it faced an additional difficulty—that of translating its interactively and metonymically described meanings into Koiné Greek, the first-century middle Eastern trade language, a language that was able to express static literal and allegorical meanings but not internally interactive meanings, as Indo-European culture did not generally recognize internal interaction until Hegel in 1807.

A literal hint of corporate interaction *is* provided in Mark 2:1–12, which is hidden by translation into Western language. Four friends of a paralyzed man bypassed a crowd around Jesus by digging through the roof and letting him down near Jesus. The passage continues:

> [5]When Jesus saw their [the *friends*] faith[fulness], he said to the paralytic, "Son, your sins are forgiven." [Some scribes complained] [7]"Why does this fellow speak in this way? It is blasphemy! Who can forgive sins but God alone?" [9][Jesus asked] "Which is easier, to say to the paralytic 'Your sins are forgiven' or to say 'Stand up and take your mat and walk'? [10]But so that you may know that the Son of Man has authority on earth to forgive sins"—he said to the paralytic—[11]"I say to you, stand up, take your mat and go to your home." [12]And he stood up, and immediately took the mat and went out before all of them.

Who forgives the paralytic? The Western answer—ranging from middle- and neo-Platonic Origen, Augustine, and Luther (chapter 4) to modern Schleiermacher and Harnack, (chapter 6)—agrees with the Scribes: "God alone" (at verse 6–7 above and with the later editorial addition verse 10) "... the Son of Man ...." But the Semitic *corporate answer* is, for once, *literally indicated* in verse 5: "When Jesus saw their [the four friends] faith, he said to the paralytic, 'Son, your sins are forgiven.'" The English literal noun *faith* translates as a figurative Aramaic verb, "engages constructively in community internal interaction with"; and the word *forgive* translates as, "acts to restore broken two-way constructive interaction." Unbelieveably for the West, that non-Platonic non-modern creative internally interacting culture thinks the *harmed ones*, the ones destructively interacted with by the sinner, are the best positioned to act to "forgive" that harmer—that is, to *restore* that *dysfunctional* community member to constructive interaction. Such *member originated* creative interactive moves are disallowed by the West's all-originating *logos*. Scripture speaks of a God giving "dominion" to the human *community* as a whole and thus to its participating subcommunities and individual members, not to separate individuals (Gen 1:26); and calling it (Gen 3 and throughout Scripture) *as a community* to *itself* use this *shared* essence-creating responsibility to *build* its ongoing interactive community life.

The New Testament records a Judean effort to counter a European *cultural* invasion, which is an intrinsic part of colonization. Judea's interactive culture worked both in Judea to resist this cultural invasion and in the dispersion to counter-invade the West by converting it to corporate social interaction. As we have seen, their success in both efforts was partial.

The Western Christian ambivalence toward the Old Testament turns out also equally to be an *unrecognized* Western Christian ambivalence toward its New Testament.

# 4

# A Millennium of Neo-Platonic Theology

*Allegorizing Interpretation of Both Testaments*

THE CHRISTIAN MISSION TO the Indo-European world found itself facing the same issue Judea faced under Western colonial rule: a middle-Platonic (later neo-Platonic) cosmological orientation that claimed an eternal truth or *logos* transcending time and human culture. This orientation was quite incompatible with the biblical call for every community member to share in joint interactive creation of a thus ever-changing interactive life together. Western intellectuals, at home in the controlling class, resisted conversion to such an inconvenient commitment.

## I PROTOTYPES OF REJECTION OF BOTH TESTAMENTS AS CORPORATE HISTORY

Ever since Christianity's introduction into the West, its Old and New Testaments have both faced explicit or implicit rejection: (1) explicit rejection as not cosmological or modern, or (2) implicit rejection by mistaking its base as cosmological or modern.

### 1 Explicit Rejection: Marcion

Marcion, excommunicated about 140 CE from the Christian congregation at Rome, erected a biblical canon that omitted the Old Testament and took from the New only purged versions of Luke's gospel and ten Pauline epistles.[1] Marcion interprets the Old Testament literally[2] as a

---

1. Tertullian, *Adversus Marcionem*, 4 (esp. 4.2), 5; Irenaeus, *Contra Haereses*, 1.27.2.

2. Origen, *Commentaria in epistolam ad Romanos*, 2.13.

valid record of the relation between a demiurge creator and the world he created. He interprets his purged New Testament as a record of the penetration of that world by Christ (an agent of a different God alien to the demiurge and his world) to save individuals generically from that world and their legalistic relation with its demiurge creator.[3] Christ suffered on the cross to purchase individuals from the demiurge whose rightful property they were, not to reconcile an estranged humanity with God.[4] Marcion was a gnostic in the fundamental sense that he understood salvation to be escape from the world.

Thus, with Marcion salvation is of generic individuals, not of corporate communities. Tertullian says Marcion taught that whereas the Old Testament prophesies a Christ who would save the community Israel, his purged New Testament tells of a Christ who comes to save every one generically "as if the Jewish Christ were ordained by the [demiurge] Creator for the restoration of the people alone from its dispersion, whilst [Marcion's Christ] was appointed by the supremely good God for the liberation of the whole human race." Yet this universal liberation is a generic one of individual proselytes rather than of nations: "[Marcion] ask[s], who among the nations can turn to the Creator, when those whom the prophet names are proselytes of individually different and private condition?"[5]

For Marcion, the God of the New Testament is totally alien to the world and those persons enslaved within it had no share in bringing it into existence, and is under no fatherly obligation to care for it. His choice to liberate individuals from the world is an act without a past: it is without a prior relationship, without a prophetic or typological prediction, without a salvation history, without a need for human repentance for past sins, without a need for divine mercy. It is totally new, totally discontinuous from what preceded it.[6]

An individual whose salvation is assured has no need to practice a positive social morality but is called to a negative ascetic obstruction of the world and its creator. Clement of Alexandria writes, "Marcion . . . [forbids] the use of this world's goods on the ground of opposition to the

3. Origen, *De principiis*, 2.5.1.
4. Origen, *Homiliae in Exodus*, 6.9; Irenaeus, *Contra Haereses*, 5.2.1.
5. Tertullian, *Adversus Marcionem*, 3.21.
6. Origen, *De principiis*, 2.5.1; Origen, *Commentaria in Ioannem*, 2.34; Tertullian, *Adversus Marcionem*, 1.28, 3.2–3.

Creator." "On this ground, that they do not wish to fill the world made by the Creator-God, they decide to abstain from marriage. Thus they are in opposition to their Maker."[7] Marcion rejects the Old Testament because of its corporate, worldly, historical, social subject matter. His system is generic, unworldly, ahistorical, and antisocial.

### 2 Implicit Rejection: Philo

The extreme *self-as-such* gnosticism of Marcion separated the self not only from the corporate human solidarity of the two Testaments but also from the cosmologically ordered world of Platonism. More traditional Hellenistic theologians retained the individual's place in a pre-ordered cosmos, thus still not recognizing human creativity in community interaction.

Philo (c.30 BCE–c.45 CE) was a scholar in the Jewish dispersion in Alexandria. He allegorized the Torah to make it fit the middle-Platonism, Stoicism, and Neopythagoreanism of his day—a prototype of implicit rejection of the Hebrew Scriptures as corporate salvation history. He did not dismiss the literal meaning of the Scriptures altogether, asking that in "a more full and exact investigation of what is not seen and in what is seen to be stewards without reproach."[8] Yet he recognizes that some statements in the Scriptures are not to be taken literally, as that a woman came out of a man's side or that God planted a paradise in Eden.[9] Philo says literal interpreters are only citizens of a petty state, whereas allegorizers are "cosmopolitan," citizens of the whole world.[10] To paraphrase Philo, the literal Scriptures are only an anecdotal history of one people, but allegory extracts the universal principles behind this history-bound material for the cosmopolitan world, which is not historically oriented and certainly does not view the history of Israel as its history.

Philo's commentaries on the Old Testament universalize and dehistoricize it to make sense of it for the middle-Platonic Alexandrian intellectual. Middle Platonism is the version of Platonism between the Plato (427–347 BCE) of "The Republic" and the neo-Platonism of Plotlines (205–270 CE). Leading middle Platonists were Antiochus of Ascalon

---

7. Clement of Alexandria, *Stromata*, 3.4.25.
8. Philo, *De migratione Abrahae*, 89.
9. Philo, *Legum allegoriae*, 2.7.19; 1.14.43.
10. Philo, *De somniis*, 1.39.

(c.100 BCE), who influenced Philo, and Albinus in Origen's time. For example, in *De cherubim* 40–130, Plotinus says that Moses was too wise to have written his Torah merely about particular mortals (e.g., 32). He wrote rather about universal matters. "Man" is mind (57), "woman" is sense-perception (40, 57), and "virgin" is virtue (42). Usually mind has intercourse with sense-perception, producing thought as offspring (57), which is figuratively stated as Adam knowing his wife Eve with the result Cain (40). Abraham, Isaac, Jacob, and Moses, unlike Cain, were lovers of wisdom and rejected sense perception—Moses never says these four knew their wives (40). Their helpmates Sarah, Rebecca, Leah, and Zipporah were virgins, i.e., virtues (41), and virtue is too good to have intercourse with mortals (44); instead, it has as offspring wisdom begotten by God, Gen 21:1–2 "The Lord visited Sarah as he had said, and the Lord did to Sarah as he had promised. And Sarah conceived, and bore Abraham a son..." (45). The union of human beings for the procreation of children turns virgins into women, but when God consorts with the soul he makes a woman into a virgin again, Gen 18:11: God visited Sarah after "it had ceased to be with Sarah after the manner of women" (50). The meaning is figurative: God does not have relations with changeable virgins at all but only with "virginity, the idea which is unchangeable and eternal. For particulars within a class are of their nature such as to come into being and pass out of it again, but to the potencies which give their form to the particulars is allotted an existence indestructible" (51). The Platonic Form "virgin" represents God's control unstained by human contribution. For Philo, Scripture is an allegorical exposition of a middle-Platonically understood world that is only properly controlled by God alone. Philo's ahistorical reinterpretation of the corporately oriented Old Testament historical narrative requires a decontextualizing method like allegory that recognizes no internal essence-changing relation among historical events. His Greek term *virgin* implies purity of essence; that is, specified from God hence free of any creative human community input.

Philo, an upper-class middle-Platonic dispersion Jewish philosopher in Alexandria, the intellectual capital of the Roman Empire, interpreted the Jewish Scriptures in precisely the way his contemporary Jesus of Nazareth (they were unknown to each other) gave his life in Judea to oppose. Jesus encouraged non-elite peasants to continue their essence-creating interactive participation in Judean community life against the

Roman program to "civilize" them—to bring them to submission to European middle-Platonic eternal Forms.

Philo's allegorical interpretation takes itself as a purifying abstraction from Israel's ethnic historical relativity. But what the Old Testament offers is neither expressible nor comprehensible within such a middle-Platonic orientation. Rather, it calls the Hellenistic world *from* static conformity to Platonic Forms *to* essence creating interaction within and among the many particular ethnic and religious communities of the Roman Empire; that is, to abandon its European cosmic God for the Old Testament corporate God.

## II MIXED ACCEPTANCE OF THE TESTAMENTS: THE CHURCH FATHERS

When the earliest Christian theologians, the "church fathers," came to interpret the Old and New Testaments, they had before them the three kinds of interpretation we have analyzed so far, (a) history-applying methods of typology and fulfillment of prophecy as in the New Testament's use of the Old Testament, (b) explicit rejection of Old Testament history as not being salvation history as with Marcion, and (c) implicit rejection of it by allegorizing it as with Philo. To be a church father included being orthodox in the eyes of the coiners of the term "church father"; thus, none of them took option (b). And because the church fathers belonged to the Western world as well as the Christian movement, their interpretations of the two Testaments could include at best a little (a) and much (c).

### 1 Systematic Theology as Allegory: Origen

Origen (c.185–c.254) headed the Christian catechetical school at Alexandria and later taught in Caesaria of Palestine. His philosophical base was Alexandrian middle Platonism. Origen further systematized the Christian middle-Platonic exegetical and theological tradition developed by Justin Martyr, Eusebius, Clement of Alexandria, and others to a form which, slightly modified into neo-Platonism by Augustine, was to reign until Thomas Aquinas in the 13th century and still to maintain substantial influence today. Origen was highly respected as a Christian scholar and leader, and was a prolific writer who equaled Augustine in output. Everything he wrote was directly or indirectly exegesis of the Bible, both Old and New Testaments.

The central theme in Platonic philosophy is the determining status of the unchangeable abstract universal over the changeable concrete particular—that is, of the reality of Plato's Forms (or middle-Platonism's mind of God), as compared with the imperfect and changing character of sensible particulars that reflect them. The Forms, or the divine mind, are with God; changeable particulars are far from God. The goal is for the individual to move from the historical particular toward the non-historical universal, from the world toward God. Origen typically concatenates several short biblical passages to show that Scripture is given us to take us to this goal, as in his *Commentary on John*:

> If the Word became flesh [John 1:14] and the Lord says "unless you eat the flesh of the Son of Man and drink his blood, you have no life in you" [John 6:53] . . . , perhaps this is the flesh of the lamb which takes away the sin of the world [John 1:29] . . . . One must not, therefore, eat the flesh of the lamb raw [Exod 12:9], as the slaves of the letter do . . . . But let us, by means of the . . . fiery words given by God, such as Jeremiah's received from the one who said to him, "Behold I have placed my words in your mouth as fire" [Jer 5:14], roast the meat of the lamb so that those who partake of it say, as Christ speaks in us [2 Cor 13:3] "Our heart was burning in the way as he opened the Scriptures to us" [Luke 24:32]. . . . Let this prophecy of the lamb, however, . . . nurture us only for the duration of the night of darkness in this life. For we must leave nothing of this nourishment, which shall thus be useful to us only in the present time, until the dawn [Exod 12:10] of the day of those things which follow this life.[11]

In the fourth book of his *De principiis*, Origen systematically distinguishes three levels of meaning in biblical passages, in ascending order of abstraction or universality, for the stepwise upward formation of the reader. The three levels, like the three parts of a human being, are called the *body*, *psyche (soul)*, and *spirit* of a passage (4.2.4).

*Bodily* meaning, the lowest of the three, is a bare, lifelessly literal, earthly, particular, non-abstract meaning. Origen recognizes the truth of such a meaning in many Old Testament historical passages, such as those reporting that Abraham was buried at Hebron, or that Solomon built the temple in Jerusalem (4.3.4). Taken alone, such meaning would be only the lifeless body, the carcass, of the passage. Such a bare meaning fits the only history known in Hellenism, an anecdotal history of bare

---

11. Origen, *Commentaria in Ioannem*, 10.99–108.

events without any internal meaning relation among them, a history rather like nineteenth century critical history.

This non-abstract bodily meaning does not include figures of speech, which abstract from one context to another. Hence, a passage with only figurative (abstractive) meaning has no bodily meaning at all. "Who is so silly as to believe that God, after the manner of a farmer, 'planted a paradise eastward in Eden'?" (4.3.1), Origen asks. (Philo echoes this example, as we have seen above). Origen says that God has arranged the impossibilities in bodily meaning of some passages to drive the reader to a higher meaning (4.2.9).

*Psychic* meaning, the next higher meaning, is directed to the moral life of the human individual—that is, paraenetic allegory as in 1 Clement (above, page 81). Origen's example is 1 Cor 9:9–10 = Deut 25:4, "You shall not muzzle an ox while it is treading out the grain," which he interprets: "God who gave the law says the words . . . not for the oxen but for the apostles, who were preaching the gospel of Christ" (4.2.6, 2.4.2). Origen finds in the passage a statute (*body*) and its heavenly and allegorically related meaning (*psyche*), both spoken by God from heaven. In contrast, Paul (above, page 94) claims a share in God's delegated authority to interacting humanity here on earth which empowers him to apply the earlier bodily statute typologically (interactively) to a later historical situation.

*Spiritual* meaning is at the third and highest level. Origen says, "When God is said to 'walk in the paradise in the cool of the day' and Adam to hide himself behind a tree [Gen 3:8], I do not think anyone will doubt that these are figurative expressions which indicate certain mysteries through a semblance of history and not through actual events" (4.3.1). Origen is saying the passage does not have an earthly, anecdotal historical meaning but a figurative meaning outside history, a "semblance of history," a "mystery," a spiritual truth capable of drawing the reader closer to God. In contrast, the Genesis passage itself, certainly figurative, nevertheless does recount a historical event—the early loss of innocent creative internal relation in human society. The figure used is not allegory but rather first-family for humanity *metonymy*. But middle-Platonism looks for an unchangeable Platonic Form governing proper behavior rather than a metonymy between community past experience and a present issue.

Origen delights in exegeting biblical passages so as to show that their spiritual meaning *is* that we need to search for spiritual meaning in biblical passages. We saw an example above from his *Commentary on John*. An example from *De principiis* is his conversion of the parable Matt 13:44 "The kingdom of heaven is like treasure hidden in a field" from a metonymy into an allegory: Origen continues "Now let us consider whether the outward aspect of scripture and its obvious and surface meaning does not correspond to the field as a whole, full of all kinds of plants, whereas the truths that are stored away in it and not seen by all, but lie as if buried beneath the visible plants, are the hidden 'treasures of wisdom and knowledge' [Col 2:3], which the Spirit speaking through Isaiah calls 'dark and unseen and concealed' [Isa 45:3]" (4.3.11). For Origen spiritual meaning is from above, from a different context, not to be drawn by us from the same context but to understand by *analogy*. But the Matthew parable itself, like all New Testament parables, is not an abstract allegory but an interacting *metonymy* between the material and the internal interactive relational aspects of the *same* community activity.

Again, Origen argues for spiritual meaning in Scripture by spiritually exegeting John 2:6 "six stone water jars for the Jewish rites of purification, each holding two or three firkins." He says the faithful "are purified through the word of the scriptures, which contain in some cases 'two firkins,' that is, so to speak, the soul [psychic] meaning and the spiritual meaning, and in other cases three, since some passages possess, in addition . . . a bodily [literal] sense as well" (4.2.5). But John intends none of these three. Jesus at the wedding feast diverts legalistic means for purification to community means for interaction. Jesus' actions are a *sign*, antitype, metonymy of his future crucifixion for the same community interaction purpose. Middle-Platonic Origen sees only *allegory*, never *metonymy*: "the reader must endeavor to grasp the entire meaning, connecting by an intellectual process the account of what is literally impossible with the parts that are not impossible but are historically true, these being interpreted allegorically in common with the parts which, so far as the letter goes, did not happen at all. For our contention with regard to the whole of divine scripture is, that it all has a spiritual meaning" (4.3.5).

Most of Origen's writing directs us to the spiritual sense. Another example is the exegesis of Gen 1:7 "And God made the dome and separated the waters that were under the dome from the waters that were above the dome." Origen first contrasts the two heavens, the heaven of Gen 1:1 and the dome: "Although God had already previously made heaven, [v. 1] now he makes . . . the firmament [dome, v. 7], that is, the corporeal heaven . . . . That first heaven indeed, which we said is spiritual, is our mind, which is also itself spirit, that is, our spiritual man which sees and perceives God. But that corporeal heaven, which is called the firmament, is our outer man which looks at things in a corporeal way." Then he contrasts the two waters: "Let each of you, therefore, be zealous to become a divider of that water which is above and that which is below. . . . By participation in that celestial water which is said to be above the heavens, each of the faithful becomes heavenly, that is, when he applies his mind to lofty and exalted things, . . . 'seeking the things which are above, where Christ is at the right hand of the Father' [Col 3:1]."[12]

All of Origen's exegeses say Scripture's purpose is to draw the individual toward heaven where one's mind is fixed on unchanging lofty and abstract things. God relates generically to an individual through that individual's conformity to an abstract *Logos* or *Word* in heaven.

Origen does recognize the fleshly incarnation: "in these last times [Heb 1:2] he emptied himself [Phil 2:7] and was made man, was made flesh [John 1:14], although he was of God."[13] But Origen understands the incarnate Word as imparting God's wisdom to individuals, not as representative leader of God's people: "He is called 'Word' [*logos*], because he removes everything irrational [*alogon*] from us and makes us truly rational beings who do all things for the glory of God. . . . For if, by participating in him, we arise and are enlightened, and perhaps also are shepherded or ruled, it is clear that we also become rational in a divine manner."[14] And the Word in Scripture is as active in joining the individual to God as is the incarnate Word. "The creator knew [the soul] would be capable of corruption, and hence subject to overpowering sins. And so just as he prepared medicine for the body from herbs, so he also prepared medicine for the soul in his words sown and scattered in divine scriptures. . . . for he has bequeathed the art of medicine, of which the chief physician is the Savior who said of himself 'Those who are well

---

12. Origen, *In Genesim homiliae*, 1.2, *Homilies on Genesis and Exodus*, 48–50.
13. Origen, *De principiis*, 1.praef.4.
14. Origen, *Commentaria in Ioannem*, 10.267–68.

have no need of a physician, but those who are sick' [Matt 9:12]"[15] The Matthew passage itself does not allegorize sin with illness, but sees both as *social*, as impediments to constructive community internal interaction, and both to be overcome by that same social interaction.

Origen defends human free choice against the gnostic fatalism of his time. He says the individual was created good, but at the same time "the Creator granted to the minds created by him the power of free and voluntary movement, in order that the good that was in them might become their own, since it was preserved by their own free will; but sloth and weariness of taking trouble to preserve the good . . . began the process of withdrawal from the good. Now to withdraw from the good is nothing else than to be immersed in evil" (2.9.2). Sensations incite toward evil, but for "one who has undergone more instruction and discipline . . . the sensations and incitements are there, but his reason, having been . . . confirmed towards the good by right doctrines, . . . repels the incitements and gradually weakens the desire" (2.9.4). Finally, Christ will himself "instruct those who are able to receive him in his character of wisdom . . . until such time as he subjects them to the Father [1 Cor 15:28] . . . . then even their bodily nature will assume that supreme condition to which nothing can ever be added" (3. 6.9).

Thus, Origen defends free choice but only a choice for each individual separately to follow or not that individual's predetermined heaven-given rationality—a choice quite different from the scriptural call to the human community for each member to make free creative interactive moves initiating and responding as *co-creators* of community internal interaction with one another and with God—to "be fruitful . . . and have dominion" (Gen 1:28).

Jean Daniélou in his *Origen*[16] (1955) criticizes Origen for his scriptural interpretation of mixing two kinds of "spiritual" meanings, (a) those in the mind of God, that is, biblically described using a word already used in a historically earlier *biblical* account, which he calls *typology*, and (b) those in analogy with use of the term in classical *Western* culture, which he calls *allegory*. Category (a) obviously includes all formal-similarity flags for corporate typological relations (above, page 79). Neither Daniélou nor Origen recognize the thus flagged internally interactive typology of Paul and of Goppelt (chapter 2.II.2, above) but

---

15. Origen, *Homilia prima in Psalmum* XXXVII 1, 1369.
16. Daniélou, *Origen*, 139–40, 185–86.

only non-interactive analogy. Daniélou says, "The genuinely biblical element mingles with a stream flowing from the culture of the time. The amalgamation first took place in Philo." He says when Origen interprets the seating by fifties and hundreds at the feeding of the multitude, with 'fifty' meaning forgiveness as in Jubilee and Pentecost, and 'hundred' meaning perfection as in Ovid, "he is combining the legitimate symbolism of the Bible with pagan symbolism."[17] And when Origen has the sea represent both evil as with biblical Leviathan, and the passions as in his own culture, he "slips from symbolism into Hellenistic."[18] The different distinctions made by Origen and by Daniélou are all only between eternal *Forms*, those of generic classical culture and of a genericized Christianity.

Origen specifically denies any direct relation between historical events: "We must not suppose that historical things are types of historical things, and corporeal of corporeal. Quite the contrary, corporeal things are types of spiritual things, and historical of intellectual."[19] Middle Platonism does not allow internal relation; any relation between historical events is at most an identity or other static similarity between their respective Platonic Forms. The two historical events cannot be in historical internal interaction; they can at most only be each in a separate analogical relation with the same heavenly Form, each a half of a static allegorical relation between the two events.

In *De principiis*, Origen interprets 1 Cor 10:11 = Num 21:5, 6, 16:41–49 "These things happened to them to serve as types" by saying that Paul "gives hints to show what these things were figures of, when he says: 'For they drank of that spiritual rock that followed them, and that rock was Christ'" (4.2.6). And he interprets Rom 11:4 = 1 Kings 19:18 "I have left for myself seven thousand who have not bowed the knee to Baal" as showing "Here Paul has taken it to stand for those who are Israelites 'according to election,' for not only are the gentiles benefited by the coming of Christ, but also some who belong to the divine race" (4.2.6). In each case Origen merely claims the two items, used in the treatment above to flag typology, are statically similar as figures of the same heavenly fixed "type." Neither he nor his culture could conceive the earlier thereby flagged *worldly* internally interacting *historical hu-*

---

17. Origen, *Commentaria in Matthaeum*, 11.3; Ovid, *Fasti*, 3.125.
18. Ibid., 10.12.
19. Origen, *Commentaria in Ioannem*, 10.18.110.

*man continuity* into which Paul as missionary is trying to bring Indo-Europeans and Europeanized dispersion Jews.

Quite arbitrary, and equally devoid of shared interactive meaning, are many of Origen's Old Testament interpretations not related to New Testament interpretations. For example, Origen takes the union of Abraham and Sarah as the spiritual union of a wise man and virtue,[20] a middle-Platonic interpretation we saw above in Philo. Another example: Origen relates Num 23:24 "[Israel] does not lie down until it has eaten the prey and drunk the blood of the slain" to the eating and drinking of the Eucharist.[21] But can celebrating victory over an enemy suggest the passing on of prophetic responsibility from a victim to his followers? The two events have opposite meanings.

Origen assembled and substantially stabilized an Alexandrian middle-Platonic Christian *systematic theology* that was ultimately to dominate Western Christianity for a millennium, and be substantially in control for another. This project is announced in chapter 4 of *De principiis*:

> The aim of the Spirit . . . was preeminently concerned . . . that . . . man . . . devoting himself to the "deep things" [1 Cor 2:10] revealed in the spiritual meaning of the words become partaker of all the doctrines of the Spirit's counsel. . . . doctrines concerning God and His only-begotten Son; of what nature the Son is, and in what manner he can be the Son of God, and what are the causes of his descending to the level of human flesh and completely assuming humanity; and what, also, is the nature of his activity, and towards whom and at what times it is exercised . . . (4.2.7).

The other books (1–3) of *De principiis* offer a construction of such an abstract systematic theology of the Christian religion, using both testaments. Two examples illustrate Origen's procedure. The relation of the Son to the Father is handled thus:

> The Son of God . . . is the invisible image of the invisible God, just as according to the scripture narrative we say that the image of Adam was his son Seth. It is written thus: "And Adam begat Seth after his own image and after his own kind" [Gen 5:3]. This image preserves the unity of nature and substance common to a father and a son. For if "all things that the Father doeth, these also

---

20. Origen, *In Genesim homiliae*, 6.1.
21. Origen, *Homilia in Numeros*, 16.9.

doeth the Son likewise" [John 5:19], then in this very fact that the Son does all things just as the Father does, the Father's image is reproduced in the Son. (1.2.6)

The absence of the holy spirit in sinners is handled thus:

> At the time of the flood, when "all flesh had corrupted God's way" [Gen 6:12], it is written that God said, as if speaking of unworthy men and sinners, "My spirit shall not remain in those men for ever, because they are flesh" [Gen 6:3]. Here it is clearly shown that God's spirit is taken away from all the unworthy. It is also written in the Psalms; "Thou wilt take away their spirit and they will die, and return to their earth; thou wilt send forth thy spirit and they shall be created, and thou wilt renew the face of the earth" [Ps 104:29f], which passage clearly points to the Holy Spirit who, after sinners and the unworthy have been taken away and destroyed, creates for himself a new people and "renews the face of the earth," when through the grace of the Spirit men "put off the old man with his doings" [Col 3:9] and begin "to walk in newness of life" [Rom 6:4]. And this is why the passage fitly applies to the Holy Spirit, because he will dwell not in all men, nor in those who are flesh, but in those whose "earth has been renewed" (1.3.7).

In these examples, Origen concatenates passages whose only relation to one another is that their spiritual meaning (as abstracted by Origen) can be used as a component in constructing a systematic theology. This method is a generalization of the allegorical method for spiritual interpretation of single passages we have seen above, which also concatenates several passages. Construction of a systematic theology thus amounts to allegory in disguise.[22] The use of the Old Testament as source for an abstractly conceived theology continues to the present and reaches perhaps its zenith in the organization of some nineteenth and early twentieth century Old Testament theologies around the systematic "God—human individual—salvation" scheme.[23] It has, however, been challenged by the communally oriented interpretation of Walther Eichrodt and Gerhard von Rad and others who reject an allegorically

---

22. So also Grant: "In short, all Christian doctrine ultimately rests on allegorization," *The Letter and the Spirit*, 93.

23. Steudel, *Vorlesungen über die Theologie des Alten Testaments*; Haevernick, *Vorlesungen über die Theologie des Alten Testaments*; Sellin, *Theologie des Alten Testaments*; Köhler, *Theologie des Alten Testaments*.

constructed interpretation for a typologically based one (below, chapter 8).

Such allegorically related abstract systematic theology misses the central point of the biblical advocacy—the delegation by God to the *community* (not members separately) of "dominion,"—ability and authority *interactively* to *create* its interactive structure, culture, Torah—and invites or *calls* the community to do so through complementary creative internal essence-creating interaction with God, one another, and nature. Systematic theology can be a useful tool in both the practice of, and the ongoing transmission of, this biblical tradition so long as wisdom remains subordinate to corporately interacting history as it is at the subordinate pole of the wisdom strand of apocalyptic (above, pages 121, 127, 146).

### 2 Allegory Distinguished and Condemned: the Antiochian School

The Antiochian school of exegesis, including theologians Diodore of Tarsus (c.330–c.390), Theodore of Mopsuestia (c.350–428), and Theodoret (c.393–c.460), and influential preacher John Chrysostom (c.347–407), set out to correct what it considered the neglect of the historical meaning of the Old Testament by the Alexandrian abstracting method. Antiochian philosophy was moderated by an empirical strain in Aristotelianism and a stronger and less hellenized Judaism in Syria. The Antiochian theologians recognized in Scripture an internally interacting history at the anthropological level, essential to the scriptural message but invisible to the Alexandrian middle-Platonic philosophical world. They vigorously opposed the Alexandrian scriptural interpretation for its non-recognition of the text's corporate historical meaning.

The Antiochian school found three levels of sense in Scripture: literal sense, spiritual sense, and typological application.

The Antiochian *literal* meaning, on which the other two meanings must be based, is *the meaning intended by the writer of the Scripture passage*, thus taking language as community interaction (as in Genesis 2:19 and in Wittgenstein as in chapter 1.IV.4, above) rather than carrier of a Platonic *logos*. Antiochian literal meaning is internal to the culturally structured community out of which and for which a Scriptural text was written, a meaning that includes its metaphors and other figures. For example, Diodore finds the figurative meaning in Ps 80:8 "You brought a vine out of Egypt" to be made explicit in the parallel second half of the verse, ". . . you drove out the nations and planted it."[24] And Theodoret, writing on difficult passages in Numbers, did not bother, as Origen did above, to explain Num 23:24: ". . . [Israel] does not lie down until it has eaten the prey and drunk the blood of the slain," since the verse itself indicates it is a characterization of Israel under the simile of a lioness: "Look, a people rising up like a lioness . . ."[25]

The Antiochian *spiritual* meaning of Scripture, *theoria*, or insight, is the relation between God and his people constituted by the historical events described by the writers—including, of course, those figuratively described. Diodore wrote, "We do not forbid the higher interpretation and *theoria*, for the historical narrative does not exclude it, but on the contrary is the basis and support of higher insights. It is necessary only to guard against the *theoria* opposing the historical basis, for the result would then be no longer *theoria*, but allegory." Diodore uses the term allegory in the sense used in this study and hastens to add an apology for differing from Paul's usage in Gal 4:24:

> The apostle has not done away with the historical sense by introducing *theoria* and calling it allegory. He did this not because of ignorance of the terms but to teach us that even if the term allegory is used for the higher thoughts, it is to be understood according to the rules of *theoria*, rather than as understood by those who displace the historical narrative. But innovators with holy scripture, or those who are wise in their own conceit, or are incompetent in or betrayers of history, introduce allegory, not in the sense of the apostle, but, through their own vanity, making the readers understand some things in place of others.[26]

The third principle of Antiochian interpretation is the application of the spiritual meaning, *theoria*, of remembered earlier situations to current ones by applying them *typologically*, thus including the latter in the historical tradition sharing the *theoria* that incorporated the original events into the overall record of God's relation with his people. For example, Theodore accepted the sprinkling of the doors with blood at the Exodos as type of deliverance through Christ's blood; the bronze serpent raised up by Moses (Num 21:9 = John 3:14) as type of the con-

---

24. Diodore of Tarsus, *In Psalmum*, Ps 118 prol., 92.

25. Theodoret, *In loca dificilia scripturae sacrae quaestiones in Numeros*, 43.

26. Diodore of Tarsus, *In Psalmum*, praef., "Extraits du Commentaire de Diodore de Tarse sur les Psaumes," Greek text, 88.

quest of death by Christ's death; and Jonah's experiences as type of the saving results of Christ's death and resurrection.[27] All are in agreement with New Testament interpretations and use former events as resource in understanding later issues.

The Antiochian exegetes distinguished the literal meaning of prophecy (the prediction intended by the prophet in his own historical situation) from a later typological application of a prophecy to some event unknown to the original prophet, which we earlier called "typology in disguise" (above, page 87). For example, Theodore limited the literal meaning of the prophecy Amos 9:11 = Acts 15:16 "On that day I will raise up the booth of David that is fallen" to a prediction about the return from captivity but also allowed it as a type of Christ.[28] Theodore recognized a literal meaning for prophecy as warning in its own day.

The Antiochian school was cautious in accepting typological interpretations, requiring a close similarity in the way type and anti-type show the same continuing saving historical relation with God. For example, Theodore rejected a typological extension to Christ of Micah's literal prophecy of a return from exile, "Many nations shall come and say: 'Come, let us go up to the mountain of the Lord'" (4:1–3), since Jesus said worship will no longer take place on a mountain: "The hour is coming when you will worship the Father neither on this [Samaritan] mountain nor in Jerusalem" (John 4:21).[29] Here, Theodore is more cautious than the New Testament itself—John 4:21 simultaneously applies to Micah both directly and antithetically: it includes the Samaritans and condemns exclusive temple worship. Such a conclusion, brought out in interactive repartee by Jesus and the Samaritan woman, would be clear in the Middle East but would be less comprehensible as one approached the Alexandrian middle-Platonic scholarly orientation.

Thus, the Antiochian exegetes allowed typological but not allegorical interpretation. They understood the biblical message to be about a saving *historical* relation between God and a creatively interacting historical people capable of transmitting such a human culture through time. The saving historical meaning of a past event could be used typologically to interpret an event current or under consideration by the

---

27. Theodore of Mopsuestia, *Commentarius in Ionam prophetam*, praef. and 2.8–9.

28. Theodore of Mopsuestia, *In Amosum prophetam commentarius*, 9.11–12.

29. Theodore of Mopsuestia, *Commentarius in Michaem prophetam*, 4.1–3. Theodore is treated in Devreesse, *Essai sur Théodore de Mopsueste*.

same historical people, but creative historical meaning could not be abstracted from its historical context.

The Antiochian school had no impact on the West, while Origen's middle Platonism, strengthened by Plotinus's neo-Platonism, captured Augustine and so was determinative.

### 3 Systematic Theology Continued: Augustine

The Christian exegetical and systematic theological writing of Augustine (354–430) continued in the spirit of Origen's Hellenistic accomodation. The young Augustine, a classically educated teacher of rhetoric, was attracted by style, eloquence, the persuasive power of language, and the material, sensible world of affairs in which rhetoric was used. But he was also a hearer in the Manichaean sect, which taught an esoteric salvation through isolation of the good rational soul from the unredeemably evil material part of the person with its irrational emotions, self-indulgence, and violence. The sect used a Christian vocabulary but interpreted the worldly Old Testament literalistically and rejected it as evil. Augustine recounts his torturous conversion to Christianity in books 5–9 of his *Confessions* (397). He decided that Manichaeism did not give a satisfactory account of the material world (5.3). In this unsatisfied state, he came upon the neo-Platonic writings of Plotinus and rejoiced at being liberated from having to reject the world as merely materialistic (7.9–20):

> I wondered how it was that I could appreciate beauty in material things on earth . . . and what it was that enabled me to make correct decisions about things that are subject to change. . . . and I realized that above my own mind, which was liable to change, there was the never changing, true eternity of truth. . . . For unless, by some means, [my mind] had known the immutable, it could not possibly have been certain that it was preferable to the mutable. And so, in an instant of awe, my mind attained to the sight of the God who IS (7.17).

An incredibly clear statement of the West's neo-Platonic faith!

Augustine, escorting his Christian mother to church, was already admiring Milan bishop Ambrose's preaching for its rhetorical style. With this conversion to neo-Platonism, he now also understood Ambrose's message, based as it was on the middle-Platonic theological tradition of Origen with its allegorical rather than typological interpretation of Scripture. Required catechetical scriptural study before baptism brought an additional conversion. "I believe that it was by your will that I came across those books [of Plotinus] before I studied the Scriptures, because you wished me always to remember the impression they had made on me, so that later on, when I had been chastened by your Holy Writ and my wounds had been touched by your healing hand, I should be able to see and understand the difference between presumption and confession, between those who see the goal that they must reach . . . and those who see the road to that blessed country" (7.20). Augustine's goal was still union with a God beyond history, but he was beginning to see a practical path within history. He was baptized in 387 and within a decade was bishop of Hippo in North Africa.

Augustine, like his theological predecessors, understood himself to be basing everything he wrote on Scripture. He wrote *De utilitate credendi* (391) to a former fellow hearer in Manichaeism, advocating the neo-Platonic figurative interpretation of the Old Testament he now saw in the New Testament against the literalistic Manichaean interpretation. Augustine claims the New Testament writers found four senses in Old Testament Scripture: "The whole Old Testament Scripture . . . is handed down with a four-fold sense—historical, aeteological, analogical, allegorical. . . . In all these senses our Lord Jesus Christ and his apostles used Scripture" (3.5–6).

The *historical* sense is the anecdotal sense. Augustine's example is the account of young David violating the ceremonial code to feed his hungry rebel army, seen as analogous to the hungry disciples' picking grain on the sabbath (1 Sam 21:3–6 = Matt 12:4). The New Testament itself, of course, went beyond this formal similarity and saw a typological historical continuity between the reform movements of David and Jesus, each giving reform of Israel priority over ceremonial law, the kind of historical relation outlawed by Origen.

Augustine's *aeteological* sense explains how historical events fit their own historical context. Augustine's example is Jesus' saying that Moses allowed divorce "because you were so hard-hearted" (Matt 19:8 = Deut 24:1–4), which Augustine gives an aeteological sense by claiming "Moses properly gave permission owing to the circumstances of the time, while Christ gave his commandment under different circumstances" (3.6). Augustine says these different circumstances are part of God's fixed order, not the result of any human creativity: "It would take a long time to explain the changes of the times and the order of change which is fixed and settled by a wondrous disposition of divine providence" (3.6). The Matthew passage reports Jesus contrasting his critics' torturous use of a precept on a different issue (remarriage to a first wife after divorcing a second) with his call for responsibility in social relations for one corporate body, expressed metonymically in Gen 2:24 "a man shall ... be joined to his wife, and the two shall become one flesh."

For Augustine, the *analogical* sense "shows the agreement of the two Testaments"—that is, the frequent similarities of New Testament-described events to Old Testament events (above, Chapter 2.II.2 and 3). As a neo-Platonist, Augustine could only interpret these similarities as allegories, as his neo-Platonic orientation could not recognize essence-changing metonymic relations.

For the *allegorical sense*, Augustine gives three examples of New Testament allusions to the Old Testament: Matt 12:40 "An evil ... generation asks for a sign, but no sign will be given to it except the sign of the prophet Jonah"; 1 Cor 10:1–11 "... our ancestors were all under the cloud ..."; and Gal 4:22–26 "Now Hagar is Mount Sinai in Arabia.... But the other woman corresponds to the Jerusalem above; she is free" (3.8). Again, these three examples are *formal similarities* used by the New Testament to flag typological uses of the Old (above, page 79) but are recognized by Augustine only as similarities. In the first, Augustine ignores the antithetical typological contrast of repentant Ninevah with "this" "evil ... generation." The second is a Pauline explication of typology (above, page 78). In the third, Paul claims against his legalistic opponents that the covenant calls for a delegated creative freedom rather than passive obedience. Like Origen, Augustine's three non-literal senses of Scripture all describe formal-similarity flags, but his neo-Platonic base cannot recognize the thus flagged corporate interactive historical relation.

Augustine provides a systematic rationale for biblical interpretation in his *De doctrina Christiana* (396). He explains and advocates seven rules of interpretation given by the contemporaneous Donatist theologian Tyconius in *Liber Regularum*. Augustine illustrates the first rule, "On the Lord and his Body," by saying (3.31.44) that Old Testament passages sometimes refer simultaneously to both Christ and the church, as in Gen 13:15 = Gal 3:16 "all the land that you see I will give to you and your seed," and sometimes they refer to them separately, as in Isa 61:10 = Rev 21:2 "... as a bridegroom decks himself with a garland, and as a bride adorns herself with her jewels," and in the latter case we should take care "which applies to Christ and which applies to the Church." These two examples reproduce the formal analogies flagging the typologies of Galatians 3:16 and Rev 21:2, but Tyconius's first rule does not specify a typological relation; it does not expect a diachronic internally interactive relation within a continuing historical community.

For the fourth rule "On species and genus" (3.34.47–49), Augustine says that a "species" (a particular city or people) is a part of the "genus" (the whole human race), ignoring as he admits "the difference between a part and a species," and that some things written literally in the Scriptures about a species are only rightly understood when extended to the genus. "When a transition is made from the species to the genus, as happens sometimes when the Scripture has been considering the species for some time, the reader should maintain a vigilant attitude lest he seek in the species what may be better and more certainly found in the genus." As an example, Augustine understands the *condemnation* of Israel, Ezek 36:17–19 "So I poured out my wrath upon them for the blood that they had shed . . . ," as applying specifically to Israel and "not exceeding the species." However, he takes the immediately following prediction of the *restoration* of Israel, Ezek 36:23–29 "I will remove from your body the heart of stone and give you a heart of flesh" as "exceeding the species" and applying to the universally baptized known world of the Roman Empire: "No one who reads this passage doubts that the 'laver of regeneration,' [Titus 3:5] which we now see given to all peoples, is here promised." Whereas Ezekiel predicts a change of heart in the corporate body of the particular nation Israel so that it will better represent God to the other nations, Augustine's fourth rule explicitly predicts a universal generic change of heart in each individual: "This spiritual Israel is to be distinguished from that carnal Israel [and] is one people by newness of grace, not by nobility of descent, by their minds and not by their race." Thus, "exceeding the species" is not intensifying typology within a continuing historical community as in the New Testament but is a genericizing jump away from corporate historical Israel to a generic humanity. The fourth rule also simplifies cosmological control of the world by dropping Platonism's organic ethnic and class distinctions. The result makes all human relations generic—a simplification of the cosmological perspective generally continuing to the present. In contrast, Scripture, from the birth of Israel in Gen 12:3 "all the families," to the birth of the church in Acts 2 "each . . . in our own native language," takes organic social distinctions among classes and cultures (both synchronic and diachronic) as part of the community structure needed for corporate creative interaction.

Augustine's interpretation of Old Testament passages, unrelated to any New Testament flag for typology, is pure allegory—like those of Origen. For example, Song 4:2 "Your teeth are like a flock of shorn ewes that have come up from the washing, all of which bear twins . . ." is interpreted by Augstine as, "the teeth of the church cutting off men from their errors, . . . as shorn sheep having put aside the burdens of the world like so much fleece, and as ascending from the washing, which is baptism, all to create twins, which are the two precepts of love . . ." (2.6.7).

Augustine also allegorizes the Old Testament repeatedly for paraenetic purposes as, for example, his use of Exod 24:19: "Moses was on the mountain for forty days and forty nights" as admonishment for Christians "to live chastely and continently without temporal delight, or, that is, to fast for forty days" (2.16.25). Augustine's interpretation here is not paraenetic typology, but number-symbolic allegory independent of any historical relation among the events. The number 40 has the symbolic meaning $40 = 4(3 + (3 + 4))$, where the first 4 is time (the four seasons), 3 is God (the Trinity), (3 + 4) is human being (3 parts of life: all our heart, all our soul, and all our mind; and 4 parts of the body), and the paraenetic application comes by multiplying time by the sum of God and human being to get "living chastely and continently without temporal delight."

With Augustine, the relation between God and humanity is not corporate in two interrelated respects: no independent creative contribution from the human side is allowed, and humanity is treated as a collection of generic selves rather than an interacting society. Both absences show up in Augustine's scriptural exegesis. They come together in his doctrine of sin and grace, developed in his controversy with his contemporary, Pelagius.

Augustine exegetes Rom 5:12 in the Old Latin version: "sin came into the world through one man, and death came through sin, and so death spread to all in which all have sinned."[30] Augustine exegetes the

---

30. Augustine, *De peccatorum meritis et remissione*, 1.10; *De nuptiis et concupiscentia*, 2.15; and twenty five other passages in thirteen other anti-Pelagian writings in *NPNF* 5.

passage thus: "By the evil will of that one man all sinned in him, since all were that one man, from whom, therefore, they individually derived original sin."[31] He says the passage means either "in which *sin* all have sinned" or "in which *man* all have sinned" and in either case "this indicates propagation, not imitation."[32] Imitation is Pelagius's term for cultural transmission of sin. In contrast, Paul's Greek reads, "in that all [ἐφ' ᾧ πάντες] have sinned"; that is, all sin by interactive participating membership in the dysfunctional human community *adam*—not by Augustine's "propagation" nor by Pelagius's "imitation" (both generic relations taking *Adam* as generic first individual). But for Genesis and Paul, *Adam* is the ongoing interacting human community, and its fall is the historical decrease in responsible essence-building interaction among members over time as economic units become larger and impersonal. Scriptural narrative indirectly describes an interactive transmission of culture using both nature and nurture, a biologically transmitted ability of persons to acculturate through participation in their culture's creative intrinsic interaction. Pelagius's generic imitation is a gesture toward the corporate.

Augustine says baptism remits the guilt of original sin, allowing an individual to be in relation with God, "but as many of them as become parents, beget children from the circumstance that they have not yet put off the entire remains of their old nature."[33] In one place he says more specifically that the act of procreation is still controlled by lust rather than individual will, hence the children are born with original sin,[34] to be corrected afterwards with baptism. Here we have an extreme example of the neo-Platonic (and Manichaean) unredeemability of the human urge to engage creatively in communal relations, and the need to purify the individual by separation from them. It is an implicit recognition and explicit rejection of the creative potential within human communal relations, a potential that is an anathema to the neo-Platonic project but is the central arena of the biblical project.

And, because sin is generic, the grace to overcome it is also generic: "It is . . . by a secret, wonderful, and ineffable power operating within,

---

31. Augustine, *De nuptiis et concupiscientia*, 2.15.
32. Augustine, *De peccatorum meritis*, 1.11; 1.10.
33. Ibid., 2.11.
34. Augustine, *De nuptiis et concupiscientia*, 1.27.

that God works in men's hearts not only revelations of the truth, but also good dispositions of the will."[35]

Augustine treats the relation between human free choice and divine power more subtly than Origen does. Augustine reports Pelagius saying, "We distinguish . . . three things . . . . We put in the first place *ability*, in the second *volition*; and in the third *actuality*. . . . The first . . . properly belongs to God, who has bestowed it on his creature; the other two . . . must be referred to man, because they flow forth from the fountain of the will. For his willing, therefore, and doing a good work, the praise belongs to man."[36] Augustine disagrees; he says the second and third also belong to God and quotes Phil 2:13 "it is God who is at work in you, enabling you both to will and to work for his good pleasure."[37] God "works all things to the point that He works in us to will also."[38] "God works in men's hearts to incline their wills to whatsoever way He wills."[39]

The issue here is not the modern one of empirical determinism *versus* free will. Both Pelagius and Augustine hold that the individual has free choice against the common fatalism of the age. Both ask, *what does God require to be pleased?*, thus giving God and the individual each a part in what happens. But for the rather stoically oriented Pelagius, God deals with the individual at arm's length—he gave free choice to the individual at creation and is now pleased if the individual can manage to use it to do a good work. At the other extreme, neo-Platonic Augustine assigns the individual a more passive role—God gives free choice but works things out so the individual decides to do it God's way.

Neither recognizes the biblically proclaimed internal relation between humanity and God requiring creative, innovative contributions from both sides—a relation inexpressible within Stoic or neo-Platonic conceptuality. Both assign some activity to the individual, but because both maintain that God is the only source of truth, salvation for the individual means drawing near to this truth, not helping to create it. In a *corporate* relation, the free choices of the parties are intrinsically limited by the (thus, also limited) free choices of the others; so that the relation is a joint creation. Accordingly, Scripture says that God shows "stead-

35. Augustine, *De gratia Christi*, 1.25.
36. Ibid., 1.5.
37. Ibid., 1.6.
38. Augustine, *De praedestinatione sanctorum*, 18.37.
39. Augustine, *De gratia et libero arbitrio*, 21.43.

fast love"; he limits his own free choices to allow humanity to exercise its delegated "dominion" (its delegated responsibility to maintain creative multilaterally internal community interaction), which constitutes salvation for the community. Thus, both human creative responsibility and human salvation are delegated to historic human communities, not isolated individuals. Since neo-Platonic theology has God relating with each individual separately, such a historic social human creativity and salvation cannot even be conceived, much less allowed. The best Augustine can do is to use original sin to ontologize the individual's experience of being enmeshed in the dysfunctionality of the community. Augustine's role for humanity is passive compared to, say, the description in Gen 18:23–32 of the nation Israel (represented by Abraham) winning an argument with God, or the claim by Paul (Gal 5:1) "Christ has set us free" from a micro-managing law. Scripture gives to humanity (when understood as an internally interacting body) both a responsibility and a corresponding freedom that if recognized would appear to a Platonic religion as blasphemy.

Yet, Augustine is closer to Scripture than Pelagius is. Augustine uses a first-person psychological analysis within the generic individual to draw as close as he can to the biblical view without adopting its corporate perspective. He understands free choice to be choosing what one desires rather than acting under compulsion. God influences one's free choice by making additional choices known or by making them desirable. "Men are unwilling to do what is right, either because what is right is unknown to them, or because it is unpleasant to them. . . . But that what was hidden may come to light, and what was unpleasant may be made agreeable, is of the grace of God which helps the wills of men."[40] Furthermore, Augustine continues, one should choose for the desirable rather than against the undesirable. "You should not be driven to live a good life by the fear of punishment, but you should be persuaded to it by the attraction and love of justice."[41] In fact, "he is guilty in will who would willingly do what it is unlawful to do, but who does not do it because he cannot escape punishment."[42] The unlawful may be a compulsion rather than a choice, as in the old struggle against human passions from Manichaean days: "The human will . . . cannot be called free so long as it is subject to the assaults and enslavement of

---

40. Augustine, *De peccatorum meritis*, 2.17 (26).

41. Augustine, *Epistola*, 166.

42. Ibid., 165.

the passions."[43] A positive free choice is closely connected with grace. "Do we then by grace make void free will? God forbid! Nay, rather we establish free will.... For neither is the law fulfilled except by free will; but by the law is the knowledge of sin, by faith the acquisition of grace against sin, by grace the healing of the soul from the disease of sin, by the health of the soul freedom of will, by free will the love of righteousness, by love of righteousness the accomplishment of the law."[44]

This pastoral bishop writes differently from the young academic just finding the church. His first-person conception of love is closer to Scripture than, say, Heidegger's authentic self. But Augustine's love is still a "love of righteousness," not an interactive relation with God internally related to one's interactive relation with neighbor, not a love of social creativity and responsibility, and not a love of flesh and blood. Later we will find the passivity of Augustine's "righteousness" to be quite active in the twentieth century, for example, in Karl Barth's "God does not need helpers" (below, page 243).

The sack of Rome by the Goths in 410 drove traditional Roman aristocrats to North Africa, bringing to this remote province their elitist intellectual attachment to the classical pagan epic tradition. Against this influence, Augustine began in 413 a new work, *The City of God*, in which he contrasted the potentially universal Christian community with classical Roman culture, to the disadvantage of the latter. His comparing two histories, the pagan Roman epic and the scriptural Hebrew-Christian epic, forced Augustine, uncharacteristically for a neo-Platonist, to allow some sort of historical meaning to both.

Augustine seeks to change the meaning of (to secularize) the account of the founding of Rome. For example: "How is it that neither Juno ... nor Venus herself, could assist the children of the loved Aeneas [son of Venus and reputed ancestor of the Romans] to find wives by some right and equitable means? ...The Romans, then, conquered that they might, with hands stained in the blood of their fathers-in-law, wrench the miserable girls from their embrace—girls who dared not weep for their slain parents, for fear of offending their victorious husbands" (3.13). "Why allege to me the mere names and words of 'glory' and 'victory'? ... Away, then, with these deceitful masks, these delud-

---

43. Ibid., 163.

44. Augustine, *De spiritu et littera*, 30 (52). Historian Peter Brown in *Augustine of Hippo*, 365–75, displays this push against neo-Platonic limitations.

ing whitewashes" (3:14). Augustine asks: if the great Assyrian kingdom lasted twelve hundred and forty years "without the aid of the gods, why is the . . . [less] long duration of the Roman empire to be ascribed to the Roman gods?" (4.7).

In contrast to the pagan tradition of glorious Rome in an otherwise barbarian world, Augustine describes a much purer, if less pretentious biblical tradition, also with two communities: the city of God and the city of the world:

> Cain was the first born, and he belonged to the city of men; after him was born Abel, who belonged to the city of God. For as in the individual . . . each man . . . is first of all born of Adam evil and carnal, and becomes good and spiritual only afterwards, when he is grafted into Christ by regeneration: so was it in the human race as a whole. . . . Accordingly, it is recorded of Cain that he built a city, but Abel, being a sojourner, built none. For the city of the saints is above, although here below it begets citizens, in whom it sojourns till the time of its reign (15.1).

Analogous to the organic harmony of the parts of the human body is the peace between humanity and God, the peace of the family and of the civil body. "The peace of the body then consists in the duly proportioned arrangement of its parts. . . . Peace between man and God is the well-ordered obedience of faith to eternal law. . . . Domestic peace is the well-ordered concord between those of the family who rule and those who obey. Civil peace is a similar concord among the citizens. . . . The peace of all things is the tranquility of order. Order is the distribution which allots things equal and unequal, each to its own place" (19.13). Thus, Augustine, coming under the necessity of analyzing community, does so by comparing its order with the organic unity of the individual human body understood as "duly proportioned" according to "eternal law." But that corresponding order in the earthly city, a law understood as Platonic *logos*, requires the obedience of its members. "The earthly city, which does not live by faith, seeks an earthly peace, and the end it proposes, in the well-ordered concord of civic obedience and rule, is the combination of men's wills to obtain the things which are helpful to this life" (19.17). But Augustine does not relax his neo-Platonic cosmological requirement that "the changes of the times and the order of change . . . is fixed and settled by a wondrous disposition of divine providence" (above, page 179). The defective worldly order is still influenced by God:

"though the miserable . . . are severed from that tranquility of order . . . , nevertheless, inasmuch as they are deservedly and justly miserable, they are by their very misery connected with order. . . . they are wretched because, although not wholly miserable, they are not in that place where any mixture of misery is impossible" (19.13).

As said, the heavenly community participates temporarily in the humanly created structures of the earthly community while on pilgrimage here. "The heavenly city, or rather the part of it which sojourns on earth and lives by faith, makes use of this peace only because it must, until this mortal condition which necessitates it shall pass away. Consequently, so long as it lives like a captive and a stranger in the earthly city, . . . it makes no scruple to obey the laws of the earthly city" (19.17). "Use money as, in an inn, a traveler uses the table, the cup, the pitcher, the bed: as one who is going to leave, not going to stay."[45] Augustine recounts the history of this pilgrimage from Abel through the Old Testament epic, the incarnation of Christ, and the persecutions of Christians, to the relative success of the church in his time (15–18). Finally, at the last judgment the citizens of the earthly community will be condemned, and those of the heavenly community will have the perfect peace that was not possible while they were pilgrims (20–21).

Augustine has implicitly recognized in the old Roman aristocratic tradition the understanding of Rome as community, "city," that transmitted through its history an ordered tradition, a tradition he had grown up in and now found himself implicitly trying to amend by means of interaction with another ordered human community—"city," the church, in which he held institutional leadership authority as bishop, itself an implicitly interactive role. He found himself involved in a struggle between two communities with different traditions, to both of which he belonged. The accommodations at the inn were to be abandoned, yet also to be left in order for the next guest. Yet, ultimately, Augustine rejects what he has recognized: he maintains a potentially cosmologically conforming Christian community, generically gathering members from among the condemned, and waiting for escape to a perfectly neo-Platonically ordered other world.

In contrast, the biblical people of God do not wait for escape from this world: they are called to live interactively in this world; they are responsible under God for improving their interactive community struc-

---

45. Augustine, *In Ioannis evangelium tractatus*, 40.10, FOTC 88.

ture by working within that worldly structure itself. Augustine takes the extreme generic position at the sect pole of the servant-sect range in apocalyptic (above, page 134). He has managed to make all Christendom into a righteous remnant waiting to leave the world.

## III THE AUGUSTINIAN HERITAGE: THOMAS AND LUTHER

Augustine's skirmish with the meaning of history in his reply to the Roman epic glanced on the conflict between the Western cosmological perspective and the biblical corporate perspective. We meet now in Thomas Aquinas a reconciliation of a different ambivalence, this one within the Western cosmological perspective itself, between other-worldly neo-Platonism and this-worldly Aristotelianism. In the following section we will find Luther dividing the church at the Alps by vigorously returning from Thomas's Aristotle to Augustine's neo-Platonism.

### 1 Adding Aristotle to Neo-Platonism: Thomas Aquinas

Augustine's comprehensive statement of the neo-Platonic theological settlement, made just at the disintegration of the Roman Empire, remained dominant for eight centuries in European theology. But in the thirteenth century, an active Aristotelian tradition passing through the Arabic philosophers Ibn Sina (Avicenna) (980–1037) and Ibn Roschd (Averroës) (c.1126–1198) tantalized European academic thought: It offered an understanding of the sensible world by human transcendental reason rather than by divine revelation. Theologians resisted, but a synthesis of *logos*-based neo-Platonism and Aristotle's transcendental reason, as written in his *de Anima*, was accomplished by Thomas Aquinas (1225–1274) in his *Summa Theologiae*,[46] a theological system with room for both active human reason and the reception of divine revelation. Thomas says, "The human intellect has a form, namely the intelligible light itself, which is sufficient of itself for the knowledge of certain intelligible realities—those, namely, acquaintances with which it can reach by way of sensible realities. But the human intellect cannot know more profound intelligible realities unless it is perfected by a stronger light, say the light of faith or prophecy; and this is called the light of grace, inasmuch as it supplements nature" (1a2ae.109.1).

---

46. Thomas Aquinas, *Summa Theologiae*. Translations are from the Blackfriars edition.

In this synthesis, Thomas claims a human ability to know the world, gained empirically through the five senses as in Aristotle's *De anima* (and again after five more centuries in modern Kant's *Critique of Pure Reason*). But the relation with God, known through revelation or prophecy, remains Augustinian and neo-Platonic: "Prophecy is firstly and principally a knowledge; prophets in fact know realities which are remote from the knowledge of men. . . . But because 1 Corinthians [14:12] says . . . 'strive to excel for the building up of the Church,' it follows that prophecy secondarily consists of utterance or speech, . . . and [prophets] proclaim this knowledge for the edification of others; as is said in Isaiah [21:10], 'What I have heard from the Lord of hosts, the God of Israel, I announce to you'" (2a2ae.171.1). "In prophecy it is needed that the capacity of a mind should be raised to the point of perceiving divine truth. . . . This . . . is brought about by a movement of the Holy Spirit. . . . Revelation brings about the removal of the veils of ignorance and obscurity" (ad 4). Scripture discloses revelation: "Before all else the New Law is the very grace of the Holy Spirit, given to those who believe in Christ. . . . the New Law is first and foremost an inward law, and secondarily a written law. . . . There is nothing in the written text of the Gospel except what is concerned with the grace of the Holy Spirit, either by disposing us for it or by providing directions for the exercise of this grace" (1a2ae.106.1). Revelation remains neo-Platonic, a fixed body of teaching, conveyed generically to each individual.

The *Summa* is a systematic treatise. Thomas lists (1a.1.10) the four conventional medieval senses of Scripture: literal; allegorical to relate the two testaments; tropological or moral; and anagogical or eschatological. He reconciles this list with Augustine's list of New Testament uses of the Old Testament in *De utilitate credendi* (above, page 178), and then ignores both lists. He uses several thousand biblical passages in constructing his theological system; but because he is synthesizing, these passages are mixed with a similar number of passages from Aristotle, other philosophers, Augustine, and other theologians. He draws on all parts of both testaments—from doctrinal passages in Sirach, Paul, and John, to passionate poetic praise in the Psalms—treating all as abstract doctrine. His drawing a systematic theology from the Bible is not a new allegorizing method—he follows the neo-Platonic systemizing tradition going back to Origen (above, page 173). He ignores any relation of the meaning of quoted passages to their literary context or the historical and cultural situation of their writers. He offers no typological interpretation, nor does he ever borrow the formal-similarity aspect of New Testament typological use of the Old Testament (above, page 79) as Origen and Augustine did. He does not share Augustine's slender biblically induced late interest in salvation history. Thomas's treatise on the understanding of the sensible world by unaided human reason (1a.75–89) amounts to a philosophy of mind (how human beings understand the world) rather than an epistemology (whether they understand it correctly). This treatise is based on Aristotle's *De anima*, the medieval textbook on philosophy of mind, rather than his *Posterior Analytics*, the textbook on epistemology. Thomas follows the *De anima* as a middle view between the pre-Socratic Ionians and the Platonists, both of which hold that only *like* can affect *like*. For the Ionian Empedocles, the mind can understand the material world because both are material; both are made of earth, air, fire, and water—while the Platonists claim the mind is immaterial and can only know the immaterial Platonic Forms. Thomas, taking Aristotle's middle way, sets forth a two-level cognition with a *material sense* and an *immaterial intellect* that is able to understand a *material* world *immaterially* (1a.84.6).

In the classical view, a material thing has immaterial form and material matter. Its *substantial form* is what makes it be the kind of thing it is; its *matter* is what distinguishes it from other things. The substantial form of, say, a vase is what there is about it that makes it *be* what we call "vase" (such as esthetic shape and a place for flowers). In addition, this vase also has *accidental forms*, like particular shape, color, or fragility—forms which can vary among vases. Accidental forms help distinguish one vase from another, but different matter distinguishes two vases with identical accidental forms.

In Plato, all vases reflect one *universal* substantial Form for vase, existing abstractly and independently of whether there are any particular vases at all (hence *Form* is written with 'F' not 'f'). Whereas, what *exists* for Aristotle and Thomas are only *particular* vase forms, with each having the form of a particular material vase. Both Plato and Aristotle claim that to know a thing intellectually is to know it in an abstract, universal, immaterial way—to know its form. With Plato, each human psyche or "soul" is born with pre-existing *a priori* knowledge of all Forms, enabling it to recognize and understand the universal Forms of vase, cat, beauty, and the like—whenever such things present themselves to the senses. But for Aristotle and Thomas, there are no independently existing universal Forms, only particular forms of material objects; and when an object is apprehended by the senses, the human psyche must actively create or *abstract* a non-material universal form from the impression of the object's particular material form on the senses in order to understand it. As Thomas puts it:

> For Plato, the [F]orms of things in the physical world subsisted non-materially and could therefore be understood, since it is non-materiality that makes a thing actually able to be understood. These he called species or ideas. And he argued that physical matter was formed by participation in these . . . . and also that our minds were formed by participation in them, so that they could have knowledge of the kinds and types of things. But Aristotle did not think that the natural forms in the physical world subsist immaterially. . . . So it was necessary to posit a power of the intellectual order which made things actually able to be understood by abstracting the thought of them from their material conditions. This is why we speak of the [*active intellect (intellectus agens)*] (*Summa* 1a.79.3, Aristotle, *De anima* 3.5).

Thus, Thomas rejects the Platonic Forms and moves to an Aristotelian-based theology, a foretaste of the modern movement position to come four hundred years later.

Animals and human beings share similar *sensory powers*, passive and active. The five external senses (sight, hearing, etc.) are passive; they receive particular forms of material objects impressed on them by the objects. The four internal senses are active; they are the *unifying* sense combining sense impressions from different external senses; the *cogitative* sense (or, for animals, instinct) calculating among particular sense impressions; the *sense memory* storing them; and the *imagination* fantasizing, decontextualizing, and combining them as *phantasms* (*phantasmata*)—for example, combining "gold" and "mountain" to imagine a gold mountain (*Summa* 1a.12.9 ad 2; 1a.78.3–4; Aristotle, *De anima* 3.4).

But the human being, the "rational animal," differs from the other animals by also having *intellectual powers*—the ability to think in terms of abstract universal forms (here agreeing with Plato). These powers take the form of an *active intellect* (abstracting forms from phantasms in the sensory area) and a *receptive intellect (intellectus possibilis)*, or abstract memory, for storing them. This receptive intellect is initially a "blank page" (*tabula rasa*) (*Summa* 1a.79.2; *De anima* 3.4 430a1) (here differing from Platonism in not having already known them eternally) that retains abstract thought produced by the active intellect, including its abstracted concepts, judgments about them, and skills such as language competence (1a.79.4; *De anima* 3.5).

The material object actively impresses its particular form directly on the passive external sense, so that the form in the knower is the same as in the known. Similarly, the active intellect abstracts directly from the phantasm in the imagination to realize the universal form of the object. Thomas says, "We read in Aristotle that the sensible actualized is the sense in activity, and the intelligible actualized is the intellect in activity (*sensibile in actu est sensus in actu, et intelligibile in actu est intellectus in actu*)" (*Summa* 1a.14.2; *De anima* 3.2 426a16; 3.4 430a3). Sugar's tasting sweet *is* the tongue's tasting sweetness. The passive external senses, unless sick, make no change in the form of the thing sensed, although the active internal senses may affect the final understanding (1a.17.2). This direct view of perception bypasses the epistemological question of whether we understand things correctly.

The human intellect not only abstracts from the phantasms of material things, but refers back to their phantasms when thinking about them because the abstract intellect does not picture them itself. "Our intellect both abstracts species from [phantasms]—in so far as it considers the natures of things as universal—and yet, at the same time, understands these in [phantasms], since it cannot understand even the things from which it abstracts species without turning to [phantasms]" (1a.85.1 ad 5). To deal with a world of material things, sense and intellect must work together. "Cognitive faculties are proportioned to their objects. . . . The proper object of the human intellect . . . is a nature or 'whatness' found in corporeal matter . . . . [which] cannot be known truly and completely except in so far as it exists in a particular thing. . . . The intellect must needs turn to [phantasms] in order to look at universal natures existing in particular things" (*Summa* 1a.84.7; *De anima* 3.7 431a16, b2). And, "When we want to help someone understand something, we propose examples to him so that he can form images for himself in order to understand" (1a.84.7).

In addition, non-material realities, including God, can be understood only by turning to phantasms: "We know incorporeal realities, which have no [phantasms], by analogy with sensible bodies, which do have [them] . . . . God we know . . . as cause about which we ascribe the utmost perfection and negate any limit" (1a.84.7 ad 3). Thus, we understand incorporeal things only through *perfection* and *negation* (*per excessum et per remotionem*) of sensible things—that is, through intensifying and antithetical *analogy* with them. For instance, once knowing God as cause (through reason or revelation); we can then understand him through intensifying and antithetical analogies between sensible effect and incorporeal cause (for example, intensifying, "God is good" and antithetical, "God is *in*finite").

Thomas relates thinking and language. With Aristotle, he holds that all rational, "intellectual" activity is either a "definition" or a "judgment," a *thinking of* or *thinking that* (for example, thinking of an apple or thinking that an apple is red). Thus, every abstract thought could be expressed in language—*thinking of* expressed with words like "apple" and *thinking that* with sentences like "The apple is red." As Thomas puts it, the active intellect, informed by phantasms from the imagination, "formulates either a definition [*intelligentia indivisibilium*] or else an affirmative or negative statement [*intelligentia composito et divisio*], which is then signified by words. Thus the meaning which a name signifies is a definition, and an enunciation . . . signifies the intellect's combining or separating" (1a.85.2 ad 3). This implies a close correspondence between two species-specific abilities in human beings: the ability to think abstractly and the ability to use language. But thinking remains primary: "Words are signs for thoughts and thoughts are likenesses of things" (1a.13.1; Aristotle *De interpretatione* 1.1 16a3).

Before Wittgenstein in 1953 (above, chapter 1.IV.4), Western philosophy has always taken language as secondary, as only a report on individual human thought. Language only names or describes forms that are already in the mind of the speaker. With Plato and Augustine these forms are part of cosmological order, already in the individual's intellect ready to be recalled, or reminded of, by Scripture. But for Aristotle and Thomas the memory at birth is a *tabula rasa*, and the forms are sensed as part of the sensible world and then abstracted by the individual's active intellect and stored in the memory. Kant's twelve inherent human categories (above, page 15) systemize Aristotle's categories and support Thomas's intellectual synthesizing of sense intuitions into judgments. Yet all of the forms and categories are fixed prior to human community. But Wittgenstein (above, pages 47–53) finds the source of the abstracted forms to be the community language, not the cosmos nor the individual mind. Individuals learn the forms by learning their community language. "How do I know that this color is red?—It could be an answer to say: 'I have learnt English.'" Members then participate interactively, using the language thus far created, in the continuing creation of further abstractions represented by new words or extended meanings for existing words. The forms do not dictate the culture as in the cosmological and generic perspectives, but are tools culturally fashioned by the community to facilitate its own interaction. The meaning of language *is* its use as tools in community interaction. These tools, and indeed the toolroom, the *tabula rasa* where they are stored, belong to the community. If one forgets a word, one can ask a neighbor. Such a community origin for language, first recognized explicitly in Western philosophy sixty years ago, was already being proclaimed three millennia ago in the middle East in Gen 2:19: "whatever [האדם, *ha adam*, the adam, *the human community*] called every living creature, that was its name."

In a cosmologically oriented system, the substantial form of a thing (its essence in the terminology of chapter 1) is fixed, so that any *relation* between things can at most change their accidental forms, not the intrinsic essence of either. Thus, there are *no intrinsic relations*—all relations are *extrinsic*. Among these remaining extrinsic relations, Thomas calls a relation *real* for one of its parties if it involves the party materially (for example, being attracted gravitationally) or *logical* if the party is only related conceptually (for example, being known unawares by someone else) (1a.28.1). Sometimes each party is in real relation with the other (for example, a thing being changed and the thing changing it), and sometimes the relation is real to one but not the other, (for example, real to a person knowing another but not real to the person being known unawares). All relations with God are non-reciprocal in this way: "being related to God is a reality in creatures, but being related to creatures is not a reality in God.... we can apply words implying temporal sequence and change, not because of any change in him but because of a change in the creatures" (1a.13.7). Thus, no relation is intrinsic or internal, and a relation with God is at most "real" in one direction. In contrast, the Old Testament, not written within the cosmological perspective, is free to portray a transcendent God who nevertheless condescends to enter two-way real and bilaterally intrinsic relations with humanity, as he wishes its members to do with one another.

For Thomas, besides the apprehending powers of sense and intellect, the human psyche also has appetitive powers—the potential to be drawn passively toward some good or end. *Love* is the effect of such attraction. It is "an effect produced in the [appetitive power] by the desirable object" (1a.2ae.26.2). Sense appetites are drawn toward things known through the senses, intellectual appetites toward things known through the intellect—including abstract goods like knowledge and virtue—and particulars sharing those goods (1a.80.2).

Love is "wanting good things for someone," be it oneself or another. The thing wanted is the object of love-of-desire (*amor concupiscentiae*), the one it is wanted for is the object of love-of-friendship (*amor amicitiae*) (1a2ae.26.4; Aristotle, *Ethics* 8–9). The first can be love of oneself or of another based on convenience or pleasure for oneself (ad 3). The second is based on similarity between oneself and another: "two men are at one in their membership of the species 'humanity,' and two white men at one in . . . 'whiteness.' The result is that the affections of the one are bent upon the other as being one with himself, and he wishes well to the other as to himself. . . . But a person's love for himself is greater than his love of any other person, for he is one with himself in actual substance, whereas he is one with another person only through some similarity of form" (1a2ae.27.3). Both kinds of love are based on self-love.

To *will* is to be affected by an intellectual appetite. Thomas says the will of necessity seeks the individual's ultimate fulfillment, but has a choice, a power of free decision, in selecting among the many possible means toward that end (1a.82.1, 83.1). "The will can tend towards nothing that is not conceived to be good. But because there are many kinds of good thing it is not by any necessity determined to any particular one" (1a.82.2 ad 1). Although true happiness consists of being joined to God, "before the certitude enjoyed through seeing God proves the necessity of this link the will clings by necessity neither to God nor to the things of God. But the will of one who sees God's essence necessarily clings to God, because then we cannot help willing to be happy. Obviously, then, the will does not by necessity will whatever it wills" (1a.82.2). Thomas is compatible with Augustine.

Thomas calls *sanctifying grace* the grace from God by which an individual is united to God and non-sanctifying (or *freely bestowed grace*) the grace by which one individual cooperates with another so the other also might be brought to God (1a2ae.111.1). Of the two, sanctifying grace is primary (1a2ae.111.5 *ad* 2). Thus, the relation with God is fundamentally with the generic individual and secondarily with usefulness in bringing other generic individuals into relation with God. Thomas remains within neo-Platonic orthodoxy.

Thomas, following Aristotle's *Ethics*, defines *justification* as a movement toward justice. With Aristotle, justice can be taken *literally* as right order in an individual's action toward another individual or for the common good of the group (*Ethics* 5.1), or *metaphorically* as right order in an individual's interior disposition (*Ethics* 5.11)—the latter of which Thomas takes in neo-Platonic fashion as subjection of the lower human powers to human reason and human reason to God. Both these senses of justification are generic: they are defined in terms of the individual. Whereas Aristotle emphasizes the first sense, Thomas moves quickly to the second—defining sin as a defect in interior disposition toward God—so that justification is the removal of a defect in that disposition (*Summa* 1a2ae.113.1).

The removal of sin is reconciliation, but a reconciliation that does not make a change in God as the offended party. "An offense is only forgiven someone when the mind of the offended party is reconciled to the offender. And so sin is said to be forgiven us when God is reconciled to us. Now this reconciliation and peace consists in the love with which God loves us. But God's love, as far as the divine act is concerned, is eternal and immutable; but as to the effect which it impresses on us, it is sometimes interrupted, namely when we sometimes fall away from it and sometimes regain it" (1a2ae.113.2). As for the change in the offender, God respects his creation; reconciliation with an individual does not violate the free choice of the individual. "Now God moves all things according to the mode proper to each. . . . And so the motion from God towards justice does not take place without a movement of free choice in someone who can exercise free choice; but he infuses the gift of justifying grace in such a way that at the same time he also moves the free choice to accept the gift of grace" (1a2ae.113.3). Although for God the relation between God and sinner is not "real" but only "logical" (above, page 194); the relation does require a choice by the sinner, unlike, say, gravitational pull, hence within the sinner sanctification is in "real" relation to justification. Luther, below, will disagree.

This sketch of Thomas's system will have to suffice. And system it is. Definitions of terms act as axioms around which are based the categorizations, the taxonomies, and the pervasive interrelations of the system—unlike definitions in current dictionaries that give usages of terms without rationalizing them into one system. Origen and Augustine allegorized the corporate worldly biblical religion into an otherworldly neo-Platonized religion for the passive generic individual. Thomas passed this tradition on under the rubric of revelation, but under the rubric of reason he used Aristotle to bring it back to the active world, and brought the two together through the intellect's turning to phantasms even for knowing God—a remarkable synthesis of opposing Western traditions. Yet thirteenth-century academic culture, with its generic parameters, lacked the resources for reaching biblical human solidarity: it could only reach a proto-bourgeois world of active human dealings at arms length.

## 2 Back to the Bible or Back to Augustine? Martin Luther

Martin Luther (1483-1546) was an Augustinian Professor of Biblical Theology at the University of Wittenberg from 1512 to his death. He inherited Thomas's Scholasticism, a synthesis of Augustine and Aristotle, and its partial undoing in the nominalism of John Duns Scotus (1265-1308), William of Occam (c.1298-c.1350), and, closer to Luther's time, Gabriel Biel (?-1495). But Luther himself was no synthesizer; he was a radical and passionate iconoclast determined to smash the scholastic system in order to recover what he believed was a pure biblical gospel of God's forgiveness. His anti-systematic position was already clear in his university *Lectures on Romans* on Paul's letter to the Romans in 1515-1516, written two years before the Reformation. The Reformation was a Germanic revolt against Italian power politics and church abuses triggered November 1, 1517 by the surreptitious translation into German, forwarding to the local bishop, and posting for university discussion of Luther's Latin agenda, the "Ninety-five Theses on the Power of Indulgences."

General councils of the Western church at Vienne (1311-1312), Constance (1414-1418), Basle (1431-1447), and Fifth Lateran (1512-1517) all tried without success to curb an increasing entrepreneurial focus in the church's institutional life, with bishoprics, abbotships, sacraments, licenses, dispensations, and indulgences all for sale—with God's favor treated as a marketable commodity. Luther was well aware of the abuses—"The worship and the service of God have become a market place" (*Lectures on Romans* p. 339, on Rom 12:8)—but he believed a more basic reform was needed, a change in theological education away from medieval scholastic system and back to the Bible and church fathers. "I just simply believe that it is impossible to reform the church unless the canon law, the decretals, scholastic theology, philosophy, and logic as they are now taught are eradicated, and . . . . the pure study of the Bible and the holy fathers recovered"[47] He believed he had found the original gospel message in Scripture and Augustine. In a preface to an anonymous anti-systematic treatise *Theologia deutsch* Luther wrote, "Except the Bible and Saint Augustine, there has not appeared a book from which I have and will learn more what God, Christ, humanity, and all things are."[48] The Wittenberg theological faculty agreed with their colleague Luther, and months before the "95 Theses" Luther wrote, "Our theology and St. Augustine progress well, and are dominant in our university . . . . Aristotle moves slowly toward his imminent end. . . . the only lecturers who can hope for students are those who are committed to teaching the Bible or St. Augustine, or other neglected doctors of the Church."[49] Wittenberg University rapidly became the largest in Germany, with its graduates spreading the new perspective over Europe.

The first sentence of *Lectures on Romans* announces Luther's *theological revolution* against the Scholastic theological settlement. "The sum and substance of this letter is: to pull down, to pluck up, and to destroy [Jer 1:10] all wisdom and righteousness of the flesh (i.e., of whatever importance they may be in the sight of men and even in our own eyes), no matter how heartily and sincerely they may be practiced, and to implant, establish [Jer 1:10], and make large the reality of sin (however unconscious we may be of its existence)" (p. 3). "For God does not want to save us by our own but by an extraneous righteousness which does not originate in ourselves but comes from beyond ourselves, which does not arise on earth but comes from heaven. . . . That is why our own personal righteousness must be uprooted" (p. 4). Luther says our righteousness is sinful, and God's forgiveness "covers" it with his righteousness. Commenting on Rom 4:7–8 = Ps 32:1–2 "Blessed are those whose iniquities are forgiven, and whose sins are covered" Luther says:

---

47. Luther, Letter to Jodocus Trutvetter, 1.170.33–38, No. 74.
48. Luther, Preface to *Theologia deutsch*, 1518, 1.378.21–23.
49. Luther, Letter to Johann Lang, 1.99.8–13, No. 41.

> The saints are intrinsically always sinners, therefore they are always extrinsically justified; but the hypocrites are intrinsically always righteous, therefore they are extrinsically always sinners. "Intrinsically" means as we are in ourselves, in our own eyes, . . . and "extrinsically," how we are before God and in his reckoning. Hence, we are extrinsically righteous in so far as we are righteous not in and from ourselves and not by virtue of our works but only by God's regarding us so. For his reckoning is not dependent upon us and does not lie in our power. Therefore, our righteousness, too, is not of our own making and it does not lie in our power (p. 124).

Luther's "extrinsic" righteousness comes to the individual from outside, without intrinsic (as we use the word) change. It comes through an extrinsic, non-essence-changing relation with God.

Nevertheless, God's forgiveness requires the individual's acceptance; and acceptance brings a change in the one accepting forgiveness. "God in his mercy forgives [sin] by his nonreckoning to those who acknowledge and confess and hate it and ask to be healed from it . . . he will redeem [the sinner] from sin in order, in the end, to make him perfectly whole and sound. And, therefore, he is perfectly whole in hope, while he is in fact a sinner, but he has already begun to be actually righteous" (pp. 126–27). Redemption does not change the individual's essence, it only restores it, makes the individual "perfectly whole and sound." Thus, redemption remains within the limits allowed by neo-Platonism, which does not allow intrinsic changes. Luther allows the individual a choice similar to the limited free choice allowed by Augustine (above, page 183) As in Augustine, salvation is predestined. According to Luther Rom 9:15 = Exod 33:19: "I will have mercy on whom I have mercy" means "to whom I have mercy in the moment of predestination, to him I shall be merciful in fact also later. . . . 'So then, it is not of him that wills, nor of him that runs, but of God that has mercy' [Rom 9:16]. . . . A man owes his ability to will and to run, not to his own power, but to the mercy of God who gave him this power to will and to run. . . . In the same way, the apostle says in Gal. 2:20 'I live, yet not I.' And Christ says: 'my teaching is not mine' [John 7:16]. And Eccl 9:11: 'I saw that the race is not to the swift, nor the battle to the strong . . .' Whose is it then . . . , to those that sit and yawn? . . . Certainly not! But they are all the instruments of God who 'works all in all' [1 Cor 12:6] (pp. 268–70).

Luther interprets Rom 7:23, "I see in my members another law at war with the law of my mind" in good neo-Platonic fashion as being a war inside the generic individual who is simultaneously sinner and righteous (pp. 199-209). This war is not the participation of a member in a community struggle between four evil social powers and the power of Christ as Paul does (above, page 140).

Luther does not see the section Rom 9–11 as proclaiming historical continuity between Israel and Christianity as Paul does (page 144, above). Luther is speaking of the election of individuals, not nations. For Luther the section merely continues the denial of self. On the passage Rom 9:2-5 "I could wish that I myself were accursed and cut off from Christ for the sake of my own people" Luther says, "This passage . . . . finds delight and sweetness in bitterness and sorrow, because it takes upon itself the misery and suffering of others. . . . Now this inverted love is the strongest and utmost kind of love: utter self-hatred becomes the sign of the highest love for another. So then, he wants to see the Jews really saved, and in order that they may achieve this, he is ready to forego his own salvation" (pp. 260-61). He contrasts this sacrificial love with the love based on self-interest in Thomas (above, page 195) and even in his esteemed Augustine, implicitly in the first-person oriented anti-Pelagian writings and explicitly in the *City of God*, where "love your neighbor as yourself" is based on self-love.[50] Luther says, "with due respect for the judgment of others [implying Augustine] . . . and speaking like a fool, I say . . . 'as yourself' [does not mean that] the one who loves is the model according to which he loves his neighbor" (p. 407 on Rom 15.2). He continues, "These words will appear strange and even foolish to those who regard themselves as holy and who love God with a covetous love, i.e., for the sake of their own salvation and eternal rest and for the purpose of avoiding hell, in other words, not for God's sake but for their own sake. They are the ones who babble that ordered love begins with itself and that everyone must first of all wish his own salvation and then his neighbor's as his own" (p. 262). Here Luther has been successfully led by biblical Paul to turn neo-Platonism on itself to reject its giving the initiative in reaching God to the self-serving human individual. But the same neo-Platonism still prevents his developing this insight to reach the biblical call, invitation, to an internal God-humanity relation

---

50. Augustine, *City of God*, 19.14; also *De doctrina Christiana*, 1.26.27.

with a creative internally interacting human community (rather than with separate individuals).

Luther expresses his negation of the human in the dialectical style of the fifth-century mystic Pseudo-Dionysius:

> For our good is hidden and that so deeply that it is hidden under its opposite. Thus our life is hidden under death, self-love under self-hatred, glory under shame, salvation under perdition, the kingdom under banishment, heaven under hell, wisdom under foolishness, righteousness under sin, strength under weakness. And . . . every yes we say to any good under a no, in order that our faith may be anchored in God . . . whom we cannot possess or attain to except by the negation of all our affirmations. Thus, "the Kingdom of Heaven is like unto a treasure hidden in the field" [Matt 13:44]. The field is something dirty and is trampled upon, in contrast to the treasure which is singled out. And yet, the field hides the treasure (p. 264).

With Luther, the dirty field is *allegory* for the individual's impotence covered by God's goodness; whereas in Matthew, the field is *metonymy* for creative cooperation between food-growing community and God.

With the closing ethical section, Rom 12–16, Luther makes paraenetic application of the same "uprooting of man's own prudence and self-will" (p. 321). The gifts listed in Rom 12:6–7 (prophecy, ministry, teaching, exhortation, giving, leading, and being compassionate) are interpreted as counsel for passive generic obedience (pp. 333–40)—just opposite their Pauline meaning as creative contribution to an interacting "one body." Luther says, "Every Christian . . . should be very apprehensive when he has his own way. I say this not only with respect to the desires of the flesh, but also with respect to our greatest achievements of righteousness" (p. 328). "'To be transformed by the renewing of your mind [Rom 12.2]' . . . is the same as to hate yourself, to will against your own will, to [understand against] your [understanding], to concede over against the objection of your own righteousness that you are sinful, and to give an ear to foolishness against the objection of your own wisdom" (p. 330). But again, Paul is against self-will and is for the creative use of one's will in *interactively deciding how* to build God's kingdom.

Luther concedes the possibility of a call to some to rule over others:

> Yet all this is addressed only to those who have the power to act and are responsible for themselves. But the matter is different in the case of those who are set over others, for they are not their own agents but the agents of God. Hence, it is their responsibility to rule their subjects with justice and not to permit them to inflict wrong upon one another. They are not empowered to tolerate everything, and patience is out of place for them. For God expects of them, not humility and patience and submission, but readiness to pass judgment, to exercise power, and to impose punishment. They are his representatives (pp. 331–32).

Thus, rulers are delegated to act unilaterally in the same way God is presumed to do. Here Luther maintains the classical Platonic structure with its different classes and a God-controlled cosmological order with rulers called to rule, others to obey. However, for Luther, the classes are in organic relation with one another rather than frozen in a generic structure.

So Luther justified his own life's work (a passionate teacher in an aggressive reform movement) as a work that obeyed a unilateral call by God to be a unilaterally acting teaching agent, similar to God's call to agent rulers to keep world order. In 1520 Luther wrote to an associate, "What honor does this wretch seek, who has no other desire than to be private and most hidden from public affairs? . . . But at the same time I say: if not permitted to be free from my office of teacher and minister of the word, I am at least free *in* exercising it."[51] In the same year he refused to obey the pope's order to recant his teaching. Although in consequence, Luther was banned by the emperor from the empire—itself an authorization for anyone in about half of Europe to kill him on sight—but he continued to teach, preach, and dispute at Wittenberg to the end of his life, thus in fact actively participating in the Reformation struggle.

Consistently with his rejection of all human righteousness, Luther interpreted the sacraments as only a proclamation or promise of God's forgiveness of sin to the individual. In *The Babylonian Captivity of the Church* (1520) he says, "The mass is the promise of the forgiveness of sins made to us by God; and such a promise as has been confirmed by the death of the Son of God. . . . If the mass is a promise, . . . then access to it is to be gained, not with any works, or powers, or merits of one's own, but by faith alone. For where there is the Word of the promising God,

---

51. Luther, Letter to Georg Spalatin, 2.135.22–26, No. 309.

there must necessarily be the faith of the accepting man" (pp. 38–39). Thus, the mass is not to be an offering or sacrifice, either of human work or of Christ's work, as suggested by the words "these gifts . . . presents . . . holy sacrifice . . . offering" in the eucharistic prayer. "The same thing cannot be received and offered at the same time" (p. 52). Luther's deletion of this liturgical "oblation" accomplishes his reform project (the elimination of the entrepreneurial arms-length exchange of works for individual salvation) but leaves intact the arms-length extrinsic relation between a unilaterally controlling God and a merely obedient human individual, or a generic human community, so central a feature of his underlying neo-Platonic conceptuality. In contrast, the first-century corporately oriented church understood that accepting a gift of interactive responsibility as ecclesial Body of Christ is precisely an *offering back to the giver* of acceptance of this offered interactive community responsibility. Such a return gift could not be by individuals separately but only by or within a community that accepted such interactive responsibly. Luther's position was prepared for by a centuries-earlier corresponding theological demotion of the church from "Body of Christ" to "mystical Body of Christ."

For Luther, God acts unilaterally. Luther says the bread is a sign of the promise of forgiveness, as the rainbow is a sign of God's promise to Noah or water is a sign of the promise in baptism. The sacraments, like the word, are non-interactive, although subordinate. "The word of Christ is the testament, and the bread and wine are the sacrament. And as there is greater power in the word than in the sign, so there is greater power in the testament than in the sacrament" (p. 44). The promise is offered generically: "Each one can derive personal benefit from the mass for himself only by his own personal faith" (p. 49). Luther specifically excludes the communal meal of John 6 (starting with a boy's offering of five barley loaves and two fish) as explication of the Eucharist (p. 19).

Luther eliminates all sacraments other than baptism and Eucharist. Penance lacks a sign and is a mere renewal of baptism, while confirmation, marriage, and unction are not about the promise of forgiveness. As for the sacrament of order: "Here Christian brotherhood has perished, here shepherds have been turned into wolves, servants into tyrants, churchmen into worse than worldlings" (p. 112). Luther has no corporate view of priesthood as an office that facilitates (not controls) a congregation's creative interaction within itself to make itself effective as agent for spreading the same within its wider community. He says, "all of us who have been baptized are equally priests" (p. 112). This generic "priesthood of all believers" is justified by 1 Pet 2:9 "You are a chosen race, a royal priesthood," a passage actually using Exod 19:5–6 typologically to urge a priesthood of the church as a whole toward the world. Luther continues: "ordination can be nothing else than a certain rite by which the church chooses its preachers.... They are also called pastors because they are to pasture, that is, to teach" (p. 113). Holy order was discredited by corruption and in an increasingly generically oriented age, it more fundamentally was losing its corporate, or even organic, meaning as sign of synchronic and diachronic community interaction. Being a passionate iconoclast, Luther throws out a corrupt corporate infrastructure rather than working to reform it—its original purpose is invisible to him and generally to the ruling class. His own subsequent measures to maintain order in the Reformation struggle were not interactive but *ad hoc*.

Middle- and neo-Platonic Christian theology from Origen to Luther is caught between its own Platonic call for the *individual* to *conform* to a *preexisting righteousness*, and a biblical call for the *community* to interact among its members and with God to *create* an ever new *social interaction*. The two calls are in contradiction, and in this chapter we have traced the attempts to append those parts of that biblical call that can be conceived within a neo-Platonic system (above, Origen, page 169; Augustine, page 185; Thomas, page 196). But with a generic individual in relation with an all-sufficient, unchanging neo-Platonic God, God does not need help; and interactions between persons are not internal (do not change the interactors' essences). Hence, the only interest the individual can have in either is a self-serving one, whether an active individual seeks to please God (as in a pre-ordered classical neo-Platonism) or a passive but obedient individual waits for God to make his will known (as in a genericized neo-Platonism). These two alternatives, given the names "*eros*" and "*agape*," are precisely the base of Anders Nygren's *Agape and Eros* (1930), written within a neo-Platonic horizon on the historical struggle between these two so named alternatives. Nygren sees the struggle ended with Luther's theologically defining choice of the latter one, "*Agape*." But placing all the work with God does not remove the relation's self-serving significance for the saved individual. The Western theologians treated in this chapter before Luther all try to bend active human self-serving purposes to something resembling the biblical call to responsible community participation. However, they cannot deny their ultimately self-serving end. Luther, still neo-Platonic but driven as reformer to conform to Scripture's *not basing the relation with God on a self-serving motivation* in the human individual, consistently condemns any human *creative* choice in behavior. From the corporate perspective, such an exclusion negates the actual individual (above, page 202). But the corporate biblical perspective, whose God *calls for creative contributions from both sides* and so cannot negate the creative individual, claims there is another human resource not recognized by the neo-Platonic perspective that can be used for making non-passive creative contribution toward God's purposes *without* being self-serving, namely, *human capacities for relating internally with one another*, which can be redirected from self-serving to creative community purposes.

In the next chapter we find a tiny community of Calvinist (hence even more extreme) reformists discovering themselves forced under extreme circumstances of economic survival for a short time actually to be *themselves corporately creating* a piece of their God's corporate kingdom here on earth.

# 5

# Forty Years of Corporate Orientation in New England

## *A New Society Requires an Old Testament*

UNLIKE THE GERMAN REFORMATION, which was powered politically by revolt from sub-alpine abuse of power and ideologically by a Luther-led return from Thomas's Aristotelian scholasticism back to Augustine's neo-Platonism, the English reformation on its second try in 1558 was a pragmatic move to avoid revolution in England. On her accession, a popular Elizabeth I acted quickly to bring to order a country on the brink of Calvinist Puritan revolution, breaking a second time with Rome but tacitly tolerating only sufficient Calvinist deviation to manage the continuation of a single established church for all England. A systematic theological foundation for this political settlement developed with a functional corporate community component remarkable for its time, and appeared in print incrementally in Richard Hooker's *Laws of Ecclesiastical Polity*, finalized in 1594.

Elizabeth's accommodation lasted the best part of a century, until the mismanagement of King Charles brought on the 1643 Puritan revolution. During this interval most reformation-minded (that is, "puritan" as contrasted with the revolutionary "Puritan") clergy were *nonconformists* rather than *separatists*; that is, they did not conform with civil law on use of the Book of Common Prayer and vestments, yet they with their followers did not separate themselves from the one established church, but remained influential spiritual leaders within it. These leaders preached from the New Testament a generic Reform theology within the neo-Platonic tradition of Augustine, Luther, and Calvin against their opponents—the more corporately oriented establishment theologians like Hooker who relied more on the Old Testament to support the monarchy's attempt to hold both church and England together as non-sectarian.

But the tiny band of New England Puritan-minded but rather upper-class intellectual settlers in 1629 quickly found themselves hungry, cold, sick, and dying; and the accompanying Puritan-oriented clergy, finding themselves to be the establishment, quickly changed their preaching base back from the New to the Old Testament to urge an interactive social responsibility they could take for granted in England. In England, establishment theologians urged corporate social responsibility over individual piety to counter Puritan revolutionary tension; in early Massachusetts, Puritan clergy quickly found themselves urging the same for the economic survival of their small isolated community in the wilderness.

The relative corporate and generic usage of the two testaments in twelve representative sermons preached by members of the three groups—English establishment theologians, English puritans, and New England colonists—is tabulated on the next page.

## 1 English Establishment Theologians, English Puritans, New England Puritans

The group designated in the table as English establishment theologians includes Richard Hooker (1553–1600), Lancelot Andrewes (1555–1626), and William Laud (1573–1645). Andrewes was chaplain to Elizabeth I and James I, and Bishop of Winchester. He was dean of English preachers and was considered a person of great spiritual depth. Laud was chief advisor to Charles I, and Archbishop of Canterbury. He was narrow but sincere, imitating Andrewes' spirituality. He forced hundreds of puritan-minded clergy out of their teaching positions or parishes for nonconformity and effectively silenced others. He was executed by the Puritan revolutionary government in 1645.

The group designated as English puritans in the table includes Thomas Cartwright (1535–1603), William Perkins (1558–1602), William Ames (1576–1633), and John Cotton (1584–1652) (who is also part of the American colonial group). Cartwright was deprived of his professorship in divinity at Cambridge for nonconformist views. Perkins was a fellow of Christ's Church Cambridge, a renowned preacher and writer, and a leader in the Puritan movement. Ames codified dissenting thought and was in close contact with New England leaders. Cotton was

# CHRISTIAN AMBIVALENCE TOWARD ITS OLD TESTAMENT

**Bible Citations in Seventeenth-Century Preaching**

| | English Establishment Theologians | | | | English Puritans | | | | New England Puritans | | | |
|---|---|---|---|---|---|---|---|---|---|---|---|---|
| preacher | Richard Hooker | Lancelot Andrewes | Lancelot Andrewes | William Laud | Thomas Cartwright | William Perkins | William Ames | John Cotton | John Cotton | Samuel Willard | Samuel Willard | Increase Mather |
| title | A Remedy against Sorrow and Fear | Upon the Third Commandment | Before the King at Whitehall Easter-Day | To King James on the King's Birthday | Commentary upon Colossians, Serm. 1-10 | Discourse of Conscience | Subst. of Christian Religion, Lect. 1-10 | The Life of Faith | God's Promise to His Plantations | A Sermon Preached upon Ezek 22:30,31 | The Duty of a People Concerning Every Man's Birth Sin | Sermon |
| date | c. 1590 | June 11, 1592 | April 13, 1623 | June 19, 1621 | before 1603 | 1596 | before 1633 | before 1630 | 1630 | 1679 | March 17, 1680 | June 21, 1719 |
| **Old Testament** | | | | | | | | | | | | |
| fulfillment of prophecy | 4 | 17 | 32 | 7 | 1 | 2 | | 14 | 16 | 16 | 6 | 11 |
| typology | 4 | 35 | 17 | 15 | 9 | 2 | | 38 | 35 | 52 | 6 | |
| typology, NT summary | 1 | | | | | 1 | 1 | | 3 | | | |
| legal citation | | 25 | | 1 | | 6 | | 3 | | | | |
| proverbial citation | | | | | 12 | 8 | 15 | 9 | 7 | 4 | 4 | 2 |
| abstract doctrine | 10 | 7 | 5 | 5 | 22 | 61 | | 213 | | 16 | 2 | 16 |
| **New Testament** | | | | | | | | | | | | |
| fulfillment of prophecy | 1 | 1 | 7 | 1 | 1 | | 2 | 7 | 1 | 2 | 3 | |
| typology | 7 | 9 | 22 | 3 | 13 | 6 | | 30 | 5 | | | 2 |
| fulfillment in NT | | | 14 | 4 | 2 | 1 | | 1 | | | | |
| legal citation | | 10 | 1 | | 1 | 7 | | 3 | | | | |
| proverbial citation | 3 | 4 | 3 | 3 | 10 | 4 | | 4 | 8 | 1 | 1 | 22 |
| abstract doctrine | | | | | 84 | 150 | 62 | 313 | | | | |
| **totals** | | | | | | | | | | | | |
| OT | 19 | 84 | 54 | 28 | 44 | 80 | 16 | 280 | 61 | 72 | 16 | 30 |
| NT | 11 | 24 | 47 | 11 | 111 | 168 | 64 | 358 | 14 | 3 | 5 | 24 |
| ratio: OT/NT | 1.73 | 3.50 | 1.15 | 2.55 | 0.40 | 0.48 | 0.25 | 0.78 | 4.36 | 24.00 | 3.20 | 1.25 |
| history-preserving | 17 | 97 | 93 | 31 | 27 | 25 | 3 | 99 | 60 | 70 | 16 | 14 |
| universalizing | 13 | 11 | 8 | 8 | 128 | 223 | 77 | 539 | 15 | 5 | 5 | 40 |
| ratio: hist-p/universalizing | 1.31 | 8.82 | 11.63 | 3.88 | 0.21 | 0.11 | 0.04 | 0.18 | 4.00 | 14.00 | 3.20 | 0.35 |

vicar of St. Botolph's in Boston, Lincolnshire, for twenty years, enjoying a reputation as preacher and theologian. When forced to resign for nonconformity, Cotton went to New England in 1633 and became teacher of the Boston church.

The Puritans, as the reform party in the English church, specifically targeted the formalism of worship in the Book of Common Prayer and the hierarchical structure in church governance, which were represented by episcopacy and the use of vestments. Prayer Book, episcopacy, and vestments were concrete manifestations of both the church's diachronic solidarity in preserving its tradition and its synchronic solidarity in corporate participation in that tradition. The Puritans, in common with continental Protestants, found the tradition corrupt and urged a return to the non-formalist and non-hierarchical church practice they saw in the Bible. Thus, they urged a more generic relation among Christians, both synchronically (elimination of hierarchy) and diachronically (return to a simpler practice). Historians with a modern perspective sometimes excuse rigidity in English Puritanism by comparing it with an equally rigid conformity expected by the Establishment, but the two conformities are different—the Puritans wanted everyone to be similar, while the Establishment wanted everyone to belong to one institution and taking complementarily interactive roles within it.

The group designated as New England Puritans in the table includes Cotton, Samuel Willard (1640–1707), and Increase Mather (1639–1723). Cotton was the leading New England cleric in the first generation; Willard and Mather were the leaders in the second. Willard was born in Concord, Massachusetts, graduated from Harvard in 1659, and was teacher of the South Church in Boston and acting president of Harvard. Mather was born in Dorchester, Massachusetts, graduated from Harvard in 1656, received an M.A. from Trinity College, Dublin, and after a short career in England during the puritan revolutionary period returned to be teacher of the Second Church in Boston, representative of Massachusetts to England, and president of Harvard.

The New England Puritan clergy, unlike Puritan clergy in England, found themselves in a civil leadership role similar to that of the establishment theologians in England and, as we will see when we come to their sermons, their concerns shifted accordingly. The ability of Puritans in circumstances of overall civil responsibility to make a rapid adjustment to a more corporate perspective suggests that English Puritanism took its counter-cultural reforming stance only in conjunction with an implicit dependence on the interactive elements in the institutions and culture it was trying to reform.

### 2 Analysis by Classifying Bible Citations in Sermons

Theological differences among the three groups will be analyzed by comparing the use of the two testaments in representative sermons. The seventeenth-century sermon in both England and New England was a major theological statement, carefully written, and continually referring to the Bible in a manner reminiscent of the intimate literary relation of the New Testament to the Old as described in chapter 2.I, above. The seventeenth-century sermon adequately reproduces the theology of its writer and reveals in an intimate but unselfconscious way the kind of acceptance that the writer accords the Old Testament.

The sermons are analyzed by classifying their use of biblical passages, using the categories developed in chapter 2 for the New Testament (fulfillment of prophecy, typology, allegory, legal citation, and proverbial citation), doubling them to allow separate treatment of the two testaments and otherwise adapting them to the new situation.

Uses of Biblical Passages in Seventeenth Century Sermons

Old Testament passages

Fulfillment of prophecy

Treating an Old Testament passage as prophecy either fulfilled in New Testament times or still in eschatological tension

Typology

Treating an event described in an Old Testament narrative passage as historical type of events either in New Testament times or later

Typology, using New Testament summary of Old Testament passage

Treating an Old Testament narrative passage typologically but using a convenient New Testament summary of it

Legal citation

A New Testament citing of a legal statute or precedent from the Old Testament

Proverbial citation

Applying an Old Testament passage of wisdom or generalized knowledge to the situation in the preacher's time

Abstract doctrine
> Abstracting systematic doctrines (e.g., original sin) from the Old Testament

New Testament passages
Fulfillment of prophecy
> Treating a New Testament passage as prophecy still in eschatological tension

Typology
> Treating an event described in a New Testament narrative passage as historical type of later events

Fulfillment in New Testament
> Treating an event described in the New Testament as fulfillment of an Old Testament prophecy or antitype of an Old Testament type

Legal citation
> Citing a legal statute or precedent from the New Testament

Proverbial citation
> Applying a New Testament wisdom passage (parables, ethical teachings) to the situation in the preacher's time

Abstract doctrine
> Abstracting systematic doctrines (e.g., preexistence of Christ, atonement) from the New Testament

Allegorical use is not included as a category because there is essentially no simple allegorical use of biblical material in seventeenth-century preaching.[1] However, the category "abstract doctrine" under each testament (the abstracting of systematic theological elements from biblical material) is allegory in disguise, as shown with Origen in chapter 4.II.1, above.

The categories "fulfillment of prophecy" and "typology" for both testaments relate events in the preacher's time to earlier biblical events through the participation of both in the ongoing creative historically interactive relation between God and his people. They differ in that for "fulfillment of prophecy" the Old Testament passage is understood as itself referring to a future event; whereas, for "typology" the relation

---

1. A rare exception: Perkins, *A Discourse of Conscience*, 148. Perkins allegorizes to the individual conscience the claim in Deut 7:22 that God clears away the nations gradually, lest the wild beasts grow.

to the later event is understood as first emerging when the later event occurs (see chapter 2, page 87, above). These categories differ between their Old Testament and New Testament versions only in that for the Old Testament the fulfillment or antitype can be found either in the New Testament or later; whereas, for the New Testament passages both necessarily occur later.

The categories "legal citation" and "proverbial citation" for both testaments are the citing of a legal precedent or the application of a wisdom passage to the situation in the preacher's time.

The new category "typology, using New Testament summary of Old Testament passage" is of cases where the preacher replaces a long Old Testament narrative passage with a New Testament summary of that passage, which he then treats as having the same significance as the Old Testament passage itself. An example is John Cotton's allusion to Matt 12:42 "The Queen of the South . . . came from the ends of the earth to hear the wisdom of Solomon" as a convenient summary of 1 Kings 10:1–10 or 2 Chron 9:1–12 to justify traveling to gain knowledge.[2] Cotton ignores the Solomon-Christ typological scheme in the Matthew passage. He intends, rather, a typological relation between the queen's travel to learn from Solomon and the travel of the puritans to New England, a relation depending only on the meaning of the original Old Testament passages. The use of New Testament passages in this way is classified under use of the Old Testament—the intention is identical with that in direct typological use of the Old Testament.

The new category "fulfillment in New Testament" is of New Testament passages treated by the preacher as describing the fulfillment of Old Testament prophecy or as claiming a typological relation between a New Testament event and some event in the Old Testament. Prophecy and typology are grouped together in this category.

The use of the passages by the seventeenth-century preachers is what is classified, not the significance the passages might have for theologians today. Examples are Cotton's use of Job 19:25 "I know that my Redeemer lives" as a prophecy rather than as Old Testament wisdom[3] and Richard Hooker's typological use of Ps 73:3 "For I was envious of the arrogant, when I saw the prosperity of the wicked" as confession by David of his sin (by which David "himself hereby openeth both our common and his

---

2. Cotton, *God's Promise to his Plantations*, 8.
3. Cotton, "The Life of Faith," 369.

peculiar imperfection"), rather than as lament by either generic Israelite or corporate Israel.[4]

Biblical references in the sermons range from a several page long analysis of a biblical chapter to a mention of a passage in passing. Most references are indicated by chapter and verse in the sermons. Only the most specific other biblical allusions are included in the totals. For example, all the biblical references in a short Cotton sermon are listed in an appendix at the end of the chapter. The works of Cartwright, Perkins, Ames, and the English Cotton are not individual sermons but collections of sermon material, representing ten or more sermons from each writer. The lower part of the table gives the totals, and the ratios, of Old Testament and New Testament citations for each sermon, and the totals and ratios of history-preserving and universalizing citations. The history-preserving categories are the first four categories under each testament, fulfillment of prophecy, typology, and legal citation, and they treat the cited passage as part of the history that defines the preacher's community. The other two categories under each testament, proverbial citation and abstract doctrine, are universalizing categories that are abstracted away from history. The arguments for this polar grouping of the categories are the same as for the categories of chapter 2 from which they are derived, except that proverbial citation is here counted as universalizing rather than neutral on the issue. History-preserving citations reflect a corporate element and universalizing citations reflect a generic element in this very early New England culture.

The four sermons in each group are chosen to represent the orientation of that group. The distribution of biblical citations among the categories is, of course, influenced by the subjects of the particular sermons, as can be noticed, for example, by comparing the two sermons of Andrewes. The representative nature of Laud's seven published sermons, preached before the king, could possibly be questioned, but there was likely some favoring of sermons of wide civic significance in the published work of all the preachers. Yet in spite of such variations the tabulated sermons reveal significant differences in the perspectives of the three groups.[5]

---

4. Hooker, "A Remedy against Sorrow and Fear," 3.645.

5. An earlier, simpler analysis, not based on the categories of chapter 2 above, appeared in Adams and Blair, "Changing Biblical Imagery," summarized in Adams, *Meeting House to Camp Meeting*, chapter 5.

### 3 The Sermons

All the *English establishment theologians* favor the Old Testament over the New and also favor the history-preserving methods of fulfillment of prophecy, typology, and legal citation over the universalizing methods of proverbial citation and abstracting of doctrines. For example, William Laud's sermon to King James on his birthday[6] favors the Old Testament over the New 28 to 11 (a ratio of 2.55) and history-preserving categories over universalizing categories 31 to 8 (a ratio of 3.88), as noted on the chart. The sermon is built around Psalm 122 "I was glad when they said to me, 'Let us go to the house of the Lord!' . . . Pray for the peace of Jerusalem," a psalm that Laud takes to have been written by King David to be sung at the solemn entry of the ark into Jerusalem (2 Sam 6) and to refer to David as "the peace of Jerusalem." Laud extends this meaning for the psalm prophetically (i.e., typologically) in stages—to the building of the temple under Solomon, to the return from exile, to Christ, and finally to King James himself:

> [T]he eye of the prophet was clear, and saw things farther off than the present. . . . David that saw not the Temple built, foresaw that it was to be built by his son: and so fitted the psalm both to a present Tabernacle and a future Temple. And it is not improbable, but that he saw farther; or if he did not, the Spirit of God did; and so fitted his pen, that the same psalm might serve the Jews at their return from Babylon, to re-edify the ruins of both City and Temple . . . . Nay, I make no question but that he saw farther yet. For what would hinder the prophet, but that he might look quite through the Temple, which was but the figure, or shadow, and so see Christ, His Church, and Kingdom (p. 4).

The final step in the chain is King James:

> I cannot be so unthankful to God and my text, but that I must fit one circumstance more to *rogare pacem*, "pray for peace." And it is "pray for it" this day. . . . surely we have a Jerusalem, a State, and a Church to pray for, as well as they; and this day was our Solomon, the very peace of our Jerusalem, born . . . . for the good and welfare of both State and Church; and can you do other than *rogare pacem*, "pray for peace," in the day, nay, nativity, the very birth-day, of both Peace and the Peace-maker? (p. 15).

---

6. Laud, *A Sermon Preached before His Maiesty*. Pagination is from vol. 1 of *Works*.

The *English puritans* preached quite differently. They favored the New Testament over the Old, and universalizing uses of the Bible over history-preserving ones. For example, William Ames, in the first 10 homilies of his *The Substance of Christian Religion: or, a plain and easie Draught of the Christian Catechisme, in LII Lectures, on chosen Texts of Scripture, for each Lords-day of the Year, Learnedly and Perspicuously Illustrated with Doctrines, Reasons, and Uses* favors the New Testament over the Old 64 to 16, and universalizing categories over history-preserving ones 77 to 3. Each homily is organized around the establishing of several abstract "Doctrines" from its biblical text. In the third homily (pp. 17–23), for example, the text is Rom 5:12 "Therefore, just as sin came into the world through one man, and death came through sin, and so death spread to all because all have sinned," and it is treated through the establishing of two "Doctrines": "Doct. 1. Sin entered into the world, not by God's creation, but by man's defection" (p. 18), and "Doct. 2. Through Adams first disobedience sin passed from Adam upon all his posterity" (p. 19). Establishing doctrines from biblical texts is a universalizing generic project. And the arguments for both doctrines are explicitly generic: sin is passed from single Adam, not Adam the human community, "by way of propagation or natural descent" (p. 19) rather than culturally through interaction. Whereas English establishment sermons are saturated with typological and prophetic connections between seventeenth-century corporate England and ancient Israel, English puritan sermons universalize the New Testament with proverbial citation or the extraction of general doctrines.

But in the *New England wilderness the Puritans* changed abruptly from the English Puritan position to an establishment orientation. The change is evident in John Cotton, who belonged to both groups. Whereas Cotton's *The Life of Faith*, almost certainly preached in England, is weighted 358 to 280 in favor of New Testament citation over Old Testament citation and 539 to 99 in favor of universalizing citation from both testaments over history-preserving citation, his *God's Promise to his Plantations* favors the Old Testament over the New 61 to 14 and history-preserving categories over universalizing categories 60 to 15. *God's Promise to his Plantations* was the charter sermon of the Massachusetts Bay experiment, preached by Cotton in Southampton as farewell on the departure of John Winthrop's fleet of ships carrying the seat of government and most of the stockholders of the Massachusetts Bay Colony to

New England in 1630. Its text is from the account of the making of the Davidic covenant, 2 Sam 7:10 "And I will appoint a place for my people Israel and will plant them, so that they may live in their own place, and be disturbed no more." The sermon is a tissue of typological and prophetic applications of the biblical tradition to the present undertaking to justify it as part of God's saving relation with his people in a joint venture as a community. Since it was delivered as part of the founding of the new community, it is here classified with the New England sermons.

Samuel Willard's *A Sermon Preached upon Ezek 22.30,31. Occasioned by the Death of the much honoured John Leveret Esq; Governour of the Colony of the Mattachusets. N-E*, preached nearly fifty years later, is equally centered on the colony as a people and community of God, as an antitype and fulfillment of ancient Israel. Old Testament references outnumber New Testament references 72 to 3 and history-preserving biblical references outnumber universalizing ones 70 to 5.

The sermon text is Ezek 22:30–31 "And I sought for anyone among them who would repair the wall and stand in the breach before me on behalf of the land, so that I would not destroy it; but I found no one. Therefore I have poured out my indignation upon them." According to Willard, Ezekiel's expression "standing in the breach" means thrusting oneself "between a sinning people, and a provoked God" to "both intercede with God and bear a due testimony against sin" (p. 6)—something needed in New England at the time, according to Willard. The New England experiment had at first required the utter loyalty of every person for its corporate survival, but after fifty years it seems to have passed the peak of its members' commitment to the common good. "We are a sick people. The Symptoms are visible and manifest, and if we do indeed consult our own health, it ought to be our care to seek the chiefest and ablest Physitians: and if you will have Mountebanks take you in hand, that will heal the wounds slightly, thank yourselves if they break out again with more rancor than ever" (p. 13). As the sermon proceeds it gradually becomes clear to the listeners that the late governor now being mourned is the one who stood in the breach, an antitype of the types Moses, Phineas, David, Hezekiah, and Josiah. Standing in the breach belongs to the calling of political leadership, both civil and ecclesiastical. "When Rulers in Common-wealth and Church are not such men, there are none at all, it exceeds the advantage of men in a private capacity to be so" (p. 8). The sermon ends with an appeal to the people of God—that is, New England, to provide and support good leaders.

Willard's sermon at the death of Governor Leveret resembles Laud's sermon to King James on the King's birthday, treated above. More deference is required when preaching before a live king than a dead governor, yet the theme of both sermons is the same: the dual representative role of a political leader of God's people, a leader thus placed in the middle, "in the breach," of the complementary relation between God and the community, a theme expounded using the typological relation between contemporaneous king or governor and ancient political leaders in Israel.

In Willard's time, another antitype of ancient Israel began to contest the colony's preeminence as antitype and is the subject of another of Willard's sermons that was preached about the same time: *The Duty of a People that have Renewed their Covenant with God. Opened and Urged in a Sermon Preached to the second Church in Boston in New-England, March 17. 1679/80. after that church had explicitly and most solemnly renewed the Ingagement of themselves to God, and one to another.* Whereas in Willard's previously analyzed sermon in which God's covenant with Israel continues in his covenant with Massachusetts, in this one it continues in a covenant with Second Church. The previous sermon has 72 references to the Old Testament; this one has 16. The previous sermon is built around the typological relation of political leader in Massachusetts to political leader in Israel within the larger typological relation of the community Massachusetts to the community Israel. The present sermon starts with a typological relation between the covenant made at Second Church and the covenant made by Israel in Joshua 24, "Choose this day whom you will serve." But after this start the bulk of the sermon is given over to an extended paraenetic application of the Joshua covenant to Second Church and its members. The paraenetic application has a double meaning throughout—it can be taken as applying to the members of Second Church as part of a corporate congregation or as applying to them generically as selves in their own right. The closing of the sermon with Eph 3:16 "that . . . he may grant that you may be strengthened in your inner being with power through his Spirit" maintains this ambiguity to the end. The possibility for generic interpretation associated with paraenetic typology (above, page 100, item (f)) is held open. In Eph 3:16

itself, of course, the context indicates that the "you" (plural) addresses a corporate body rather than a plurality of generic individuals.

Willard's second sermon thus reveals the beginnings of a sectarian shift, a move away from concern for the well-being of the New England community to concern to do one's duty as required by a group set apart, and beyond this an abstract generic duty, rather than a duty to interact within the community to change community essence.

Increase Mather was a contemporary of Willard but the sermon to be analyzed here is his very late "A Plain Discourse Concerning every Man's Birth Sin" preached on his eightieth birthday, forty years after the Willard sermons analyzed above, and ninety years after the Cotton sermon. In this sermon the 24 New Testament citations nearly equal in number the 30 Old Testament citations, and the 40 universalizing biblical citations overwhelm the 14 history-preserving ones. The corporate perspective has taken second place.

The topic is "Birth Sin," which according to Mather has been called original sin since Augustine (p. 6), and the text is Ezek 16:5 "for you were abhorred on the day you were born." The sermon specifies that the Ezekiel citation belongs to our "abstract doctrine" category: "Thus by Parabolical and Allegorical Expressions the Prophet sets forth the Miserable state of the Jewish Nation when in Aegypt. There is also a Mystical Spiritual Meaning intended in the words; Namely to signify that such as this is the case of all the Elect of God, till He shall please to Regenerate them. . . . It is true of every man that comes into the World, that he is altogether born in Sin" (pp. 2–3). In support of birth sin he cites Gen 8:21 "the inclination of the human heart is evil from youth" (p. 3) and specifies the category of this citation also (it too is abstract doctrine): "Thus it is with *Man*, not with this or that Man, but with every Man, and this from their *Youth*" (p. 3). Mather understands Adam as representative not of corporate humanity but of the generic human being. "Why should we be punished for Adam's Sin? We could not help what he did in eating the forbidden fruit. But it should be considered that *Adam* was not a particular but universal Person, the *Representative* of all Man-kind: now the act of a Representative is justly imputed to those he does represent; tho' we did not chuse *Adam* for our Representative, God chose him for us" (p. 13). Generic, universalizing application of the biblical passages is Mather's wont.

This sermon suggests that the non-puritan survival-based re-creation of corporate community responsibility is over. Augustine's generic base in Plotinus's neo-Platonism, to which Luther's and Calvin's reformation returned, is dominant. As with Augustine, so with Mather a generic original sin requires a generic salvation: "Grace is a Personal Property which is not Propagated, but Original Sin is a property of Nature, thence does continue to be Propagated" (p. 14). Mather interprets the salvation offered in 2 Cor 5:17 "if anyone is in Christ, there is a new creation" in the same generic way (p. 20), thus differing from the communal reading of Paul's "in Christ" as creative participation in the work of a corporate "body," as in Rom 12:4–6 "We, who are many, are one body in Christ" (above, page 144).

The shift to a generic perspective, so advertised in this sermon, preceded the coming of the Enlightenment to New England. It is a shift, not to the straightforward generic anthropological position soon to be victorious, but back to the generic cosmologically oriented English puritan tradition coming through Luther and Calvin from Augustine and neo-Platonic Plotinus, and again attractive when a denser New England population allowed the luxury of a loss of interest in maintaining its earlier corporate orientation.

The arrival a few decades later in New England of the individual-based Enlightenment did nothing to eliminate the generic perspective or the loss of interest in the Old Testament. For example, Jonathan Edwards's sermon *Christ the Great Example of Gospel Ministers* in 1749 cited the New Testament 42 times and the Old Testament 8 times.

### 4 A New Society Requires an Old Testament

The abrupt early New England shift from Puritan individual ethical accountability to a community responsibility exceeding even the English establishment position did not escape the attention of English Puritans. In about 1650, former New England resident Sir Richard Saltonstall wrote to Cotton from England criticizing the persecution of non-conformists for their conscience, suggesting that Cotton not "practice those courses in a wilderness which you went so far to prevent." Cotton wrote back, "Do you think the Lord hath crowned the state with so many victories that they should suffer so many miscreants to pluck the crown of sovereignty from Christ's head?"[7] There was no room for a generic conscience in New England's early struggle to build a survivable community.

Why did the first two generations of Puritans in New England abandon the reformation position they had held in England before, and to which they returned after, this short period? And how were they able to change positions so readily and so completely?

The Puritan idealists going to New England had been not individual separatists but non-conformists working within the English church. The preachers among them had taken a leadership role in promoting the New England project and now suddenly found themselves to *be* the establishment for a collection of righteous individualists (now cold, hungry, sick, and dying in the wilderness) and so were forced with the others to find a way to lead in a joint building of a functionally *inter*acting *community* capable of *creating* its own community survival rather than just being righteous as individuals. The result was a commitment quite different from that of the non-conforming English group they came from, and its inspiration: Reformation Germany with Luther remaining as "teacher" while emperor, nobility, and administrators still maintained a viable social order from above. The settlers found biblical "faith" to be shared creative *interaction*, not individual passive *belief*.

Later, when the growth of population and commercial relations with England had stabilized the New England economy, there was a separation of functions again and the New England church leaders went back to the earlier English puritan generic stance, leaving the biblically advocated community maintenance to the civil authority.

The New Testament was valuable to the non-conformist Puritans in England in its advocacy of a "from below" reform of, rather than withdrawal from, an Israel under imposed Roman rule from above. But the Puritans in England, like Westerners generally, had not been able to recognize that New Testament reform as from perennially oriented Western culture itself, imposed on Judea and maintained in Europe by its upper class rulers—a social class conveniently unable to conceive the corporate orientation. The West rationalized the New Testament as requiring each individual Christian to follow a fixed scriptural "Law." The division of the church in the continental Reformation was held back in England by Elizabeth's compromise and rationalized by a theology from the Old Testament that explicitly supported sufficient freedom to

---

7. Cotton, Exchange of letters with Richard Saltonstall, 2.127–34.

preserve some community interactive responsibility. But New England separatist-leaning Puritans, finding themselves in the wilderness without any community structure to resist, needed help *creating* a responsibly structured community. They found that help most readily and directly available in the Old Testament literal account of just such an active *creation* of community by its members, rather than in the New whose *continuation* of such creation by typological application of the Old was, for them as Westerners, a giant interactive typological step further from their recognition.

The New Testament cannot be understood as proposing a reform away from theoretically oriented Western culture by that theoretically oriented culture itself. It can only be understood outside that orientation through what the West would call a practical orientation, one not *discovering* but rather *creating* a structure for community interaction, as ancient Israel both did and recounted in practical figurative typological relational language rather than theoretical systematic imperative literal language. The early New England community in the wilderness found a type for itself in Israel's acceptance of a call to a responsible creating of interacting community as agent people-of-God and took itself as an antitype, a "New Israel," in John Winthrop's prophetic words on the ship going over, "wee shall find that the God of Israell is among us . . . . wee shall be as a citty upon a hill."[8]

---

8. Winthrop, "A Modell of Christian Charity," 295.

## APPENDIX

Biblical citations in John Cotton, *God's Promise to his Plantations*

### Categories:

| | Old Testament | | | New Testament |
|---|---|---|---|---|
| O-1 | fulfillment of prophecy | | N-1 | fulfillment of prophecy |
| O-2 | typology | | N-2 | typology |
| O-3 | typology using New Test. summary of Old T. | | N-3 | fulfillment in New Testament |
| O-4 | legal citation | | N-4 | legal citation |
| O-5 | proverbial citation | | N-5 | proverbial citation |
| O-6 | abstract doctrine | | N-6 | abstract doctrine |
| Incl | subsequent references to same biblical passage | | | |

### Biblical citations:

| Pg. | Passage | Cat. | Pg. | Passage | Cat. | Pg. | Passage | Cat. |
|---|---|---|---|---|---|---|---|---|
| 0 | 2 Sam 7:10 | O-2 | 8 | Prov 31:14 | O-5 | 15 | Isa 56:5 | O-2 |
|   | Ps 22:27–31 | O-1 |   | Matt 13:45–46 | N-5 |    | Mal 4:2–3 | O-1 |
| 2 | 2 Sam 7 | Incl |   | unjust steward | N-5 |    | John 15:1–2 | N-1 |
| 3 | Acts 17:26 | O-3 |   | thief in night | N-5 |    | David temple | O-2 |
|   | Deut 2:5–9 | O-2 | 9 | Acts 16:12 | N-2 | 16 | Isa 27:1–2 | O-1 |
|   | Ezek 20:6 | O-2 |   | Joseph | O-2 |    | Job 34:29 | O-5 |
|   | Exod 19:4 | O-2 |   | Luke 12:48 | N-5 |    | Isa 65:22 | O-1 |
| 4 | Ps 80:9 | O-2 |   | 2 Chr 11:13–15 | O-2 |    | Jeroboam | O-2 |
|   | Gen 26:17–22 | O-2 | 10 | Mic 2:6–11 | O-2 |    | Ahab | O-2 |
|   | Ps 44:2 | O-2 |   | 1 Thess 4:6 | O-3 |    | Ahaz | O-2 |
|   | Gen 23:9–16 | O-2 |   | 1 Sam 22:1–2 | O-2 |    | after David | O-2 |
|   | Gen 45:10 | O-2 |   | Acts 13:46–47 | N-2 |    | vine | Incl |
|   | Adam | O-2 | 11 | Matt 8:9 | N-5 |    | seed | O-2 |
|   | Noah | O-2 |   | Ps 32:8 | O-5 | 17 | Jer 24:5 | O-1 |
|   | Gen 26:22 | Incl |   | Rom 1:11–12 | N-5 |    | Jer 11:17 | O-1 |
| 5 | Gen 34:21 | O-2 |   | 1 Cor 16:12 | N-5 |    | in David | O-2 |
|   | Gen 21:25 | O-2 | 12 | Macedonia | N-2 |    | Isa 4:5–6 | O-1 |
|   | Gen 1:28 | O-1 |   | Ps 24:1 | Incl | 18 | 1 Sam 4:22 | O-2 |
|   | Gen 9:1 | O-1 | 13 | Acts 17:26–27 | N-2 |    | Isa 27:2–3 | O-1 |
| 6 | Ps 24:1 | O-5 | 14 | Ps 89:21–22 | O-1 |    | Ps 122:6 | O-2 |
|   | Jer 10:7 | O-5 |   | Ps 92:13 | O-1 |    | Ps 129:5 | O-1 |
|   | Deut 10:14 | O-5 |   | Amos 9:15 | O-1 | 19 | Ps 133:1–2 | O-1 |
|   | 2 Chr 25:11–14 | O-2 |   | Ps 80:8–11 | O-2 |    | Phil 2:4 | N-5 |
|   | Gen 12:7 | O-2 |   | Ps 1:4 [1:3] | O-5 |    | Acts 4:32 | N-2 |
|   | Exod 15:17 | O-2 | 15 | Isa 61:3 | O-1 |    | Jer 2:21 | O-2 |
| 7 | Ruth 2:12 | O-2 |   | Solomon | O-2 |    | Ninevites | O-2 |
| 8 | Matt 12:42 | O-3 |   |   |   |    |   |   |

# 6

## The Modern Perspective

*Explicit Rejections of the Old Testament*

### I NINETEENTH-CENTURY LIBERAL THEOLOGY

MODERN PHILOSOPHY, IMPELLED BY sixteenth century bourgeois mentality and seventeenth century natural science (starting with Descartes's rationalism in 1637 and Hobbes's empiricism in 1651 and blossoming in Kant's critical philosophy in 1781) replaced the predestining otherworldly god of neo-Platonism and Aristotelian-based Scholasticism with its cultural descendent, the god of human rationality and objective empirical knowledge.

Nineteenth century Protestant *liberal theology*, flourishing in the Germanic and Anglo-Saxon world between Kant and the Second World War, was based on modern philosophy as its predecessor had been on the perennial philosophies of their times. Liberal theology continues the Western non-recognition of multilaterally internal relation needed for typological application of Scripture to current social issues. It continues the Western tradition of applying Scripture allegorically, although now directly rather than relayed to heaven and back through two allegories as in Origen, (above, chapter 4.II.1). Legal biblical material, now no longer understandable perennially as regulation according to timeless *Forms*, and not yet understandable corporately as statute law created by the community under a God-delegated responsibility for facilitating corporate interaction, is now based theoretically on the self interest of a majority of individuals. Apocalyptic New Testament narrative and parables using part-for-whole metonymy continue to be interpreted literally, generically, and sometimes allegorically in one of the five ways in the table "Five Opportunities for Modernist Genericizing of the New

Testament" in chapter 3 (above, page 151). In liberal theology, The Old Testament becomes *explicitly* rejected and the New is taken literalistically as proclaiming a new religion; it is certainly not viewed as an attempt to reform Israel from perennial back to its corporate prophetic stance it had before the European conquest. Whereas both biblical and neo-Platonic theologies were built on tissues of multiple references to Scripture, liberal theology clearly reveals the bare bones of modern philosophy.

Picked here to represent liberal theology are Friedrich Schleiermacher, who stands at its creative beginning, and Adolf von Harnack, whose orthodox liberalism is characteristic of its end.

Nineteenth-century liberal theology held Christianity (1) to be a new religion rather than a continuation of Old Testament religion, (2) viewed Jesus as its "founder," (3) rejected the Old Testament, (4) argued for a generic universality in Christianity against Old Testament organic complementarity, and (5) took faith to be a passive generic *feeling* by individuals rather than intentional creative corporate *interaction* by community members.

*1 The Feeling of Absolute Dependence: Friedrich Schleiermacher*

Friedrich Schleiermacher (1768–1834), dean of the theological faculty at Berlin, stated all of these five views in his *The Christian Faith* (1822–1831).

1. Christianity is independent of Judaism: "Christian piety, in its original form, cannot be explained by means of the Jewish piety of that or of an earlier time, and so Christianity cannot in any wise be regarded as a remodeling or a renewal and continuation of Judaism" (p. 61). "The relations of Christianity to Judaism and Heathenism are the same, inasmuch as the transition from either of these to Christianity is a transition to another religion" (pp. 60–61). "We can find rendered with some exactness in Old Testament passages only those of our religious emotions which are of a somewhat general nature without anything very distinctively Christian. For those which are distinctively Christian, Old Testament sayings will not provide a suitable expression, unless we think certain elements away from them and read other things into them. And that being the case, we shall certainly find quite as near and accordant echoes in the utterances of the nobler and purer Heathenism" (p. 62).

2. Jesus is "founder" of Christianity: "Jesus is Founder of a religious communion simply in the sense that its members become conscious of redemption through him. . . . Only through Jesus, and thus only in Christianity, has redemption become the central point of religion" (pp. 56–57).

3. The Old Testament is explicitly rejected:

> The Old Testament Scriptures owe their place in our Bible partly to the appeals the New Testament Scriptures make to them, partly to the historical connexion of Christian worship with the Jewish Synagogue; but the Old Testament Scriptures do not on that account share the normative dignity or the inspiration of the New. . . . The ecclesiastical status of the Old Testament was due to its historical connexions, so that its gradual retirement into the background lies in the nature of the case. . . . The real meaning of the facts would be clearer if the Old Testament followed the New as an appendix (pp. 608–11).

4. Christianity is universal whereas Judaism is particular: "Even in the prophetic books most of the contents relate to the legal dispensation and the circumstances of the people as such, and the spirit in which they originate is simply the spirit of the people: it is therefore not the Christian Spirit, which as One Spirit was to break down the wall of partition between this people and all others" (p. 609).

5. Finally, faith, or *piety*, is generic; it is independent of relation. Influenced by an aspect of German romanticism, Schleiermacher inserts *feeling* (*Gefühl*), a pre-theoretical and pre-practical consciousness more immediate than Kant's theoretical and practical reason, into the notion of piety, that is, piety is a particular way of feeling. "The piety which forms the basis of all ecclesiastical communions is, considered purely in itself, neither a Knowing nor a Doing, but a modification of Feeling, or of immediate self-consciousness" (p. 5); that is, piety is a self-awareness, an "immediate" feeling, a knowing about self, such as self-approval or self-reproach (p. 7).

Life is "an alternation between an abiding-in-self [*Insichbleiben*] and a passing-beyond-self [*Aussichheraustreten*] on the part of the subject." Both Knowing and Doing involve passing-beyond-self, whereas Feeling "is entirely an abiding-in-self" (p. 8). Yet it "falls to Piety to stimulate Knowing and Doing, . . . otherwise . . . piety would be something isolated and without any influence upon the other mental functions of our lives"

(p. 9). The two elements, abiding-in-self and passing-beyond-self, "correspond in the subject to its *Receptivity* and its (spontaneous) *Activity*" (p. 13), and thus to its simultaneous feeling of dependence and of freedom, hence of reciprocity in one's relation with a *World* (pp. 13–15).

But we cannot at all provide ourselves with a World. The consciousness of a necessarily pre-given self and world "is itself precisely consciousness of absolute [*schlechthinig*, come-what-may, unavoidable] dependence; for it is the consciousness that the whole of our spontaneous activity comes from a source outside of us" (pp. 15–16); that is, spontaneous activity, partly free and partly dependent, is unavoidably dependent on there being an I and a world to interact. Consciousness of this is *Piety*: "The . . . essence of piety is this: the consciousness of being absolutely [come what may] dependent, or, which is the same thing, of being in relation with God" (p. 12).

Thus, Schleiermacher calls the source for the being of an I and a World 'God.' He says, "the Whence of our receptive and active existence, as implied in this self-consciousness, is to be designated by the word 'God'. . . . This 'Whence' is not the world . . . For we have a feeling of freedom . . . in relation to the world, since we are . . . continually exercising an influence on its individual parts" (pp. 16–17). And piety, the consciousness of being dependent, belongs to the individual: "The feeling of absolute [unavoidable] dependence, expressing itself as consciousness of God, is . . . an essential element of human nature" (p. 26). Redemption, being freed to bring the feeling of unavoidable dependence into all human states of consciousness (pp. 54, 98) also belongs to the individual—"the more the subject, in each moment of sensible self-consciousness, with his partial freedom and partial dependence, takes at the same time the attitude of absolute dependence, the more religious is he" (p. 22).

God and human nature are inseparably and jointly involved in human unavoidable dependence, and in the education of one's consciousness of it. Hence, redemption is "a human state which not only would obtain the fullest recognition from the common human reason, but in which also it is impossible always to distinguish, even in the same individual, between what is effected by the divine Spirit and what is effected by the human reason" (p. 65). The "supernatural" pervades nature as well: "But if the supernatural in the Christian self-consciousness consists in the fact that it cannot . . . be produced by the activity of reason, it by no means follows . . . that the expressions given to this self-consciousness must also be supra-rational. For in the same sense in which the Christian self-consciousness is supra-rational, the whole of Nature is supra-rational too" (p. 66). A gracious nod to pre-Enlightenment neo-Platonic theology!

The feeling of unavoidable dependence is the basis for Schleiermacher's theological system. *The Christian Faith* has a three-tiered organizational scheme. Doctrine consists of three elements: "descriptions of human states" of mind, "conceptions of divine attributes," and "utterances concerning the constitution of the world" (p. 125). Each part or sub-part of the book, aside from the introduction and conclusion, is divided into three "SECTIONS" (pp. ix-xii) according to these three elements of Christian doctrine. Of these elements, "we must declare the description of the human states of mind to be the fundamental dogmatic form; while propositions of the second and third forms are permissible only in so far as they can be developed out of propositions of the first form; for only on this condition can they be really authenticated as expressions of religious emotions" (p. 126). Doctrine is to be based on "piety", that is, on the individual's consciousness of being unavoidably dependent.

The feeling of unavoidable dependence does not occur abstractly or spontaneously, rather the capacity for this feeling must be developed within some particular religious system: "The positive religions are just the definite form in which religion must exhibit itself."[1] "A peculiar and noble capacity of man underlies religion, a capacity which, of course, must be educated."[2] "No man as a mere single being can come to actual existence. By the very fact of existence he is set in a world, . . . and a religious man, by attaining his individual life, enters by this very fact into a common life, which is to say into some definite form of religion."[3] All piety, including Christian piety, is thus intersubjective: "Christian piety never arises independently and of itself in an individual, but only out of the communion and in the communion, there is no such thing as adherence to Christ except in combination with adherence to the communion" (p. 106).

But the intersubjectivity of faith is a *generic* intersubjectivity, not a *corporate* one. All community is based on similarity: "Fellowship

1. Schleiermacher, *On Religion*, 217.
2. Ibid., 214–15.
3. Ibid., 230.

... is demanded by the *consciousness of kind* which dwells in every man" (p. 27). Any feeling, and in particular the feeling of unavoidable dependence, in one person is awakened in another by imitation through consciousness of kind (p. 27). A church or communion is a group of individuals who through such reciprocal influence possess a core of identical religious affections: "When people speak of a particular religion, this is always with reference to one definite 'Church,' and it means the totality of the religious affections which form the foundation of such a communion and are recognized to be identical in the various members" (p. 29). The Christian church is historical in the sense that it was founded by Christ, but its function is merely to be the locus of a generically shared common faith whose impact on the individual is identical with the impact that would have been experienced in meeting the original historical Jesus: "If, however, the faith of the later generations, and consequently of our own, is to be the same as the original one and not a different faith ... then it must still be possible to have the same experiences.... But there is given to us, instead of His personal influence, only that of His fellowship.... Our proposition, therefore, depends upon the assumption that this influence of the fellowship in producing a like faith is none other than the influence of the personal perfection of Jesus Himself" (p. 363). Schleiermacher's frequent term *Gesamtleben, community life*, is rendered "corporate life" in the MacIntosh edited translation (pp. 358–536), but in the terminology of the present book it is "generic common life", as is clear from the context. Schleiermacher specifies a community united by *similar feeling*; Scripture advocates a community united by *complementary creative internal interaction to accomplish a community project*, something Jesus as individual could not do, but could do as "Christ" representing and encouraging the people of God. For Schleiermacher, community consists in a common piety and a generic mechanism for spreading it, making the faith of all individuals similar diachronically as well as synchronically. As in critical history, historical distance is completely overcome.

Progress, an Enlightenment ideal, is kept under control. The various world religions and their subdivisions can be classified according to their value, with the highest level being the German Evangelical church resulting from the union of Lutheran and Reformed churches in Schleiermacher's time (pp. viii, 31–52, 101–7). Yet this relative perfection consists in a maximizing of the feeling of unavoidable dependence among current members of the communion independently of any historical relation with the past: "Christ and the Apostles themselves refer to the books of the Old Testament as divine authorities favorable to Christianity. But from this it does not in the least follow that for our faith we still need these earlier premonitions, since we have actual experience; and the New Testament approves of men ceasing to believe on the ground of such witness when once they have gained immediate certainty through their own perception. [note] John 4:42 [It is no longer because of what you said that we believe, for we have heard for ourselves]" (pp. 610–11). Schleiermacher holds that Catholicism is a more primitive form of piety than Protestantism because it takes tradition more seriously than the immediate generic relation to Christ that he advocates: "that Church which places the communion above the relation to Christ also most easily takes over matter from the earlier religious communions, and consequently . . . whatever has a certain flavour of the Jewish or the Heathen is more in keeping with the Roman Church, just as every opposition to these elements, even in earlier times, contained something akin to Protestantism" (p. 107). Schleiermacher speaks to an academic elite. German Evangelical Church liturgy and piety retained significant explicit practices and their implied implicit corporate orientation from its pre-Reformation past, including its parent Israel, and this was an embarrassment for Schleiermacher.

Thus, history and tradition receive short shrift in Schleiermacher. Piety is transmitted over the centuries, but it is a one-way transmission of a fixed recognition of dependence, an "education" of a natural generic propensity, authenticated by current experience, with no further need for reference to prior, more primitive forms. It is an immediate conscious state in the generic individual, coming from God, steadily available. Schleiermacher has found the classical Greek Platonic ghost behind the Enlightenment machine.

Because Schleiermacher holds that God-consciousness is induced in German Evangelical Christians from the German Evangelical Christian community, a community whose defining theological confessions both claim and display dependence on the Bible (pp. 112–13), he is under some compulsion to reconcile his system with the biblical material.

Substantial parts of the book do not refer to the Bible at all. In those portions that do, Schleiermacher's disagreement with the Old Testament perspective often surfaces as, for example, his disagreement with the complementary relation between humanity and God in Exod 32:14 "And the Lord changed his mind about the disaster that he planned to bring on his people" (p. 206). He discounts any corporate material in the New Testament as, for example, its conception of sin as a social structure in eleven New Testament passages (p. 165). He frequently uses the New Testament negatively as, for example, claiming Rom 1:19–20 "what can be known about God ... [has] been understood ... through the things he has made" as basis for eliminating a literal Old Testament account of creation from church dogma (p. 150). He misunderstands and rejects New Testament typological use of the Old Testament: "a proof from prophecy of Christ as the Redeemer is impossible; and in particular, the zealous attempt to seek out for this purpose prophecies or prototypes which relate to accidental circumstances in the story of Christ must appear simply as a mistake" (p. 74). Such use of the Old Testament is powerless to cause faith: "it is never asserted that faith sprang from the proof, but from the preaching" (p. 70). The New Testament itself, of course, used past prophecy and types not to prove *facts* to *individuals* but to persuade the *community* to make *choices* based on its past community experience.

Schleiermacher's approving uses of the New Testament are generic: They exploit all five of the opportunities for genericizing the New Testament outlined in table "Five Opportunities for Modernist Genericizing of the New Testament" in chapter 3, page 151 above.

(1) Schleiermacher exploits the first of these opportunities, taking the new age as being discontinuous with the old, anticipating existentialist Bultmann by a hundred and thirty years (above, page 154). On Paul's treatment of Abraham's faith, Schleiermacher takes the more discontinuous version in Galatians 3 over that of Romans 4 to justify a stand at the discontinuous pole of the eschatological strand of apocalyptic. But Schleiermacher goes much further than Paul; he does not allow that Abraham actually possessed faith: "The promise to Abraham, so far as it has been fulfilled in Christ, is represented as having had its reference to Christ only in the divine decree, not in the religious consciousness of Abraham and his people. And since we can only recognize the self-identity of a religious communion when there is a uniformity of the religious consciousness, we can no more recognize an identity between Christianity and Abrahamitic Judaism than between it and the later Judaism or Heathenism" (p. 61). The discontinuity between Judaism and

Christianity, which in Schleiermacher is an abstraction of the eschatological discontinuity between the two ages, is absolute.

(2) The second opportunity listed in the table for a genericizing interpretation of the New Testament is the misreading of first-century corporate "powers" sociology as a generic analysis of society by bringing the conflict with the power of sin from within the community to inside the generic individual. Schleiermacher refers to Paul's social powers of sin, flesh, and spirit (pp. 272–81), but interprets Paul in accordance with Augustine and the Reformation confessions that hold sin to be generic and internal to the individual. For Schleiermacher, sin, like faith, is generic at two levels. At the first level, sin is "that inherent quality of the acting subject which is a part condition of all his actual sins and is anterior to all action on his part" (p. 281), either innate or due to education (p. 279), "our evil nature" (p. 280). At the second level, sin is "the sinful acts which are due to the individual himself" (p. 281). But the two are related: "we recognize our evil nature as being also our own sin, since, instead of having overcome it by our action, we voluntarily perpetuate it" (p. 280). Schleiermacher brings the conflict with sin inside the individual because in his generic conceptuality there is no other possible location for it.

(3) With the third opportunity for genericizing the New Testament, taking the resurrection of Christ as singular rather than as first-fruits of resurrection of the community, Schleiermacher is more extreme than Bultmann (page 156, above). Whereas Bultmann makes the resurrection of Christ available only for each individual generically, Schleiermacher makes it irrelevant because God-consciousness in the disciples directly (and in subsequent individual Christians indirectly) is induced generically from Jesus before his resurrection: "The facts of the Resurrection and the Ascension of Christ, . . . cannot be laid down as properly constituent parts of the doctrine of His Person. . . . The disciples recognized in Him the Son of God without having the faintest premonition of His resurrection and ascension, and we too may say the same of ourselves" (pp. 417–18). The resurrection of Christ and related doctrines "are accepted only because they are found in the Scriptures; and all that can be required of any Protestant Christian is that he shall believe them in so far as they seem to him to be adequately attested" (p. 420). For Schleiermacher, the resurrection of Jesus is irrelevant to Christian faith; that is, to individual feeling of unavoidable dependence. In contrast,

Torah and Prophets urge throughout resurrection of the community to both the freedom and responsibility needed to create a functional, internally relating community, not the resurrection of separate individuals to feel unavoidably dependent. Moreover, the Gospels characterize the resurrection of Jesus precisely as the passing on of responsibility to the disciples for continuing this work: "as the Father sent me so I send you," not to feel something but to do something: "Whose sins you forgive, they are forgiven" (John 20:22–23).

(4) The largest number, but least spectacular, of Schleiermacher's genericizing uses of the New Testament is the misreading of promotion of active corporate participation in community interaction as a passive generic submission. For example, Schleiermacher interprets the two passages John 1:45 "Philip found Nathanael, and said to him, 'We have found him about whom Moses in the law and also the prophets wrote, Jesus,'" and Matt 16:15–18: "Peter answered, 'You are the Christ . . .' And Jesus answered him, '. . . you are Peter, and on this rock I will build my church,'" as saying they followed Jesus because he made pervasive their feeling of unavoidable dependence (pp. 68–69), rather than joining his work at restoring Israel to its pre-colonial corporate interactive life.

(5) The fifth opportunity for Schleiermacher's genericizing the New Testament is the reading of the servant remnant as sect remnant, mistaking an interacting community offering inclusion to all as being an exclusive saved community. Schleiermacher goes further: he does not recognize any remnant, servant, or sect: Schleiermacher has no interest in communities, only in recognition of individual unavoidable dependence on a world, learned by example from others.

For Schleiermacher, religion frees one for a generically shared passive primordial feeling of unavoidable dependence, whereas Scripture calls for internally interactive participation in creation and maintenance of community. To maintain his position within the nineteenth century academic Christian theological tradition, Schleiermacher explicitly rejects the Old Testament and genericizes the New in the five ways here analyzed.

*2 The Universal Kernel of the Gospel: Adolf von Harnack*

A century later, Adolf von Harnack (1851–1930) was still promulgating Schleiermacher's same five views on the independence of Christianity from the Old Testament and genericizing the New Testament in the same second five ways. Although Harnack's specialty was church history, not theology, his popular theological essay *What is Christianity?* (1900) reflects a widespread consensus among liberal theologians of his time.

Christianity is independent of Judaism: "Jesus was the 'Messiah,' and was not the Messiah; and he was not the Messiah because he left the idea far behind him; because he put a meaning into it which was too much for it to bear" (p. 141).

> The new principles displayed great vigor and pointed far beyond Judaism.... The new experience of a direct union with God makes the old worship with its priests and mediations unnecessary.... It was the path upon which a deliverance from historical Judaism and its outworn religious ordinances was capable of gradual attainment.... Someone had to stand up and say "The old is done away with"; he had to brand any further pursuit of it as a *sin*.... The man who did that was the apostle Paul, and it is in having done it that his greatness in the history of the world consists.... It was Paul who delivered the Christian religion from Judaism.... This religion, born in Palestine, and confined by its founder to Jewish ground, in only a few years after his death was severed from that connexion (pp. 173–78).

In chapters 2 and 3, above, we found the opposite: Paul worked to keep "the old" against western culture.

For Harnack, the essence of Christianity is the teaching of Jesus: "That Jesus' message is so great and so powerful lies in the fact that it is so simple and on the other hand so rich.... His words speak to us across the centuries with the freshness of the present" (p. 51).

The Old Testament is explicitly rejected: "The possession of this book has not been an unqualified advantage to the church.... There was always a danger of an inferior and obsolete principle forcing its way into Christianity through the Old Testament. This, indeed, was what actually occurred" (p. 186). Two decades later he was even more explicit: "The repudiation of the Old Testament in the second century would have been a mistake which the great church properly refused to make. Its retention in the sixteenth century was a fate which the Reformation was not yet able to avoid. But its continued preservation since the nineteenth century as canonical document in Protestantism is the result of a religious and ecclesiastical paralysis."[4]

---

4. Harnack, *Marcion*, XI and 248–49.

Christianity is generic and universal, whereas Judaism is particular: "The Gospel is in nowise a positive religion like the rest; ... it contains no statutory or particularistic elements; ... *it is, therefore, religion* itself" (p. 63). "The founder had his eye upon *man* in whatever external situation he might be found—upon *man* who, fundamentally, always remains the same" (p. 17). Of Paul he says, "It was he who perceived that religion in its new phase pertains to the individual and therefore to all individuals, ... he carried the Gospel to the world and transferred it from Judaism to the ground occupied by Greece and Rome" (p. 177).

Finally, faith is generic and universal rather than corporate and particular. Harnack's philosophical presuppositions are neo-Kantian: He analyzes in terms not of pre-theoretical and pre-practical immediate self-consciousness as Schleiermacher did but in terms of *facts* and *values*. History is understood as a critical history of *facts:* "In history absolute judgments are impossible. . . . History can only show how things have been; and . . . we must not presume to think that by any process of abstraction absolute judgments as to the value to be assigned to past events can be obtained from the results of a purely historical survey. Such judgments are the creation only of feeling and of will; they are a subjective act" (p. 18). "In taking up a theological book we are in the habit of enquiring first of all as to the 'stand-point' of the author. In a historical work there is no room for such enquiry."[5] Religion, on the other hand, is understood as a *value*, and judgment of its value lies outside of history. He says in the case of the gospel writings one is driven to value it by an essence that leaps off the page: "The Gospel in the Gospel is something so simple, something that speaks to us with so much power, that it cannot easily be mistaken. . . . No one who possesses a fresh eye for what is alive, and a true feeling for what is really great, can fail to see it and distinguish it from its contemporary integument" (p. 14).

In answering the question "What is Christianity?" Harnack himself exercises this judgment, looking for an essence, or kernel, of Christianity that is *new and different* from the culture of its time, and *universal, timeless, and generic* in its application to each individual. Harnack remains within the non-interactive Enlightenment perspective.

The kernel must be new and different: "The historian's task of distinguishing between what is traditional and what is peculiar . . . in Jesus' message of the kingdom of God is a difficult and responsible one" (p. 55).

---

5. Harnack, *The History of Dogma*, author's preface to the English edition, 1.vii.

Using as example the scholars of his own age, including himself, he says: "Some day the knife will be applied and pieces will be cut away where as yet we do not feel the slightest inclination to distinguish. Let us hope that then we may find fair judges, who will measure our ideas not by what we have unwittingly taken over from tradition and are neither able nor called upon to correct, but by what was born of our very own, by the changes and improvements which we have effected in what was handed down to us or was commonly prevalent in our day" (p. 55). In Harnack's world, an academician is judged by what in his work will stand out as new, and thus Harnack seeks to evaluate Jesus as the "great teacher." But the New Testament actually shows Jesus calling Israel to resist European colonization and maintain its own tradition.

Harnack looks for a universal and generic kernel in the culturally bound husk of Jesus' teaching and finds a simple three-fold expression of it:

*Firstly, the kingdom of God and its coming.*

*Secondly, God the Father and the infinite value of the human soul.*

*Thirdly, the higher righteousness and the commandment of love.*
(p. 51)

Only such a universal kernel could apply to individuals across the ages: "There are only two possibilities here: either the Gospel is in all respects identical with its earliest form, in which case it came with its time and has departed with it; or else it contains something which, under differing historical forms, is of permanent validity. The latter is the true view" (pp. 13–14). As Philo universalizes Scripture into middle-Platonic precepts (above, page 163), so Harnack's universal kernel is based on modern empiricism. The biblical gospel itself is not "valid" as "fact," rather it calls the *community* to *create* a continuing ever-changing essence-building interactive life together.

In reaching his generic version of Jesus' teaching, Harnack exploits all five of the opportunities for genericizing the New Testament (above, page 151) by misreading its position on the five key corporate-generic ranges in the apocalyptic idiom in which it is written.

(1) Harnack takes the discontinuous pole of the eschatological strand over the salvation-history strand: "the kingdom of God is the rule

of God ... in the hearts of individuals.... From this point of view everything that is dramatic in the external and historical sense has vanished; and gone, too, are all the external hopes for the future" (p. 56). The new age is totally discontinuous from the old; history is eliminated.

(2) Harnack reads first-century corporate "powers" sociology as a generic analysis of society by bringing the conflict with the power of sin inside the generic individual. "It is not a question of angels and devils, thrones and principalities, but of God and the soul, the soul and its God" (p. 56). He does not recognize Paul's "powers" as social dysfunctionality.

(3) Harnack applies the resurrection of Christ generically to each individual, for example: "Whatever may have happened at the grave and in the matter of the appearances, one thing is certain: This grave was the birthplace of the indestructible belief that death is vanquished, that there is a life eternal.... mankind, so far as it believes in these things, has attained to that certainty of eternal life for which it was meant.... This feeling first established faith in the value of personal life" (pp. 162–63) a generic interpretation.

(4) Harnack reads an active corporate participation by a broader range of individuals as being a generic participation, thus taking the individual pole in the whole-individual range: "As individualism becomes a stronger force, so the relation of God to the individual was prominently emphasized.... the individual belief in Providence appears side by side with the political belief, and combines with the feeling of personal worth and responsibility.... The products of this inner development are an interest in personal salvation, and a belief in the resurrection" (pp. 133–34). "If anyone wants to know what the kingdom of God and the coming of it meant in Jesus' message, he must read and study his parables.... The kingdom of God comes by coming to the individual, by entering into his soul and laying hold of it.... Take whatever parable you will, the parable of the sower, of the pearl of great price, of the treasure buried in the field—the word of God, God himself, is the kingdom" (p. 56).

(5) Harnack, like Bultmann and Schleiermacher (above, pages 157 and 232), recognizes no remnant, servant, or sect. But like Bultmann and Schleiermacher, Harnack's omission of any servant role for the righteous places him closer to the sect remnant position.

Harnack isolates value-free critical history from fact-free religion, abstracting each from other practices and from one another.

For Harnack, religion is as antiseptic, objectified, unchangeable, and uninfluenceable—as is critical history. The human community does not participate in the creation of either. Hence, Harnack necessarily misses the corporate biblical message by genericizing in the typical nineteenth century way.

In Harnack's own day, communally inclined theologians Alfred Loisy and Ernst Troeltsch[6] of the history-of-religions school criticized his "essence of Christianity" as missing both Christianity's interactive essence and its purpose for the human community in which it was incarnated. But such communal leanings in theology were eclipsed after the First World War by the rise among liberal theologians of a new school (existentialist theology), prolonging for another half century the prominence in Protestant theology of a militant individualism, to the development of which we now turn.

## II TWENTIETH CENTURY: ABANDON OR INTENSIFY LIBERAL THEOLOGY?

### *1 Search for a Replacement for Liberal Theology: Karl Barth*

Nineteenth-century European academic belief in progress through individual freedom and education was shattered by the First World War. Neo-Kantian "facts" and "values" and liberal theology seemed to be as stultifying as scholasticism had seemed to the Renaissance. For university graduate Karl Barth (1886–1968), that nineteenth century academic world was shattered a few years earlier than for the others. As a young pastor from 1911 to 1921 of the tiny Swiss-German town of Safenwil, he immediately recognized his theological education (from teachers including Harnack at Berlin, Kant-Schleiermacher disciple Wilhelm Herrmann, and neo-Kantian philosopher Hermann Cohen at Marburg) as irrelevant to his pastoral responsibilities to his parishioners—proletarians struggling against Safenwil's two bourgeois factory owners (also parishioners) in the notorious early stages of the continental industrial revolution. Barth became active in the Socialist Union movement—preaching, speaking at union meetings, and searching for some theological base adequate to his parishioners' distressed situation. After

---

6. Loisy, *The Gospel and the Church*, 1–22; Troeltsch, "The Dogmatics of the 'Religionsgeschichtliche Schule,'" 12.

intellectual struggle, he took haven in Luther's choice of Augustine's negation of all human righteousness, a choice against liberal theology but also against finding an answer to the proletarian dilemma. In 1921, he returned to the academic world, a world where this last choice would also fit his new environment. From 1932 to 1968 he produced his systematic *Church Dogmatics* in 13 "part-volumes". In none of his positions, from his early pastoral involvement in socialism to his last *Dogmatics* sections, did Barth ever recognize the scriptural bilateral corporate relation between God and the interacting human community.

In 1911, still pastor in Aargau, Barth was asked to speak to the cantonal labor union and chose as his address title "Jesus Christ and the Socialist Movement."[7] He began by asserting, "Jesus *is* the socialist movement and the socialist movement *is* Jesus in the present" (pp. 386–87 [19]); "Socialism is a movement from below to above. . . . what Jesus Christ was and intended and achieved, seen from the human side, was throughout a *movement from below*" (pp. 391–92 [23]). Barth condemns the church for avoiding the problem:

> [F]or eighteen hundred years the Christian church, when faced with social misery, has always referred to the Spirit, to the inner life, to heaven. The church has preached, instructed, and consoled, but she has *not helped*. . . . That is the great, momentous apostasy of the Christian church, her apostasy from Christ. When social democracy then appeared with its gospel of heaven on earth, . . . she accused social democracy of vulgar materialism, and beat on her breast saying "Lord, we thank you that we are not as they are, that we are still idealists who place spirit first and believe in heaven" (p. 395 [26]).

He adds, parodying Harnack, "before and after, religion is ever a matter between God and the soul, the soul and God" (p. 404 [34]). He apologizes for the church with its liberal theology: "Jesus is not the Christian world view and the Christian world view is not Jesus." "What Jesus has to bring to us are not ideas, but a way of life" (p. 391 [22]). Accordingly, in his address he alludes to some 52 Gospel passages but only one Pauline passage.

As in socialist literature, Barth says, "The proletarian is not always poor, but his existence is always dependent on the power and good will

---

7. Barth, "Jesus Christus und die soziale Bewegung," ["Jesus Christ and the Movement for Social Justice"].

of his employer, the manufacturer. Here socialism enters . . . . to make independent the dependent, with all the consequences for their external, moral, and cultural life which that would bring with it" (p. 391 [23]). Here Barth specifies independence, but not multilaterally internal *interdependence*, what early Marx's *German Ideology* (above, page 26) called non-alienation. Barth says Jesus "created new people in order to create a new world. . . . we need people of the future to create the state of the future, not the reverse" (pp. 397–98 [28])—a call for one-way influence from God through "new" individuals rather than through responsible interaction within the already existing community, as in Marx's *German Ideology*. The lack of internal relation between member and community also appears when Barth claims, "The opposite to God is not the earth, not matter, not the outward appearance, but evil, . . . the demons, the devils who live in the person" (p. 396 [27])—the typical Western substitution of an evil inside the person for Paul's claim for the impact on individuals of "principalities and powers" of corporate social dysfunction. Thus, Barth implies that when he cries, "how do we pray: '*my* Father!' or '*our* Father!'? Is not thus already everything said—that for Jesus there was only a social, solidarist God; hence also only a social, solidarist religion!" (p. 405 [34]), he is claiming only that God relates with all individual community members, not with the whole community as a social structure created by the internal interaction of its members.

Barth helped organize three unions, and at the outbreak of the First World War took the politically sensitive step of enrolling in the Social Democratic party to support its internationalism against Swiss nationalism, as he was to do again in 1931 in Bonn when he joined the German Social Democrats to help against rising National Socialism.

But after the war started, the confederation of younger Swiss pastors (the "Christian socialists") pulled apart; Hermann Kutter, pastor in Zurich, emphasized a more spiritual approach and Leonhard Ragaz, pastor in Basel, wanted more practical social action. For Barth, crucially, this disagreement came down to a simple question: Who is going to save Europe—God or the socialists? Barth could never imagine the corporate scriptural answer: both together! In a 1914 lecture he said, "God does not need us, but we him,"[8] a non-bilateral refrain that will continue to appear in Barth and whose pedigree in Western theology is obvious. In a 1916 lecture "The Word of God and Theology," Barth

---

8. Barth, "Evangelium und Sozialismus," 732.

subordinated everything to the "Word." "The Bible teaches not at all . . . how we should speak to God but what he says to us, not how we find the way to him but how he has sought and found the way to us. . . . The Word of God stands in the Bible."[9] Barth looked for a "Word," a "theology," a Form, abstracted above both the socialist movement in Europe and the analogous Jesus movement portrayed in the Gospels. Searching with his friend Eduard Thurneysen, pastor of a neighboring village, he did not pick the Gospels that he alluded to 52 times in his 1911 speech but to the same starting place that another reformer, Luther (above, chapter 4) had picked: *Romans*, the most systematic book in the New Testament, written by Paul, the "from above" intellectual. Like Luther, Barth could not recognize Paul's corporate orientation. The result was Barth's passage-by-passage commentary on *Romans*, his *The Epistle to the Romans*, first edition (1919).

The preface begins: "Paul, as a child of his age, addressed his contemporaries. But much more important than this fact is the other, that he as prophet and apostle of the kingdom of God speaks to all people of every age" (p. 3 [V]). This opening statement resolves the problematic relation between theology and particular events and cultures—it simply lifts us out of all historical contexts, even Paul's. It is as ahistorically and generically oriented as Harnack's: "The founder had his eye upon *man* in whatever external situation he might be found—upon *man* who, fundamentally, always remains the same" (above, page 234). The speaking and hearing are outside the historical setting of speaker and of hearer. Instead, a disembodied Paul, or disembodied Word through Paul, speaks to generic individuals, "all people of every age," to be reached directly, independently of their different internal relations with different cultures in different ages.

This return to theology places Barth above the practical worlds of both first-century Roman oppression and early twentieth-century bourgeois oppression. On the passage Rom 2:1: "in passing judgment on another you condemn yourself" he writes: "Church and mission, personal true-heartedness and morality, pacifism and social democracy do not represent the kingdom of God, but rather in new form the kingdom of the world . . . . The calling to faith is not a calling to anything already at hand" (p. 42 [24]). We are back to the separation of the two

---

9. Barth, "Die neue Welt in der Bibel," 28 [*The Word of God and the Word of Man*, 43].

cities in Augustine's *City of God*. On Rom 10:3 "being ignorant of the righteousness that comes from God, and seeking to establish their own, they have not submitted to God's righteousness." Barth says of God: "*He* will be the savior. *He* will make justice through *his* power. For only what *he* does and accomplishes is really and finally new and good" (p. 398 [297]). Barth has recovered from his brief flirtation with socialism, a socialism intuiting internal bilateral relation as solution for the rampant alienation of the age but unable to state it theoretically (as early Marx did do imperfectly). Henceforth, Barth's escape *from* a liberal theology, which is hopelessly inadequate to deal with the alienation he had found in his congregation, will be an escape *to* Luther, which means back to Augustine and neo-Platonism. Academic-minded Barth has found what will be a permanent home.

In 1921 Barth was called to serve as a professor to Göttingen, just as he finished a second, completely rewritten, definitive edition of his *Romans*. This edition added Luther's Pseudo-Dionysian dialectical negation of human righteousness with Kierkegaard's escape of the self from system, all to destroy liberal theology's "criminal arrogance of religion" (p. 37).

Amplifying the quoted first sentence from his 1919 introduction, Barth renounces two kinds of distancing of God's message, either *objectifying* it by analysis of Paul or of his Romans (rather than directly seizing its message for oneself), or *subjectifying* it by seeing it as about Paul's situation or the reader's (rather than about God himself).

For the first, Barth says in his second edition preface: "Intelligent comment means that I am driven on till I stand with nothing before me but the enigma of the matter; till the document seems hardly to exist as a document; till I have almost forgotten that I am not its author; till I know the author so well that I allow him to speak in my name and am even able to speak in his name myself" (p. 8). Here Barth eliminates the "objective" distance from the document so prized by nineteenth century liberalism, but far from bringing author and reader into interaction, Barth seeks to identify their situations. As in both cosmological and modern perspectives, he wants the reader to apply Paul's insights directly to the present rather than to see a complementary corporate relation between tradition and present issues. He does not leave room for *interpretation* of Paul's message metonymically into our situation. The third edition preface (1922) repeats this rejection of any distinction between Paul and his reader: "The question is whether or no [the commentator] is to place himself in a relation to his author of utter loyalty. Is he to read him, determined to follow him to the very last word, wholly aware of what he is doing, and assuming that the author also knew what he was doing? . . . Anything short of utter loyalty means a commentary ON Paul's Epistle to the Romans, not a commentary so far as is possible WITH him" (p. 17).

And for the second kind of distancing, Paul's message is not to be avoided by any consideration of Paul's own situation. "Paul is authorized to deliver—the Gospel of God. . . . Yes, precisely—*of God!* The Gospel is not a religious message to inform mankind of their divinity or to tell them how they may become divine. . . . The Gospel is . . . not an event, nor an experience, nor an emotion—however delicate!" It is rather "the Word of the Primal Origin of all things, the Word which, since it is ever new, must ever be received with renewed fear and trembling" (p. 28). The gospel is not about the human "criminal arrogance of religion" but about God. It fits Paul's situation and all others in the same way.

Barth's first point is directed against Harnack's reliance on critical-historical "fact," and his second point is directed against Harnack's religion as "value" and Schleiermacher's *a priori* religious "feeling." Together Barth's two points unify all subjects with one another and with the object in a way that excludes internal, interactive relation among them—and corrects their separation in liberal theology and in neo-Kantianism by reuniting them neo-Platonically.

Barth interprets Paul's use of Old Testament tradition. When he comes (pp. 145–48) to Paul's treatment of Abraham's justification, Rom 4:23–24 "Now the words 'it was reckoned to him,' were written not for his [Abraham's] sake alone, but for ours also," he uses the passage to passionately advocate a relation between past and present beyond critical history, but still not the typologically expressed corporate relation found above (chapter 2.II.2) in Paul. *Against* critical history: "It is possible to blot out the radiance with which the past is illuminated, and to describe the wisdom of the book of Genesis as a wisdom of the past. Abraham can be depicted as a Bedouin sheikh, belonging to a bygone age" (p. 147). *For* Platonic unity: "particular episodes in history can be of universal importance. . . . The Genesis narrative opens its mouth and utters the non-historical truth that to Abraham his faith was reckoned as righteousness. In so far as his situation is ours also, our ears too can be open to hear. History reveals its importance, when, through such communing, the present becomes aware of the unity of meaning that is in all history" (p. 145). This is precisely middle-Platonic "biblical typology" taken as allegory relayed through heaven as in Origen (above, page 171) rather than transmitted interactively through history—an unchanging principle of justification-through-faith that passes from Abraham to others, with the Pauline epistle as a messenger delivering this Platonic Form, this "Word," of Abraham as prototypical justified individual (just as Augustine takes Adam as prototypical sinning individual). In contrast, Scripture uses the two, in reverse order, as eponyms for dysfunctional human community and for an Israel restored to some degree of responsible corporate interaction and charged to work historically for the same with and in the other nations.

Barth reproduces Luther's radical understanding of justification as a state of simultaneously being sinner and righteous, an understanding going back to Augustine and Pseudo-Dionysius (above, page 201). "Before ever we read the story of Abraham, we are in the same uncertainty as Abraham was. We stand at the barrier between death and life, between deep-seated human corruption, which is the denial of God, and the righteousness of God, which is the denial of men..." (p. 147). Between God and the human individual there is a radical dialectical relation in which God's *No* to all that the human person is in nature, psyche, culture, and history is God's *Yes* to that person shattered by God. "Men can apprehend their unredeemed condition only because they stand already within the realm of redemption; they know themselves to be sinners only because they are already righteous; they perceive their death, only because they are alive. Only in God can men be so utterly dismembered. If they had not passed into the land of freedom beyond the frontier of all human possibility, how could they perceive that even the loftiest human possibility is insignificant and unreal, save as the boundary which marks their slavery?" (p. 286). Barth is even more eloquent than Luther.

Thus, all the work of salvation is done by God, none by us. "His death is the means by which men are able to apprehend themselves in God.... This apprehension, however, must not be identified with some peculiar maturity of human experience. The sign of baptism reminds us of this invisible fellowship with God, which rules out any question of being the fellow or disciple of Christ except in the bearing of His Cross" (p. 196). That is, God does not need our help. "[The Gospel] does not require representatives with a sense of responsibility, for it is as responsible for those who proclaim it as it is for those to whom it is proclaimed.... God does not need us" (p. 35). This neo-Platonic denial of human creative responsibility underlies practically every page of Barth's *Romans*, as it does of Luther's *Romans*. Calling the relation with God "invisible" is to say that it cannot be seen in a changed God or a changed human being—it is extrinsic. If "God does not need us," then the relation is not intrinsic to God; and if the relation "must not be identified with some peculiar maturity of human experience," then it is not intrinsic to the faithful. Such a view stands in contrast with the biblical corporate conception of covenant between God and his people that requires dedication of complementary resources from both sides: help from God, and resourceful, active service in the world from Israel. Because Barth, like Origen, Augustine, and Luther, does not accept a complementary relation between God and humanity, he is forced (as they are) to ask for an utterly passive will in the justified human being, to match God's impassability.

Barth exploits the five opportunities for genericizing the frequent corporate apocalyptic New Testament passages unrecognizable to Western culture as metonyms (table "Five Opportunities for Modernist Genericizing of the New Testament," page 151, above), as Schleiermacher and Harnack did before him (above in this chapter) and Bultmann after (above, chapter 2.III.2). Barth takes the first opportunity, moving to the discontinuous pole in apocalyptic's eschatological strand, with his claim for God's dialectical *No* to all that is human, thus also implicitly rejecting the Scripture's call for a functionally interacting human community. As for the second opportunity, in Barth the Pauline battle between the self and the social *power* of sin (Rom 7:13–25) is placed inside the generic individual: "Religion breaks me into two halves. One half is the *spirit* of the inward man, which delights in the law of God.... The other half is the *natural* world of my members" (p. 268). As for the third opportunity, in Barth the resurrection of Christ is related not corporately to the community of sent disciples but generically to the new life of the individual: "So then, just as I am visibly one with the dying Christ, so I am invisibly one with this 'Other,' the risen Christ; and I am therefore the man who lives in God; I am the individual, soul and body, who stands in my place" (p. 206). Barth's use of the fourth opportunity, replacing corporate salvation of the community with salvation of the individual, is evident in the immediate relation between God and the individual. As for the fifth opportunity, any servant function of the faithful is explicitly denied: "God does not need us" (p. 35). Thus Barth continues the unwitting literalization in Greek translations of apocalyptic metonyms, missing the core corporate nature of salvation in both Testaments, a concept nonexistent in both neo-Platonism and modern theology (but central to the nineteenth century communal theology of Möhler and Newman, treated below in chapter 7; and the twentieth century blossoming of communal theology, described in chapter 10).

Barth's writing is untouched by explicit rejection of the Old Testament so characteristic of nineteenth century liberal theology. Rather, as we have seen, he tries to reestablish a diachronic identity with it. But without the philosophical resources to recognize it as carrier of a corporate tradition for the people of God, Barth could only bring the individual into close, but extrinsic, engagement with an ahistorical and acultural "Word of the Primal Origin of all things" (p. 28), as he supposes some Old Testament individuals also were.

Although sharing existentialism's passionate revolt against nineteenth century system, Barth was not an existentialist as Bultmann was to be. As a socialist, Barth was politically active in Germany against National Socialism to the point of being deprived of his professorship (Heidegger and Bultmann were not). His Lutheran-based *No* to all that is human excludes existentialism's human individual as authentic self. He soon distanced himself from any existentialist influence in his *Romans*. In its fifth edition preface (1926) he says: "When I wrote the book, did I simply put into words what was everywhere in the air—specially in Germany after the War? Did I say what was readily acceptable to the 'rulers of the world' in our generation, and what men's ears itched to hear? . . . Have [my readers] been presented with . . . a rehash, resurrected out of Nietzsche and Kierkegaard and Cohen? . . . As it becomes more and more clear how much there remained to be done after the book was written, I often wish that I had never written it" (pp. 21–23).

In his lectures on the incarnation in 1932, Barth maintains his negation of all active human contribution. He says God used human means at the incarnation "only in the form of *virgo Maria*, that is, only in the form of a non-willing, non-accomplishing, non-creative, non-sovereign person, only in the form of a person who can merely receive, merely be ready, merely let something happen to and with itself."[10] For Barth, early twentieth-century Swiss rural alpine culture's ideal daughter exemplifies the human passivity needed by God. In contrast, Luke 1:46 presents a Mary as aggressive as the Hannah of 1 Sam 2.

Nevertheless, Barth maintains a passive, organic, but not corporate socialism. As late as 1960 he wrote,[11] "Jesus Christ from the beginning did not intend separate followers, disciples, or witnesses but rather a plurality of them united through him with himself, but thus also with one another." "They . . . may have received, taken up, and carried out their ministry of witness in very different ways—yet in no case as separated monads in some private discipleship on their own responsibility." Thus, Jesus does not utilize any already existing human community but rather forms individual selves into a nominally organic community around himself. "Thus what unites Christians and makes them siblings is not, as several have recently understood and depicted, the propensity for those of common situation, beliefs, and mind-set to come together. . . . Jesus Christ himself, who calls the many selves together, also mutually binds them." In contrast, Scripture describes a Jesus *re*invigorating an already existing community Israel that is already in covenant with God in order to reinvigorate the whole human community—an Israel that already has been given original delegated responsibility for interacting corporately.

In *Church Dogmatics* 3.1[12] Barth takes the image-of-God passage Gen 1:26–28 as saying that each individual is an image of God simply in the sense of being a creation of God. It "is not a quality of a person. . . . It is not anything that a person is or does. It consists in a person-as-such being God's creation" (pp. 206–7 [184]). Thus, rather than a gift to a community of ability and responsibility for multilateral internal interaction, the "image of God" is a mark of non-bilateral extrinsic dependence of each self on God. The passage explicitly protects Augustine's generic doctrine of original sin. In fact, "the sexual differentiation is the only differentiation with which humankind is created. The creation or existence of human beings in groups and kinds, in races and peoples and the like, never comes in question; no real differentiation and no real relation is given except that from individual to individual, and in its earliest and most concrete form from man to woman, from woman to man" (p. 208

---

10. Barth, *Die Kirchliche Dogmatik,* 1.2.209 [*Church Dogmatics,* 1.2.191].
11. Ibid., 4.3.2, 780–82 [*Church Dogmatics,* 4.3.2, 681–83].
12. Ibid., 3.1 [*Church Dogmatics,* 3.1].

[186]). Thus, he explicitly rejects taking the biblical use of the male-female distinction as metonymy for the many biblical distinctions (parent and child, prophet and priest, king and people, Israel and the nations) that make complementary creative relation necessary and possible. He does not recognize literal biblical *"the adam"* in literally intended Gen 1 but not in several centuries earlier metonymically intended Gen 2 as interacting human community—the social frame through which God relates with individuals. Louis-Marie Chauvet says, "in spite of appearances, Barth responds to Scholasticism as a Scholastic. He has in no way overcome the metaphysical dualism between the 'natural' and the 'supernatural.'"[13]

Barth attacked nineteenth-century theology based on the self with a massive neo-Platonic *Church Dogmatics*. But his earlier struggle with community problems lapsed into his early *Epistle to the Romans* that brought Bultmann to an influential existentialism.

### 2 Dehistoricization: Rudolf Bultmann

Rudolf Bultmann was already well established as a liberal New Testament scholar when his conversion (adding existentialism to his liberalism) was revealed in his review in 1922 of the second edition of Barth's *Romans*.[14] His theological position did not change basically after that time. He accepted the Kierkegaardian and Nietzscheian elements—that is, the existentialism—he found in early Barth and then more radically in early Heidegger.

The early Barth had moved the center of theology away from the individual to a God in heaven; and this move, not a corporate one, nevertheless denied the liberal position. Bultmann accepts the centrality of God as in Barth, but unlike Barth retains the existential human self as the locus of that centrality. Bultmann begins his 1924 essay "Liberal Theology and the Latest Theological Movement" like a Barthian by saying, "The object of theology is God, and the complaint against liberal theology is that it dealt not with God but with the human individual. God implies the radical negation and sublimation of the individual." But he ends the essay much closer to both liberal and existentialist positions with: "The object of theology is indeed God, and theology speaks of

---

13. Chauvet, *Symbol and Sacrament*, 544.
14. Bultmann, "Karl Barth's *Epistle to the Romans*," 100–120.

God by speaking of the individual as he is confronted by God, that is, from the standpoint of faith."[15] After the Second World War, the position expressed in the latter sentence became the celebrated program of demythologization (the program of understanding all Scripture solely in terms of its existential meaning for the single self), abstracting it from any historical, mythological, psychological, or scientific vehicle.[16]

We have already seen (in chapter 2, page 110, above) Bultmann's argument in his *New Testament Theology* that the New Testament message, unlike that of the Old Testament, transcends history. In addition, Bultmann devoted two essays specifically to the relation of the Old Testament to the Christian faith.

In the first of these, "The Significance of the Old Testament for the Christian Faith" (1933), Bultmann asserts all of the five characteristic positions of nineteenth-century liberal theology listed at the beginning of this chapter, except that for the second position he moves the founding from Jesus even later to the community of apostles (pp. 11–12).

Bultmann begins the essay by rejecting the modern critical-historical approach to relating New Testament religion to Old Testament religion and replacing it with the "genuinely historical" question of "what basic possibility [the Old Testament] presents for an understanding of human existence" (p. 13). "Genuinely historical" means existential: "A genuinely historical inquiry of the Old Testament is one which, prompted by one's own question concerning existence, seeks to reactualize the understanding of human existence expressed in the Old Testament, in order to gain an understanding of his own existence" (p. 14).

With this groundwork laid, Bultmann goes on to assert that in New Testament times, which still had an existential relation to the Old Testament, the existential understandings expressed in the Old and New Testaments were contrasted as Law and Gospel. "Only he who knows himself to be limited by God's demand . . . can understand the preaching of the Gospel. . . . Christ is the end of the Law; but precisely so that he can be understood as the end of the Law . . . everyone who hears of him must also have heard of the Law" (pp. 14–15). Thus, Bultmann says,

---

15. Bultmann, "Die liberale Theologie und die jüngste theologische Bewegung," 1.2, 25. Jürgen Moltmann makes this interpretation of the Bultmann passages in *The Theology of Hope*, 59, an interpretation essentially inaccessible through the opaque filter of the standard English translation of the Bultmann passages, *Faith and Understanding*, 29, 52.

16. Bultmann, "New Testament and Mythology"; *Jesus Christ and Mythology*.

the Old Testament as law is presupposition for the grace in the New Testament—a presupposition that can be replaced for us by the law in our own culture. The cultic laws of the Old Testament are bound to a primitive stage of a particular people, and we have analogous demands in our own culture. And the truly moral demands "spring out of human relationship as such and not out of its concrete historical form," and hence, "are not specifically Old Testament demands" (p. 16). The Old Testament has significance for the New only in dehistoricized terms, and "the pre-understanding [Heidegger's *fore-structure*, page 35 above] of the Gospel which emerges under the Old Testament can emerge just as well within other historical embodiments of the divine Law" (p. 17). Bultmann's argument is the same as Schleiermacher's argument that "the relations of Christianity to Judaism and Heathenism are the same" (above, page 224). Bultmann implies that both are examples of *community*, the very thing the New Testament liberates us from.

For existentialist Bultmann, the Old Testament condemns itself. In the Old Testament, the individual seeking self-understanding "is not referred to the universal, the cosmos, so that he may see himself as a part of this realm, nor is he referred to the Logos so that he may find true being in the timeless. Rather he is directed into his concrete history with its past and future, with its present that lays before him the demand of the moment in concrete relation with the 'neighbor,'" (p. 20). Out of the ethnic history in the Old Testament can be read the existentiality (the "historicity") of the individual as a pre-understanding for approaching what for Bultmann is its opposite, the New Testament. For existentialist Bultmann, the Old Testament contains its own condemnation—it leads to the very existentialist understanding under which it emerges in the New as law rather than gospel, as impediment rather than help.

Within the Old Testament, Bultmann says that existence under the law is grace for a particular people—God chooses this people, concludes a covenant with them, forgives them, and sends the prophets with the message of eschatological hope. But it is only hope. In the New Testament this hope is fulfilled, the individual's relation to God is bound to Jesus, the new age is dawned—the age in which God's forgiving grace no longer comes in the history of a people but in the proclaimed "word" (pp. 28–29). He continues

> In the Old Testament God's revelation is bound to the history of a particular people. . . . What God has done in this history he

> has done unto each individual in so far as this individual has an integral place within his people and his people's history.... In the New Testament, God's deed in Jesus Christ is not understood in the same way.... For [Jesus] is the eschatological deed of God which makes an end of all ethnic history as the sphere of God's dealing with man. The contemporaneity of the saving event accomplished in him is not mediated through the continuous ethnic history.... The message of the forgiving grace of God in Jesus Christ is not a historical account about a past event, but rather it is the Word which the Church proclaims, which now addresses each person immediately as God's word.... For in this Word the individual is confronted immediately by God.... The Church is not a sociological entity, an ethnic or cultural community bound together by the continuity of history; but is constituted by the proclaimed word of God's forgiveness in Christ (pp. 29–30).

Thus, for Bultmann, in the Old Testament God reaches the individual through the ethnic community; but in the New Testament, God reaches the individual directly, generically, through the "word" or proclamation—and the second method fits the existentially realized self much better than the first. Bultmann concludes: "Israel's history is not our history, and in so far as God has shown his grace in that history, such grace is not meant for us.... But this just means: to the Christian faith the Old Testament is not in the true sense God's Word" (pp. 31–32).

In his essay "Prophecy and Fulfillment"[17] (1949), Bultmann sharpens his critique of the Old Testament. He says the Old Testament was a prophecy fulfilled only in its inner contradiction, in its miscarriage (p. 183 [72]). The contradiction consists in the covenant as being contracted with a community but having a validity based on the moral behavior of the individual. "It is a contradiction in terms to speak of a covenant which distinguishes an empirical historical people and assures it of God's help, if the validity of the covenant is bound up not at all with the existence of the empirical historical people as a people, but with the moral behavior of the individuals in the people" (p. 172 [60]), that is, the contradiction of a covenant with the *community* that depends on the behavior of *individuals* within it. Bultmann wants saved individuals; the Old Testament wants a saved community.

---

17. Bultmann, "Weissagung und Erfüllung." Page numbers in brackets refer to English translation.

The "contradiction" arises from Bultmann's genericizing one of the biblical component's terms and not the other. The Old Testament does not bind the covenant generically "with the moral behavior of the individuals in the people" as, say, a generically applicable neo-Platonic "Law" does, but rather with community internal interaction creatively constituting the essence of the community and, thus, of each individual member's essence as its interactive role in the community. Such a covenant cannot save a self separately: Individual salvation *is* creative participation in the ongoing joint community interaction and *is* an internally related part of community salvation. Old Testament "Law" or Torah is not pre-assigned: The covenant specifically delegates to the community the creation of its social structure needed for community interaction.

For Bultmann, the same contradiction does not arise in the New Testament because he genericizes the New Testament community as well (using the fourth opportunity offered by the apocalyptic style), misreading active corporate participation by a broader range of individuals as generic participation (above, page 151). Using the New Testament passage Matt 3:9, "God is able from these stones to raise up children to Abraham," Bultmann argues (p. 172 [60]) that the New Testament fulfills, or resolves, the contradiction by replacing the historical Israel with the non-historical eschatological congregation. "And so the people of God is no longer an empirical historical entity—it does not exist as a people needing institutional rules for its organization" (p. 183 [71]). "The idea of the people of God shows itself as unrealizable in an empirical national community, since this requires state apparatus, law, and authority" (p. 184 [73]). Rather, "encountering God's grace makes one recognize God's activity as eschatological in the true sense, that is, as withdrawing one from the world" (pp. 184 [73–74]). As a result of the New Testament fulfillment "we get the right to interpret that contradiction . . . as one that belongs to human existence as such—to be created by God, to be called to God, and yet to be imprisoned in worldly history" (p. 185 [74]). Thus, Bultmann resolves the contradiction by desocializing the New Testament individual and rejecting the obstinately corporate Old Testament.

From the point of view of the communal scholars (outlined in chapter 2 and 3, above), Bultmann has unwittingly rejected the New Testament as well. Those scholars' recognition of the corporate nature of the New Testament moves the contradiction from *within* the Old Testament to *between* the biblical call to shared responsibility with God for the world in both testaments *and* the non-interactive Western orientation in all its variations (perennial, modern, or existentialist—the last of these most clearly bringing the contradiction into focus).

The two essays show that, for Bultmann, the whole Old Testament is law rather than gospel. Law, in this case, is not created through excessive legalism but exists because the individual in society has to deal with an "empirical historical people" and is "imprisoned in worldly history"—that is, because living in society includes anti-existentialist accountability to society. This is a more radical version of the fifth characteristic of nineteenth-century liberal theology, understanding faith to be generic rather than corporate (above, page 157), than we found in liberal theology itself: Bultmann has not just made earthly historical community irrelevant to faith, he has given earthly community as such the color of evil, something to be saved from. Bultmann has reached an anthropological equivalent of cosmologically based gnosticism.

Bultmann, like the second century gnostic Marcion (above, page 163), identifies law with the historical world, taking Paul's polemic against self-serving exploitation of the law, "the law, weakened by the flesh" (Rom 8:3), as polemic against law itself, against tradition, against Torah and Prophets. Like Marcion, he sees the conflict between history and grace, between world and God, between works and faith, between Old Testament and New, as resolvable only by escape of the self from the former to the latter.

This extreme position can be accounted for in part as polemic against National Socialism (the dates of the two essays neatly bracket the period of National Socialist rule in Germany) and Bultmann's dislike of excesses in Germany during this period cannot be doubted. Yet others, not existentialists, or those disillusioned with existentialism, have doubted that the proper individual response to corporate evil is escape. They have come to believe instead that a call to abandon society in search of salvation precisely sets the conditions for such horrors. A rising chorus in the sixties and seventies speaks against existentialism in general and Bultmann in particular. Some voices in that chorus are these:

Hans Jonas (whose 1934 existentialist demythologization of antique gnosticism[18] had been a model for Bultmann) writes in 1964:

---

18. Jonas, *Gnosis und spätantiker Geist*.

*The Modern Perspective* 253

> When, many years ago, I turned to the study of Gnosticism, I found that the viewpoints, the optics as it were, which I had acquired in the school of Heidegger, enabled me to see aspects of gnostic thought that had been missed before. . . . Then after long sojourn in those distant lands returning to my own, the contemporary philosophic scene, . . . the extended discourse with ancient nihilism proved—to me at least—a help in discerning and placing the meaning of modern nihilism: just as the latter had initially equipped me for spotting its obscure cousin in the past . . . . The meeting of the two, started as the meeting of a method with a matter, ended with bringing home to me that Existentialism, which claims to be the explication of the fundamentals of human existence as such, is the philosophy of a particular, historically fated situation of human existence. . . . In other words, the hermeneutic functions become reversed and reciprocal—lock turns into key, and key into lock: the "existentialist" reading of Gnosticism, so well vindicated by its hermeneutic success, invites as its natural complement the trial of a "gnostic" reading of Existentialism.[19]

This is a reading Jonas then proceeds to make.

Eric Voegelin writes, "The attempt to come to grips with the problems of personal and social order when it is disrupted by gnosticism, however, has not been very successful, because the philosophical knowledge that would be required for the purpose has itself been destroyed by the prevailing intellectual climate."[20] "[A] critical examination of the principles which have induced Bultmann to deny theological relevance to the Old Testament is forced into definite form by certain characteristics of his work, the decisive one being the vein of Gnosticism running through it."[21] For scholastically oriented Voegelin, gnosticism is an attempted escape from a cosmologically ordered world rather than a historically ordered one, but for both positions the *self-as-such* anthropological position is gnostic.

Roger Johnson says that for Bultmann, "the new understanding of self and world, actualized in Christian faith, remains consistent in its ontological structure with the new understanding of self and world

---

19. Jonas, Epilogue "Gnosticism, Existentialism, and Nihilism," *The Gnostic Religion*, 320–21.
20. Voegelin, *Science, Politics, and Gnosticism*, vi.
21. Voegelin, "History and Gnosis," 64.

which appears—albeit only in intention and then with distortion and partiality—in Gnosticism."[22]

Walther Zimmerli prefaces his book *The Old Testament and the World* (1971) with the statement, "The lectures . . . were provoked by Rudolf Bultmann's thesis that the biblical proclamation experiences its 'de-secularization' in the message of the New Testament, and that the Old Testament retains its significance in the Christian Church only by its 'failure.'" Zimmerli goes on to relate Bultmann's position to that of Marcion.[23]

Samuel Terrien speaks of "Bultmann's Marcionitic and docetic tendencies."[24] Of Bultmann he says, "In transforming New Testament theology into an anthropology of existential self-understanding, he failed to grasp the existential involvement of the church in the political, moral, and cultural realities of history."[25]

Ernst Käsemann writes, "I now find myself at variance with my own past, with the school of theology in which I grew up and particularly with my teacher, Bultmann."[26] "The earliest Christian theology cannot adequately be interpreted from an existentialist starting-point, if decisive weight is to be given to its fundamental understanding of itself."[27]

Johann Baptist Metz says, "The deprivatizing of theology is the primary critical task of political theology. . . . No doubt there is an emphasis on the individual in the message of the New Testament. . . . It is our contention that theology, precisely because of its privatizing tendency, is apt to miss the individual in his real existence."[28] The German original of Dorothee Sölle's *Political Theology* bears the title "Political Theology: A Critical Conversation with Rudolf Bultmann." Jürgen Moltmann, in discussing Bultmann's eschatological doctrine, says, "For the subject in search of himself, 'world' and 'God' thereby become radical alternatives. . . . There is no need to mention

---

22. Johnson, *The Origins of Demythologizing*, 243.

23. Zimmerli, *The Old Testament and the World*, vii, 2.

24. Terrien, *The Elusive Presence*, 38–39.

25. Ibid., 38. Unfortunately, we shall find in chapter 9, below, that this criticism, with Old Testament replacing New Testament, can also be leveled against Terrien himself.

26. Käsemann, *Essays on New Testament Themes*, preface to the English edition (1963), p. 8.

27. Käsemann, "On the Subject of Primitive Christian Apocalyptic," 117.

28. Metz, *Theology of the World*, 110.

that this view of "God" and "world" as alternatives has a previous history in gnosticism and mysticism."[29]

Leonhard Goppelt writes, "Bultmann considered apocalypticism and Gnosticism to be equally important as means of interpretation in the New Testament, and he justified his existential approach because of the tension between the two.... Gnosticism ... is the basis of Bultmann's analysis of the New Testament."[30] Ben F. Meyer writes of Bultmann's demythologization program, "The terms into which Jesus' eschatology was transposed were new but the strategy itself was at least as old as Gnosticism.... As for the systematic translation of apocalyptic eschatology ... into ... existentialist self-understanding, the suspicion arises ... that the integrity of the faith has fallen victim to the translation."[31] J. Christiaan Beker says of Paul's theology, "What is husk for Bultmann belongs in our construal to the core."[32] And, correspondingly, John H. Yoder says of Bultmann's proclamation of the offer of restored selfhood, "This is just the ... wrapping paper thrown in when you buy the 'meat.'"[33]

As early as 1952, Karl Barth (not using the anti-gnostic vocabulary of the sixties and seventies) wrote, "Bultmann attaches such an exclusive importance to his use of existentialism, and indeed it is the very hallmark of his theology[,] which is what makes it such a problem.... As we seek to understand the New Testament, our first reaction is bound to be one of self-defense against its strangeness.... We shall always be trying to confine this strangeness within the straight jacket of our prior understandings and preconceptions.... But have we any right to elevate all this into a methodological principle?"[34]

For half a century Bultmann dominated the thinking of many who disagreed with him as well as those who agreed. But a continuing "critical conversation" with Bultmann, and with liberal and existentialist theology as a whole, contributed to increased interest in the corporate orientation, always latent in ordinary lay church life, and starting to regain

---

29. Moltmann, *Theology of Hope*, 65.
30. Goppelt, *Typos*, 1964 appendix, 211.
31. Meyer, *The Aims of Jesus*, 244–45.
32. Beker, *Paul the Apostle*, 18.
33. Yoder, *The Original Revolution*, 31–32.
34. Barth, "Rudolf Bultmann—An Attempt to Understand Him," 121, 124.

academic respectability in the early nineteenth century. This recovery is the subject of the next chapter.

# 7

## The Communal Orientation

*First Western Corporate Understanding of Scripture*

I THE GENESIS OF COMMUNAL SYSTEMATIC THEOLOGY

### *1 Intrinsic Justification: Johann Adam Möhler*

DURING THE PERIODS OF cosmologically and generically oriented theology (analyzed in the three preceding chapters), the church with its Semitic Scriptures, sacraments, and order continued to practice (unthematized) some semblance of corporate interaction. In chapter 4 we saw a series of neo-Platonic theologians trying to support corporate biblical practices with non-corporate philosophical resources, such as Luther's use of "Word of God" to justify his strategic use of teaching authority to control a reformation that had become a power struggle. And in chapter 6 we saw early Barth's Gospel-based flirtation with social democracy.

Chapter 5 exhibited two temporary outbreaks of a more explicitly corporate theology, namely Hooker's theological rationalization of Elizabeth's political preservation of church unity in England and early New England puritan preaching calling for a corporately responsible community. The occasions for both arose from contemporaneous political or natural exigencies and the forms for both were drawn typologically from the Old Testament.

Political and cultural circumstances also contributed to the rise of an explicitly corporate theology in Germany in the early nineteenth century. Napoleon had confiscated large holdings of Catholic Church land in Germany, demolishing the wealth and political influence of the ecclesiastical establishment. At the same time the new Romantic Movement countered the Enlightenment's dry interest in emancipation through reason with a new concern for living human relations. In 1817, Johann Sebastian Drey established a Catholic theological faculty at Tübingen alongside the Protestant faculty for the purpose of renewing the prevailing scholastic theology to make it once again a living expression of the faith and life of the church. This program reached an explicitly corporate orientation in the work of Johann Adam Möhler (1796–1838) before being submerged by growing ultramontanist influence from Rome and reactions by European governments to the revolutions of 1848.

Möhler's *Unity in the Church* (1825) is written to advocate creative interaction among complementary members as essential to church community: "As the Catholic principle binds all believers into a unity, the individuality of the believer is not to be lost, for the individual should continue as a *living* member in the whole body of the church" (1.4.35.114). "The choir is formed when the voices of the different members, men and women, boys and girls, each with its own character, resolve themselves into a harmony. Without difference and variety there is flagging, enervating monotone, not sonority but dissonance" (1.4.46.152). Antitheses are essential for unity: "True life consists only in the penetration of what stands opposite it. Hence, . . . in heresy no true Christian life is possible since there are no antitheses in heresy, and no antitheses because no unity" (1.4.46.154).

Möhler's *Symbolism: Exposition of the doctrinal differences between Catholics and Protestants as evidenced by their symbolical writings* (1832–1838) claims the relation between God and humanity is as corporate as the relation among the faithful claimed in his *Unity*. The doctrinal differences between the communions are shown by comparing doctrinal statements from the Protestant Reformation and Catholic Counter-Reformation. Since the core Reformation issue was justification of the individual, Möhler devotes the first 254 pages of *Symbolism* (covering original justice, original sin, justification, faith, works, and sacraments) to building his case for intrinsic relation between God and the faithful *individual*, arguing explicitly against Lutheran and Calvinist extrinsic justification. In the next section on the doctrine of the church (pp. 255–349), Möhler extends the corporate orientation with God from the individual to the human community. His argument against Protestantism is also implicitly directed against non-corporate leanings in neo-Platonic and Enlightenment Catholic theology. He says of the Catholic pastor, "we may hope that discourses on the doctrines of the Catholic faith, will be rendered more solid, more comprehensive, more animated, and more impressive, when those doctrines have been studied by him, in their opposition to antagonist confessions" (p. xiii).

The central argument of Möhler's *Symbolism* is that all the differences between Protestant and Catholic theology come from a single difference, the one between the Protestant-held *extrinsic* relation between God and members of a *generic* faithful community and a Catholic-held *intrinsic* relation between God and a *corporate* faithful community, a position in fact opposing neo-Platonic and scholastic tendencies shared by both theologies.

At the first level, the God-individual relation, Möhler describes the contrasting positions on justification as follows: The Catholic view attributes free will to human beings, a free will that survives the fall so that not all human actions are sinful. Justification occurs when the sinner, helped by God, both outwardly through preaching and inwardly through prevenient grace, hearkens to God's call, and, cooperating freely, leads a virtuous new life, becoming really just in the sight of God. "According to Catholic principles, in the holy work of regeneration we find two operations concur—the Divine and the human; and when this work succeeds, they mutually pervade each other, so that this regeneration constitutes one theandric work. . . . The Divine Spirit worketh not by absolute necessity, though he is urgently active: His omnipotence suffers human freedom to set to it a bound, which it cannot break through, because an unconditional interference with that freedom would bring about the annihilation of the moral order of the world, which the Divine wisdom hath founded on liberty" (pp. 86–87). Here Möhler says plainly what the Old Testament makes so clear: God is actually capable of limiting his own will sufficiently (unlike those who play God) to have a creative two-way relation with others, that he gives humanity both ability and authority to interact with him in a way that depends on the choices of both. Thus, Möhler identifies faith and love and, also, justification and sanctification. Reconciliation is not an arms-length exchange with God; the human being alone does not have the means for satisfying God. Reconciliation is a joint action, at the same time an act of God toward the sinner, and the free and faithful response of the sinner to God.

By contrast, according to Möhler, the Protestant view holds that the human being from before the fall had no freedom but was under divine necessity in all activity. Justification occurs as follows: "when the sinner has been intimidated by the preaching of the law, which he is conscious of not having fulfilled, and hath been brought to the brink of despair, the Gospel is announced to him. . . . With a heart stricken with fear and terror, he grasps at the Redeemer's merits, through faith, which alone justifieth. God, on account of Christ's merits, declares the believer just, without his being so in fact; though released from debt and punishment, he is not delivered from sin" (p. 84). Good works—that is, sanctification—may follow but are distinct from justification. Through it all, the sinner, lacking free will, is passive. The doctrine of predestination follows naturally from the absence of free will.

Continuing for the time being at the level of the God-individual relation, Möhler says a sacrament according to the Catholic view is an outward earthly sign that conveys the offering of justification *and* sanctification. Human cooperation is elicited and is required for the sacrament's effectiveness. The circle of seven sacraments provides for this mutual cooperation at each passage in life. By contrast, in the Protestant view of the sacraments, consistent with the Protestant conception of justification, there is no sanctifying grace, "just as if the Reformers dreaded being sanctified" (p. 205). The sacraments are thus one-sided pledges of God's promise of forgiveness and thus serve only to assure the receiver that the receiver's debt of sins is remitted. They are effective when the recipient possesses faith in the forgiveness of sins. The number of sacraments is reduced to two in part because of the difficulty of viewing matrimony and holy order as instituted for the purpose of God's forgiving the individuals receiving them.

Möhler reaches the second stage in his argument, adopting a corporate perspective also at the anthropological level, when he comes to the doctrine of the church (pp. 255–349). The human individual is naturally socially formed. "The power of society in which man lives, is so great, that it ordinarily stamps its image on him, who comes within its circle" (p. 267). And God relates with humanity as a social entity. "Man [is] by his very nature . . . compelled to receive the [manner of] worship of the social state in which he has been fixed, as the true expression, the faithful image of religious truth" (p. 267). "We speak here . . . of a direction given to the will by a living membership with an all-embracing, religious society. An ancient philosopher has, with reason, defined man to be a social animal" (p. 269). "The more polished and civilized the members of a state, the more are they bound together by wise ordinances, holy laws, venerable customs and manners, which wisely determine the mutual relations of rights and duties; so that in fact, with every higher degree of internal freedom the outward bonds are proportionably straitened" (p. 270). That is, internal freedom requires external restraint—only a society with an adequate corporate interactive structure provides a context within which a member is free to act creatively.

Correspondingly, the church, according to the Catholic view, is a corporate body called to cooperate with God under his influence—a society called into existence to "be the living exposition of the truth" (p. 265), in which "the works wrought by [Christ] during his earthly life, for the redemption and sanctification of mankind, are, under the guidance of the spirit, continued to the end of the world" (p. 258).

A visible church is needed to continue the visible work of the incarnate Christ:

> The ultimate reason of the visibility of the Church is to be found in the *incarnation* of the Divine Word. Had that Word descended into the hearts of men, without taking the form of a servant, and accordingly without appearing in a corporeal shape, then only an internal, invisible Church would have been established. But . . . . [T]he Deity having manifested its action in Christ according to an *ordinary human fashion*, the form also in which His work was to be continued, was thereby traced out. The preaching of his doctrine needed now a *visible, human* medium, and must be entrusted to visible envoys . . . ; men must speak to men, and hold intercourse with them, in order to convey to them the word of God. And as in the world nothing can attain to greatness but in society; so Christ established a community; and his divine word, his living will, and the love emanating from him exerted an internal, binding power upon his followers; so that . . . . [A] living, well-connected, visible association of the faithful sprang up, whereof it might be said—there they are, there is his Church, his institution wherein he continueth to live, his spirit continueth to work, and the word uttered by him eternally resounds. Thus the visible Church, from the point of view here taken, is the Son of God himself, everlastingly manifesting himself among men in a human form, perpetually renovated, and eternally young—the permanent incarnation of the same, as in Holy Writ, even the faithful are called "the body of Christ" (p. 258–59).

Thus, according to Möhler, because humanity is social, the incarnation of God in human form is continued in social human form. As internal freedom depends on external restraint, so in the church "those very bonds, which exhibit the reality of the community, produce a result the very reverse of restraint, and establish the internal freedom of man, or promote the purest *humanity*; for this expression may be used, since God became man. Without external bonds, there is no true spiritual association" (p. 271).

The church is both divine and human as Christ was. "She has a divine and a human part in an undivided mode, so that the divine cannot be separated from the human nor the human from the divine. . . . The divine without the human has no existence for us" (p. 259). Although the church is subject to the vicissitudes of human culture in each age—"Her priests and bishops fall not from the skies; as she must take them out of the description of men that the age can furnish" (p. 275)—the church has the same authority as Christ: "accordingly, we can say of the Church, that she is the Christian religion in its objective form—its living exposition" (p. 259). The church is a visible corporate human agency of God for the corporate salvation of humanity; its acts are at the same time the acts of a human community and the acts of God through that human community.

By contrast, Möhler says, the Reformation view of the church was that God approached each believer independently and the true church was the invisible class of all such believers (a generic collection whose only connection with one another is possession of the common characteristic of being justified). "As each believer was deemed to be instructed by God alone, and capable, without human aid, of attaining to Christian knowledge; so . . . an outward Christian ministry could not even be conceived: God, by means of Scripture, was the sole teacher" (p. 318). The visible church, with its community structure, can have no part in the salvation of the individual because no human effort can have such a part—God does not need helpers. "The believer . . . is . . . instructed by God only, exclusively of all co-operation of human activity, whether it be his own, or that of other men" (p. 324). Möhler quotes to this effect Luther's "The Papacy in Rome": "We pray in the Creed, 'I believe in the Holy Spirit, the communion of saints.' This community or assembly means all those who live in true faith, hope, and love. Thus the essence, life, and nature of Christendom is not a physical assembly but an assembly of hearts in one faith."[1] A phrase in Luther's next sentence supports Möhler's generic interpretation: ". . . as long as each one preaches, believes, hopes, loves, and lives like the other."

Möhler says the divergence of the Protestant doctrine of a generic invisible church from the Catholic doctrine of a visible one, like the other doctrinal divergences, proceeds from the same single difference between intrinsic and extrinsic relations between God and humanity. "The one . . . determines the other. Since for them [the Protestants] justification is not internal, the Church cannot be external. When justification is not internal to the individual, it is powerless to extend the invisible successfully out into the visible and thus enable the internal church at the same time to be indubitably external."[2] That is, the same individual who cannot relate internally with God also cannot be an internally related part of a visible church relating as a corporate whole with God, and for God with the world.

In this second stage of Möhler's argument, adopting a corporate perspective also for the relations within humanity, Möhler broadens some doctrinal positions enunciated in the first stage that had not yet challenged a generically orientated humanity. For example, in the first stage baptism appears as regeneration of the individual (p. 219) and in the second stage as incorporation of the individual into the church: "Baptism is the *introduction* into the Church—the reception into the community of the faithful" (p. 261). According to Möhler's argument, these two (regeneration and introduction) are *the same*.

In Möhler's view, for Protestants the priesthood of all believers is not the priesthood of the corporate church as with Catholics but the priesthood of each generic believer. "Ordination, as a sacrament, became no longer necessary; since this presupposes the necessity of a continuance of the divine work of salvation, by the mediation of the Church. . . . The exterior ordination becomes transmuted into a purely internal act, whereby God imparts the consecration of the Spirit, not to this or that individual in a special manner, but to all in an equal degree" (p. 318). Möhler says Luther allows that, "although now all be qualified for, and possess the right of exercising the priestly functions, yet, *in order to avoid disorder* they must delegate to one or more of their body the general right, to be

---

1. Luther, "The Papacy in Rome," 39.65; Möhler, *Symbolism*, 324.
2. Möhler, *Symbolik*, 129 [*Symbolism*, 103].

exercised in their place, and in their name" (p. 319).³ Thus, this office-holder represents not the corporate body of believers as a community but each individual believer generically.

Möhler considers Luther also to have excluded the corporate institutional community from an essential role in salvation, diachronically as well as synchronically. To exclude the church as a diachronic medium in salvation, Luther needed some method of connecting the present believer back to the earthly Christ without human mediation. This was done by absolutizing the Bible. "As . . . the Reformers represented all human concurrence in the work of salvation . . . as impossible, . . . so they indulged in the idea, that whoever addressed himself immediately to Holy Writ, obtained an immediate knowledge of its contents. They rejected the mediating authority of the Church, . . . because they wished to avoid *every* thing human, without apprehending that the subjectivity of the believer would, thereby, be . . . confounded with the objective revelation" (p. 313)—"just as if it were the same thing to read the inerrable Scripture, and to be forthwith inerrable" (p. 314).

Möhler on the contrary asserts, as with legal hermeneutics, that the Bible cannot be applied directly to a present situation as though every situation were literally similar. Rather, the Bible must be interpreted, and interpreted by the community. That is, it can only provide a metonymic (internally relating) context for making a creative decision by the church in a new situation. Of the "oft-repeated assertion that the Bible is the judge in matters of faith" Möhler says, "it is one thing to say 'the Bible is the source of the doctrine of salvation;' and another to say, 'it is the judge to determine what is the doctrine of salvation.' The latter can as little be, as the code of civil law can exercise the functions of the judge: it forms indeed the rule of judgment, but it doth not itself pronounce judgment" (p. 313). The church interprets the Scriptures, according to Möhler, in terms of its very life as a community, transmitted by itself through time from its origin in its founder. This is tradition. It includes the content of the Bible *and* the doctrine of the inspiration and canonicity of the Bible (p. 293). This tradition remains the same in substance but develops in outward form (p. 289) as the church meets ever new situations.

Möhler supports his corporate position from the Bible. He uses mostly New Testament passages, especially from Paul and John, calcu-

---

3. Möhler is paraphrasing a passage in Luther, "De instituendis ministris ecclesiae," *WA* 12.189 ["Concerning the Ministry," *Luther's Works* 40.34].

lated to present to theoretically oriented Western culture the strongest possible biblical witness for a corporate conception of the church: John 20:21 "As the Father has sent me, so I send you" (p. 265), and 1 Cor 12:29 "Are all apostles? Are all prophets? Are all teachers?" (p. 320). Although Möhler's attention is not drawn to the Old Testament by his polemical situation, he makes a corporate interpretation of the New Testament that is commensurate with its continuity with the Old, and considers the whole Bible as part of a living tradition transmitted in the church. In the following section, we will find Newman, seven years later, treating the transmission of tradition in great detail and using passages from both testaments without distinction.

Möhler was the first Western corporately oriented theologian since the fourth century Antiochian Fathers (above, chapter 4.II.2), as 25 years earlier Hegel had been the first *philosopher*. Möhler has found a fundamental identity between *Christology*, messiahship, representative leadership role, and its complement, *ecclesiology*, the role of the group so led, chrismated. Corporately oriented Möhler argues on two fronts, with Protestants and with Catholics. For Möhler, God and humanity are at the same time distinct enough from, and open enough toward, each other to allow a creative internal relation between them. Both the distinctness and the openness are upheld in corporate Scripture, but the openness is missing in generic modern theology and the distinctness is missing in neo-Platonic theology.

The issue of intrinsic *versus* extrinsic justification persists today but, as hinted by Möhler, is shared by both Catholics and Protestants. The Catholic-Protestant academic theological difference at the Reformation was between neo-Platonisms with and without scholasticism, that is, with or without Aristotle's *de Anima*, with neither compatible with scriptural intrinsic justification. The Protestant-Catholic difference grew with Protestant liberal theology, but began to dissipate when both sides began to recognize the corporate base revealed in mid-twentieth century biblical studies, which led to a scripturally based corporate theology (treated in chapter 10 below). On October 31, 1999 Edward Cardinal Cassidy, president of the Pontifical Council for Promoting Christian Unity, and Ishmael Noko, general secretary of the Lutheran World Federation, solemnly signed a declaration that held that the differences on justification are not "church dividing."

## 2 Development of Doctrine: John Henry Newman

John Henry Newman's *An Essay on the Development of Christian Doctrine*[4] (1845) promotes a corporate understanding of the church as Möhler's *Symbolism* does. Newman says, "The view on which it has been written . . . has recently been illustrated by . . . Möhler."[5] Newman, like Möhler, was a patristics scholar. Then-current English polemics allowed him to add the Old Testament to the base Möhler used for typological development of doctrine.

The German romanticism of Johann Fichte and Friedrich Schelling, opposing the Enlightenment perspective, came to England through the poet Samuel Taylor Coleridge (1772–1834) and others. The Anglican Church, like Möhler's German Catholic Church under Napoleon, had lost political standing in the 1820s and 1830s as membership in the House of Commons was opened to non-Anglicans; middle class representation in parliament was increased and church finances were rationalized. In 1833, Richard Froude, John Henry Newman (1801–1890), John Keble, and soon thereafter Edward Pusey, inaugurated the Oxford Tractarian movement that urged renewal in the Church of England through recognition of its historical calling as the English part of the one catholic, i.e., all-including, church, thus transcending the issues of scholasticism, nationalism, Reformation, and Enlightenment. Newman was the theologian of the movement, developing the diachronic corporate understanding of the church that supported it. But twelve years later in 1845, he resigned his cure in the Anglican Church, wrote his *Essay*, and then was received into the Roman Church.

In the *Essay*, Newman parodied the Anglican Church's use of the Vincentian canon, according to which pure doctrine is "what has been believed always, everywhere, and by all"[6] to justify "cutting off and casting away as corruptions all usages, ways, opinions, and tenets, which have not the sanction of primitive times" (p. 10). Newman unmercifully pillories the use of Vincent's criterion. It "is congenial, or, as it may be said, native to the Anglican mind, which takes up a middle position, neither discarding the Fathers nor acknowledging the Pope" (p. 11).

---

4. Newman, *Essay*, final revision, 1878. Page numbers from "new edition".

5. Newman, *Essay*, first edition, 90.

6. Vincent of Lérins, *Commonitorium Primum* 2. Fifth century Vincent himself allowed a development of doctrine, *Commonitorium Primum* 23, as Newman points out (p. 172).

"What is meant by being 'taught *always*'? does it mean in every century, or every year, or every month? Does '*everywhere*' mean in every country, or in every diocese?" (p. 12). Newman says that an application of Vincent, strict enough to reject characteristic Roman and Protestant doctrines, eliminates characteristic Anglican doctrines as well. An application rejecting the primacy of the see of Peter also eliminates the Augustinian doctrine of the Trinity and the real presence of Christ in the Eucharist—two Anglican-held doctrines in which their nineteenth-century forms are clearly developments from their early forms. Newman gives multiple examples showing there is no historical period, early or late, when Christian doctrine was stated in an explicit form commanding diachronic universal acceptance. The search for a fixed body of teaching, directly applicable to every age, ignores the need for interpretation. Like appeal to the Bible in continental Protestantism, it attempts to bypass an intervening historical transmission and application of tradition.

According to Newman, a historical movement like Christianity is known under a number of *aspects*, varying according to times and individuals. No one aspect exhausts its content which, rather, corresponds to the total of all possible aspects. These aspects must be learned piecemeal. "It is characteristic of our minds, that they cannot take an object in, which is submitted to them simply and integrally. . . . Whole objects do not create in the intellect whole ideas, but are . . . thrown into series, into a number of statements, strengthening, interpreting, correcting each other, and with more or less exactness approximating, as they accumulate, to a perfect image. There is no other way of learning or of teaching. We cannot teach except by aspects or views, which are not identical with the thing itself which we are teaching" (p. 55). A new movement requires time for the various ramifications of its living principle to develop, for the various aspects under which it can be known to emerge (pp. 36–39). Moreover, a historical movement not only affects but is affected by the circumstances in which it is active: It must risk corruption to be effective (pp. 39–40).

New aspects of a fixed Christian principle emerge as the need arises. An example is the development of papal polity out of episcopal polity. "It is true, St. Ignatius is silent in his Epistles on the subject of the Pope's authority. . . . St. Ignatius directed his doctrine according to the need. . . . Christians at home did not yet quarrel with Christians abroad; they quarrelled at home among themselves. St. Ignatius applied the fitting remedy. The *Sacramentum Unitatis* was acknowledged on all hands; the mode of fulfilling and the means of securing it would vary with the occasion; and the determination of its essence, its seat, and its laws would be a gradual supply for a gradual necessity" (p. 149). Here the unity represented and effected by the sacrament of holy order is the unchanging substance, while episcopacy and papacy are the aspects that developed respectively under conditions of conflict within dioceses and between dioceses.

A doctrine develops a more precise form under challenge. "Few but will grant that Luther's view of justification had never been stated in words before his time. . . . It is equally certain that the [counter] doctrine of justification defined at Trent was, in some sense, new also. The refutation and remedy of errors cannot precede their rise" (p. 58). "No doctrine is defined till it is violated" (p. 151). Newman's "aspect," like Frege's "sense" (above, page 46), is public: It is located in a historical community, not in separate individuals.

Newman says doctrines undergo developments that are political, logical, historical, ethical, or metaphysical. For the doctrine of the incarnation, "the Episcopate, as taught by St. Ignatius, will be an instance of political development, the *Theotokos* of logical, the determination of the date of our Lord's birth of historical, the Holy Eucharist of moral, and the Athanasian Creed of metaphysical" (p. 54). "Certainly it is a sort of degradation of a divine work to consider it under an earthly form; but it is no irreverence, since our Lord Himself, its Author and Guardian, bore one also" (p. 57).

Newman says biblical fulfillment of prophecy and typology are examples of the development of doctrine. In prophecy and typology "the event which is the development is also the interpretation of the prediction; it provides a fulfillment by imposing a meaning" (p. 102). He says, "the method of revelation observed in Scripture abundantly confirms" the development of tradition:

> For instance, Prophecy, if it had so happened, need not have afforded a specimen of development; separate predictions might have been made to accumulate as time went on . . . by communications independent of each other. . . . But the prophetic Revelation is, in matter of fact, not of this nature, but a process of development: the earlier prophecies are pregnant texts out of which the succeeding announcements grow; they are types. It is

> not that first one truth is told, then another; but the whole truth or large portions of it are told at once, yet only in their rudiments, or in miniature, and they are expanded and finished in their parts, as the course of revelation proceeds (p. 64).

An example is the development of the Messianic idea: "The Seed of the woman was to bruise the serpent's head; the sceptre was not to depart from Judah till Shiloh came, to whom was to be the gathering of the people. He was to be Wonderful, Counsellor, the Prince of Peace. . . . Every word requires a comment. Accordingly, it is no uncommon theory with unbelievers, that the Messianic idea, as they call it, was gradually developed in the minds of the Jews by a continuous and traditional habit of contemplating it, and grew into its full proportions by a mere human process" (p. 65).

Newman continues:

> But the whole Bible, not its prophetical portions only, is written on the principle of development. As the Revelation proceeds, it is ever new, yet ever old. St. John, who completes it, declares that he writes no "new commandment unto his brethren," but an old commandment which they "had from the beginning." And then he adds, "A new commandment I write unto you." [1 John 2:7, 8] The same test of development is suggested in our Lord's words on the Mount, . . . "Think not that I am come to destroy the Law and the Prophets; I am not come to destroy, but to fulfill." [Matt 5:17] He does not reverse, but perfect, what has gone before (p. 65).

Newman similarly traces the development of the understanding of sacrifice through the Old Testament, the New Testament, and the early church.

> First the rite is enjoined by Moses; next Samuel says, "to obey is better than sacrifice;" then Hosea, "I will have mercy and not sacrifice;" Isaiah, "Incense is an abomination unto me;" then Malachi, describing the times of the Gospel, speaks of the "pure offering" of wheatflour; and our Lord completes the development, when He speaks of worshipping "in spirit and in truth." If there is anything here left to explain, it will be found in the usage of the Christian Church immediately afterwards, which shows that sacrifice was not removed, but truth and spirit added (pp. 65–66).

An Old Testament revelation having been developed, that is, fulfilled, later in the Old Testament itself is no bar to further development in the New. "We rightly feel that it is no prejudice to our receiving the prophecy of Balaam in its Christian meaning, that it is adequately fulfilled in David; or the history of Jonah, that it is poetical in character and has a moral in itself like an apologue" (p. 103). The same kind of development is to be expected, says Newman, in the history of the church. "Now it is but a parallel exercise of reasoning to interpret the previous history of a doctrine by its later development, and to consider that it contains the later *in posse* and in the divine intention; and the grudging and jealous temper, which refuses to enlarge the sacred text for the fulfillment of prophecy, is the very same that will occupy itself in carping at the Ante-nicene testimonies for Nicene or Medieval doctrines and usages" (p. 106). Anglicans Richard Hooker and Jeremy Taylor in the sixteenth and seventeenth centuries had explicitly asserted a continuing development of doctrine, as Newman points out (p. 22). Newman's historical (rather than philosophical) theology has brought him to the corporate orientation.

Elizabeth as queen had a choice in 1558 between unity with Rome and avoiding revolution in England. In 1845 Newman had a choice only between uncertain influence in the Roman Church and influence in a disappearing unity at home. He chose the former, becoming a Cardinal Deacon, but his theological influence, along with that of its cousin Tübingen theology, was submerged in the mid-nineteenth century European conservative political reaction to the revolutions of 1848. Yet, his Tractarian movement in the Anglican church survived and blossomed under mid-twentieth century communal biblical studies and a liturgical reform in Western Christianity (chapter 2 above and 7.II and 10 below). In addition, Newman's *Essay* anticipated von Rad's conception a century later of transmission of tradition and the Old Testament's part in it (below, this chapter, II.2).

### 3 Post-Critical Pragmatism in Theology: Henry Nelson Wieman

Henry Nelson Wieman offers a theology within the conceptuality of the pragmatism of the philosopher Charles S. Peirce (above, chapter 1.IV.5), the communally oriented post-critical philosophy of science in the New England of Wieman's time. Wieman interprets present acts as part of a net of synchronic and diachronic internal relations within and among present situations, future relations, and past tradition, including the Old Testament. He makes use of the philosophy of language of his time.

Wieman's system, as outlined in *The Source of Human Good* (1946), is built around the concepts *qualitative meaning* and *creative event*. *Qualitative meaning* is "that connection between events whereby present happenings enable me to feel not only the quality intrinsic to the events now occurring but also the qualities of many other events that are related to them" (p. 18). Qualitative meaning is a relation among events enabling some events to be signs of others. "Signs are those events belonging to the structure which serve to represent the structure as a whole" (p. 21). Such a structural connection between events transforms instrumental good into intrinsic good:

> When I chop wood to sustain that other structure of happenings called "the life of my family in our home," the values of the activity may be purely instrumental if the qualities pertaining to life in my home cannot freely enter conscious awareness as I chop. However, if bonds of meaning are developed between my chopping the wood and the life of my home, so that the lives of the children and the affection of the wife are vivified in conscious awareness by the very act itself, then the activity ceases to be merely instrumental. Then chopping the wood has taken on those qualities pertaining to the total structure of events called "the life of my home." It is an intrinsic good, no matter how fatiguing it may be (pp. 54–55).

Thus, one finds a structural connection among events (a qualitative meaning), making them a meaningful whole with some events acting as signs of that whole. "As more events become signs, as these signs take on richer content of qualitative meaning, as these meanings form a network of interconnective events comprehending all that is happening in the world, this universe . . . . becomes more deeply and pervasively meaningful. It becomes the house of the human spirit" (p. 23). Qualitative meaning also relates events diachronically into a live history or tradition that is needed to interpret the present. Signs "conserve the qualities of past events by which alone the present can have depth and richness of meaning" (p. 22). Wieman, who was interested in the philosophy of language, here gives a corporate anthropological analysis of signs similar to the way John's Gospel uses the seven signs as keys to seven interactions, each in turn an interacting sign of the whole of Jesus' ministry, a metonymic relation quite different from Tillich's abstract analysis of symbols (the nearest equivalent to Wieman's signs) in which a symbol represents something by participating in its "reality"—its Platonic Form (below, page 306).

According to Wieman, the *creative event* is the "process . . . [which generates] new meanings, integrating them with the old, endowing each event as it occurs with a wider range of reference" (p. 56). An existing structure of qualitative meaning becomes demonic when it becomes an idol, losing its interactive relation with the original creative event—in our terminology when extra-contextual allegory replaces intra-contextual typology.

The creative event is made up of four constitutive subevents: "emerging awareness of qualitative meaning derived from other persons through communication; integrating these new meanings with others previously acquired; expanding the richness of quality in the appreciable world by enlarging its meaning; deepening the community among those who participate in this total creative event of intercommunication" (p. 58). Both synchronic and diachronic relations in community are, thus, essentially involved in the creative event. Wieman's paradigmatic example of creative event with its four subevents is the sequence of originative events of the Christian tradition: (1) "Jesus engaged in intercommunication with a little group of disciples with such depth and potency that . . . . the thought and feeling of each got across to the others. . . . Not something handed down to them from Jesus but something rising up out of their midst in creative power was the important thing." (2) "The meanings, thus derived by each from the other, were integrated with what each had previously acquired. Thus each was transformed." (3) "Since they could now see through the eyes of others, feel through their sensitivities, and discern the secrets of many hearts, the world was more rich and ample with meaning and quality." And (4) "There was more depth and breadth of community between them as individuals with one another and between them and all other men" (pp. 39–41). This creative event depended on the community and its tradition. "The creative transformative power . . . . required many other things besides [Jesus'] own solitary self. It required the Hebrew heritage, the disciples with their peculiar capacity for this kind of responsiveness, and doubtless much else of which we have little knowledge" (p. 41). After Jesus, there came "the formation of a fellowship with an organization, ritual, symbols, and documents by which this dominance of the creative event over human concern might be perpetuated through history" (p. 41).

Wieman rejects the modern non-interactive empiricism of Hume for what Wieman calls the communal "empiricism," that is, the "pragmatism" of Charles S. Peirce and John Dewey (p. 6). Wieman's emphasis on the practical meanings of events eradicates the modern period's distinction between theoretical and practical reason. To the modern objection that empirical inquiry can only discover the "is" and not the "ought," Wieman replies: "Unless there is an actually existing demand imposing an 'ought,' there can be no 'ought.' Therefore, the 'ought' must be generated by something actually in existence, and this ought-imposing existence must be discovered by empirical [i.e. pragmatic] inquiry. I claim that empirical inquiry discovers this ought-imposing existence to be the creativity herein described."[7]

Wieman rejects any generic anthropological perspective. "Western culture has made a tragic blunder in conducting society upon the theory that the minimal social unit is the individual human being" (p. 237). He also rejects the cosmological perspective. "We shall have no recourse to any 'transcendental grounds, orders, causes or purposes' beyond events, their qualities, and relations" (pp. 6–7). Although the creative event transcends humanity in the sense that "it creates the good of the world in a way that man cannot do," it is "functionally transcendent but not metaphysically so" (pp. 76–77).

Half of Wieman's 16 page essay "Intellectual Autobiography"[8] is devoted to distancing himself from Tillich and Alfred North Whitehead, at that time the chief contemporaneous representatives respectively of the classical and process cosmological orientations. In the essay "Reply to Barth"[9] Wieman says, "the living God, creating, sustaining, renewing, cannot be the Primordial Order of Whitehead or the ontological Ground of Being according to Tillich." On Tillich's he says, "When one is vividly aware of this scope and depth of being, one may be filled with awe. . . . To equate religion with this feeling of awe is to put it away on a shelf, to be taken down whenever this feeling comes over you, but to do nothing

---

7. Wieman, "Reply to Weigel," *Empirical Theology*, 368–69.
8. Wieman, "Intellectual Autobiography," *Empirical Theology* 3–18.
9. Wieman, "Reply to Barth," *Empirical Theology*, 304.

about it because the unknown provides no hint of what should command and direct all the resources of human action in commitment."[10]

Wieman also rejects Whitehead's modification of the Platonic doctrine of Forms to allow for change, development, and storage of temporarily unused Forms, insisting instead on the community's ongoing creation of its culture by essence-creating interaction among all its members, as do the Old and New Testaments.

Thus, Wieman belongs neither to the modern anthropological orientation nor to the cosmological orientation, in either its classical or its process version. His position is unabashedly a corporate anthropological one. It is anthropological: "The revelation of God in Jesus Christ did not occur in cells and atoms nor in the cosmic whole as viewed by modern science. It occurred as a transformation brought about in the life of man. . . . Our primary religious responsibility is with human life and not with cells and atoms."[11] It is also corporate, at both intimate and institutional levels. For the intimate group, "The human being simply is not human except in relation to the intimate group. Human sexuality rising to heights of love; its pervasive character, weaving webs of meaning through an entire neighborhood; its reaching-out into all the resources of culture to find nourishment and enrichment; its need of wide and deep association with others beyond the two—all these, combined with the prolonged dependency of the human infant and the need of parents to draw upon the whole of the resources of culture and social institutions for the care of the child, reveal the socializing potency of human sexuality."[12] And at the macro-sociological level Wieman says, "The hope of the world lies in modifying all the basic institutions of society in order to provide conditions favorable for the higher dominance of creative interchange to all social relations."[13] (Here the term "creative interchange" replaces the earlier term "creative event").

Wieman calls on the Old Testament as source for the corporate anthropological perspective he advocates. "The Jewish tradition declares that the sovereign good works creatively in history. . . . The Greek tradition, on the other hand, declares that the sovereign good is essentially a

---

10. Wieman, "Reply to Smith," *Empirical Theology*, 263.
11. Ibid., *Empirical Theology*, 261.
12. Wieman, *Empirical Theology*, 237.
13. Wieman, "Reply to Bernhardt," *Empirical Theology*, 209–10. All subsequent references in this section are to *Empirical Theology*.

system of Forms or a Supreme Form. The one tradition gives supreme authority to the creative event, the other to the Form. Our interpretation follows the Jewish tradition in giving priority to the *creative event*" (p. 7). Wieman traces the recurrent crises in the history of the people of God that enabled creative good to triumph over an idolized created good: the flight from Egypt under Moses; the establishment of the covenant between Israel and God; the birth of classical prophecy—Jeremiah, Second Isaiah, Jesus, Paul, Augustine, Luther (pp. 270–71). "Through this progressive sequence of transformative events, the source of good won supremacy in man's devotion over all created good and formed a tradition continuing as one strand in history. The winning of this supremacy by the creative event was a difficult struggle, conducted not by man but by God, and scarcely yet won. But it is won in the sense that World War II was won at Stalingrad" (p. 271).

Wieman rejects the traditional transcendence of God. "There is one respect, being naturalistic, in which we depart from the Jewish Christian tradition: we ignore the transcendental affirmation in the Jewish Christian tradition of a creative God who not only works in history but resides beyond history. The only creative God we recognize is the creative event itself" (p. 7). But the biblical perspective itself is closer to Wieman than to its Western interpretation. The biblical perspective itself is not Western; it does not confuse transcendence with "residing beyond history," unlike its long-time Western perennial interpretation. The creative event is, in the terminology used here, the typological application of a qualitative meaning to a wider historical context, the method both Wieman and Scripture use to build a corporate relation between God and human community. The God of Scripture is sufficiently distinct from the world to be in corporate relation with it but is not removed from it. Hegel said the same (above, page 21) but communally oriented European biblical studies and theology, ready in 1946 to blossom in Europe, were unknown in North America. Wieman's theology received little notice, but it does show how close to the surface the internally interacting world is.

### 4 A Shunt Around Neo-Platonism: Martin Buber, Emmanuel Levinas

The Jewish religious philosopher Martin Buber (1878–1965) advocated a two-way internal relation between God and the human individual, and between one human individual and another, in his early *The Legend of the*

*Baal-Shem* (1907)[14] by distinguishing between *legend* and western *myth*. Myth "knows multiplicity but not duality. Even the hero only stands on another rung than that of the god, not over against him: they are not the I and the Thou." In contrast, "The god of the legend calls forth the son of man—the prophet.... The legend is the myth of I and Thou, of the caller and the called, the finite which enters into the infinite and the infinite which has need of the finite." Buber is distinguishing myth as a figurative description of similarity ("multiplicity") and legend as conveying a two-way complementary relation ("duality") between essentially different persons continually changing without either absorbing the other. At age 29 Buber had found in the Hassidic tradition the core of what is here called the corporate perspective. But he did not start there.

Buber grew up with his grandfather, a scholar in the Haskalah or Jewish Enlightenment, and with his father made visits to a non-Enlightenment Hasidic settlement, both in the Galicia region of Eastern Europe. In 1904, Buber completed the doctorate in philosophy at Vienna, influenced by Kant, Dilthey, Georg Simmel, Feuerbach, Kierkegaard, and Nietzsche, and also by the German mysticism of Meister Eckhart (c.1260–c.1327) and Jakob Boehme (1575–1624). In "Über Jacob Boehme"[15] (1901), Buber quotes Boehme: "One is member of the other, and one without the other would be nothing," but climaxes his essay by saying, "But Boehme was not satisfied with this bridge, and this is where he comes closest to us. He is driven toward a deeper unity. It is not enough that the I unite itself with the world. The I is the world ... in the sense of that great Renaissance teaching of the microcosm." Thus, Buber solidifies nineteenth century European existentialism with a little drop of cosmological cement, as so many existentialists do.

Buber became interested in socialism and Zionism and, through these and his early experience of Hasidism, he began to recognize a calling to a responsibility as a Jew toward the wider European world of which he was a part. Hasidism was an eighteenth- and nineteenth-century popular Jewish movement in Eastern Europe started by Rabbi Israel ben Eleizer, the Baal-Shem-Tov (Master of the Good Name), a mystical leader (or zaddik) of a local community of Hasidim ("pious ones"). Members of this community served God by serving others. In 1904 Buber read the Baal-Shem's testament, *Zevaat Ribesh*, and at the

---

14. Buber, *The Legend of the Baal-Shem*, 13.
15. Buber, "Über Jacob Boehme," 253.

passage "for he ... is worthy to create and is to become like the Holy One, blessed be He, when he created His world" Buber reports, "It was then that, overpowered in an instant, I experienced the Hasidic soul," the soul of one who seizes the opportunity offered by God to share in creation. "The primally Jewish opened to me, flowering to newly conscious expression in the darkness of exile; man's being created in the image of God I grasped as deed, as becoming, as task. And this primally Jewish reality was a primal human reality.... I became aware of the summons to proclaim it to the world."[16] Buber was overpowered in an instant because he recognized in this mystical folk-religious sect a legitimation of human creativity missing in both current Western culture and in Enlightenment Judaism, and in the connection between mystical state and social responsibility not present in German mysticism. But it took Buber 19 more years to reach a definitive exposition of this connection.

In "Ekstase und Bekenntnis," Buber's introduction to his collection of essays of others *Ekstatische Konfessionen*[17] (1909), Buber thematizes an alternation between ecstatic state and return to the world. He says the ecstatic experience is the experience of the unity of the *I*. "The soul that resides in it resides in itself, has itself, experiences itself, limitless" (p. 12). "[Ecstasy's] unity is solitude.... It includes the other, the others, in itself, in its unity, as world. Outside of itself it has no other, it has no more community with them, no mutuality. But language is a function of community.... Ecstasy ... is the abyss that no sounding plumb measures, the unsayable" (p. 17). The ecstatic, on returning to the ordinary world, tries to speak and act in that multiform community in accordance with the unity ecstatically experienced. "He wants to create a memorial for the ineffable ecstasy, to bring the timeless over into time—he wants to make the unity without multiplicity into the unity of all multiplicity" (pp. 21–22). Buber implies that the collected mystical writings introduced by his essay do not report the indescribable ecstatic state but attempt, after returning from that state, to apply the results of the mystical experience in the ordinary world. As before, he seeks to connect mystical state and social world but there is a difficulty.

The Kantian-Romantic-existentialist separation of the mystical and the worldly continues in *Daniel: Dialogues on Realization*, (1913), with existential concern taking the place of ecstatic experience. In *Daniel*

16. Buber, "My Way to Hasidism," 59.
17. Buber, "Ekstase und Bekenntnis," 11–22.

Buber distinguishes "orienting" and "realizing" modes of experience. The orienting mode classifies experience according to time, space, causality, and the like as means for one's ends; whereas, the realizing mode grasps the experience for its own sake (p. 64). Orienting is passive, realizing is creative (p. 63). Orienting involves only part of a person; realizing involves the whole person: "And he who had only to register in the system of experiencing, and living with only one part of his being, could come to terms with the all, must now bring forth the totality of his being in order to withstand a simple thing or event" (p. 63). Orienting happens in the person having the experience, and does not lead to reality (p. 75); realizing is creative unification, and does reach reality (p. 72). Orienting and realizing must alternate: "As in the life of the community the attained reality must ever again be inserted in the structure of experience, so in the life of the individual, hours of inserting follow hours of realization and must so follow" (p. 70). Buber again connects separate modes by alternation but, in *Daniel*, both realizing and orienting modes remain within the first-person perspective of one individual. We wait for a system reaching interaction between individuals.

In 1914 Buber gave up ecstatic mysticism in practice and in theory. In practice he abandoned it when, on not giving adequate attention to a needy visitor who approached him as he was emerging from a period of ecstatic experience, he concluded that it is irresponsible to withdraw from relation with the world: "You are not swallowed up in a fulness without obligation, you are willed for the life of communion."[18] At the theoretical level he now advocates "a realistic and active mysticism, i.e. a mysticism for which the world is not an illusion, from which man must turn away in order to reach true being, but the reality between God and him in which reciprocity manifests itself . . . without the weakening of the lived multiplicity of all for the sake of a unity of all."[19] Buber, thus, rejects even a temporary escape from the multiplicity of human community. But the alternation persists—it is now an alternation between worldly mysticism and worldly manipulation.

In *I and Thou* (1923) Buber reached his mature limited corporate perspective. Two kinds of relation, *I-Thou* and *I-It*, replace the two kinds of experience, realizing and orienting, of *Daniel*. The *I-It* relation is a

---

18. Buber, "Dialogue," 14.

19. Buber, Introduction to "The Baal-Shem-Tov's Instruction on Intercourse with God," 180.

continuation of the empirical orienting experience in *Daniel*: in the *I-It* relation the other, the *It*, is treated as object—is observed or manipulated. "I perceive something. . . . I will something. I feel something. I think something. . . . [this is] the realm of *It*" (p. 4). "The man who experiences has no part in the world. For it is 'in him' and not between him and the world that the experience arises. The world has no part in the experience. It permits itself to be experienced, but has no concern in the matter. For it does nothing to the experience, and the experience does nothing to it" (p. 5).

The *I-Thou* relation, replacing his former ecstatic mysticism, is more than the realizing experience in *Daniel*. It is not an experience, but a relation. "I do not experience the man to whom I say *Thou*. But I take my stand in relation to him, in the sanctity of the primary word [*I-Thou*]. Only when I step out of it do I experience him once more. In the act of experience *Thou* is far away" (p. 9). Buber's *I-Thou* and *I-It* relations, like all the earlier described experiences, are still described from the *I*, the first-person, side of the relation.

The *I* holds the *I-Thou* and *I-It* relations in alternation in Buber's *I and Thou*, as it does the ecstatic experience and return to the world in "Ekstase und Bekenntnis," and the realizing and orienting modes in *Daniel*. "The relation to the *Thou* is direct. . . . Every means is an obstacle. Only when every means has collapsed does the meeting come about" (pp. 11–12). Yet, the *I-Thou* relation cannot persist without the alternation: "every *Thou* in our world must become an *It*. It does not matter how exclusively present the *Thou* was in the direct relation. As soon as the relation has been worked out or has been permeated with a means, the *Thou* becomes an object among objects" (pp. 16–17). "[H]is mortal life swings by nature between *Thou* and *It* . . . . There, in the threshold, the response, the spirit, is kindled new within him; here, in an unholy and needy country, this spark is to be proved" (pp. 52–53).

Love is a direct relation with the *Thou*. "Feelings accompany . . . love, but they do not constitute it. . . . Feelings are 'entertained': love comes to pass." "[L]ove is *between I* and *Thou*. . . . Love is responsibility of an *I* for a *Thou*" (pp. 14–15). Thus, in Buber love is the responsibility in a relation: it transcends both the objective nature of the other as recognized by the I and the subjective feeling thereby induced in the *I*. Buber says the hair color of the other that I observe is objective, the resulting feeling in me is subjective, and my responsibility to the other, love, transcends both.

Buber says the *I-Thou* relation is bilateral—the *Thou* contributes as well as the *I*: "Relation is mutual. My *Thou* affects me, as *I* affect it" (p. 15). Yet Buber views the contributions from both sides only from the first-person *I* side, characterizing intentional acts by the *Thou* only indirectly in terms of their effects impinging on the *I*. The relation with God is bilateral in the same way: "you need God more than everything; but do you not know too that God needs you—in the fulness of His eternity needs you? . . . Creation happens to us, burns itself into us, recasts us in burning—we tremble and are faint, we submit. We take part in creation, meet the Creator, reach out to him, helpers and companions" (p. 82).

This relation with God, however, is one step further removed from sensible means. It is reached through other *I-Thou* relations. "Every particular *Thou* is a glimpse through to the eternal *Thou*," which "is realized in each relation and consummated in none. It is consummated only in the direct relation with the [eternal] *Thou* that by its nature cannot become *It*" (p. 75), cannot be objectified. Rather, it sends the *I* back to the world open to *I-Thou* relations with others. "[H]e who goes on a mission has always God before him" (p. 116). "[P]ure relation can be fulfilled in the growth and rise of beings into *Thou*, that the holy primary word [*I-Thou*] makes itself heard in them all. . . . [M]en's relations with their true *Thou*, the radial lines that proceed from all the points of the *I* to the Centre, form a circle. It is not the periphery, the community, that comes first, but the radii, the common quality of relation with the Centre" (pp. 114–15).

Thus, one relates with God only as a *Thou*, never as an *It*, and God is glimpsed through other *I-Thou* relations. "The eternal *Thou* can by its nature not become *It*; for by its nature it can not be established in measure and bounds, not even in the measure of the immeasurable or the bounds of boundless being . . . ; for it can be found neither in or out of the world; for it cannot be experienced, or thought . . .—'He' is also a metaphor, but 'Thou' is not" (p. 112). Buber cannot objectively describe the God he intends with twentieth-century empirical language and he gave up, earlier, the attempt to do so mystically.

Buber's criticism of the European culture of his time is radical:

> Taking his stand in the shelter of the primary word [*I-It*] of separation, which holds off the *I* and the *It* from one another, he has

> divided his life with his fellow-men into two tidily circled-off provinces, one of institutions an the other of feelings—the province of *It* and the province of *I*. Institutions are "outside," where all sorts of aims are pursued, where a man works, negotiates, bears influence, undertakes . . . . Feelings are "within," where life is lived and man recovers from institutions. . . . Neither knows the person, or mutual life. . . Institutions yield no public life, and feelings no personal life (pp. 43–44).

He goes on to say:

> Is not, indeed, the productive greatness of the leading statesman and the leading economist bound up with the fact that he looks on the men with whom he has to deal not as bearers of the *Thou* that cannot be experienced but as centres of work and effort, whose particular capabilities it is his concern to estimate and utilise? . . . And if we look from the leaders to the led, has not the development in the very nature of modern work and possession destroyed almost every trace of living with what is over against them—of significant relation. It would be absurd to wish to return on this development—and if the absurd did come about, the enormous and nicely balanced apparatus of this civilization, which alone makes life possible for the enormous numbers of men that have grown with it, would simultaneously be destroyed. (p. 47).

Thus, "[T]he separated *It* of institutions is an animated clod without soul, and the separated *I* of feelings an uneasily fluttering soul-bird. Neither of them knows man; institutions know only the specimen, feelings only the 'object'; neither knows the person, or mutual life. . . . Institutions yield no public life, and feelings no personal life" (p. 44).

But institutions and feelings can be vehicles for interaction. "True public and true personal life are two forms of connexion. In that they come into being and endure, feelings (the changing content) and institutions (the changing form) are necessary; but put together they do not create human life: this is done by the third, the central . . . *Thou* that has been received in the present" (p. 46).

"That institutions yield no public life is realized by increasing numbers, realized with increasing distress. . . . That feelings yield no personal life is realized only by a few. For the most personal life of all seems to reside in feelings, and if, like the modern man, you have learned to concern yourself wholly with your own feelings, despair at their unreality will not easily instruct you in a better way—for despair is also an interesting feeling" (pp. 44–45). Rather, those distressed by the realization that institutions yield no public life seek to reduce institutions to feelings—for example, ignoring an increasingly empty institution of marriage so that a community of love "will arise when people out of free, abundant love, approach and wish to live with one another. But it is not so. The true community does not arise through peoples having feelings for one another (though indeed not without it), but through, first, their taking their stand in living mutual relation with a living Centre, and, second, their being in living mutual relation with one another. The second has its source in the first, but is not given when the first alone is given" (p. 45).

Buber's phrase "living mutual relation with one another" transcends a phenomenological analysis of the *I-Thou* relation from only the *I* side. The eternal *Thou* relating with each *I* in the community is here given a constitutive relation with the *betweens* between each pair of I's. Shortly we will find Levinas calling on Western philosophy to analyze this relation between two I's. But neither Buber nor Levinas sees the *I* and the several differently relating *Thou*s all in a common "world" within which to relate, as Gadamer, chapter 1.IV.3 above, does.

Twentieth century University of Vienna graduate Buber, who also experienced his Enlightenment Jewish background and Eastern European Hasidic sectarianism, has over decades assimilated these three backgrounds into the development of a critique of the modern perspective. According to Buber's 1918 description the zaddik (the leader of the local Hasidic community) was

> the perfected man in whom the immortal finds its mortal fulfillment.... The perfected man is ... the helper in spirit, the teacher of world meaning, the conveyor to the divine sparks.... Is it not at base a legitimate, *the* legitimate power, this power of the helping soul over the needy? Does there not lie in it the seed of future social orders? ... And I could compare: on the one side with the head man of the province whose power rested on nothing but habitual compulsion; on the other with the [conventional] rabbi, who was ... an employee of the "directorship of the cult." Here, however, was another, an incomparable; here was ... the living double kernel of humanity: genuine *community* and genuine leadership.[20]

---

20. Buber, "My Way to Hasidism," 52–55.

Hasidism was a "spiritual" sect within minority-status dispersion Judaism, thus twice removed from direct participation in mainstream European society. With these two, Buber has experienced community based on unilateral direction from above and community centered on a leader who is helping others. Yet, he has not seen the possibility of the multilaterally interacting community proposed in the Torah and Prophets—the community Hegel gives inside-out description of as a totality of interactions with each member being the collection of that member's roles in these interactions, or Gadamer's conceptual "world" shared by more than one person, thus a world seen from the perspective of the *We* rather than the *I* so that every *You* is also an *I*, both part of a *We*, a community of shared interactive responsibility freeing each member to contribute creatively to the whole. Buber comes closest when he pictures his community's relation to God as a circle of members related to God at the center, so that the community members share their relation with God and thus are in "living mutual relation with one another" (the paragraph above).

Subsequent intense studies of the Hebrew Bible by Buber in *Kingship of God* (1932), *The Prophetic Faith* (1940), and *Moses* (1945), and his translation of the Hebrew Bible, *Die Schrift* (1954–1961) with Franz Rosenzweig, moved Buber somewhat closer to the biblical perspective. In 1933 he stated his position in terms of a person's *response* to "the other". He wrote, "Responsibility presupposes one who addresses me . . . from a realm independent of myself, and to whom I am answerable. . . . [I]t can only be experienced when one is not closed to the otherness, the ontic and primal otherness of the other, . . which . . . must not be confined to a 'wholly otherness.'"[21] In 1960 he contrasted the bases of Western and biblical thought: "The truth . . . is not the sublime 'unconcealment' suitable to Being itself, the *alethia* of the Greeks; it is the simple conception of truth of the Hebrew Bible, whose *etymon* means 'faithfulness,' the faithfulness of man or the faithfulness of God."[22]

Buber brought from Judaism to the wider Western world an awareness of relations *between* persons beyond both subjective and objective analyses of Western philosophy. His *I and Thou* reinforced a mid-twentieth-century European search for community and was taken up by the Christian theologians Friedrich Gogarten, Emil Brunner, and others

---

21. Buber, "The Question to the Single One," 45.
22. Buber, "The Word that is Spoken," 120.

who were not ready for the unreservedly corporate positions of the Old Testament, Möhler, and Newman—positions that were in eclipse at the time.

The Jewish philosopher Emmanuel Levinas (1906-1995) praised Buber for offering insights from Judaism to the wider European society: "It was he who showed the Western world that Judaism exists as a contemporary form of life and thought. But it was also he who taught Judaism itself that it was again visibly exposed to the outside world, present otherwise than by the participation of its assimilated and de-Judaized intellectuals in the spiritual life of the West."[23]

Levinas, a generation after Buber, interpreted Judaism to the Western world out of the rabbinic rather than Hasidic tradition and to a world coming after Husserl and Heidegger rather than after Boehme and Kant. Like Buber in *I and Thou*, Levinas puts the relation with a *Thou*, an *other*, beyond the reach of Western ontology: "not in synthesis, but in the face to face of humans.... First philosophy is an ethics," not an ontology.[24] Relations between persons are not ordered cosmically or generically or merely organically:

> The relation with the Other does not nullify separation. It does not arise within a totality nor does it establish a totality, integrating me and the other. Nor does the face to face conjuncture presuppose the existence of universal truths into which subjectivity could be absorbed.... Rather... the relation between me and the other commences in the *inequality* of terms, transcendent to one another.... the alterity of the other does not result from its identity, but constitutes it: the other is the Other. The Other qua Other is situated in a dimension of height and of abasement—glorious abasement; he has the face of the poor, the stranger, the widow, and the orphan, and, at the same time, of the master called to invest and justify my freedom. This inequality does not appear to the third party who would count us. The inequality *is* in this impossibility of the *exterior* point of view, which alone could abolish it.[25]

The otherness of the other in a face-to-face relation consists precisely in the impossibility of a systematic, "exterior" characterization, both of the other itself and of the other's relation to the would-be character-

---

23. Levinas, "Martin Buber's Thought and Contemporary Judaism," 5.
24. Levinas, *Ethics and Infinity*, 77.
25. Levinas, *Totality and Infinity*, 251.

izer. The relation's acceptance reaches the objectivity only of a response. "The commandment is stated through the mouth of him it commands." Namely, the one who says, "Here I am!"[26]

The otherness of the other, human being or God, is transcendent or "infinite" in the sense of being prior to the interactor's consciousness and intentionality, not reducible to the objective or the subjective, beyond the reach of the "universal truths" of perennial or Enlightenment analysis. As in Buber, the relation with God lies behind every relation with an Other: "The trace of the infinite is inscribed in my obligation toward the other."[27]

But Levinas goes beyond Buber when a second other, a third party, appears. In "Peace and Proximity" (1984) (PP) he says, "But how does responsibility obligate if a third party troubles this exteriority of two where my subjection of the subject is subjection to the neighbor? The third party is other than the neighbor but also another neighbor, and also a neighbor of the other . . . . What have they already done to one another? Who passes before the other in my responsibility?" (PP 168). In *Otherwise than Being* (1974) (OB) he says, "The other and the third party, my neighbors, contemporaries of one another, put distance between me and the other and the third party. 'Peace, peace to the neighbor and the one far-off' (Isaiah 57:19)" (OB 157).

> In the proximity of the other all the others than the other obsess me, and already this obsession cries out for justice, demands measure and knowing, is consciousness. . . . The other is from the first the brother of all the other[s] . . . The relationship with the third party is an incessant correction of the asymmetry of proximity in which the face is looked at. . . . [I]t is only thanks to God that, as a subject incomparable with the other, I am approached as an other by the others . . . I am another for the others. . . . The passing of God, of whom I can speak only by reference to this aid or this grace, is precisely the reverting of the incomparable subject into a member of society (OB 158).

Thus, God is met only through his "trace" and is met only as one's having become a member of society. The appearance of the second neighbor forces implicit recognition of the first neighbor as a member of society

---

26. Levinas, *Ethics and Infinity*, 110, 109.
27. Levinas, "The Proximity of the Other," *Alterity and Transcendence*, 106.

and, by extension, brings explicit recognition that the subject, the phenomenological "I" under consideration, is a member of society.

"Comparison is superimposed onto my relation with the *unique* and the incomparable, and, in view of equity and equality, a weighing, a thinking, a calculation, the comparison of incomparables, and, consequently, the neutrality—presence or representation—of being, . . . the necessity of thinking together under a synthetic theme the multiplicity and the unity of the world; and, through this, . . . finally, the political structure of society, subject to laws and thereby to institutions where the *for-the-other* of subjectivity—or the ego—enters with the dignity of a citizen into the perfect reciprocity of political laws" (PP 168). Having two neighbors requires one to reason, to compare, and so to thematize what cannot be totally thematized—and so to need philosophy. "[Europe's] Biblical heritage implies the necessity of the Greek heritage. Europe is not a simple confluence of two cultural currents. . . . The relation with the other and the unique that is peace comes to demand a reason that thematizes, synchronizes and synthesizes" (PP 168). "To the extravagant generosity of the for-the-other is superimposed a reasonable order . . . of justice through knowledge" (PP 169), a disciplined and disciplining offer to each neighbor out of a responsibility to each of the other neighbors in the community. Although the whole community is objectified only as an indefinite number of individual others each with neighbors, Levinas's self responsibility to *two* others takes a step toward the present book's "corporate" relation, thus beyond Buber's *I-Thou* relation with one other. But does it not also move perilously toward a Western style systemization?

Thus, Levinas seeks to replace the Enlightenment social contract based on the self-interest of each separate ego, dominant in Western philosophical analysis of human relations, with a social relation that is a "trace" of God requiring "a weighing, a thinking, a calculation, the comparison of incomparables" to reach "a reasonable order . . . of justice," a "political structure of society," starting with obsession with "the *for-the-other* of subjectivity—or the ego"—a radically different ego from the one named in the Western tradition. Such an "order" or "political structure" would require "thinking together under a synthetic theme," presumably requiring language or other symbolic means of communication for use of *Western* "neutrality—presence or representation—of being" as a tool for a very non-neutral purpose. (All the quotes are from PP 168–69 in the preceding paragraph.)

In terms of the central issues of our study, Levinas by many measures is an ally of the communal perspective. But can he use the "Greek heritage" to compare incomparables without making them comparable in the Greek sense? Can he place a judge (or a historian) in internal relation with a matter being judged without violating the Greek heritage's base in the invariance of being? Can the Greek heritage characterize "thinking together under a synthetic theme" without the parties coming to a consensus, or without obliterating the alterity of each to the other that "constitutes" them? Can it allow a complementary intersubjectivity between them in which they can interact without thinking or acting in the same way? Levinas avoids part of the Greek heritage with his Husserlian phenomenalism, a truncation of the Greek perspective costing it the power to formalize an interaction from the perspectives of several distinct participants simultaneously—shown in chapter one for similarly phenomenally oriented early Heidegger (*Sein und Zeit* 118. Also see page 37, above). Greek repair of this damage would be brought about by bringing back its banned "totality" of universally pre-known Forms.

The non-neutral purpose is, of course, primary: "justice is not a legality regulating human masses, from which a technique of social equilibrium is drawn, harmonizing antagonistic forces. . . . Justice is impossible without the one that renders it finding himself in proximity. His function is not limited to . . . the subsuming of particular cases under a general rule. The judge is not outside the conflict, but the law is in the midst of proximity" (OB 159). In the terminology of this study this is to say a judge is in internal relation with the matter to be judged. Thus, a judgment should not flow from a "totality," a "universal truth," and certainly not from Enlightenment self-interest: "It is not without importance to know—and this is perhaps the European experience of the twentieth century—if the egalitarian and just State in which the European is accomplished—and which it is a matter of founding and, above all, preserving—proceeds from a war of all against all—or from the irreducible responsibility of the one for the other" (PP 169). In another place Levinas says more directly, "it is very important, in my view, that justice should flow from, issue from, the preeminence of the other . . . . Justice, inseparable from institutions, and hence from politics, risks preventing the face of the other . . . from being recognized."[28] And the danger is practical: "My critique of the totality has come in fact after a political experience that we have not yet forgotten."[29]

In contrast, the Hebrew Bible, much of it independent of the Greek heritage, satisfies Levinas's requirements untarnished by that heritage. It starts not with the phenomenal self but with the whole human community *adam* with its multilaterally internal relations among its members, relations of incomparability making each simultaneously subordinate and superordinate to every other. The community is objectified—that is, named—but is not a "totality." Levinas's phenomenological "subject" emerges in Scripture already intrinsically a multilaterally interacting member of a community, and the "other" it confronts is also already member of a community—the same community. Whereas Levinas starts with a self intrinsically wanting to serve the neighbor it meets, Scripture starts with a human community of members inherently serving and being served by one another, with each member having a choice to what extent to "war against all" and to what extent to contribute to and accept the contributions of others, all the while being exhorted to choose the latter.

Scripture *is* a community tradition; it is composed in a language devised by a community, it is about justice, and it is a non-Greek objectification by the community of its community life as one tool for maintaining that life. Scripture narrates a human community being called by its God from its beginning to responsibility for creating and practicing a justice that distributes that interactive creativity throughout the explicitly recognized whole community (Gen 1:27–28). This includes responsibility for *creating* its own members both biologically and culturally (for example, the biological origins and long torturous social formations of the political leaders Joseph (Gen 37:20—41:57) and Moses (Exod 2:1—4:17)), inheriting and developing *capacities* both for responsibility toward their community and for self-serving at the expense of the community. The responsibility of individual members for others is *posterior* to the prior delegation of responsibility to the community for creating those members with sufficient common horizon to be capable of accepting or rejecting that responsibility when called by God through the others. When humanity demurred from its responsibility (Gen 11:1–9), a

---

28. Levinas, "Violence of the Face," *Alterity and Transcendence*, 176.
29. Levinas, *Ethics and Infinity*, 78–79.

particular *family* among the others, represented by Abraham, was called to internal mutual responsibility and to the offering of influence toward the same to the other families of the world (Gen 12:3). The choices that members make cannot be pre-calculated absolutely: they can only be creative offerings toward improving the already existing interactive relations among others (who themselves have a *choice* both whether and how to respond). Rules are needed but so are exceptions: as David's eating the bread of the presence and Jesus' disciples rubbing grain together on the Sabbath (1 Sam 21:1–6 = Luke 6:4–5). Such interpretations of later situations by typological reference to similar earlier ones in both Testaments (for example, the "second Exodus" in Isaiah 40, or the antithetical typology of Jer 22:15–16 described in the following paragraph) relate issues and solutions in different circumstances not formally, or allegorically, but as essence-changing internal relation across time that adds to the understanding of both earlier and later interactive challenges to the same community.

The biblical epic traces the adaptation of Israel's responsibilities to an ever larger community as Israel grows from patriarchal family to expatriate workforce, to tribal voluntary association, to absorption of the Canaanite communities, to empire, to client state in a world empire, to dispersion. All the while, Israel is called to create justice at home and servanthood leadership among the other communities toward the same. The prophets also take whole communities as basic. Their goal is resurrection of whole Israel: Hosea 6:1–2 "On the third day he will raise us [Ephraim and Judah] up, that we may live before him," or Ezekiel 37:1–14 "These bones are the whole house of Israel." Israel is called as Servant to the nations (Isa 49:1–6), a calling to be maintained through its political organization. The member *is* a member; salvation of the member *is* salvation of the member's role in community. Jeremiah says, "'Did not your father do . . . justice and righteousness? . . . is not this to know me?' says the LORD" (Jer 22:15–16). Jeremiah utters this not as a privately informed individual but as prophet, office holder, in whole Israel, about another office-holder, king Josiah, and directed to a third, king Shallum. Scripture gives every individual some office-holder role in the community, some responsibility for the community's justice.

Levinas often applies Scripture as in rabbinic midrash, using passages as ethical models for individuals—in the terminology of the present book, paraenetic typology (above, page 98). For example, when one suffers, "One doesn't pray for oneself" but "prays for the suffering of God, who suffers by the sin of man and the painful expiation for sin"— "Doesn't the Psalmist say 'I am with him in distress'?" (Ps 91:15)[30]—a position nearly opposite neo-Platonic Christianity's central concern with salvation of the individual. Midrashic interpretation is useful for maintaining a dispersed community with a written tradition. But Levinas is also ready himself to apply Scripture typologically, that is, prophetically, when a current community-wide issue appears. At a Jewish-Christian amity meeting in France he said, "We recognize ourselves in this relationship [kinship with Christianity] whenever we are in the presence of a world that does not know, or does not want to know, the Bible, like that Pharaoh at the beginning of Exodus—'a new sovereign who did not know Joseph'" (Exod 1:8)."[31]

Buber and Levinas engage current dispersion Israel interactively with the Western academic world, a servant role (Isa 49:6) moving that world toward a more corporate orientation (whereas Marx and Wittgenstein could so contribute only as individuals formally baptized into that world by act of parent or grandparent). Next, we see Western Christianity rediscovering directly its own canonical Old Testament and readmitting it to its tradition.

## II RECOGNIZING THE NEW TESTAMENT AS WITHIN THE TRADITION

In the mid-twentieth century, biblical scholars Walther Eichrodt and Gerhard von Rad, building on Johannes Weiss, Wilhelm Bousset, and Albert Schweitzer (chapter 3.I, above), laid out the corporate basis of the Old Testament tradition and described its typological transmission of that corporate basis throughout its history and on to the New Testament.

### *1 Bilateral Relation Between God and Community: Walther Eichrodt*

Walther Eichrodt, in *Theology of the Old Testament* (1933) solidifies the corporate understanding of the Old Testament of Möhler, Newman, and Wieman (noted previously in the chapter) against its domination by the critical-historical school. "It is high time that the tyranny of historicism

---

30. Levinas, "Violence of the Face," 182.
31. Levinas, "Beyond Dialogue," *Alterity and Transcendence*, 83.

in OT studies was broken and the proper approach to our task rediscovered" (1.31)—high time for Christians to read the Old Testament not from the interaction-free critical-historical position recognizing only empirical events but from within their own Christian tradition (recognizing the Old Testament as part of that tradition and as a major resource for the Christian movement's interpreting its present to itself). Eichrodt says:

> The historical approach had triumphed on every side. . . . The method had a particularly fatal influence both on OT theology and on the understanding of the OT in every other aspect, because it fostered the idea that once the historical problems were clarified everything had been done. The essential inner coherence of the Old and New Testaments was reduced, so to speak, to a thin thread of historical connection and causal sequence between the two. . . . One consequence of this is the fact that the OT has completely lost any effective place in the structure of Christian doctrine. Indeed, in the circumstances, it sometimes seems more from academic politeness than from any real conviction of its indispensability that it is so seldom denied all value as canonical Scripture—a step which would enable the whole subject to be transferred from the sphere of theology to that of the comparative study of religions (1.29–30).

The critical method thus makes invisible any possible current meaning of the Old Testament for the Christian or any other current tradition. It also implies the collapse of the Old Testament itself into a disjointed heap of disparate materials. "The little still left to OT theology to do, viz., the historical presentation of the Israelite and Judaistic religion, was quite insufficient to conceal, even with the help of the magic word 'development,' how serious the loss had been. There was no longer any unity to be found in the OT, only a collection of detached periods which were simply the reflections of as many different religions" (1.30–31). This lack of unity is a heritage from rationalism: "Rationalism . . . in its delight in critical analysis . . . lost its feeling for the vital synthesis in the OT and could only see the differing teachings of individual biblical writers" (1.28).

Eichrodt finds the missing unity, a unity binding the whole Old Testament together and also carrying over to the New Testament and the Christian tradition, in the concept of Israel as the people of God, as a community bound to God in a bilateral covenant relation and, thus, in its communal life representing God to the world: "every expression of the OT which is determinative for its faith rests on the explicit or implicit assumption that a free act of God, consummated in history, has raised Israel to the rank of the People of God, in whom the nature and will of God are to be revealed" (1.14)

On God's side, this relation to Israel is based neither on a blood relationship nor on God's territorial presence in the countryside but on election. "This is something on which God has entered freely and which he on his side may dissolve at any time" (1.44). On Israel's side, the relation is no extrinsic justification of Israel but has a factual historical impact on the life of the community and the individuals in it. The covenant "was always regarded as a bilateral relationship; for even though the burden is most unequally distributed between the two contracting parties, this makes no difference to the fact that the relationship is still essentially two-sided" (1.37). "It is in the name of Yahweh and in the covenant sanctioned by him that the tribes find the unifying bond, which proves a match even for the centrifugal tendencies of tribal egoism and creates from highly diversified elements a whole with a common law, a common cultus and a common historical consciousness" (1.39).

Eichrodt recognizes a development in the concept of covenant: "in the whole long process of adjusting the Mosaic religion to the environment of Canaanite religion and culture it is round this crucial issue that the struggle fluctuates to an fro, now assimilating, now rejecting, striving in part toward distortion, in part toward new understanding and sharper definition of the covenant concept" (1.45). For example, the classical prophets understand very well the two-sided relation between God and Israel but generally avoid the term "covenant" because of the legal character it tends to impart to the relation (1.51–52); while in the Deuteronomic period there is an embracing of this very legal character (1.54). Thus, Eichrodt traces the development of the bilateral covenant relation, not just the empirically described evolving states of Israel as with the history-of-religions school.

The relation between God and the community includes a personal relation with each member *as* actively interacting member. Eichrodt specifically rejects a "collectivistic" generic understanding of Old Testament piety in which the individual has no individual part in the shaping of his own thought and action, contrasted with the still generally held concomitant "individualistic," thus generic, understanding of the New Testament as the victory of relationships purely between God and individuals. Eichrodt continues, "The practice of drawing a distinction between these two patterns of living and then playing them off one against the other was, however, something that grew up in the soil of philosophical idealism; and to transfer it to the conditions of ancient society can lead only to misunderstanding" (2.232). Eichrodt finds that in the Old Testament the individual is related to the community by a sense of solidarity, he is "welded into a social unit outside which there can be no meaningful life for the individual" (2.233). The common life of the members "is founded on a spiritual and psychical unity in which each individual is a representative of the whole, and in turn has his entire private attitude to life shaped by the whole" (2.233). And "the sense of the spiritual unity of all members of the tribe leads to a vigilant responsibility on the part of each individual member, and to willing commitment to the welfare of the whole" (2.234).

On the basis of this solidarity, Eichrodt concludes, "solidarity provides free scope for a thoroughly personal relationship with God" (2.239).

> But Old Testament faith knows nothing, in any situation or at any time, of a religious individualism which grants a man a private relationship with God unconnected with the community either in its roots, its realization or its goal. Just as it is the formation of a divine *society* which gives meaning to the divine demand that summons the individual and enlists him in its service, so it is in serving his brethren that the obedience of the one who is called is proved, it is in the common cultic festivals that his religious life finds its natural expression, and it is toward a perfected people of God that his hope is directed (2.265).

And specifically: "eschatological universalism never implies a flight from the hope for the nation's future into an individualistic ideal world, but affirms that it is precisely the national ties which provide the framework within which the divine community of the future is to be realized. Prophetic thought does not see community and individual in mutually exclusive opposition, but in fruitful interaction" (2.266–67). He admits the presence of "the rudiments of a purely individualistic piety" in postexilic wisdom writers but excuses it by saying, "they enter into the type of teaching given by their opponents, and then use *reductio ad absurdum* to destroy it with its own arguments" (2.267). This differs from the claim in chapter 3 above that prophecy in a European ruled colony spoke in metonymy rather than explicitly.

Eichrodt's table of contents shows that his coverage of all the previously usual topics of an Old Testament theology is under the rubric of covenant: the covenant statutes—that is, law and cultus; the nature of the covenant God; prophets, priests, and kings as instruments of the covenant; covenant breaking and the judgment of Israel; the eschatological fulfilling of the covenant; God and humanity in the world; and the relation of the individual to God. This treatment requires the use of the critical-historical method, but Eichrodt's program is to use that method as a tool to recover the past as part of the wider post-critical project of merging its horizon with his current western readers own. "In treating individual religious concepts the major elements of their historical background must be taken into account. Only so can we hope to do justice to the great unitive tendency that runs through the whole religious history of Israel and makes it with all its variety a self-consistent entity" (1.32). This unitive principle is to be discovered, not imported from some other horizon: "It is impossible to use a system which has been developed on a basis quite different from that of the realm of OT thought to arrive at the OT belief about God" (1.32). The Enlightenment's systematic three-part frame for Old Testament study "God, self, salvation" misses the unitive principle and substitutes an incompatible modern principle.

Eichrodt has been criticized for trying to place all the diversified themes in the Old Testament under the one concept of covenant, yet this is exactly Eichrodt's intention. Israel preserves its Old Testament history for metonymic interaction with its present in its continuous joint interactive creation of community (with God, among its members, and in creative mission to other communities in the world) because this is the very basis for the existence of the Israel whose story this is: "without which indeed Israel would not have been Israel" (1.18).

### 2 Living Within a Tradition: Gerhard von Rad

Gerhard von Rad further analyses the hermeneutical method Israel used during two millennia of cultural change to transmit the covenant-people tradition found by Eichrodt.

In his *Old Testament Theology* (1957–1960) von Rad, like Eichrodt, distinguishes Old Testament theology from the history of Old Testament religions. "The subject matter which concerns the theologian is, of course, not the spiritual and religious world of Israel and the conditions of her soul in general, nor is it her world of faith . . . : instead, it is simply Israel's own explicit assertions about Jahweh" (1.105). Israel's assertions about God are not made abstractly but by recounting a history. "The Old Testament writings confine themselves to representing Jahweh's relationship to Israel and the world in one aspect only, namely as a continuing divine activity in history" (1.106).

The Old Testament understanding of history is *not* the modern critical understanding of history:

> We are of course thinking, when we speak of divine acts in history, of those which the faith of Israel regarded as such—that is, the call of the forefathers, the deliverance from Egypt, the bestowal of the land of Canaan, etc.—and not of the results of modern critical historical scholarship, to which Israel's faith was unrelated. . . . These two pictures of Israel's history lie before us—that of modern critical scholarship and that which the faith of Israel constructed. . . . It would be superfluous to emphasize that each is the product of very different intellectual activities. The one is rational and "objective," that is, with the aid of historical method and presupposing the similarity of all historical occurrence, it constructs a critical picture of the history as it really was in Israel . . . . The other activity is confessional and personally involved in events to the point of fervour (1.107).

The narration of an event in the Old Testament for a confessional purpose, is always an interpretation of that event. Often several different interpretations of the same event are present or are reconstructible. For example, in the adaptation of the stories of the patriarchs into the Yahwist epic, the Gods of the patriarchs were reinterpreted as the God of Israel: "In the promise of a land made to the ancestors, Jahwism recognized the voice of its own God. . . . This at once brought the old patriarchal stories into an entirely new light, for what a difference it must have made when Jahweh took the place of the 'strong one of Jacob'! From the hermeneutic point of view, this meant a complete reinterpretation of the old tradition . . . . Jahwism transferred the old promise of a land to the horizon of a different and much more distant point of fulfillment, namely the conquest under Joshua" (2.322). A second example is the successive reinterpretations of the story of Jacob wrestling at Jabbok (Gen 32:24–32; von Rad 2.325–26). From a pre-Yahwistic wrestling with a river demon who took flight at dawn, the story shifted in the Genesis account to an encounter between God and Jacob who said, "I will not let you go, unless you bless me." Then in Hosea 12:2–6 Jacob is indicted for deceit and importunity. And finally, assuming continuity between the testaments, Jacob's seeing God face to face takes on christological implications (e.g., 1 Cor 13:12 "now we see . . . dimly, but then face to face" and John 1:18 "No one has ever seen God; the only Son . . . has made him known"). A third example is the shift of the election tradition under the classical prophets from blessing to judgment (2.323). For the critical-historical school, these differences (in the three examples) are differences in Israel's religion in different ages. For the transmission-of-tradition school, they are typologically related examples of the exercise of the same religion in different cultural circumstances. The tradition does not start over from scratch in each age.

Thus, the bulk of the Old Testament material is a series of ever-recurring reinterpretations of older traditions. "No generation produced a perfectly independent and finished historical work—each continued to work upon what had been handed down to it, the Elohist working upon the Jahwist, the Deuteronomist upon copious older material, while the Chronicler in turn built further upon the foundation of the Deuteronomist" (1.119). As the tradition accumulated, traditions conflicting in perspective were retained, sometimes even side-by-side in a dialectical manner as, for example, the two accounts of creation (Gen 1, 2) and the two accounts of the rise of the monarchy (1 Sam 8–12).

This accumulation of tradition is very different from a critical history of the same period. "It would be a very hasty conclusion if critical historical scholarship were minded to be itself taken as the only way into the history of Israel, and if it denied to what Israel reports in, say, her sagas a foundation in the 'real' history. In some respects, this foundation is an even deeper one" (1.108). He further says, "The picture given by modern critical history is also interpreted history, interpreted from premises in the philosophy of history that exclude from consideration any participation by God in history and understand the human being alone as creator of its history."[32]

Recovery of the course of this transmission of tradition is significantly assisted by use of the critical-historical method, but for von Rad this is not the end but only one means toward that end. Von Rad's end, as

---

32. Von Rad, *Theologie des Alten Testaments*, 2.9. This passage was omitted from the English translation.

biblical theologian rather than critical historian, goes beyond recovery of the critical history of the transmission of traditions to the relation with God transmitted—a relation outside the critical-historical horizon and available for further such transmission to the New Testament period and on to his own age.

The application of an early tradition to later events intensifies the significance of the earlier events, giving them an eschatological cast. "The later story-tellers are so zealous for Jahweh and his saving work that they . . . depict the event in a magnificence far transcending what it was in reality. These are texts which contain an implicit eschatological element, since they anticipate a *Gloria* of God's saving action not yet granted to men" (1.111). In many cases this intensification takes the form of promise and fulfillment, as in the promise of land to the patriarchs—a promise whose successive expectations of fulfillment are ever wider and more significant (2.383). The result is a tradition which always presents Israel in the eschatological position of being between type and antitype, of being between promise and fulfillment, of being in the midst of a not yet complete history of God's saving action (2.414). Israel's tradition invites its application to ever new events in the life of the community. The "continuous reinterpretation to which . . . the old stories about Jahweh were submitted, did not do violence to them. Rather they were predisposed to it from the very start. Their intrinsic openness to a future actually needed such fresh interpretations on the part of later ages" (2.361).

Von Rad extends the concept of typology as developed by Goppelt for the New Testament use of Old Testament examples (chapter 2.II.2, above): the transmission of tradition in which each age interprets community events as saving acts of God by putting them in continuity with analogous earlier saving events carried forward in the community's tradition (2.363–74). In a sketch of the history of New Testament use of the Old Testament, he distinguishes this typology from medieval allegorical interpretation after Augustine and a succession of universalizing substitutes called typology since the Reformation (2.366–67). He welcomes the new understanding of typology that makes New Testament typological use of the Old Testament equivalent to prophecy and fulfillment. "Such a transformation of the traditional material in the light of a new saving event was as proper for early Christians as were many other such transformations which had already taken place in the Old Testament itself" (2.332–33). All the main points of the analysis of typology in section 2.II.2 of the present study are present in von Rad's work.

The connections among the manifold events within the Old Testament, and with the New, realized through their typological relation within the tradition as saving interactions with God, provide a unity for the Old Testament that eluded the critical history-of-religions school. The typological relation expanded the significance of any single saving act of God to make it represent and interpret God's relation with Israel throughout Israel's history. "Here at last we come upon one unifying principle towards which Israel's theological thinking strove, and with reference to which it ordered its material and thought; this was 'Israel,' the people of God, which always acts as a unit, and with which God always deals as a unit" (1.118). Although von Rad depreciates Eichrodt's "starting point in the covenant" (2.412), he has, in this passage, come close to stating Eichrodt's thesis.

Gerhard Hasel devotes a chapter, "The Question of History, History of Tradition, and Salvation History" in his *Old Testament Theology: Basic Issues in the Current Debate*, to a critique of von Rad's system. Hasel easily deflects Franz Hesse's complaint that of the two kinds of history von Rad distinguishes (the *critical history* of the tradition and the *content* of the tradition), salvation history is the former (pp. 59–63). He also deflects, without effort, Friedrich Baumgärtel's view that neither kind of Old Testament history is relevant to the Christian faith (pp. 64–65). But Hasel agrees with Eichrodt and others (pp. 63–68) that von Rad has not successfully brought the two kinds of history together and summarizes efforts by Pannenberg to do so by subsuming both under a universal history (pp. 68–72). John J. Collins says, "Von Rad rightly saw here a central problem for biblical theology, but he cannot be said to have resolved it."[33] Neither Hasel nor Collins recognize that von Rad does bring the two kinds of history together and does so by giving them complementary roles, with critical history being a means toward the current historians' recovery of Israel's dominant corporate salvation-historical perspective, as has been shown throughout this section. Scholars with modern presuppositions reject von Rad's subordination of critical history to corporate salvation history in order to bring the two kinds of history together because they would prefer the subordination the other way around. Von

---

33. Collins, "The 'Historical Character,'" 192.

Rad's claim is that the *Old Testament* prefers the subordination of the critical.

Both Eichrodt and von Rad give first place to God's interaction with the community. Eichrodt's program is precisely the abstract characterization of the unifying principle of the Old Testament as being the ongoing bilateral relation between God and the community Israel as the people of God. And von Rad's complementary project is to show that the purpose and function of the Old Testament was and is the bringing forward of God's past saving acts in Israel as context for understanding the continuing saving relation between God and his corporate people. Although the emphasis is synchronic in Eichrodt and diachronic in von Rad, Eichrodt also allows a diachronic development of the bilateral relation; and von Rad's diachronic bilateral relation is synchronic at any one time. The complementarity of Eichrodt's synchronic approach and von Rad's diachronic approach resembles the synchronic-diachronic complementarity between communal political philosophy and communal philosophy of history found in this study's chapter 1, above.

Another complementarity aspect of the two treatments is between the abstractness of Eichrodt's characterization of the essence of the Old Testament perspective and the historical particularity of von Rad's characterization of the transmission of tradition. Von Rad's historical characterization is a communal advance over Eichrodt, which von Rad points out several times.[34] It holds up the intrinsic typological or eschatological nature of the relation between Israel and God more naturally than when that relation is characterized abstractly. It characterizes in terms of particular diachronic and synchronic corporate structures in the specific community. Yet, all universalization cannot be avoided—language itself uses it—and both Eichrodt and von Rad depend on universalizing critical history as a tool. The issue between them is the same as a methodological issue handled in chapter 1, above, by characterizing the difference between modern and communal thought (both abstractly with the cosmological-corporate distinction and historically in terms of particular philosophical traditions), even though some of the contrasted traditions (like the corporately conceived Old Testament and generically

---

34. E.g. von Rad, *Old Testament Theology*, 1.114, 2.338, 2.411, 2.412. By 1957 Eichrodt accepts the diachronic approach also with some reservations, "Is Typological Exegesis an Appropriate Method?," 224–45.

conceived modern theology) are not themselves written with any conscious awareness of a generic-corporate distinction.

Although von Rad excels as a communal theologian on this issue, Eichrodt excels with his development of the human contribution in the bilateral relation between God and Israel. In von Rad, the transmission of the tradition is a corporate activity within Israel; but his description of that tradition gives the saving acts of God toward Israel more prominence than the complementary acts of Israel toward God, which are equally or more so part of the biblical story. This emphasis is clear in the first two quotations in this section on von Rad. The unilateral nature of the relation with God in neo-Platonic and modern theology is not explicitly challenged as it is in Eichrodt.

Both writers explicitly interpret the Old Testament from within the Christian tradition to which they and their prospective readers belong—not because the Old Testament requires this but because the Old Testament requires interpretation from *some* context that understands itself to be in internal typological interactive relation with the Old Testament as the two scholars' Christian context does. In fact, any speech or writing requires some openness to its interactive intention to be understood.

Eichrodt and von Rad complete the radical break with neo-Platonic, liberal, and existentialist perspectives begun by the communal-leaning study of the Old Testament in the history-of-religions school,[35] thus accomplishing a communal turn in biblical studies away from a merely critical historicism. Empirical critical study has transcended itself by revealing a position beyond empiricism and this break emerges exactly where one might expect: in critical study of the Old Testament which, unlike the New, was not written in the two-valued Greek vocabulary of first-century Apocalyptic culture. New Testament studies were to follow suit starting in 1960 (above, chapter 2.II.2). With these two events, the Old Testament has been readmitted to the Christian tradition, and the New Testament has begun to be recognized as a radically corporate document invading Europe, bringing with it that non-Platonic, non-Perennial, non-Existentialist but instead *corporate* tradition. This story continues in chapter 10, below.

---

35. Including Johannes Weiss, Wilhelm Bousset, and Albert Schweitzer on apocalyptic in the New Testament (Chapter 3.I above); William Wrede and Schweitzer on justification by faith in Paul (page 139 note 26 above).

# 8

# Contemporary Perennial Theological Systems

THE PERENNIAL CLASSICAL WESTERN cosmological orientation is still a living option in Christian theology. This chapter analyzes two influential mid-twentieth century perennial systems, those of Tillich and of Rahner. Both Tillich and Rahner try to meet existentialist yearnings within a cosmological orientation. Both are basically uninterested in the Old Testament.

## *1 The Logos: Paul Tillich*

Paul Tillich, in his *Systematic Theology* (1951–1963), offers a theological system based explicitly on the classical Western cosmological philosophical orientation. According to Tillich, philosophy is "that cognitive approach to reality in which reality as such is the object. Reality as such, or reality as a whole, is not the whole of reality; it is the structure which makes reality a whole and therefore a potential object of knowledge" (1.18).

Tillich rejects the turn of modern philosophy toward the subject. "Epistemology, the 'knowledge' of knowing, is a part of ontology, the knowledge of being, for knowing is an event within the totality of events. Every epistemological assertion is implicitly ontological" (1.71). Epistemology is derived from ontology. The generic human being can understand the world because the human cognitive function shares in the reason, the structure, the being, the *logos*, of reality as a whole: "The philosopher looks at the whole of reality to discover within it the structure of reality as a whole. He tries to penetrate into the structures of being by means of the power of his cognitive function and its structures. He assumes—and science continuously confirms this assumption—that there is an identity, or at least an analogy, between objective and subjective reason, between the *logos* of reality as a whole and the *logos* working in him. Therefore, this *logos* is common; every reasonable being participates in it, uses it in asking questions and criticizing the answers received" (1.23).

Tillich distinguishes the classical ontological concept of reason from the technical concept of reason dominant since the middle of the nineteenth century. "According to the classical philosophical tradition, reason is the structure of the mind which enables the mind to grasp and to transform reality. It is effective in the cognitive, aesthetic, practical, and technical functions of the human mind. . . . Its cognitive nature is one element in addition to others; it is cognitive and aesthetic, theoretical and practical, detached and passionate, subjective and objective" (1.72). With the dominance of positivism and existentialism, technical reason (the discovery of means for given ends) has been divorced from ontological reason. "While reason in the sense of Logos determines the ends and only in the second place the means, reason in the technical sense determines the means while accepting the ends from 'somewhere else.' . . . Since the middle of the nineteenth century . . . the ends are provided by nonrational forces, either by positive traditions or by arbitrary decisions serving the will to power" (1.73). Tillich bemoans the current loss of a *rational* structure that provides a meaning and goal for existence. Of ontological and technical reason he says, "the former is predominant in the classical tradition from Parmenides to Hegel; the latter, though always present in pre-philosophical and philosophical thought, has become predominant since the breakdown of German classical idealism and in the wake of English empiricism" (1.72). Hegel's actual corporate position (above, chapter 1.IV.1) was not then widely recognized.

In Tillich, "being" is a term for the structure, the meaning, the aim of existence—it engages our *ultimate concern*. "Our ultimate concern is that which determines our being or not-being. . . . The term 'being' in this context does not designate existence in time and space. . . . The term 'being' means the whole of human reality, the structure, the meaning, and the aim of existence" (1.14). In Tillich, these terms (*logos*, being, ontological reason, structure of reality, reality itself, and reality as a whole) refer to the structure or order in the cosmos, and to the reflection of that structure in the human mind. Tillich thus explicitly exposes his Platonic cosmological philosophical presuppositions. His theological system is built on these presuppositions.

According to Tillich, reason as actualized in the world is fallen and subject to salvation: "Although the essence of ontological reason, the universal *logos* of being, is identical with the content of revelation, still reason, if actualized in self and world, is dependent on the destructive structures of existence and the saving structures of life. . . . Its actualization is not a matter of technique but of 'fall' and 'salvation.' . . . One must distinguish . . . ontological reason in its essential perfection from its predicament in the different stages of its actualization in existence, life, and history" (1.74–75). The fall is the Platonic fall of existence away from essence: "Existence for Plato is the realm of mere opinion, error, and evil. . . . True being is essential being and is present in the realm of eternal ideas, i.e., in essences. In order to reach essential being man must rise above existence. He must return to the essential realm from which he fell into existence. . . . On this point, the Platonic and the Christian evaluations of existence coincide" (2.22–23). In contrast, others have found Scripture using "fall" not as of single selves from fixed "eternal ideas, i.e. . . . essences" but of whole humanity from ongoing essence-*creating* corporate interaction; and salvation not as conforming to a pre-existing fixed reality but as interactively *creating* an ever richer interactive reality.

According to Tillich, the theologian's sources are different from the philosopher's sources. "The philosopher looks at the whole of reality to discover within it the structure of reality as a whole. . . . There is no particular place to discover the structure of being; there is no particular place to stand to discover the categories of experience. The place to look is all places; the place to stand is no place at all; it is pure reason" (1.23). The source of the *theologian's* knowledge, however, "is not the universal *logos* but the Logos 'who became flesh,' that is, the *logos* manifesting itself in a particular historical event. And the medium through which he receives the manifestation of the *logos* is not common rationality but the church, its traditions and its present reality. He speaks in the church about the foundation of the church. And he speaks because he is grasped by the power of this foundation and by the community built upon it" (1.23–24). Theology, as distinguished from philosophy, relates everything to a quest for the *New Being*: "The material norm of systematic theology today is the New Being in Jesus as the Christ as our ultimate concern" (1.50).

The Logos stands behind the *logos*. "God acts through the Logos which is the transcendent and transcending source of the *logos* structure of thought and being" (1.57). "In Jesus Christ the Logos has become flesh" (1.18). The Logos brings together the concrete and the universal. "Priestly and prophetic theologies can be very concrete, but they lack universality. Mystical and metaphysical theologies can b very universal, but they lack concreteness. . . . Only that which has the power of representing everything particular is absolutely concrete. And only that which has the power of representing everything abstract is absolutely universal" (1.16). "If Jesus is called the Christ he must . . . be the point of identity between the absolutely concrete and the absolutely universal. In so far as he is absolutely concrete, the relation to him can be a completely existential concern. In so far as he is absolutely universal, the relation to him includes potentially all possible relations and can, therefore, be unconditional and infinite" (1.17). The cosmological and existential are joined.

The union of the concrete and the universal is a paradox:

> All biblical and ecclesiastical assertions about the final revelation have a paradoxical character. . . . They cannot be expressed in terms of the structure of reason but must be expressed in terms of the depth of reason. . . . The final revelation does not give us absolute ethics, absolute doctrines, or an absolute ideal of personal and communal life. It gives us examples which point to that which is absolute; but the examples are not absolute in themselves. . . . The absolute side of the final revelation . . . involves the complete transparency and the complete self-sacrifice of the medium in which it appears. . . . No situation which Jesus faced and no act through which he met it establishes an absolutism of dogmatic or moral character. . . . Although potentially absolute, they are sacrificed in the moment they occur. . . . The paradox of final revelation, overcoming the conflict between absolutism and relativism, is love. . . . The absoluteness of love is its power to go into the concrete situation, to discover what is demanded by the predicament of the concrete to which it turns (1.150–52).

The corporate position would applaud Tillich's recognition of the paradox of uniting the *concrete* and the *universal*, a paradox he can perhaps avoid only by moving away from human community toward the isolation of mysticism. The corporate orientation avoids this paradox by recognizing *internal* interaction, interaction that changes the essence of the interactors. Thus static universals are disallowed: A member cannot know the precise effect of an action in advance because the member's co-interactors have a creative choice how to respond.

Tillich's sacrificial love is conceived not in corporate but in singular terms. The "New Being in Jesus as the Christ" is the overcoming in the one person Jesus of the fall of existence from essence and could only appear fully in an individual:

> The New Being has appeared in a personal life, and for humanity it could not have appeared in any other way; for the potentialities of being are completely actual in personal life alone. Only a person, within our experience, is a fully developed self, confronting a world to which it belongs at the same time. Only in a person are the polarities of being complete. Only a person is completely individualized, and for just this reason he is able to participate without limits in his world. Only a person has an unlimited power of self-transcendence, and for just this reason he has the complete structure, the structure of rationality. Only a person has freedom, including all its characteristics, and for just this reason he alone has destiny (2.120).

No group can present the new being as an individual does. "Neither the Jewish nation as a whole nor the small 'remnant' groups to whom the prophets often referred were able to overcome the identification of the medium with the content of revelation. The history of Israel shows that no group can be the bearer of the final revelation, that it cannot perform a complete self-sacrifice. The breakthrough and the perfect self-surrender must happen in a personal life, or it cannot happen at all" (1.143). The new being can then spread by Platonic "participation" from this one person Jesus as the Christ to the whole universe. "What happens to man happens implicitly to all realms of life, for in man all levels of life are present . . . For this reason the philosophers of the Renaissance called man the 'microcosmos.' He is a universe in himself. What happens in him happens, therefore, by mutual universal participation. . . . This gives cosmic significance to the person and confirms the insight that only in a personal life can the New Being manifest itself" (2.120–21).

Tillich has reduced cosmological Platonism's organic community order among three interacting social classes to generic order for each individual: Platonic conformity of the individual to its class's assigned *community role* is thus reduced to conformity to its individual generic essence. Mary Daly (next chapter) used Tillich to justify her existentialism—namely that social responsibility is just "being who you really are."

Scripture, by contrast, asks for socially responsible community interaction, with Jesus the Christ (i.e., anointed) as the creatively interacting representative leader of a creatively interacting Israel. Scripture sees Jesus' excellence not as individual microcosmic image of cosmic order but as interactive agent for Israel's return to its original God-delegated responsibility as a nation to interact as internally relating community at home and as interactive "light to the nations" abroad. The issue is: does the biblical God ask for individual conformity to a *fixed essence* for each individual or does it ask for *community* responsibility for continuous *essence-creating*, thus essence-changing, *interaction* among all individuals?

For Tillich, as for Plato, *participation* (human or non-human), is unilateral conformity to the unchanging form of the thing participated in, so that: "Revelation and salvation are final, complete, and unchangeable with respect to the revealing and saving event; they are preliminary, fragmentary, and changeable with respect to the persons who receive revelatory truth and saving power" (1.146). "The concept of participation has many functions. A symbol participates in the reality it symbolizes; the knower participates in the known; the lover participates in the beloved; the existent participates in the essences which make it what it is, under the condition of existence; the individual participates in the destiny of separation and guilt; the Christian participates in the New Being as it is manifest in Jesus the Christ" (1.117). "Every human being participates in the universal *logos*" (1.176). With Tillich, *participation* means Platonic participation: "sharing the abstract form of," not "interacting with," as it does in the biblical perspective. The relation is unilateral, not bilateral; it asks for *similarity* whereas bilateral internal relation requires *complementarity*.

Because everything participates in the universal *logos*, everything participates in everything else indirectly as resultant of the participations of each in the *logos*. Hence, "no person is separated from other persons and from the whole of reality in such a way that he could be saved apart from the salvation of everyone and everything." (1.147).

"Communion" is participation by one human being in another:

> When individualization reaches the perfect form which we call a "person," participation reaches the perfect form which we call "communion." Man participates in all levels of life, but he participates fully only in that level of life which he is himself—he has communion only with persons. Communion is participation in another completely centered and completely individual self. . . . The person as the fully developed individual self is impossible without other fully developed selves. If he did not meet the resistance of other selves, every self would try to make himself absolute. . . . One individual can conquer the entire world of objects, but he cannot conquer another person without destroying him as a person. The individual discovers himself through this resistance. If he does not want to destroy the other person, he must enter into communion with him. . . . Individualization and participation are interdependent on all levels of being (1.176–77).

The individual human essence is fixed but is fulfilled by communion with fixed others, leaving the essence of all parties unchanged.

Tillich allows a secular development in history: "Everything new in history keeps within itself elements of the old out of which it grows. . . . But Hegel did not take seriously the ambiguity of this structure and its destructive possibilities" and did not recognize "the tragic character of history" (3.343). In particular:

> [T]he ambiguity of power lies behind the ambiguities of historical integration. . . . [S]ince God as *the* power of being is the source of all particular powers of being, power is divine in its essential nature. . . . every victory of the Kingdom of God in history is a victory over the disintegrating consequences of the ambiguity of power. . . . its conquest involves a fragmentary reunion of subject and object . . . . and conquers, even if only fragmentarily, that compulsion that usually goes with power and transforms the objects of centered control into mere objects (3.385).

Hegel, in contrast, recognizing the ambiguity, sees that ambiguity rather precisely as opportunity not for the conformity of Platonic participation but for intentional interaction among complementary parties. Tillich does not recognize a covenant between God and community sharing "dominion" (Gen 1:28; Rom 5:17), a sharing of responsibility for appropriate use of power, as Paul claims for the "power of Christ" exercised by the church as Body of Christ. For Tillich this power is to be controlled by each individual's Platonic participation in—that is, conformity to—the power of being. The church must emphasize "the vertical line of salvation over against the horizontal line of historical activity. And . . . the vertical line is primarily the line from the individual to the ultimate" (3.391). Such salvation through individual conformity maintains the Western passive-individual neo-Platonic reduction of Paul's active justification through faith to passive obedience, as analyzed for Luther on page 197, above.

For Tillich, the individual's need to overcome the fall of its *subjective reason* from the *universal logos* brings together *ultimate concern* as subjective attitude in the individual and *ultimate concern* as object: "In terms like ultimate, unconditional, infinite, absolute, the difference between subjectivity and objectivity is overcome. The ultimate of the act of faith and the ultimate that is meant in the act of faith are one and the same."[1]

Tillich places Hegel as the climax of a supposed German-Romantic return to "the classical tradition from Parmenides to Hegel" (1.72). He says that Hegel "took non-being into the very center of his thought; he stressed the role of passion and interest in the movement of history; he created concepts like 'estrangement' and 'unhappy consciousness'; he made freedom the aim of the universal process of existence. . . . But he kept all these existential elements from undermining the essentialist structure of his thought" (2.24). Thus, Tillich sees Hegel as gathering up all these existentialist goals and showing them satisfied by participation in the universal *logos*. Tillich, like the then Western world generally, could not grasp Hegel's radically innovative corporate position. In Tillich's *method of correlation* relating the self and the Logos, his existentialist-leaning age is allowed to raise the existentialist issues, but the answers are predetermined by the Logos. "The Christian message provides the answers to the questions implied in human existence . . . Their content cannot be derived from the questions, that is, from an analysis of human existence. They are 'spoken' *to* human existence from beyond it. Otherwise they would not be answers, for the question is human existence itself" (1.64). But the Old and New Testaments (chapters 1–3, above) and Hegel's *corporate* position (chapter 1.IV.1, above) specifically assign to the human community the continuous interactive creation of thus ever-changing essence-creating corporate interaction. Hegel says

---

1. Tillich, *Dynamics of Faith*, 11.

the *community* has "retained for itself the principle of change" (above, page 23)—the community interactively creates its own essence.

Tillich is also not a liberal theologian. Although he admits a near equivalence of Schleiermacher's "feeling of absolute dependence" (above, page 226) with his own "ultimate concern," he claims this common element has a different position in the two systems. With Schleiermacher it is a source, with Tillich it is a medium. "Criticism must be directed against Schleiermacher's method in his *Glaubenslehre (The Christian Faith)*. He tried to derive all contents of the Christian faith from what he called the 'religious consciousness' of the Christian. . . . This was an illusion. . . . The event on which Christianity is based . . . is not derived from experience; it is *given* in history. Experience is not the source from which the contents of systematic theology are taken but the medium through which they are received" (1.42). And under the fallen conditions of existence, this medium is not totally dependable: "Only if [an individual's] spirit and the divine Spirit in him were one could his experience have divine character . . . . There may be revelation through him. . . . But this revelation comes against him and to him and not from him" (l.46). Schleiermacher's source is the unavoidable dependence of the human individual; Tillich's source is a pre-Platonic Logos; and Scripture's source is the human community's covenant-delegated responsibility for creative corporate interaction.

How accountable is systematic theology to the Bible? For Tillich, "the material norm of systematic theology today is the New Being in Jesus as the Christ as our ultimate concern. This norm is the criterion for the use of all the sources of systematic theology" (1.50).

> The Bible is a collection of religious literature written, collected, and edited through the centuries. Luther . . . . gave a material norm . . . justification through faith. In the light of this norm he interpreted and judged all the biblical books. . . . The Old Testament was never directly normative. . . . The New Testament was never equally influential in all its parts. Paul's influence almost disappeared in the post-apostolic period. . . . The Bible as such never has been the norm of systematic theology. The norm has been a principle derived from the Bible in an encounter between Bible and church (1.50–51).

This is an encounter that, for Tillich, resulted in the norm's identifiability with the classical Greek *logos* and was taken as answer to the ultimate concern of the individual believer.

Tillich says, "For the followers of a world religion, the event of their foundation is the center of history. This is true not only of Christianity and Judaism but also of Mohammedanism, Buddhism, Zoroastrianism, and Manichaeism.... the question is unavoidable as to how Christianity can justify its claim to be both rooted in time and based in the universal center of the manifestations of the Kingdom of God in history." Tillich's answer: by having "a theology which calls Jesus as the Christ the central manifestation of the divine Logos" (3.367). We may here raise the question whether on this basis original biblical religion is any better than the others mentioned, any one of which, had it become sufficiently politically significant in the middle- and neo-Platonic West, would have been Platonized as Christianity was (and as Manichaeism was) into having its central principle be the Greek *logos*. Chapter 2, above, describes a twentieth-century flowering of communally oriented biblical studies daring to find a substantial biblical content contradictory to, and incomprehensible to, this perennial Greek orientation.

Missed by Tillich's neo-Platonic position is the opening biblical claim that God gave the human community responsibility ("dominion") for *interactively creating* its own culture and warned it that attempts by any human agency to control others unilaterally ("acting like 'the gods'") would be the death of interactive communal life. This opening is followed by a two millennium account of successes *and* failures (the "Tradition"), which is intended as a tool for community learning by its own mistakes, a tool used by the New Testament from the Old Testament on average of every other verse. This biblical program offers an ongoing "reality" to be continuously interactively created by the human community with God's help—it is not a pre-made reality ready for individual human consumption.

## 2 Transcendental Thomism: Karl Rahner

Transcendental Thomism, begun by Joseph Maréchal and continued by Karl Rahner, attempted to reconcile scholastic Thomas with neo-Platonic and existentialist concerns by extending Kantian transcendental reason (above, page 15) beyond empirical judgments to judgments on immaterial realities including God, thus going beyond Kant's (and Aristotle's) prohibition of "dialectical illusion." In a 1957 preface to his early theoretical work *Spirit in the World* (1939) Rahner explained, "What I tried to do ... was this: to get away from so much that is called 'neo-Scholasticism' and to return to Thomas himself, and by doing this to move closer to those questions which are being posed to contemporary philosophy" (p. xlvii)—a move in fact *away* from Thomas's Aristotelian base back toward neo-Platonism.

Rahner helped bring theology out of a 90-year-long ghetto of textbook neo-scholasticism and into creative dialogue with the culturally pluralistic modern world, a dialogue confirmed by the Second Vatican Council (1962–65). This opening encouraged Catholic interest in current academic biblical study and a resulting reemergence of a communal approach in the political, liberation, and liturgical theologies of Johann Metz, Gustavo Gutierrez, Louis-Marie Chauvet, and others (chapter 10, below). But Rahner himself overcame neo-scholasticism, not with a biblical communal theology but with a scholastic Thomas modified to admit generic and existentialist elements from modern philosophy. Whereas Tillich merely correlated existentialist question and cosmological answer, Rahner incorporated an implicit *self-as-such* analysis of the individual as part of his modified cosmological system.

Rahner starts by seeking to unify being and being known. "One cannot ask about being in its totality without affirming the fundamental knowability, in fact a certain *a priori* knownness of being as such . . . . Being itself is the original, *unifying* unity of being and knowing in their *unification* in being known. . . . being is of itself knowing and being known, . . . being is being-present-to-self" (pp. 68–70). For Platonism, all being is eternally implicitly known by each person. Thomas brings knowing and the being of immaterial things together partly by reason and partly by revelation. Kant and early Heidegger bring knowing and phenomenal being of material things together for both *present-at-hand* and *ready-to-hand* objects. Now, how will Rahner bring knowing together with objects-in-themselves, material or metaphysical?

Rahner starts with Thomas's *Summa Theologiae* 1a.84.7 ad 3, according to which one understands already otherwise known immaterial things through intensifying and antithetical analogy—that is, *excessus* and *negation*—with the phantasms of material things (see page 193, above). In the corpus of *1a.84.7* on knowledge of material things Thomas says, "cognitive faculties are proportioned to their objects." Rahner makes this reciprocal: "the intrinsic possibility of knowledge is based on the intrinsic possibility of knowability, and vice versa; . . . knowing and object are one in a more original way and do not seek a relationship to each other only subsequently to their own possibility" (p. 36). When Rahner comes to Thomas's *ad 3* on knowing incorporeal realities by analogy with corporeal ones through *excessus* and *negation*, he moves Thomas's *excessus* from one of the two means for analogy to make it the integrating element for analogy and negation. He says *excessus* is to be "understood in such a way that it encompasses the [analogy] and [negation] in itself as moments of its own essence in the one fundamental act of metaphysics" (p. 53).

This elevation of *excessus* is a modification of the abstractive function of Thomas's active intellect. The active intellect "is not the power to imprint on the possible intellect [memory] a spiritual image of what has been sensibly intuited.... [It] is rather the capacity to know the sensibly intuited as limited, *as* a realized concretion, and only to that extent does it... liberate the form from its material concretion." It can abstract "only if, antecedent to and in addition to apprehending the individual form, it comprehends of itself the whole field of these possibilities and thus, in the sensibly concretized form, experiences the concreteness as a limitation of these possibilities, whereby it knows the form itself as able to be multiplied in this field. This transcending apprehension of further possibilities ... we call 'pre-apprehension' ('*Vorgriff*'). Although this term is not to be found literally in Thomas, yet its content is contained in what Thomas calls '*excessus*'" (p. 142).

Here Rahner's *excessus* takes over not only the function of Thomas's analogy and negation but of the whole active intellect—a move away from Thomas and Aristotle toward Kant and the modern perspective's ancestor, Plato. Communal language philosopher Wittgenstein would agree with Rahner and Plato that the abstract idea as class of possibilities ("pre-apprehension") is *already in* the individual intellect *but* he would hold that it, the abstract idea as class of possibilities, was there because the community had already taught it to the individual as part of teaching the word for it. That is, a creatively interacting community builds for itself a community cultural "active intellect," an abstracting community language analogous to the single person's abstracting active intellect of Aristotle and Thomas. In addition, the community simultaneously acculturates each of its members with that language as an individual pre-apprehension, which is similar to the individual pre-apprehension in Plato and Rahner. Is this, the community, where Platonism itself unwittingly discovered its individual pre-apprehension?

Rahner proceeds, "This possibility of placing over against oneself as object what is had in the sense intuition as identical with sensibility, and of so doing in a true judgment affirming a universal about it, is grounded in a pre-apprehension. . . . This pre-apprehension attains to *esse*. The breadth of this pre-apprehension is not merely the totality of what is representatively imaginable in sensibility, . . . but [is] absolute being" (pp. 397–98). Rahner's pre-apprehension is an *a priori* horizon in the generic human knower reaching both material and immaterial realities. It takes on whole the work Thomas divides between abstraction for forms of material realities, and revelation or reason followed by analogy for other realities. It, Rahner's preapprehension, extends the Kantian transcendental capacity of the human individual to apprehend and make judgments about sensible realities to include Kant's forbidden dialectical judgments. Rahner's combining Thomas and Kant violates both.

Rahner's *excessus* reaches judgments, not just concepts. He says, "the *excessus* essentially takes place only in the judgment, and so the judgment is only the expression of the dynamic desire of the spirit for being as such. This also explains how absolute being can be given without being conceived. . . . [S]ince this light [of the active intellect] is the *a priori* and merely formal condition of the objectivity of the world, metaphysics does not consist in the vision of a metaphysical object, perhaps of being as such, but in the *transcendental reflection* upon that which is affirmed implicitly and simultaneously in the knowledge of the world" (p. 398). "The analogy of being in Thomas is not merely a construction designed to help towards the conceptual, negative definition of the essence of God, but already has its starting point where the experience of world is transcended in a pre-apprehension through *excessus* and negation" (p. 402). With Rahner, the material world is also apprehended metaphysically; and Kant's phenomenal world *is* the noumenal world.

In "Anonymous Christians" Rahner says this pre-apprehension "determines man's nature . . . . The express revelation of the word in Christ is . . . only the explication of what we already are . . . . In the acceptance of himself man is accepting Christ as . . . guarantee of his own anonymous movement towards God by grace." Thus, individual secular European Platonists, and perhaps existentialists, may well be "anonymous Christians."

Contemporaneous non-transcendental neo-Thomists reject Rahner's pre-apprehension. They hold Thomas's turn to the phantasm as only enabling a judgment on the contingent existence of a material thing known and the *excessus* as only a component in understanding by analogy an immaterial thing already known through reason or revelation. Not only does Rahner's pre-apprehension-*excessus* lean more toward the Platonistic individual-as-microcosm than toward Thomas's Aristotelian-derived active intellect, it also reflects Heidegger's reversing Kant's phenomenal being as relation between thing-in-itself and knower (above, page 16) into Heidegger's phenomenal *ready-to-handness* (above, page 35) as prior to *present-at-handness*.

In *Hearer of the Word* (1941) Rahner asks: what does this pre-apprehension, *Vorgriff* (striving, anticipation, horizon) reach toward? Rahner reports three possible answers:

> There are in the history of Western philosophy three typical directions in which an answer to this question has been attempted: the direction of the perennial philosophy which, in this case, goes from Plato to Hegel, the direction of Kant, and that of Heidegger. The first one answers: the range of the *Vorgriff* extends towards being as such, with no inner limit in itself, and therefore includes also the absolute being of God. Kant answers: the horizon, within which our objects are conceptually given to us, is the horizon of sense intuition, which does not reach beyond space and time. Heidegger says: the transcendence which serves as the basis for man's existence, goes toward nothingness (p. 49).

In the terminology of the present study, these three directions are: the perennial (Plato), modern (empirical), and *self-as-such* (in 1941 Heidegger was taken as existentialist). What Rahner does not mention is a fourth "typical direction," the communal direction with *Vorgriff* provided by corporate society, as in intrinsic relation (Möhler) and aspects (Newman), followed a century later by transmitted tradition (Gadamer, von Rad), public language (Wittgenstein), political relations (Metz and Gutiérrez), and sacraments (Chauvet). The last three are treated in chapter 10, below. Later, Rahner recognizes the existence but not the substance of this fourth direction in "Theology and Anthropology" (below, page 320).

To show how Rahner's early theoretical position is reflected in his voluminous later applications, samples of his treatment of Christology and of development of doctrine are given.

Rahner's Christology is central to his system. In "The Theology of the Symbol," Rahner applies the equivalence of being and knowing to God. Rahner says, "all beings are by their nature symbolic, because they necessarily 'express' themselves in order to attain their own nature" (4.224). They begin by expressing themselves to themselves. "The original unity . . . maintains itself while resolving itself and 'dis-closing' itself into a plurality in order to find itself precisely there" (4.227). Becoming plural through expressing oneself to oneself also applies to God. "The Father is himself by the very fact that he opposes to himself the image which is of the same essence as himself, as the person who is other than himself; and so he possesses himself. But this means that the Logos is the 'symbol' of the Father, in the very sense which we have given the word; the inward symbol which remains distinct from what is symbolized, which is constituted by what is symbolized, where what is symbolized expresses itself and possesses itself" (4.236).

This expressing oneself to oneself is the basis of one's expressing oneself to others. "It is because God 'must' 'express' himself inwardly that he can also utter himself outwardly; the finite, created utterance *ad extra* is a continuation of the immanent constitution of 'image and likeness'" (4:236–37). Thus, the "immanent" and "economic" Trinity are one—the immanent relation of the Logos to the Father as his expression of himself to himself is exteriorized in his expression, his making present of himself, to others.

Rahner's unity of being and knowing, and its use to justify God's immanent relation in the Trinity, both derive from Hegel, but Rahner's *self-as-such* origin for relation reverses Hegel's *interactive* origin of trinitarian being-for-another (above, page 21). And the exteriorization to the world is not in Thomas, for whom being present to others and expressing oneself to others is not an intrinsic or a real but only a logical relation (above, page 194).

According to "Christology within an Evolutionary View of the World," although God's self-expression impinged on the world before the incarnation, its complete acceptance by the man Jesus makes the incarnation the climax of God's communication of himself. "This Saviour, who represents the climax of this self-communication, must therefore be at the same time God's absolute pledge by self-communication to the spiritual creature as a whole *and* the acceptance of this self-communication by this Saviour; only then is there an utterly irrevocable self-communication on both sides, and only thus is it present in the world in a historically communicative manner" (5.176). God's making himself present through the Logos, and its complete acceptance by the man Jesus, constitute a "hypostatic union" between God and a human being. This union in the one person Jesus is an offering and pledge of God's grace to all persons. "The Hypostatic Union takes effect interiorly *for* the human nature of the Logos precisely in what, and really only in what, the same theology prescribes for *all* men as their goal and consummation, viz. the direct vision of God enjoyed by Christ's created human soul" (5.180–81). Jesus is, then, the example for us.

But we are not examples in turn. "The Hypostatic Union does not differ from our grace by what is pledged in it, for this is grace in both cases (even in the case of Jesus). But it differs from our grace by the fact that Jesus is our pledge, and we ourselves are not the pledge but the recipients of God's pledge to us" (5.183). Thus, God does not need helpers. The people's role is to be generic recipients of grace, and in fact the church is described as the medium for this process: "The Church as the people of God in a socially organized form is the enduring historical presence of the eschatologically triumphant grace of God and of Christ in the world for the individual."[2] It "continues the symbolic function of the Logos in the world. . . . The sacraments make concrete and actual, for the life of the individual, the symbolic reality of the Church as the primary sacrament."[3]

Thus, Rahner's Christology and his doctrines of the Trinity, incarnation, church, and sacraments make generic and non-interactive application of a cosmological and *self-as-such* base. The symbol is firstly the expression of an individual to itself, thus within the *self-as-such* perspective. The plurality of the Trinity is a plurality intrinsic to a single individual, not a corporate plurality of distinct individuals. Secondarily, a symbol also expresses an individual to other individuals but generically to each of them separately. The incarnation is the hypostatic union of God with one human individual, and it presents generically to each individual the opportunity to respond similarly to God's grace, but without authority to impart such grace to others. Although the church is "an enduring historical presence" in "a socially organized form," its function and purpose is to mediate God's grace generically to each member.

2. Rahner, *The Church and the Sacraments*, 22–23.
3. Rahner, "The Theology of the Symbol," 4.240–41.

In contrast, the New Testament sees Jesus not as the pledge of God's grace to the generic individual but as messiah and king—offices of representation of the already existing people of God (Israel) as a creative corporate anthropological (that is, *incarnate*) agency with already delegated responsibility for interactively mediating God's grace into the human communities of the world (Gen 12:3 = Acts 3:25 "in you all the families of the earth shall be blessed," Isa 49:6 = Luke 2:32 "a light to the nations"). Rather than such a leader inciting creative action by the church, Rahner presents the complete acceptor of "the offering and pledge of God's grace to all persons" as generic example for those "who are not the pledge but the recipients of God's pledge." Neo-Platonism, bent toward the extreme of generic human impotence as in Luther (above, page 197), shows its continuing strength.

Both Tillich's and Rahner's systems are christocentric. With Tillich, the Christ is the Logos (the principle of order in the universe) who becomes incarnate to overcome the Platonic fall of existence from this order. In Rahner, the second person of the Trinity is the principle of the Father's expression or making present—including both the immanent making present of the Father to himself and the economic, external making present of the Father to generic human beings. Rahner's Christology is based first on the existentialist expression of one individual to itself and then derivatively on the expression of one individual to generic others in parallel. Both Rahner's and Tillich's Christologies are cosmological; neither is corporate. In both, the generic is dominant over the organic, an adaptation to a generic and existentialist age.

Development of doctrine is the other sample area of Rahner's system in which the philosophical cast of his results are investigated here. Rahner's material on the development of doctrine fills out his Trinity-incarnation-church-individual system, described above, by showing just how "the Church as the people of God in a socially organized form is the enduring historical presence of the eschatologically triumphant grace of God and of Christ in the world for the individual" (as quoted above).

According to Rahner in "The Development of Dogma," doctrine and living experience existed together dialectically in the church of the apostles:

> Christ, as the living link between God and the world, whom they have seen with their eyes and touched with their hands, is the objective content of an experience which is more elemental and

> concentrated, simpler and yet richer than the individual propositions coined in an attempt to express this experience—an attempt which can in principle never be finally successful. The vivid experience of Christ's relationship to sin, ... his death, his attitude to Peter and a thousand other experiences of the kind, which the Apostles lived through in an unreflexive and global way, *precede* the doctrinal propositions (1.65–66).

With the apostles themselves there is a development of dogma, a development that is not a logical deduction of proposition from proposition but "a connexion between what becomes partially explicit in a proposition and the unreflexive, total spiritual possession of the entire *res*" (1.67).

This process did not stop with the apostles. "It is not only propositions about their experience that the Apostles bequeath, but their Spirit, the Holy Spirit of God, the very reality, then, of what they have experienced in Christ. . . . But just this 'successio apostolica,' in a full and comprehensive sense, hands on to the post-Apostolic Church, and precisely with respect to knowledge in faith, not simply a body of propositions. but living experience" (1.68). In the church, propositional doctrine and living experience coexist in historical interaction. "Original, non-propositional, unreflexive yet conscious possession of a reality on the one hand, and reflexive . . . , articulated consciousness of this original consciousness on the other—these are not competing opposites but reciprocally interacting factors of a single experience necessarily unfolding in historical succession. Root and shoot are not the same thing; but each lives by the other" (1.64–65). Even explicitly stated propositions convey more than their explicit content. For example, "died" in the saying "Christ died for our sins" does not refer to "just a physiological exit. The whole human experience of death can be really stated . . . and heard . . . in this word, an experience which neither speaker nor hearer has ever translated adequately and objectively into propositions" (1.72).

The dialectical relation between experience and propositional formulation implies the necessity of making all new theological formulations in the light of both current living faith and the dogmatic formulations of the past:

> In the long run the correctness of our arguments and deductions from the propositions of faith can only proceed from the heart of a faith known by being lived, that faith which still possesses all in

> undivided unity and totality. But this original faith can only be explicated when we attend to the binding formulations in which it has never failed to express itself, and necessarily in objective propositional form. Neither is wholly possible without the other. For it was only to the Church as a whole that the promise was made that she should possess the original faith entire and unclouded. She alone, and not every isolated individual, has the organs which, without fear of error, can bring this reflexion to completion with universal binding authority (1.76).

In contrast, Newman (chapter 8, above) sees the development of doctrine as a diachronic *hermeneutic* process, a continuous discursive reformulation of the same non-discursive gospel necessarily resulting from the continuous creative application of that same Gospel to new circumstances. Rahner's dialectic is between theory and individual experience. Newman's dialectic is between corporate life and the different practical world circumstances under which it must be lived.

In the development of dogma, Rahner never draws on the Old Testament as Newman does. Rahner does refer once to the Old Testament, but negatively: "If formerly, before Christ, something took place in history, it was and is invariably conditioned, provisional, . . . and thus leading to death and emptiness . . . . it was still not apparent how God was going at last to respond to the human answer, usually negative, to his own initiating act: whether the ultimate utterance of his creative Word would be the word of wrath or of love" (1.49). In contrast, Newman found the Old Testament account of the continuous interacting relation between God and his community to be a vast continuing resource for interactive metonymic essence-building application to community issues which extended to the New Testament and, together with the Old Testament, continued without interruption in the Christian movement.

Rahner recognizes a social aspect of human beings and the need for an organic agency to bring salvation to them, yet he maintains that this elaborate structure is for the sake of the generic salvation of individuals:

> The individual . . . must have the possibility in his life of partaking in a genuine saving relationship to God. . . . In view of the social nature of man and the previously even more radical social solidarity of men, however, it is quite unthinkable that man, being what he is, could actually achieve this relationship to God—which he must have and which if he is to be saved, is and must be

> made possible for him by God—in an absolutely private interior reality and this outside of the actual religious bodies which offer themselves to him in the environment in which he lives.[4]

So for Rahner, it is the individual who is to be saved, a salvation possibly transmitted unilaterally through the community as a medium. It is not a salvation consisting of constructive participation in community interaction. The ecclesiology here is not as high as in the Torah, Prophets, Gospels, Paul, and communal theologians Möhler, Newman, Dodd, and Eichrodt, and, as we will see in chapter 10, Metz, Gutiérrez, Segundo, and Chauvet, for whom salvation is not of separate individuals but of their community's shared creative interactive social structure. For Rahner, the church is an organic means for generic salvation of individuals, not a community extending its essence-creating interaction into the larger community. Rahner's system starts and ends with the transcendental self.

Rahner claims this accommodation to modern philosophy's generic anthropological orientation is needed not only to adapt theology to the then-current secular philosophy, but also to the following then-just-emerging philosophy. Rahner says:

> Perhaps it might be said that the "modern period" to which this transcendental anthropology is especially adapted is already a thing of the past or in process of decline together with its philosophy. . . . If it is the case that Christian Neo-Scholastic Philosophy, together with theology, have been mostly asleep during the modern period, they cannot be spared the task set by modern philosophy on the grounds that perhaps this philosophy is declining in its contemporary form: the lost ground must be at least made up if theology is really to do justice to the spirit of the age which is to *follow* the "modern period." . . . If the topics treated in the coming philosophy are hope, society, the critique of ideology, a new form of freedom within a new social bond, . . . [then] the change to a transcendental anthropology constitutes a challenge for today's and tomorrow's theology (9.39–40).

Rahner, like Western philosophy for two millennia, never suspected that New Testament Christianity might offer precisely a turn *away* from "transcendental anthropology," that it might have offered a way of life radically incompatible with the commitments reflected in Western

---

4. Rahner, "Christianity and the Non-Christian Religions," 5.128.

philosophy as a whole. Western philosopher-theologians have converted Christianity into a Western religion based on middle-Platonism by Origen, neo-Platonism by Augustine, Aristotelian transcendentalism by Thomas, neo-Platonism again by Luther, modernism by Schleiermacher, existentialism by Bultmann, and neo-Scholasticism by Rahner. That next philosophy that Rahner predicts and describes is communal philosophy, which is a move toward the biblical orientation. If that is the coming perspective, then the coming theology's God will need to be one in creative interaction with a creatively interacting human community rather than one known by each generic human individual through an *a priori* pre-apprehension reaching a universal *esse*. Individuals will be saved not as generic enlightened and obedient selves but as creative participants in the construction of their corporately interacting, thus being saved, community. Such participation by an individual is that individual's salvation because an individual *is* its role in creative community interaction, as pointed out by Hegel (above, page 20). Such a God is the one promoted in both testaments. Was Western philosophy's move in the nineteen-sixties a move unawares to a more biblical orientation than Western Christian theology has reached over its two millennium lifetime? And will this new movement endure?—see chapter 10, below.

But first, in chapter 9, three theologians with modern philosophical perspectives will be considered, and a fourth who does recognize two-way internal interaction within and between the technological and social levels of society but only a one-way reflection from these two onto the community's ideational level.

# 9

# Contemporary Modern Theological Systems

CHAPTERS 8 THROUGH 10 sample the mix of cosmological, modern, and corporate theologies in the contemporary Western world. This chapter offers examples of the modern theologies. The theologian Mary Daly vehemently protests the imposition on the self of any complementary relation with other persons—an existentialist position, and one extreme point within the generic modern perspective. New Testament scholar Norman Perrin and Old Testament scholar Samuel Terrien each make radically generic interpretations. Norman Gottwald adds sociological analysis to traditional literary, historical, and theological analyses of the Old Testament—which is essential for a corporate understanding of it—but a positivist base for his sociology keeps his results within the modern perspective.

*1 Rejection of Complementarity in Social Structures: Mary Daly*

Mary Daly's *Beyond God the Father: Toward a Philosophy of Women's Liberation* (1973) is an aggressive denunciation of complementary relations in society. Although the book presents itself as an advocate for a feminist position, it goes beyond eradication of male domination and exploitation of women to include domination based on race, class, ethnicity, and nationality—and claims liberation ultimately requires eradication of all social structures, all roles, interactive or not. Liberation "involves the becoming of psychic unity, which means that one does not have to depend upon another for 'complementarity' but can love independently. . . . such independence means the becoming of psychologically androgynous human beings, since the basic crippling 'complementarity' has been the false masculine/feminine polarity" (p. 26). "Instead of settling for being a warped half of a person, which is equivalent to a self-destructive non-person, the emerging woman is casting off role definitions and moving toward androgynous being" (p. 41). Daly says male-female complementarity is the root of all other forms of complementarity because it occurs at the most intimate level of individual relations to others, cutting across all other forms of exploitation. Women's liberation "is not a rival to any truly revolutionary movement, but goes to the root of the evils such movements are trying to eradicate" (p. 54).

Thus Daly's agenda, "liberation" from "role definitions," with its resulting "psychic dependence" on complementary others, precisely opposes the corporate orientation as with Hegel's "person" as sum of its interactive social roles, or early Marx's claim: "The human essence is no abstraction, inherent in each single individual. In its reality it is the ensemble of the social relations."[1] Does Daly's vehement rejection of any organic relation place her as generic or as *self-as-such*? Are "androgynous" persons understood to be similar to one another beyond the mere similarity of being independent of one another?

Daly supports her position with Tillich's neo-Platonic identity of individual and cosmic ultimate concern (above, page 308). Daly says, "we have no power over the ultimately real, and . . . whatever authentic power we have is derived from *participation in* ultimate reality" (p. 29). "It is . . . like God speaking forth God-self in the new identity of women" (p. 41). Here Daly is neo-Platonic rather than Platonic—an individual's essence requires no *organic* social interaction as with the three social classes in Plato's *Republic*.

The individual's freedom from all communal structure advocated by Daly resembles Bultmann's two decades earlier existentialist freedom from both organic relation and generic similarity with others. Daly's God-given freedom liberates from the past: "women have the option of giving priority to what we find valid in our own experience without needing to look to the past for justification" (p. 74). It liberates from contemporary society as well: "The adequate meeting of the two [female and male] worlds, then, cannot be imagined as a simple one-to-one relationship between representatives of humanity's two halves, for half a person really never can meet the objectified other half. The adequate 'cosmoses' will require a breakdown of walls within the male psyche as well as within the female. It will require in men as well as in women a desire to become androgynous, that is, to become themselves" (p. 172).

1. Marx, "Theses on Feuerbach," 6.

The existentialist world, without Platonism's classes, frees each to follow its own *logos*: each shares this same "ultimate concern."

The coming androgynous persons will live not in isolation from one another but with equal status and with neither similar nor complementary roles, so that no one is in position to coerce another. Instead of patriarchy's "role models" there are "free persons whose lives communicate a kind of contagious freedom" (p. 10). When "we meet others who are on the same voyage" there is no "agreement that is *formed*" but a "profound *agreement that is found*" (p. 159). Communication "is neither 'public' nor 'private,' neither 'objective' nor 'subjective.' It is intersubjective silence, the vibrations of which are too high for the patriarchal hearing mechanism" (pp. 152–53). Thus, the social institutions of language for human communication, of exchange, either arms-length or corporate, are rejected. Rather, "When women reach the point of recognizing that we are aliens in this terrain, the sense of transcendence and the surge of hope can be seen as rooted in the power of being" (p. 28).

With Daly, the term "patriarchy" extends beyond rule by males to include any society structured with complementary roles, and so with a complex mass of hierarchical relations. The presumed ancient matriarchal society preceding patriarchal society was "egalitarian rather than hierarchical and authoritarian. . . . this kind of culture was not bent on the conquest of nature or of other human beings. In brief: It was not patriarchy spelled with an 'm.' . . . 'On top' thinking, imagining, and acting is essentially patriarchal" (p. 94). And so women are leading the emancipation because of their powerless, exploited position in a patriarchally organized society: "the women's movement is more than a group governed by central authority in conflict with other such hierarchical groups. If it were only this it would be only one more subgroup within the all-embracing patriarchal 'family'" (p. 35). "There has been a theoretical one-sided emphasis upon charity, meekness, obedience, humility, self-abnegation, sacrifice, service. Part of the problem with this moral ideology is that it became accepted not by men but by women, who hardly have been helped by an ethic which reinforces the abject female situation" (p. 100). "[T]he bearers of New Being have to be those who live precariously on the boundary of patriarchal space—the primordial aliens: women" (p. 72). "The Antichrist dreaded by the patriarchs may be the surge of consciousness, the spiritual awakening, that can bring us beyond Christolatry . . . . the Antichrist and the Second Coming of women are synonymous" (p. 96). For Daly, women can lead the way to separation because they are the most alienated part of the community. Daly sees a powerless group, women, leading the way to a world without interaction. The prophets, gospels, and Paul (1 Cor 1:27 "God chose what is weak in the world to shame the strong") see a lower, hence more interactive, class using its interactive influence to move the whole community toward creative interaction, but can Daly use such interaction to stop interaction?

The neo-Platonic-leaning church Daly knew did not help her distinguish between constructive and exploitive interaction. She says that church mission, like a "'bombing mission,' . . . is not communication but compulsion, whether this be understood as physical or psychological." The protest is telling: the counter-thrust imitates the thrust. Daly herself goes on to ask for a relation in which the "communication involved is not a thrusting of an objectified 'message' to another nor a thrusting of oneself or any model upon the psyche of another" but a mutual "interpenetration of insights coming from discovery of participation together in being, in the cosmos" (p. 168)—a "being" as in Kierkegaard: "the reproduction of inwardness in the recipient constitutes the resonance by reason of which the thing said remains absent," and in Heidegger: two "devote themselves to the same affair in common . . . [so that] their Dasein, each in its own way, has been taken hold of"[2] (page 39, above). Aggressive theologian Daly grazed on a plateau shadowed by peaks where live neo-Platonic Tillich, existentialist Kierkegaard, and phenomenalist (early) Heidegger.

Daly enjoys using the tradition's own theological terms to parody her disagreement with it. The fall is "the fall into freedom" (pp. 44–68). The doctrine of incarnation suffers from complementarity between savior and saved: "the idea of a single divine incarnation in a human being of the male sex may give way in the religious consciousness to an increased awareness of the power of Being in all persons" (p. 71). Both influencer and influenced need to be free of interaction: "When no longer condemned to the role of 'savior,' perhaps Jesus can be recognizable as a free man" (p. 96). Whereas Bultmann rejected the Old Testament (above, page 250) but accepted New Testament resurrection as "personal address which accosts each individual, throwing the person himself into

---

2. Kierkegaard, *Concluding Unscientific Postscript*, 232; Heidegger, *Being and Time*, 159.

question by rendering his self-understanding problematic" (above, page 156), the more combative Daly more consistently is willing to recognize the New Testament also as interactively oriented and rejects it as well.

Daly takes male-female complementarity as prototypical of creative social complementarity as Scripture does (above, page 6) but does so to condemn both rather than to extol community. The diachronic dimension of Scripture's communal orientation gives an importance to the procreation and rearing of children that is bypassed in Western philosophy and disappearing in modern culture. Daly's announcement of freedom not only from any corporate past but from any corporate future places procreation and rearing of children by a nurturing community completely outside her permitted horizon.

From the communal perspective, Daly herself carries out an inverse "bombing mission" of "publicly" "thrusting an objectified model" of *self-as-such* social practice "on our psyches" with as much "psychological compulsion and coercion" as she can muster. Her perspective is so immune to any offer of bilaterally creative relation from another that it could not recognize the inverse violence done to the other by refusing such an offer.

Daly did not issue *Beyond God the Father* neutrally under the pseudonym Johanna Climaca. Publication of this work involved complementary interactive roles beyond her allowed non-verbal sharing of delight in essence, roles including reformer, tree cutter, paper manufacturer, printer, distributor, bookseller, even readers. The project of liberating individuals from complementary roles must be paid for with complementary roles.

Daly speaks for a feminist movement seeking freedom from community responsibility. But there is another feminist movement that shares the corporate orientation's advocacy of multilaterally creative relations among members, hence values the complementary differences among them. The feminist theologian Phyllis Trible says Genesis 2–3 presents the sexes as interacting in a creative complementary manner before the fall: "The two are neither dichotomies nor duplicates. . . . In responding to the woman, man speaks for the first time and for the first time discovers himself as male. No longer a passive creature, *ish* comes alive in meeting *ishshah*." But the complementarity becomes an alienating one at the fall: "Next the differences which spell harmony and equality yield to the differences of disobedience and disaster. . . . Whereas in creation man and woman know harmony and equality, in sin they know alienation and discord."[3] The feminist Old Testament scholar Carol Meyers says the complementary relation of women and men in pre-monarchic Israel was positive and creative: "female creativity and labor were highly valued in early Israel. This female worth was not biological exploitation but rather part of the full cooperation of all elements in society in pursuing the goals of the Israelite people." Later in the monarchic period, the same restriction of women to family life "became the basis for ideologies of female inferiority and subordination."[4] Both scholars treat historical and modern sexism as the perversion of creative complementary relations into alienating relations.

Daly's liberation program is the opposite of Latin-American corporate liberation theology, to be treated in the next chapter. Daly advocates liberation of individuals from social interaction. The Latin-Americans advocate liberation of society for social interaction.

## 2 The Criterion of Dissimilarity in Life-of-Jesus Research: Norman Perrin

The criterion of dissimilarity, pioneered by Rudolf Bultmann and others,[5] held that the earliest recoverable form of a saying of Jesus is authentic only if it *differs* from the position of Judaism and of the early church. The criterion was an explicit tool for critical-historical reconstruction of the "teaching of Jesus" from 1920 to 1960. It takes as *a priori* that Christianity is a new teaching, neither a reform back to Torah and Prophets nor the teaching of the early church.

Norman Perrin describes the criterion in *Rediscovering the Teaching of Jesus*:[6]

> The fundamental criterion for authenticity upon which all reconstructions of the teaching of Jesus must be built . . . we propose to call the *"criterion of dissimilarity."* . . . We may formulate it as follows: the earliest form of a saying we can reach may be regarded as authentic if it can be shown to be dissimilar to characteristic

---

3. Trible, "Depatriarchalizing in Biblical Interpretation," 38; 39, 41.

4. Carol Meyers, "The Roots of Restriction," 98, 101.

5. The criterion is from Bultmann, *The History of the Synoptic Tradition*, 205, and appears in Hans Conzelmann, *Jesus*, 16; early Käsemann, "The Problem of the Historical Jesus," 37; and Perrin, *Rediscovering the Teaching of Jesus*.

6. Perrin, *Rediscovering the Teaching of Jesus*, 15–38.

> emphases both of ancient Judaism and of the early Church, and this will particularly be the case where Christian tradition oriented toward Judaism can be shown to have modified the saying away from its original emphasis.... The teaching of Jesus was set in the context of ancient Judaism, ... But if we are to seek that which is most characteristic of Jesus, it will be found not in the things which he shares with his contemporaries, but in the things wherein he differs from them (p. 39).

Perrin adds two subsidiary criteria of authenticity: the criterion of coherence (accepting additional early material if it coheres with material authentic by the first principle) and the criterion of multiple attestation, (accepting material present in all or most of the early sources). The latter is limited to general characteristics of the teaching of Jesus (pp. 43, 45). Perrin admits the criterion may disqualify some authentic sayings of Jesus (p. 43), but its goal is objective certainty, and that requires a stringent criterion.

Let us test the criterion on the parable of the sower (Mark 4:3–8). Perrin says (pp. 155–56): "In this particular instance there is no point in attempting to reconstruct the original form of the parable.... the fate of parts of the seed sown has been described, both to add vividness and verisimilitude to the story and to prepare artistically for the contrast of the successful harvest." Thus, Perrin finds that one cannot isolate an earliest recoverable form of the saying—it does not meet the strict criterion of authenticity. In this form it says only that some win, some lose. Perrin continues, "the significant thing is simply the fact of a story of a peasant sowing and harvesting." He adds, "this parable was probably originally concerned to inculcate confidence in God's future; but for our purposes we must note only that it does look from the present to the future; from the seed-time to the harvest, from a beginning to its consummation." He lists the parable under "Confidence in God's Future."

As we will later see, if Perrin had been able to recognize the interactive nature of the "fate of parts of the seed," he would have had to disqualify its authenticity because of its similarity with the corporate profession of ancient Judaism and early church.

In his book *In Parables*, John Dominic Crossan, another disciple of the criterion of dissimilarity, compares the accounts of the parable of the sower in the four gospels and in contemporaneous Jewish and early church written material. His rather reasonable resulting earliest recoverable form is Mark 4:3–8 with omission of two repetitive phrases (pp. 39–44). But Crossan succumbs to the temptation to tell us what the parable means by suggesting, "it will be necessary for us to read much more of the poetry of Ted Roethke in order to understand these pastoral parables of Jesus" and then explicitly interpreting it as intended "to assist people to find their own ultimate encounter" with "their own experience of the kingdom, and to draw from that experience their own way of life" (pp. 51–52). This is an interpretation properly dissimilar to emphases of both ancient Judaism and early church, indicating the saying to be authentic according to Crossan's criterion of dissimilarity.

According to chapters 2 and 3 above, Jesus spoke and acted within the corporate orientation common to ancient Judaism and the early church, which implies that the modern criterion of dissimilarity rejects everything that Jesus may have said (and his Judean listeners would have been able to understand). The five decades earlier form-criticism of the more corporately oriented history-of-religions school, developed by Hermann Gunkel[7] (1862–1933) and others, identifies *forms*—that is, cultic, narrative, paraenetic, or literal language structures used for community interaction. The form-critical school would regard parable as such a form. Understanding a parable requires the hearer to have a sufficiently common cultural horizon with the speaker to be able to recognize and understand the *form*, including the analogy or metonymy needed to apply it to the hearer's situation. Thus, the parable of the sower would have conveyed a "message," an application within the Judean culture of Jesus' worker class hearers, for them to understand and pass it on orally until elite class persons who could write began to join the movement. The criterion of dissimilarity specifically excludes this Judean cultural context and, thus, excludes Jesus' intention in telling the parable—that is, it excludes its meaning, whatever that may have been.

Today we expect a well-told joke, form-critically somewhat similar to a parable, to make use of all the details in its dramatic build-up to a single denouement. Could it be the same for a gospel parable—its single point emerges at its climax and every detail contributes substantively to that meaning? Neither of the exegeses above makes use of all the details to reach their interpretations.

Similarly, the so-called parable of the "prodigal son," announced in Luke 15:11 as of *two sons*, is rather a unified part-for-whole me-

---

7. Gunkel and Begrich, *Einleitung in die Psalmen*.

tonymy on the contrast between the *younger son* capable of accepting a compassionate offer of reconciliation and an implacable *older son* self-righteously rejecting that offer. Its telling is a prophetic act. Its point was not repentance—the younger son came back seeking only arms-length paid employment. Without the whole parable one cannot reconstruct its intended meaning. Is the parable about God accepting our repentance or about *our* accepting some one else's repentance?

The hearers of the sower parable readily recognized the literally described interaction among grain, rocky soil, weeds, paths, birds, and variable harvest as metonym for their own whole Judean multilaterally internally interacting corporate community culture, resisting Westernization by the European occupation. But the three "interpretations" of the parable, introduced by the phrases "and he said" or "and he said to them," were all later editorial additions—one does not explain a parable or a joke to one's audience. In the *first*, Mark 4:9 "ears to hear" means having the corporate acculturation to perceive the intended metonymy. The *second*, vv. 10–12, quotes Isa 6:9: Isaiah's call to be a prophet, a call to two-way interaction, to interpret metonymically rather than allegorically, to recognize the sower's interactive relation with earth, plants, and birds as metonymic prophetic call for interactive relation in society. But the *third* interpretation, vv. 13–20, is a late non-interactive interpretation missing the intended non-dominating creative internal interaction of sowers, wheat, birds, paths, rocky soil, and reapers, taking the parable as allegory for the European occupation's middle-Platonic non-negotiable *logos*, "word" (diagrammed above, chapter 2.II.3)— the very position the original parable spoke against.

If Jesus acted within the context of Israel's tradition, then everything he did had some positive relation to it, and everything negative was against its distortion. An example is Jesus' answer (Mark 10:2-9) to his elite opponents' trick question on divorce, using Gen 2:24 directly against their convoluted use of Deut 24:1, both from "Moses," the Torah or tradition. The Western world has always looked for dissimilarities between Jesus and the Israelite tradition so that it could view Christianity as a new religion. But a more sophisticated approach would be to identify which parts of the Israelite tradition Jesus treated positively and which he ignored or rejected. The New Testament witness is that he treated positively the salvation-historical and prophetic parts and ignored or rejected the Persian, Hellenistic, and colonization-inspired post-exilic wisdom and legalism—that is, he took precisely the corporately oriented original parts over the imported cosmologically oriented ones. The criterion of dissimilarity specifically disallows recognition of this issue.

Whereas modern theology, descended from neo-Platonism, took Jesus as teacher of an objective truth independent of any context, the New Testament titles for Jesus (king, lord, son-of-man, servant, anointed one) name traditional representative leadership roles from Israel's corporate prophetic tradition; and their attribution to Jesus indicates his being taken as representing and leading Israel in reviving its same covenant with God to be changers of the world. Jesus spoke "with authority," that is, within the community tradition. Jesus is presented as eschatological intensification, that is, antitype, of earlier leaders in the corporate Israelite tradition, not as introducer of something completely new.

The criterion of dissimilarity is one high-water mark reached in the application of modern presuppositions in New Testament scholarship but was challenged by corporate biblical, theological, and liturgical theologies (next chapter) that flourished in the sixties and seventies until a fading memory of world war and great depression allowed a return of increased concentration of economic power, turning the tide back toward a neo-Platonic style cultural orientation to serve those who want to rule and those who want to be ruled.

But during those two decades of relatively flourishing corporate Western theology, Jesus began to appear as a prophetic representative leader, messiah, of Israel who challenged it with a call to interact creatively with other nations to maintain, or return to, its corporate covenant with its God as a community. Biblical scholar Ernst Käsemann said in 1953, "The solution . . . cannot . . . be approached with any hope of success along the line of supposed historical bruta facta but only along the line of the connection and tension between the preaching of Jesus and that of his community. The question of the historical Jesus is, in its legitimate form, the question of the continuity of the Gospel within the discontinuity of the times and within the variation of the kerygma."[8] James Robinson, following Peter Biehl, says of the criterion of dissimilarity: "The method can affirm the historicity only of that part of Jesus in which he is least 'Christian.' For its 'historicity' depends upon the demonstration that it does not present the Church's view." Robinson urges a communal view. "Material regarded as wholly 'unauthentic' in terms of positivistic histo-

---

8. Käsemann, "The Problem of the Historical Jesus," 46.

riography may not seem nearly as 'unauthentic' in terms of modern [i.e. communal] historiography."[9] And Alan Richardson writes, "The 'conclusions' of the liberal or 'historicizing' critics have been stood upon their head: what the liberals deemed to be mythology has become history and their history has become mythology."[10]

## *3 Divine Presence as Basis for Old Testament Theology: Samuel Terrien*

Samuel Terrien, in *The Elusive Presence* (1978), concedes the significance in the Old Testament of what he calls covenant ideology but claims it is secondary to what he calls the theology of presence—the concern in the Old Testament with the presence of God, actual or potential, directly to each separate individual in Israel. Terrien says, "It is the distinctiveness of the Hebraic theology of presence rather than the ideology of the covenant which provides a key to understanding the Bible" (p. xxviii).

According to Terrien, covenant was important only during certain crisis periods. "While there are explicit allusions to covenant in the Hebrew Bible and in the writings of the early church, covenant consciousness did not apparently dominate the preoccupations of the religious leaders of Israel, except Joshua in the twelfth century, Josiah in the seventh, and Ezra in the fourth . . ." The theology of presence, on the other hand, provides a central concept for the whole Bible, including the New Testament: "It is the Hebraic theology of presence, not the covenant ceremonial, that constitutes the field of forces which links across the biblical centuries the fathers of Israel, the reforming prophets, the priests of Jerusalem, the psalmists of Zion, the Jobian poet, and the bearers of the gospel" (p. 31).

Terrien is, thus, pitting his "presence" against Eichrodt's "covenant" as central unifying concept of the Bible. At the level of his argument there is no winner. Explicit consciousness of covenant as biblical theme is indeed limited as Terrien claims, but Terrien's explicit theology of divine presence to individuals is equally limited. It does not take account of the primeval history (Gen 1–11), the exodus and conquest, the issue of monarchy in Samuel, and all of the written prophets other than the visions of their calls. He is also unaware of the possibility of divine presence to an individual leader as metonymy for presence to the cov-

---

9. James M. Robinson, *A New Quest of the Historical Jesus*, 100 and 99, notes 3, 2. Biehl, "Zur Frage nach dem historischen Jesus," 56.

10. Richardson, *An Introduction to the Theology of the New Testament*, 14.

enant community being led. As we have seen, such a critique of Eichrodt misses his point—that the Old Testament is written to represent and to contribute to a *bilateral interaction* between God and *corporate* Israel (above, chapter 7.II.1). At this more basic level, Terrien's position is that the Old Testament is written to trace the actual or potential presence of God *generically* (not through community interaction) to various individuals in Israel. And for the conflict at this level there *can* be a winner.

The individuals experiencing the presence in Terrien's book are often anachronistically modern ones, preoccupied with themselves as individuals rather than with the community and their corporate function within it. Terrien says when Moses asked God what his name was (Exod 3:13), "more than intellectual curiosity was implied, for he betrayed a doubt as to the validity of his own experience.... This anxiety was not only of a psychological, sociological, and political nature ('will they believe what I say?') but was also and primarily the result of a theological *Angst*. He wanted religious certainty. He wished to see with his own power of perception. He intended to comprehend" (pp. 118–19). Of Moses' use of the tent of meeting (Exod 33:7–11) Terrien says, "The tent of meeting provided Moses with the solitariness, privacy, and isolation which have always been the mark of the encounter between God and man.... One should interpret the manufacture, use, and function of the tent of meeting as pointing to a nexus of religious activity and thinking which distantly anticipates the psychological mode of presence through the inward processes of communion" (pp. 176, 179). Of David's dancing in a linen ephod (2 Sam 6:12–23) he says, "The notorious scene in which the king danced ecstatically 'in the presence of Yahweh' testifies to the passionate character of his attachment to the God who had delivered him from all his enemies" (p. 168). "His carefree deportment seems to indicate the abandon of a soldier to his piety. Captains and politicians sometimes conceal within the intensity of their religion an urge to search for the plenitude of their being. This is one of the reasons religion partakes of the more ambiguous elements of the human psyche and may be thoroughly self-deceiving. Dancing before the ark in neglect of decorum perhaps indicated the frustration of a genius whose deeper cravings remained unfulfilled by military prowess and political achievement" (pp. 281–82).

None of Terrien's generic existentialist analyses would be proposed by a communal scholar. More significantly, Terrien offers a meaning for these stories outside the intentional horizon of the Old Testament itself, an epic portrayal not of separate individuals but of a human community interacting internally among its members, with its leaders, and with its God. Moses' asking God for his name is not from concern with the "validity of his own experience" but another attempt of the enabling role he had failed at decades earlier, when, as a youth, he fell into an officious non-enabling leadership role only to be frightened into flight by a victim of his "help" (Exod 2:14). Next, God rebukes Moses' brazen profiteering on the piety of others (when he grazes his sheep on an ungrazed holy mountain). God shames Moses into returning to Egypt to try again to lead Israel's escape from slavery. Moses asks how he should answer when the slaves ask who is saving them. God's literal answer is: "I am doing what I am doing" (Exod 3:14). In corporate Israel *I am* is *I do, I interact with you*, as discovered again for the West 37 centuries later by Hegel (above, chapter 1.IV.1). In context, God's answer means, "the God who is saving you is who is saving you, *inter*acting constructively with you, *your* community's God."

The isolation of Moses *with Joshua* (Exod 33:11) in the tent of meeting was a ceremonial act, part of their representative roles in Israel, not an isolation from the community to facilitate a generic "communion" with God. When this small delegation proved dysfunctional, seventy other elders were added and taken into the tent with them (Num 11:16); Moses also had to appoint judges over thousands, hundred, fifties, and tens (Exod 18:13–26).

And the account (2 Sam 6:16-23) of Michal's despising David in his triumphal entry is a commentary on a once charismatic but now despotic leader who no longer allows any self-respect to members of his court. It is not on a concealed urge on David's part "to search for the plenitude of his being," something Michal (early partner turned trophy) thinks David has been doing way too much recently. In each case the issue is effective interactive leadership *versus* playing God (remember the apple!). In today's Western culture everyone faces this issue constantly.

Terrien calls the divine presence *elusive* because God manifested himself to Israel on his own terms. "Israel ... entertained a unique theology of presence. She knew that her God was always free from the human techniques of ritual or moral manipulation. She conceived the presence of that God to be elusive and unpredictable" (p. 27). Nathan's judgment that David should not build the temple (2 Sam 5–8) "indicates a polemic against the notion of a static Deity, attached to a temple built by man and therefore subjected to the limitations of human worship. Nathan's prophetic word defends the freedom of Yahweh. God is near, but his presence remains elusive" (p. 170). Terrien's "elusiveness" not only implies that God cannot be manipulated but that he believes in a controlling God and so cannot recognize a God who offers a two way *interactive* relation with human community.

It is only a short step from such elusiveness of God to a Reformation denial of God's need for helpers. The characteristic Reformation extrinsic justification of the passively conforming individual lurks just below the surface. Of Abraham's binding of Isaac for sacrifice (Gen 22:1–19), Terrien follows Kierkegaard's *Fear and Trembling* (1843) in saying:

> The willingness to accept an order which pushes beyond the limits of practicality—that is, to the *ab-surdum*—the mystery and the freedom of the Godhead or the devotion of man annuls the validity of all archaic forms of religion. In the context of the Hebraic theology of presence, with the absurdity of its demands, religion no longer means the ritual exchange of sacrality with a static cosmos . . . but, on the contrary, the courage to face the abyss of being, even the abyss of the being of God, and to affirm, at the risk of assuming all risks, the will to gamble away not only one's ego but even one's hope in the future of mankind (pp. 83–84).

A communal analysis, in contrast, would find Abraham's sacrifice of Isaac representatively actively offering *and* passively accepting of corporate Israel's interactive covenant relation with God as the family through which "all the families of the earth shall be blessed" (Gen 12:3). And this covenant made no "absurd demands"—Abraham could win a reasonable argument with God (Gen 18:23–33). The sacrifice of Isaac was antitype for the sacrifice of the Christ. Would Terrien say the crucifixion was absurd?

Terrien places presence above covenant. "To look at covenant as the determining factor . . . is also to confuse the means with the end, for the rite and ideology of covenant are dependent upon the prior reality of presence. . . . The ritual and legal structure of covenant offers a tool, original and effective as it may be, by which the recollection and the hope of the presence are mediated to the rank and file of the people and transmitted to posterity from generation to generation" (p. 26). But

Israel itself would say the covenant is not means or end—it *is* the corporate interaction between God and Israel together in constructing and maintaining Israel. Yet Terrien sees the "peoplehood" of Israel as their generic sharing in the divine presence. "Israel maintained her historical existence as a people only in so far as she remembered and expected the manifestation of divine presence. It was the presence which created peoplehood. An individual member of that people partook of the life of the community only in so far as he shared in the presence, either through cultic celebration or by associating himself with the mediators of presence who had experienced its immediacy" (p. 42). The cult thus emerges as substitute for presence for the generic and passive individual. "A cultic form of presence was sacramentally available. A God who remained historically absent manifested his proximity to the average man through cultic communion" (p. 29). Behind these passages stands a conception of the cult as a system for delivery of religious services to individual consumers, rather than liturgical interaction part of and representing the whole of Israel's interactive community life in covenant with God to interact internally within itself and with the other nations.

Samuel Terrien attempts what theologians of the modern perspective (Schleiermacher, Harnack, Bultmann) and the corporate perspective (Newman, Dodd, Eichrodt, von Rad) both agree is improper: a generic interpretation of the Old Testament. A communal critique of Terrien's position would make two counterassertions. Firstly, in the biblical horizon God can only be present to an individual through the mechanism that makes the individual *be* an individual, namely that individual's corporate participation in a community: God cannot be present to an individual generically since human individuality itself is not generic. And secondly, divine presence is only *half the covenant relation*, with the other half, Israel's presence in the relation, *equally or more so* the subject of the biblical story. The choice between Terrien's presence and Eichrodt's covenant is precisely a choice between modern and communal philosophical presuppositions, and this is no mere choice between conceptual methods but a choice between religious commitments, between behaviors.

Old Testament scholar Walter Brueggemann[11] groups Terrien's book with two other books also published in 1978 (Claus Westermann's *Elements of Old Testament Theology* and Paul Hanson's *Dynamic*

---

11. Walter Brueggemann, "A Convergence in Recent Old Testament Theologies."

*Transcendence*) as evidence of a then-current tilt in Old Testament studies away from Eichrodt's and von Rad's sole emphasis on a historical-covenantal tradition and toward a more "balanced dialectic" between a historical-covenantal tradition and a blessing-esthetical-systematizing tradition that occurs throughout the Old Testament (but is most prominent in its wisdom material). However, of the three books analyzed by Brueggemann, only Terrien's claims that the generically interpretable material is more fundamental than, and the basis of, the relational material. Westermann separates salvation into two components: *deliverance*, the "mighty acts" of God (the central concern from Exodus to Numbers) and *blessing*, the continuous bestowing of growth, success, increase, and provision. Both are covenantal. In the blessing component, God's contribution is commissioning humanity to responsible stewardship of the earth, its cultivation and maintenance, these the concern of Old Testament wisdom. Westermann says, "When Adam and Eve are commanded during creation to cultivate and maintain the garden, wisdom as a coming to terms with life is implied in this commission."[12] Thus, wisdom as skill, itself universalizing and generic, finds its place as a resource in carrying out the interactive covenant commission. Westermann's book is not a tilt from corporate to generic perspective but a subsuming of generic wisdom under an overall corporate perspective. And the third book, Hanson's, approximately reproduces Westermann's deliverance-blessing dichotomy in his teleological-cosmic dichotomy, with the cosmic aspect subsuming wisdom.

### 4 Economic Determinism in Sociology of the Old Testament: Norman Gottwald

Norman Gottwald in *The Tribes of Yahweh* (1979) offers a valuable sociological study of premonarchic Israel, filling a significant gap in late twentieth century literary and historical study of early Old Testament history. Yet an existentialist kernel hides behind an empiricist-based sociological method masking the Old Testament's corporate ideological base, a base stated abstractly in Hegel and early Marx and presumed in Eichrodt's and von Rad's Old Testament work. This section presents

---

12. Westermann, *Elements of Old Testament Theology*, 99.

Gottwald's significant contribution to pre-monarchic Israel but also clarifies his deviation from its corporate base.[13]

Gottwald distinguishes three levels in society: *technological*, *social*, and *ideational*. The first nine parts of Gottwald's eleven part book integrate findings at the technological and social of the three levels with the results of historical and literary study, showing significant interaction between the technological and social levels. But in parts ten and eleven he treats the relation of these with the third, the ideational level (Israel's "religion" or ideology), presenting it as passively dependent on the technological and social levels, that is, as not in internal interaction with them.

Gottwald's study at the *technological* and *social* levels of characteristics of Israel that distinguish it from other communities includes the following: between 1250 and 1000 BCE the "feudal" network of petty city-states in Canaan (which were vassals of Egypt) was replaced by a retribalized non-statist coalition of former *apiru* (brigand mercenaries), Shosu (a particular tribe of bandits), peasants, and transhumant pastoralists (village-based herders and shepherds). These groups were already resident in the region; they did not differ ethnically from the population still under feudal control. By the end of the period the coalition, which called itself Israel, included by conversion the bulk of the population of central Canaan. Control of the means of production was moved from the feudal hierarchy to the extended family level. The priesthood was decentralized and there was no professional military. The economic tribute structure of the Canaanitic-Egyptian "feudal" system was unnecessary and not replaced; and its military defense system, not so necessary in a period of weak empires, was replaced by temporary voluntary assistance from neighboring units when needed. Gottwald says the basic distinguishing characteristic of premonarchic Israel compared to other communities was *egalitarianism*, or *social equality*, which he defines (p. 798 n. 635) as equal status and equal access to resources. Gottwald describes this society as having an interactive structure at the technological and social levels.

As for the *ideational* level, Gottwald defines its chief concepts "Yahweh" and "covenant" as follows: "The chief articles of Yahwistic faith may be socioeconomically 'demythologized' as follows: 'Yahweh'

---

13. I am indebted to Professor Gottwald for suggesting to me in 1978 corporately oriented critics supporting my early formulation of this critique.

is the historically concretized, primordial power to establish and sustain social equality in the face of counter-oppression from without and against provincial and nonegalitarian tendencies from within the society. . . . 'Covenant' is the bonding of decentralized social groups in a larger society of equals committed to cooperation without authoritarian leadership and a way of symbolizing the locus of sovereignty in such a society of equals" (p. 69). Thus, Gottwald has "Yahweh" stand for Israel's power to gain and retain the egalitarian structure Gottwald attributes to it, and has "covenant" symbolize the decentralized sovereignty of equals he finds in it.

In contrast, a communal interpretation would demythologize 'Yahweh' and 'Covenant' to mean Israel's commitment to internal essence-creating relations in human community, with each side of a relation superior to the other side in that side's complementary contributions to essence-creating corporate community interaction.

Gottwald approves sociologist Emile Durkheim's view of religious commitment as unilateral ideal representation of social-level solidarity but rejects Durkheim's lack of "lawful" (empirical) rigor in holding that "the social facts are not the empirically observed relations among people in particular societies but are inaccessible intuitions and impulses toward human solidarity" (p. 625). Correspondingly, he criticizes Max Weber's two-directional "elective affinity" or "co-determination" of religious and social factors, used "to circumvent what Weber took as the impoverished one-directionality of the Marxian claim that social relations and religious ideas were determined by the economic base" (p. 629). Gottwald also condemns Weber's finding a non-social source for religious movements in charismatic individuals: "[T]here remains in Weber's outlook the idealist 'escape hatch' of the great personalities as the mysterious sources of religions which are subsequently adapted into a social routine. . . . there is no way of penetrating to the social matrix in which the religious innovators themselves are formed . . . . To my mind, however, we must come to terms with Moses and the prophets, as with all religious innovators, as propagandists for a religion already formed or forming in a given social field" (p. 630). In the first two of these comments Gottwald defends his separation of the technological and social levels, and in the third he places the practice of religion within the social level.

Gottwald then formalizes his position on this network of possible relations by staking out his "lawful" empirical social-scientific approach, claiming:

> This brings us finally ... to Marx, who hypothesized that at the root of all social organization and mental ideation, including religion, is the way human beings within nature act upon nature to produce their means of subsistence and thereby fashion their own social nature. As the modes of acting upon nature (technology and cooperative forms of labor) change over time, the ways people associate with and control, or are controlled by, one another (social and political organization), as well as *the ways they think about themselves* in nature and in society (religion and philosophy), also change correlatively (p. 631).

Here Gottwald says the *technical* and *sociological* levels interact and the ideational level changes correlatively.

This isolation of the ideational level, of "religion and philosophy," as epiphenomenon of the other two levels, as "thinking about themselves" rather than changing their *interaction* with one another, is a reverse ghost of the ideational level's dominance over the other two in the West from pre-classical Greece until its reversal in modern philosophy into ideational dependence on sense input. The corporate orientation, intrinsic to both Testaments, introduced to the West by Hegel, early Marx, late Wittgenstein, and Möhler, places all three levels in corporate interaction. Language is used not only to describe social interaction but as tool for interaction of the social and intellectual levels. The account of God prompting the human community Adam to name the animals (Gen 2:19) is metonymy for creating language as tool for facilitating delegated community "dominion" (Gen 1:28) at the social level. Corporately oriented scholars are still trying to "name" the concepts "internal relation" and "corporate" for use in promoting social action as *inter*action.

Gottwald quotes from Marx's *German Ideology* to support his position: "The premises from which we begin are not arbitrary ones, not dogmas, but real premises from which abstraction can only be made in the imagination. They are the real individuals, their activity and the material conditions under which they live.... These premises can thus be verified in a purely empirical way."[14] But here, corporately oriented Marx uses "empirical" to mean human understanding within a Hegelian-derived

---

14. Marx, *The German Ideology*, [Tucker, *Reader*, 113].

multilaterally internal relation among "real individuals," "their activity," and "material conditions." In a nearby Marx passage quoted by Gottwald (p. 633), Marx explicitly distinguishes (above, chapter l.IV.2) his use of "empirical," "*empirisch*," as including the internal interaction among the three levels from his use of *Empiristen* (empiricists) for the eighteenth-century empiricists like Hume: "Its premises are the people not in some imagined isolation and rigidity, but in their actual, empirically perceptible process of development under definite conditions. As soon as this active life-process is described, history ceases to be a collection of dead facts as it is with the themselves still abstract empiricists [*Empiristen*], or an imagined activity of imagined subjects, as with the idealists."[15] Marx, thus, is communal, unlike the "idealists" after Descartes and "empiricists" after Hobbes with their "collection of dead facts."

Marx writes not just to describe but to change the socio-political structure of his time. Gottwald does too, in a contrary direction, but only says so at the very end of his book.

After treating subsequent scholarly claims for ways to identify what elements in society are dominant in initiating social change, Gottwald says a "cultural-materialist hypothesis which states the priority of Israelite social relations over Yahwist religion in the initiation of cultural innovation and in the stabilization of the new cultural network. . . . moves beyond the noncommittal 'expressive totality' of a functionally described society in which the identification of variables as independent and dependent is strictly equivocal" (p. 642), and he settles for religion as a negative feedback servomechanism at the ideational level, initially formed as epiphenomenon of the technological and social levels but then useful to them in maintaining the status quo by automatic negative feedback on any change (p. 643). Thus, Gottwald gives religion an interactive stabilizing function within the social level.

How does Gottwald apply all this to pre-monarchic Israel? After praising Eichrodt and von Rad as offering the best of historical and literary studies of the Old Testament, Gottwald says, "In the end, however, both Eichrodt and von Rad fail disastrously at 'theology' because they offer disembodied idea structures unintegrated to the cultural-material and historico-social reality of ancient Israel by means of a clear methodological correlation. We are not shown by them how the structure of Israel's religious ideas was grounded in and correlated to Israel's social

---

15. Marx, *Die deutsche Ideologie*, 26f [Tucker, *Reader* 119].

system as that system evolved in its techno-economic and techno-environmental setting" (p. 794, n. 600). In other words, Eichrodt and von Rad fail disastrously because they do not use the proper correlativising techniques in showing the religion they find in the Old Testament as being related with the technological and social characteristics of Israel. In contrast, although Eichrodt and von Rad do not call on the vast sociological resources Gottwald has contributed, in chapter 7 above they are shown as opposing the dominance of the ideal in the then-prevalent liberal theology precisely by holding the ideal, social, and technological elements to be multilaterally internally related. In 1845 Marx stretched the term "empirical" to include corporate relations. More recently, the West has given that term back to Hobbes and Hume and defined the new terms "internal" and "corporate" for it.

Gottwald says, "When we take the significant results of literary, historical, and religious study of the Bible and present them within the framework of a social-scientific approach, new and illuminating patterns of interpretation emerge" (p. 16). Gottwald summarizes that social-scientific framework: Premonarchic Israel will be treated with "(1) a method that will plot the correlations between Israelite society and Israelite religion; (2) a method that will mandate the clarification of causal relationships according to laws of probability; and (3) a method that will facilitate the comparative differentiation of the Israelite religion-society complex in a field of other religion-society complexes, both historically and typically" (p. 608). The terms "plot the correlations," "clarification of causal relationships," and "comparative differentiation" all point to positivistic study of brute facts unencumbered with interactive meaning—and point to fact separated from value in favor of the former; and, most significantly, point to an ideational level not dialectically related with the other levels but rather a mere epiphenomenon of them.

Eichrodt and von Rad do not meet Gottwald's requirements. Rather they claim the two ideational structures "covenant" and "transmission of tradition" both statically characterize *and* actively mold the community Israel. These structures are internally interactive parts of it. Although critical sociological study of premonarchic Israel by Gottwald and others provides significant new raw material for understanding the premonarchic Old Testament, this help is limited in the same way as that of equally useful nineteenth-century critical history: Both force the interpreter to deal with the actual past material events to be interpreted but neither allows the past ideal structures to come into full bilateral internal hermeneutic relation with the material events of their own time or the events and ideal structures of the present investigating community.

The Old Testament, itself an ideational element, represents itself neither as mere reflection of material Israel nor merely as automatic servomechanism, but as means for intentional multilateral interaction within Israel both at the time of recording and for future internal typological application to new circumstances by subsequent hearers for "learning by one's mistakes." It does characterize and advocate premonarchic Israel's uniqueness but as a corporate, not egalitarian, society. It shows decentralization of authority, not its elimination. There are still authority-exercising roles—family patriarchs, local priests, "judges." But beyond that, an original or responding contribution of *any* individual to community interaction, with or without formal presiding authority ("status"), is *complementary* to that of others, is valued as a unique contribution from that individual needed for interaction and, thus, has a share in the community's presiding structure. If active community complementary relations provide a context for a member's contribution, then that member has a range of choices in responding to this context, making the response a *creative* one. Evidence for these views in the Old Testament includes the pervasive narration of complementary interactions among individuals that respect the creative contribution of each participant: the frequent portrayal of the decentralizing of responsibility and authority to make them accountable to the local community, and the equally frequent accounts with pejorative tone of interactions not meeting these ideals. The Old Testament characterizes Israel as attempting, with some success, a *complementary-creative-contribution* corporate structure. What is significant is not equal status but freedom to contribute creatively in relations both with and without equal status. Without the impact of such an Israel on the West, neither Gottwald's study nor the present one would exist.

The extended family was nearly economically self-sufficient. Hence, the economic life of Israel above the extended family level was, by default, a substantially parallel or generic one. This parallelism is reflected, for example, in the stories of dividing the land between two competing families (Abraham and Lot, Isaac and Abimelech, Jacob and Laban, and Jacob and Esau, Gen 13:2–12, 21:32, 30:25—31:55, and 32–33). Cooperative voluntary military defense above the extended family level, on the other hand, was corporate (Gideon, Judg 6:34–35, 7:24; the Levite, Judg 19:29—20:11).

Within the extended family there was not equal status but a division of labor and a corporate complementary relation among the members giving each a creative part in family life. The complementary roles of husband, wife, and children are illustrated in vignettes of premonarchic family life, such as the conjugal affection of Isaac and Rebecca (Gen 24:62–67) and Jacob and Rachel (Gen 29); the relation of mother and son of Rebecca and Jacob (Gen 27) and Hagar and her son (Gen 21:9–21); and the relation of father and daughter in the stories of the betrothal of Rebecca (Gen 24) and Rachel (Gen 29). Equal status is not required for non-alienating relationships: Accountability of the head to the rest of the family was maintained by both personal relationship and economic dependence. Already noted earlier (above, page 327) is the feminist theologian Carol Meyers' statement: "female creativity and labor were highly valued in early Israel. This female worth was not biological exploitation but rather part of the full cooperation of all elements in society in pursuing the goals of the Israelite people."

The Covenant Code (Exod 20:24—23:19), which retains premonarchic materials (as, for example, in Gottwald, p. 58), depicts an egalitarian structure above the extended family level and a non-egalitarian structure within the family. Social equality (equal access to resources and equal status) above the extended family level is depicted through the limitation of slavery to six years (21:2–3), punishment for murder (21:12–14), for kidnapping (21:16), for injury (21:18–19, 22–25), for injury done by one's animals (21:28–31, 35–36), various torts to equals (21:33–34, 22:1–15), regulation of loans (22:25–27), treating others equitably (23:1–8), allowing the poor to eat from fallow fields (23:10–11), and egalitarian treatment of strangers (22:21, 23:9), widows and orphans (22:22), and the poor (23:6, 11). On the other hand, within the extended family a non-egalitarian status structure is depicted through unequal status for women (21:4, 7, 22, 22:16–17), slaves (21:20–21, 26–27, 32), and children (21:4, 15, 17). The family structure was non-egalitarian, but there was mutual obligation of the parties in the unequal, complementary relationship. The persons in inferior status had some rights (21:8, 10–11, 26–27, 22:16, 23:12). Paul Hanson makes the same division of Covenant Code materials,[16] but he explains it as being due to theological

16. P. Hanson's Class I and Class II in his "The Theological Significance of Contradiction," 116.

immaturity rather than to its applying to needs at different structural levels in society.

Thus, the only generic relation in premonarchic Israel was the economic one by default above the extended family (exceptions: the law of hospitality and of draft in war), corresponding to the small scale and material simplicity above this level. Later, the monarchy was established when the scale and complexity of Israel's life among its neighbors demanded a more structured national life, with more economic interaction above the extended family level and a centralized and bureaucratized court, military, and priesthood. If complementary-creative-contribution is the basic principle of premonarchic Israel's uniqueness, then holding on to this uniqueness under the monarchy would involve calling the monarchy, bureaucracy, and estate holders to accountability to the group (rather than acting exploitively)—precisely the project the prophets took on during the monarchy. The prophets never criticized the division into complementary roles by taxation or military draft. Hosea's negative references to the king, for example, are either criticism of a particular king's behavior, condemnation of the king as symbol of the recalcitrant people, or for removal of the king as punishment of the people. Similarly, the "anti-monarchy" passage 1 Sam 8:10–18 "he will take your sons . . . to run before his chariots" is a warning of royal exploitation, placed in the usual dialectical way alongside other "pro-monarchy" passages in Samuel, and is not an inconsistency. The prophet's criticism was of use of the proceeds of the new arrangement by the leaders for an irresponsible international policy or for prestige at home—"Are you a king because you compete in Cedar?" (Jer 22:15)—rather than of responsible use for the good of Israel and other nations.

An extension of equal status and equal access down to the bare individual, thus shorn of communal support for its individuality by disallowing it any interactive role, as asked for by Daly above, would be a step historically unthinkable until after two and a half millennia of intrusion of Western culture, including the apocalyptic period's pluralistic choices (chapter 3 part III above), Hellenistic denial of the possibility of internal relations (chapter 4 above), Enlightenment genericization of the individual (page 15 above), and twentieth-century consumerization of the individual (Metz, next chapter). The distinguishing characteristic of premonarchic Israel was the non-alienating nature of its corporate interaction.

The election of Israel as *chosen people* is demythologized by Gottwald as being the uniqueness of egalitarian Israel in the midst of the near-Eastern hierarchically ordered "feudal" world. He says, "'The Chosen People' is the distinctive self-consciousness of a society of equals created in the intertribal order and demarcated from a primarily centralized and stratified surrounding world" (p. 692). When nonegalitarian stratification was later reimposed by the monarchy, Israel became like the other nations with king, state apparatus, and estate holders; and, according to Gottwald, the doctrine of the election of Israel no longer corresponded to the social reality but became "an embalmed relic and grotesque parody of the original truth" (p. 702).

Again, Gottwald's demythologization assumes the concept "chosen people" has no creative subsistence but is merely a verbalization of a material fact. But to one expecting internal dialectical relation between humanly held doctrine and social reality, the continued use of the doctrine of election during and after the monarchy would suggest that social equality is not a correct demythologization. The continuing doctrine of election might, for example, merely reflect tautologically that *chosen people* is a religious symbol of the community Israel, a relation that would continue as both social relations and the correlative conception of the symbol changed (as, for example, happened in the transformation of "Christianity" from a corporate Semitic to a cosmological Western religion in the second and third centuries). Or, more likely, the meaning of *chosen people* may include the *mission* of Israel chosen to carry the covenant with God with its complementary-creative-contribution living style to the other communities, which was acted out in the premonarchic period through the conversion of Canaan, and expressed discursively at the beginning of the monarchic period by Gen 18:18–19 "all the nations of the earth shall be blessed in [Abraham] . . . . for I have chosen him, that he may charge his children . . . to keep the way of the Lord by doing righteousness and justice," which was, in turn, expressed to leaders during the prophetic period by incessant condemnation of exploitive foreign alliances, and expressed discursively during the exile by Isa 49:6 "I will give you as a light to the nations, that my salvation may reach to the end of the earth," which was acted out in the first century through Judaism's ministry in dispersion to "God-fearers" (Acts 13:16), and acted out again in the Christian era through the spread of Christianity to a third of the world's population. The conversion of the population of

Canaan to active participation in corporately interacting Israel, so well characterized in *The Tribes of Yahweh*, is a more available technological and social basis for *mission* as the meaning of the doctrine of election in the premonarchic period than is Gottwald's choice of egalitarianism. The choice of the latter reflects a generic tendency in modern culture that includes the positivist sociology Gottwald applies. Persons with free will cannot *interact* corporately unless they are, or thereby become, *different* from one another.

Another illustration of the consequences of Gottwald's choice of egalitarianism as characterizing Israel's uniqueness as "chosen" is his handling of the conflict between contemporary feminism and the Old Testament's patriarchal orientation. Gottwald says, "contemporary feminism in church and synagogue is a logical and necessary extension of the social egalitarian principle of early Israel, which itself did not exhibit any appreciable independent feminist consciousness or praxis" (p. 797, n. 628). As noted earlier in the chapter (above, page 327), contemporary feminism comes in two versions: generic-independent and corporate-creative. The generic version *is* a logical extension of the generic principle of egalitarianism offered by Gottwald as the basis of Israel's uniqueness, but the corporate version is compatible with the Old Testament and indeed compatible not as "logical extension," but directly.

In summary, Gottwald sees the basic distinguishing characteristic of premonarchic Israel as social equality, including equal status and equal access to resources—with "Yahweh" standing for Israel's power to gain and retain this egalitarian structure, and "covenant" standing for this decentralized sovereignty of equals. In contrast, the present book has held that the Old Testament's reason for being is as tool for the continuing creation, maintenance, and spread of corporate multilaterally internally interacting, thus essence-changing, community life. Equal status as conventionally understood is not a feature of corporate relations. Rather, each participant assumes a higher status in initiating an interaction, and their responders in turn are thus offered a higher status in choosing their response.

At the end of his book Gottwald says, "Yahweh and 'his' people must be demystified.... Cogent symbols of historico-social transcendence for the future must illuminate . . . the critical intersection between lawful social process and human freedom.... where... opportunities continually emerge for ever larger numbers of us to struggle toward meeting our genuine human needs and actualizing our repressed human potentialities" (p. 708). It appears the contemporary generically leaning "meeting our genuine human needs and actualizing our repressed human potentialities" reflect not just an empiricist but also an existentialist component present all along in Gottwald's analysis. In contrast, in the next chapter the corporately oriented Latin-American liberation theologians will be found using a corporate sociology understanding the ideational level not as passively dependent on but as *internally interacting with* the other two of Gottwald's levels, and making a thoroughly corporate exegesis of the Old Testament.

10

# Contemporary Communal Theological Systems

FINALLY, WE SURVEY THE late twentieth century blossoming of communal theology, looking for versions that utilize all five manifestations of the corporate movement as characterized in chapter 1: political philosophy, philosophy of history, language philosophy, post-critical philosophy of science, and moral philosophy.

A recovery from the hegemony of cosmologically oriented neo-Scholastic (Rahner) and "neo-neo-Platonic" (Tillich) reactions against the 1848 European working class unrest emerged after 1933, a recovery led by communally oriented Old Testament interpreters Eichrodt and von Rad (above, chapter 7.II) and New Testament interpreters Goppelt, Dodd, and Lindars (above, chapter 2.III.1), a recovery supporting the Second Vatican Council (1962–65). This legitimization of a biblically based communal theology, along with a need of the European and Latin-American church to compete ideologically with the superficially similar later Marxist ideology, facilitated the emergence of political theology with Johann Baptist Metz and liberation theology with Gustavo Gutiérrez. Another spectacular communal theology was developed by Louis-Marie Chauvet from communal language philosophy. Attempts to build communal theologies on philosophy of science and moral philosophy were less successful.

## 1 Political Theology: Johann Baptist Metz

Johann Baptist Metz proposes a *political theology*, so named to indicate its understanding of the individual as interacting member of the *polis* (the city or comprehensive historical community), rather than as microcosmic reflection of the cosmos, or abstraction of a generic collectivity, or isolated *self-as-such*, or even merely in personal *I-Thou* encounter with one or two others. Although informed by Marx's secular political philosophy, Metz takes his stand against the four mentioned non-political theologies on the basis of the emerging communal interpretation of the Bible. In *Theology of the World*[1] (1968) he says, "The immediate dependence on the claims of Scripture is not gratuitous, but is based on recent exegesis, which most characteristically in the post-Bultmann period vindicates the Old Testament and interprets the well-known internal unity between the testaments as not only from New to Old but also in the reverse direction, thus holding up the Old Testament as intrinsic presupposition and dowry for New Testament concepts and language" (p. 80 [87]). Among systematic theologians before Metz, this position has been so central only with the Antiochian scholars (chapter 4, above) and Newman (chapter 7, above).

Metz claims that theology since the Enlightenment has become privatized, and that "*the deprivatizing of theology is the primary critical task of political theology*" (p. 101 [110]). The task is not to replace the individual with society but to reach the *actual individual*, who is intrinsically social. "Naturally there is in the message of the New Testament a legitimate individualizing of the person, a singling out before God, that can be considered as basic in the message, above all in its Pauline expression. This is not put in question by insisting on deprivatizing. On the contrary! For precisely through the tendency to privatize theology falls into the danger of missing the actual called individual" (p. 102 [110]). And, deprivatizing asks for a corporate rather than a cosmological perspective. "Deprivatization is aiming at a new objectivization—not in the metaphysical, but in the social and political sense" (p. 120 [128]).

In his *Faith in History and Society: Toward a Practical Fundamental Theology*[2] (1977) Metz says the then current privatization in theology emerged in the Enlightenment as a reflection of the rise of the bourgeoisie or middle class. The public life of the middle class is based on the principle of exchange. "The bourgeoisie is sustained by a new principle which supports and regulates all social relationships—the principle of exchange. Production, trade and consumption are all fashioned by it. All other values formerly forged by society but no longer contributing directly to the functioning of the bourgeois society of exchange retreat

---

1. Metz, *Zur Theologie der Welt*. Page numbers in brackets refer to English translation.

2. Metz, *Glaube in Geschichte und Gesellschaft*. Page numbers in the text from now on refer to this second work. Brackets refer to English translation.

more and more to the sphere of the private, that is, the sphere of individual freedom" (p. 32 [35]). Religion has no exchange value, hence it becomes private. "It no longer expresses a primary need" (p. 32 [35]).

For the same reason, *tradition* no longer provides a framework for the whole of life but is at best to be consumed privately. "It is the peril of bourgeois life to leave everything that does not obey the calculus of quantitative reason or submit itself to the law of the market, i.e. to profit and success, to the private preference and idiosyncrasy of the individual. As the bourgeois citizen converts religion into a utility religion to which he turns privately, so he also converts tradition into a value which he partakes of privately. 'Culture industry' is a more recent term for this procedure coming out of the Enlightenment" (p. 34 [37]).

*Authority* is also in crisis. "The bourgeois principle of exchange . . . tends precisely to assume the equality of the partners. Authority as principle of inequality and subordination automatically loses its social plausibility" (p. 36 [40]). But without some authority, some tradition, some structure within which to relate with others, it is not possible to be persons. Using the word "subject" for a person interactively in community he says "Threatened in the bourgeois society is . . . that authority the affirmation of which is the affirmation of one's being a subject or the possibility of another being a subject, the challenging authority of freedom and justice and the indicting authority of suffering. Never will such authority have much exchange value" (p. 37 [40]). When authority as tradition loses its plausibility, the church resorts either to authoritarianism or to those forms of authority that are acceptable in middle-class society, "an onslaught of experts, of bureaucrats, authority as unapproachable and systematized administration, authority as management of truth without a social basis" (p. 37 [41]).

*Reason* is in crisis. The Enlightenment moved reason from a metaphysically based mutual consent maintained by ecclesiastical and political power to the individual human subject. But this subject was a bourgeois subject. In the essay "What is Enlightenment?" Kant wrote, "Laziness and cowardice are the reasons why so many, after nature has long since discharged them from external direction, nevertheless remain under lifelong tutelage, and why it is so easy for others to set themselves up as their guardians. It is so comfortable not to be of age."[3] But, Metz says, this appeal by Kant is to the propertied citizen. "It is not a call to

3. Kant, "What is Enlightenment?", 286, quoted by Metz on p. 39 [43].

create new social conditions of freedom, but applies to those who already have . . . the social power to come of age. . . . What is supposed to come of age here is not unemancipated humankind as a whole but a particular subject actually in danger of being 'lazy,' 'cowardly,' and 'comfortable,' the propertied citizen" (pp. 39 [42–43]). "The Enlightenment served to raise the propertied citizen to bearer of political reason. . . . a new elite, a new aristocracy, a reversed mirror image of precisely what had been fought against. . . . In the logic of this reason, practice actually developed not as a practice of liberation, but a practice of domination of nature—in the interest of the market" (p. 40 [43]).

*Religion*, heretofore dependent on metaphysics, came under the same crisis. Metz says it was replaced by a natural religion based on human needs, and taken up by liberal theology, as in Schleiermacher's feeling of absolute dependence and Tillich's ultimate concern. Natural religion thus "belongs in fact only to the new human being of the Enlightenment, the citizen as rational subject. It is therefore an intensely privatized religion arranged for the domestic use of the propertied bourgeois citizen, a religion of feeling and interiority. It does not threaten, oppose, or contest the conceptions of reality, meaning, and truth which hold in the exterior bourgeois culture of exchange and success. It supports what already holds without it" (p. 41 [45]). Metz censures Enlightenment culture not just for being generic but for making its generic universalization from a small and untypical sample of humanity (the western bourgeois individual), a sample untypical among the peoples of the world and of history precisely by having compressed its corporate life into a generic mold.

Metz characterizes his own theological system as *practical* first and theoretical only in dialectical relation to practice, rejecting "practice as implementation, application, or 'concretizing' of a previously defined theory" (p. 47 [50]). He says:

> The Christian idea of God is intrinsically a practical idea. God cannot be thought of at all without such thought disturbing and infringing on the immediate interests of the one who seeks to think of him. . . . Stories of conversion and exodus are . . . not dramatic embellishments of an already conceived "pure" theology, but belong rather to the underlying impulse of this theology itself. . . . This practical structure applies with particular clarity to christological knowledge. The practice of imitation belongs constitutively to Christo*logy*, as indeed the *logos* of this Christology, like that of Christianity itself, cannot be equated with the Greek philo-

sophical *logos* for which ultimately Christ can only be "folly." . . . It is only those who imitate Christ who know with whom they have become involved and who saves them (pp. 47–48 [51–52]).

Neither Metz, nor Latin-American liberation theology (next section), nor the original Marx reduce the theoretical to mere epiphenomenon of the practical as in Marxist economic determinism. Rather, the theoretical, as part of human understanding, is a creatively interacting part of whole understanding, which is practical, that is, useful. Metz says, "Revelation in the Old Testament is not primarily assertion of fact, nor appeal, nor personal communication from God, but promise. . . . The sovereign promise inaugurates the future, it establishes the covenant as the solidarity of those who hope, for whom the world then appears for the first time as a history oriented to the future. . . . The eschatological horizon emerges most clearly in the pivotal revelation of God in Exodus 3:14, which recent exegesis teaches us to translate 'I will be whom I will be'" (pp. 80–81 [87–88]).

*Solidarity, remembering,* and *narrating* are three structuring categories in Metz's corporate practical theological system. Solidarity is the corporate presupposition itself. Remembering and narrating are essential for historical consciousness—the means for effecting corporate life.

*Solidarity* is intrinsic to being a subject before God. "The history of biblical religion is a history of the way in which a community and its constituent members become subjects in the presence of their God. Thus 'Subject' is not the isolated individual, the monad, who only afterwards convinces itself of its co-existence with other subjects. Experiences of solidarity with or antagonism against—liberation from or anxiety about—other subjects are from the beginning a part of the constitution of the religious subject" (p. 57 [60–61]). Whereas relations in a society based on exchange are on an arm's length basis between equals, the Christian position is "that an act of solidarity is not only 'for nothing' but can entail a loss, that ordinarily in the relationship of solidarity there is precisely no equality among the members, that solidarity is thus qualitatively more than a utilitarian alliance of equal partners, and humanity more than exploitation, namely a commitment without calculation in a fallen world." Solidarity "extends also to the vanquished and overrun, to those left behind in the march of progress, to the dead" (p. 206 [230–31]). Solidarity is Metz's category for expressing his thoroughgoing corporate orientation.

*Narrating* expresses the particular historical rather than abstract universal nature of solidarity. *Remembering* understands history to be practical rather than objective, transmitting *perilous remembrances* of the past suffering and defeat of those in solidarity with the ones who remember, rather than letting them be covered in forgetfulness by a history of success and progress. Perilous remembrances bring about a practical understanding of the subject's world that is not possible with neo-Platonic or modern abstract reason:

> Respect before historically accumulated suffering makes reason perceptive in a way that cannot be expressed in the abstract contrast between authority and knowledge . . . In this perceptivity, history as remembered history of suffering gets the form of a *perilous tradition* which can be avoided or domesticated neither with a purely submissive attitude to the past as in many hermeneutical theories of understanding, nor in a pure critique-of-ideology approach to the past as in many critical theories of understanding. It is in every case mediated *practically*. It happens in perilous stories in which the concern for freedom is introduced, identified and presented in narrative form (p. 173 [195–96]).

For Metz, the church is the community that transmits the perilous practical narrative remembering of the passion and resurrection. "Christianity as community of those who believe in Jesus Christ has from the very beginning not been primarily a community interpreting and arguing, but a community remembering and narrating with practical aim: a challenging narrative remembering of the passion, death and resurrection of Jesus. The logos of the cross and resurrection has an indispensable narrative structure. Faith in the redemption of history and the new people in the face of the history of human suffering transmits itself in perilous liberating stories, stories for which a hearer becomes a 'doer of the word'" (pp. 189–90 [212]). Thus, Christology and ecclesiology are explicitly related as in Dodd and Kee (above, pages 103, 108).

Remembering as eschatological category resolves the tension between *already* and *not yet*: "It all comes to this: not to dehistoricize salvation or freeze it as an 'idea,' so that the 'already' can be understood in the 'not yet,' and the state of salvation can be appropriated in hope. The 'already' is after all a determining modality of the 'not yet' inasmuch as 'not yet' claims to be different from 'not'" (p. 177 [200–1]).

Metz condemns a church that only provides religious goods for consumption. Such a "church for the people is no church of the people, is not a church in which this people understand and celebrate themselves as fellow carriers of the new history under God" (p. 124, [141]). The people should not be "mere consumers of religion or mere objects of care and attention, but the subject of the Church..., in short, the people of God" (p. 125 [141]). Salvation is joining forces with God. God *does* need helpers.

Metz praises Kant for definitively bringing theology to practical reason, but says theology still needs to be extended with Marx from individual morality to social responsibility, and from isolated theory into dialectical interaction with the practical. "With Kant individual moral imperatives replace the issues of social action and conceal that coming of age is not only a question of moral exertion by the individual but also of social structures and relationships. First through Marx it becomes clear that individual moral practice is not at all socially neutral and politically innocent, and that the so-called purely ethical interpretation of social practice always works with substitutions, speaking of 'the people' and meaning the current already domesticated bourgeois subject" (p. 50 [53]).

By reversing the point of a German fable Metz contrasts the political theology of himself, Dorothee Sölle,[4] early Jürgen Moltmann,[5] and Latin-American liberation theology (treated below) with two other contemporaneous theological schools. A hare challenges a hedgehog to a relay race in parallel furrows in a field, and the hedgehog wins by stationing his wife at the other end of his furrow so that the hare races back and forth in the adjacent furrow to his death, always finding the hedgehog at each end "already there."

Of the idealistic universal-history theology of Wolfhart Pannenberg (and others descended from a cosmologically interpreted Hegel), Metz says:

> Like the two hedgehogs they have the course of history completely in view. Because they view it from both ends they have no need to traverse it. The hare runs—and the hedgehog sits in tricky duplication at the relay points of history as a whole.... Here the ultimate salvation through history will not be revealed

---

4. Sölle, *Political Theology*.
5. Moltmann, *Theology of Hope; The Crucified God*, but less in later writings.

by running, will not be evoked, remembered, and further narrated as practical meaning experienced within historical life; life ... is not troubled by collective historical anguish or threatening sense of catastrophe, hence has no need of looking forward to any expected hope (p. 144 [162]).

Of Rahner's idealistic-transcendental theology of anonymous Christianity, Metz says, "Through their transcendental omnipresence they bait the hare to death.... The one hedgehog is like the other, the beginning like the end, paradise like the end of time, creation like the fulfillment, and at the end the beginning repeats itself. History itself ... cannot intervene. The transcendental magic circle is complete and, like the two hedgehogs, is undefeatable. The suspicion arises that the process of transcendentalization of the Christian subject may have been guided by a tendency to unburden and immunize" (p. 145 [163]).

Metz implies that the two universalizing systems shield us from the responsibility (Gen 1–2) and the pitfalls (Gen 3) of creating language, culture, and history in communal relation with a non-micromanaging God. He attacks a semi-gnostic world-denying principle lurking in neo-Platonic and scholastic theology from which modern theology also cannot escape. His critique comes from the recently rediscovered (chapter 7 above) biblical proclamation of human solidarity as basic to the gospel. "The universality of Christianity's offer of salvation is not based on either a transcendental or universal-historical concept of universality. It has the character of an 'invitation.' The inviting logos of Christianity does not in any sense compel. It has a narrative structure with a practical and liberating intention. The salvation 'for all' grounded in Christ comes not as universal idea, but as the intelligible power of a practice, the practice of belonging" (p. 147 [165]). "The memories of the failure of Christianity, the deep-rooted disappointments for individuals and whole groups and classes of people, cannot be overcome and eliminated from the world simply by explaining" (p. 148 [166]).

Metz describes a radical loss. Before the Enlightenment, a surviving Christianity based on biblical human solidarity existed among the non-privileged classes in the West, unrecognized by neo-Platonic and scholastic academic theology. But bourgeois culture reduced its victims (the consumers) to the same empty generic life as its victors (the entrepreneurs). It reduced the victims' practical religion to what academic theology had been systematizing theoretically for the previous millennium and a half, namely, how to meet one's individual needs. Metz says, "In obeying its eschatological vocation Christianity should not establish itself either as a ghetto-society or as the ideological protective shell for the existing society. Rather it should become the liberating and critical force of this one society."[6]

### 2 Latin-American Liberation Theology: Gustavo Gutiérrez, Juan Luis Segundo

Latin-American liberation theology applies the emerging theology of communal typological application of both Testaments to a corporately oriented indigenous Christian continent struggling to emerge from European colonial ecclesiastical rule, North American economic domination, and a more recent generic fundamentalist religious invasion from its northern neighbor.

Unlike in Europe where a shrinking church in a market-dominated culture was torn between sectarian strategies and anonymous-Christian explanations, the Latin-American church, still culturally significant, has struggled to disassociate itself from the power elite in order to serve rather than exploit the common people. The conference of Latin-American bishops at Medellín, Columbia in 1968, emboldened by the Second Vatican Council, reached a Latin-American episcopal consensus on the church's vocation to reform society starting from below rather than from above. This challenged the impoverished general population to assume its share of responsibility for creating a reconciled society in which all members participate creatively and, thus, saving the elite from their enslavement in an exploitive role. Only thus, could there be cultural and economic well-being for the whole, only thus, reconciliation of exploiter and exploited with each other and with God.

The new movement was called "liberation theology" by the Peruvian Gustavo Gutiérrez in a 1968 paper "Hacia una teología de la liberación" and characterized definitively in his pioneering book *A Theology of Liberation*[7] (1971). Other leaders included the Uruguayan Juan Luis Segundo, the Argentineans Enrique Dussel and José Míguez Bonino, the Chileans Ronaldo Muñoz and Segundo Galilea, the Mexican

---

6. Metz, *Theology of the World*, 96, from a Metz article in English in *The Word in History*, 8–9; the paragraph omitted in *Zur Theologie der Welt*.

7. Page numbers are to the book.

José Miranda, the Brazilians Hugo Assmann and Leonardo Boff, and the Peruvian Ricardo Antoncich.

By the time of the Medellín conference it had become clear to the reform-minded in the third world that "development," or industrialization, of "underdeveloped" third-world countries by developed nations is not the answer to oppression because private investment and first world governmental foreign aid, channeled through the Latin-American controlling class, increase the dependent status of the underdeveloped countries and their exploited poor populations—such "development" cannot effect the reconciliation of exploiter and exploited.

Liberation theology calls for freedom in Christ to relate responsibly with others. Gutiérrez says, "The freedom to which we are called presupposes the going out of oneself, the breaking down of our selfishness and of all the structures that support our selfishness; the foundation of this freedom is openness to others. . . . The fullness of liberation . . . is communion with God and with other[s]" (p. 36). Both oppressed and oppressor are called to this freedom.

Liberation theology claims that theological reflection should not be a reflection on God as in past centuries but on executing the church's active calling in the world of social relations, of politics. God and human community should be in two-way relation. Reflection should be a "second step," after practice, to correct the church's strategy and increase its effectiveness. Gutiérrez says, "Theology as a critical reflection on Christian praxis in the light of the Word does not replace the other functions of theology, such as wisdom and rational knowledge; . . . . but . . . . wisdom and rational knowledge will more explicitly have ecclesial praxis as their point of departure and their context" (pp. 13–14). Juan Luis Segundo says the gospel is interpreted within the hermeneutic circle—what revelation tells us to do today will depend on the context, the politics, of the situation today. "If Gutierrez is right when he says that theology comes 'after,' then any preliminary consideration of . . . some specifically Christian contribution to liberation . . . is senseless and hence unanswerable."[8] Segundo finds Jesus making this point by calling forward a man with a withered hand and asking the Pharisees, "Is it lawful to do good or to do harm on the sabbath?" (Mark 3:4). Segundo comments, "The Pharisees were prepared to answer a different question—an abstract, formal question of classic theology which took account of only

---

8. Segundo, *The Liberation of Theology*, 84.

the Sabbath itself, not human beings: 'Is it permitted to do *anything at all* on the Sabbath?'" [9] Followers of Jesus cannot escape making perilous practical decisions in real community contexts, and these decisions are always about political actions.

Such a church, actively supporting a social revolution toward a reconciled humanity allowing creative participation by all, must be a church "of the people." Assmann, for example, writes, "Praxis, then, becomes the basic reference point for any truly contextual theology. . . . Grassroots Christians are far more radical in their use of the new methodology. It is really their methodology, their authentic methodology, because it is a type of Christian reflection that corresponds with their own practical experience of the faith in the context of political praxis. That is why they are more radical in doing what we theologians are trying to do; that is why their expression in grassroots language is more suited to the real-life context than our sophisticated but extra-contextual talk."[10] A reform coming from the multilaterally interacting social class "below" with nothing to lose!

Gutiérrez rejects the "distinction of planes" between church and world, which he finds in an influential position of Yves Conger. According to Gutiérrez, for Conger the church "was not to interfere, as institution, in temporal matters, except . . . through moral teaching. In practice this would mean . . . acting through the mediation of the conscience of the individual Christian. The building up of the earthly city, then, is an endeavor which exists in its own right. . . . The Church is not responsible for constructing the world. . . . The planes are thus clearly differentiated." Gutiérrez says the present functions of priest and layperson are often correspondingly differentiated. The priest functions within the church plane; "to intervene directly in political action is to betray his function. The layman's position in the Church, on the other hand, does not require him to abandon his insertion in the world" (p. 57). For Gutiérrez, such a distinction of planes between church and world is inconsistent. Practically, the inconsistency shows up in lay apostolic movements that as ecclesial movements are not to interfere in temporal matters and as lay movements are unable to carry out an

---

9. Ibid., 78.

10. Assmann, "The Power of Christ in History," 135–36. See also Dussel, *History and the Theology of Liberation*, 165; and Ronaldo Muñoz, "The Historical Vocation of the Church," *Frontiers* 154.

apostolate that involves moving into the political-economic sphere (pp. 63–64). Theoretically, the distinction is inconsistent because Scripture itself delegates responsibility for the world to humanity: "Biblical faith does indeed affirm the existence of creation as distinct from the Creator; it is the proper sphere of man, whom God himself has proclaimed lord of this creation. *Worldliness*, therefore, is a must, a necessary condition for an authentic relationship between man and nature, of men among themselves, and finally, between man and God" (p. 67). And besides, as Enrique Dussel points out, the Latin-American church has never observed the distinction of planes. Despite heroic efforts on the part of early Dominicans, Franciscans, Mercedarians, and some secular clergy to treat the indigenous population as human beings (with resulting martyrdom of a number of clergy at the hands of Spanish colonial authorities), the Latin-American church has as a matter of historical fact consistently allied itself with the oppressive controlling interests.[11] That is, the church as institution does interfere in temporal matters but, according to the liberation theologians, on the side of systematic oppression and dehumanization rather than social arrangements that liberate all individuals, both rich and poor, to make their own creative contribution to the corporate whole. But now through the influence of liberation theology the church is once more beginning the effort "to shake off the ambiguous protection provided by the beneficiaries of the unjust order which prevails on the continent" (p. 101).

Thus, Latin-American liberation theology not only agrees with European political theology that the church misses the real individual unless it reaches through the individual's worldly corporate social context (above, page 350), but further claims that the institutional church must itself be an integral part of the worldly social context, and cannot avoid practical entanglement in socio-economic issues. Overcoming the bourgeois privatization of religion was not initially as important for liberation theology as it was for political theology because the Latin American church still had public standing through both its liaison with the ruling class and its integration into the folk solidarity of the masses (a solidarity only beginning to be undermined by importation into Latin America of bourgeois private religion subsidized by North American interests). Liberation theology, rather, has worked at moving church institutional involvement in the world away from radical and obvious

11. Dussel, *History and the Theology of Liberation*, 75–109.

exploitation of the masses, agreeing with Metz that the church should not become "the ideological protective shell for the existing society" (above, page 357).

Liberation theology draws heavily on the Old Testament, using it typologically in the same way the New Testament does. Dussel, for example, after telling the story of Moses and the bush (Exodus 3), says, "Moses, the comfortable herdsman, becomes the liberator of an enslaved people. It is not an honor but a harsh responsibility insofar as he had been living in the totality of his own egotism up to then. Now he will suffer the persecution of the totality that is Egypt, because he must somehow shoulder the injustice and enslavement of his people in order to free them." Thus assuming the responsibility of representing Israel includes sharing its suffering. The typological application to the present follows. "Moses *heard* a voice. It *said* something to him. This is a basic point for us because of the situation in which we find ourselves. Comfortably established in another totality, not the totality of the desert but the totality of daily life and its hubbub, we do not hear anything. We, like Moses, are being called by name continually; but we do not hear anyone or anything."[12] Ronaldo Muñoz interprets the present situation by putting it in the same history as the biblical events, allowing continuity in the saving relation of God with his people, the essential point of typology (above, page 79). "In the light of faith we can sense a line of continuity between the people in our midst who are suffering and looking for liberation and the people of Israel who were oppressed in Egypt and liberated through the intervention of Moses. We realize it is the same people whom the prophets, as men of God, championed long ago: the same poor and alienated people whom Jesus of Nazareth preferred to share his life with and who were proclaimed heirs of the kingdom of God."[13]

Gutiérrez makes similar typological use of a substantial number of Old Testament passages, including Jer 22:13–16: "Are you a king because you compete in cedar? Did not your father . . . do justice and righteousness? . . . He judged the cause of the poor and needy . . . Is not this to know me? says the Lord." Gutiérrez applies this passage typologically to the present situation in Latin America: "To know Yahweh, which in Biblical language is equivalent to saying to love Yahweh, *is* to establish

---

12. Ibid., pp. 4, 3.
13. Muñoz, "The Historical Vocation of the Church," 154.

just relationships among men, it *is* to recognize the rights of the poor. . . . When justice does not exist, God is not known; he is absent" (p. 195).[14]

And for Gutiérrez, the New Testament also is a thoroughly political document, a document thoroughly in continuity with the Old Testament. Gutiérrez's Old Testament quotations are followed by an equal number of politically relevant New Testament passages, for example, Matt 25:31–45 ". . . Lord, when was it that we saw you hungry and gave you food . . . ?" that Gutiérrez clarifies for generic Westerners:

> It is also necessary to avoid the pitfalls of an individualistic charity. . . . The neighbor is not only man viewed individually. The term refers also to man considered in the fabric of social relationships, to man situated in his economic, social, cultural, and racial coordinates. It likewise refers to the exploited social class, the dominated people, and the marginated race. . . . This point of view leads us far beyond the individualistic language of the I-Thou relationship. . . . Indeed, to offer food or drink in our day is a political action; it means the transformation of a society structured to benefit a few who appropriate to themselves the value of the work of others. This transformation ought to be directed toward a radical change in the foundation of society, that is, the private ownership of the means of production (p. 202).

Every Latin-American liberation theologian shares the condemnation of private ownership of the means of production,[15] a position more natural for those working with its victims (the third-world multinational underclass) than for the first-world industrialized nations which, in alliance with the Latin-American controlling class, effectively are the owners of the means of production in Latin America. The Latin-Americans would rather have their means of production owned by a local government they had elected than by directors elected by stockholders in New York and Houston. But all liberation theologians reject the contemporary Marxist movement's economic-deterministic tendency to reduce the issue from reconciliation to mere arms-length "justice,"[16] seeing God,

---

14. All liberation theologians apply the Bible typologically in this way. The most sophisticated and complete statement is José Miranda's *Marx and the Bible*.

15. E.g., Miranda, *Marx and the Bible*, 1–33; Segundo, "Capitalism Versus Socialism," 240–59; Dussel, *History and the Theology of Liberation*, 135–37; Antoncich, "Hermeneutical Problems," II, 5).

16. E.g., Segundo, *Liberation of Theology*, 57–62; Miranda, *Marx and the Bible*, 252, 259, 278–80; Assmann, "The Power of Christ in History," 147; Galilea, "Liberation

rather, as asking human communities to work for increased multilaterally internal interaction.

Juan Luis Segundo wrote *The Liberation of Theology* (1966) to liberate theology itself from "the naive belief that the word of God is applied to human realities inside some antiseptic laboratory that is totally immune to the ideological tendencies and struggles of the present day" (p. 7). He starts by explicating typological use of Scripture as a circular hermeneutic relation between the meaning of an event described in Scripture and the meaning of the present event being interpreted. Such a relation is reached when profound questions and suspicions of present social arrangements trigger a reexamination of our culture's whole conceptuality, including our theology, leading to suspicion that our interpretation of Scripture is inadequate, thus liberating us to better recognize what the writers of Scripture actually were trying to say. Segundo provides four examples of failure or success in this project, those of Cox, Marx, Weber, and Cone.

Segundo says Harvey Cox in *The Secular City* does not offer such a dialogical relation with Scripture to the new pragmatically oriented technological society Cox describes. Rather, Cox loses his way, only faulting this new society not based on "ultimate concern" for not asking that Tillichian question of ultimacy instead of putting Scripture in dialogue with current pragmatic humanity as-is, in the same way that Scripture did from slaves pragmatically needing escape from pragmatically wanting to get the best places at the table (Segundo, pp. 9–12).

As for Marx, Segundo says Marx does hold to a two-way relation between "spiritual" and "material" (as claimed in this study, page 25, above) and that "the process of discovering this connection abets the revolutionary forces of the proletariat"; but Marx never sees this "as an opportunity for the proletariat to convert religion into their own weapon in the class struggle through a new and more faithful interpretation of the Scriptures," and instead views religion only "as an autonomous and ahistorical monolith" (pp. 16–17).

Weber in *The Protestant Ethic and the Spirit of Capitalism* also recognizes the internal relation between religion and material history, but Segundo says Weber's detached sociological perspective "is the theological equivalent of another great ideological adversary of liberation: the so-called quest for the *death of ideologies* or their suicides on the altars of

---

Theology and New Tasks," 170.

scientific and scholarly impartiality" (Segundo, p. 25). "Death of ideologies" is the slogan of promoters of the neutral technological "developmental" model for Latin America, which is used to hide and cover over the critical relation between dependence and liberation (p. 37 n. 37).

Finally, James Cone in *A Black Theology of Liberation* says that although Blacks learned theology from white theology with its talk about the universal human being, "there is no place in Black Theology for a colorless God in a society where people suffer precisely because of their color" (Cone, p. 120), and the Black community is able to find in Exodus and the Gospels a Black God and a Black Jesus not just "loving" but actively supporting the Black community in its particular situation. Segundo says Cone succeeds in reaching the requisite bilateral internal hermeneutic typological relation between scriptural tradition and God's present people (Segundo, p. 28).

Segundo here is trying to shock his first-world audience (this was a course at Harvard Divinity School) into recognizing that oppressed communities have an advantage over their oppressors in scriptural exegesis, that Scripture is not an abstract "fixed deposit" but, rather, has writer-intended meanings that can only be captured by a reader by that reader's applying it typologically to particular practical situations that reader is facing.

The oppressors as well as the oppressed will be saved from the oppressive relationship in the new reconciled world. Dussel says, "No one enmeshed in sin can do justice. Only the person who is suffering from injustice can do justice. The process of liberation itself is the only thing which will make it possible for the oppressor to undergo a real conversion. Hence only the underdeveloped nations of the world can enable the affluent nations to discover a new, more human model of human life and existence."[17] A reform from below! The corporateness of the view is radical. Latin America is working under God not merely to save itself but to save the industrialized nations as well. The point is not missed by some first-world political theologians. Dorothee Sölle says:

> There is a root experience which grounds a liberation theology for First World citizens.... This root experience is the totalitarianism of the hedonistic culture.... Our being exploited is different from the exploitation of the Third World. Still, it is one beast that rules over us, Third World and First World people, but we in

---

17. Dussel, *History and the Theology of Liberation*, 146.

the affluent societies tend to overlook its fascist dimensions. Our immediate experience of the beast is of its hedonistic side rather than of its oppressive side.... The ruling and the exploited classes represent two sides of the same alienation from life.[18]

Liberation theology has quite naturally aroused opposition from power elites, secular and ecclesiastical. But criticism also comes from religious constituencies not belonging to the power elite. Two objections are that liberation theology has a weak Christology, and that it condones a use of violence contrary to the New Testament perspective. As for the weak-Christology objection, liberation theology's thoroughly corporate perspective takes Jesus as representative leader of the people of God, so that its strong ecclesiology is also a tacit strong Christology, something not obvious to cosmological or generic perspectives not recognizing "Messiah" or "Christ" as meaning "representative of" old and new Israel.

Other claims of a weak Christology in liberation theology may be more nearly a tacit disagreement with its Christology. Assmann, after a survey of actual pre-liberation christologies in Latin America, claims that a Christology that separates the resurrection and the crucifixion corresponds to a social separation of the victorious dominators and the impotent dominated. "There is no way of separating the cross and the resurrection without succumbing to alienating Christs. The Christ of oppressive Christologies really has two faces. On the one side are all the Christs of the power establishment, who do not need to fight because they already hold a position of dominance; on the other are the Christs of established impotence, who cannot fight against the dominance to which they are subject." What is needed in Latin America is a Christology uniting the crucifixion and the resurrection, which would then correspond to an ongoing struggle for liberation "where defeat will pave the way for victory, and where victory itself will ultimately have to meet defeat if it is to continue to be victorious."[19]

This last quotation is also the beginning of an answer to the second objection, that liberation theology condones violence. In the next section that objection will be analyzed as it is made by a corporately oriented source, the late twentieth century revival of sixteenth-century anabaptist thought, and it will appear that underlying the objection is

18. Sölle, "'Thou Shalt Have No Other Jeans Before Me,'" 9–10.
19. Assmann, "The Power of Christ in History," 149–50.

the vestige of a sectarian separating conception of the proper relation of the church to the world.

### 3 Baptist Theology: Sectarianism Versus Constantinianism

The late twentieth century North American reform position of John Howard Yoder, member of the sixteenth-century launched baptist "radical reformation" community, is surprisingly close on some issues to European political theology and Latin-American liberation theology. Radical reformation theology, from its beginnings, took the Bible as near corporately understood historical tradition defining the Christian community, but it approached the Christology-ecclesiology domain christologically, rather than ecclesiologically as political and liberation theology do. Its outstanding difference is its call to witness in the world in a manner excluding all coercive means in the interaction between church and world.

The sixteenth-century radical reformation understood the church to be a (1) freely chosen (2) community (3) of disciples of Jesus (4) as discipleship can be known from the Bible. It held three sixteenth-century central European communions, Catholic, Lutheran, and Reformed, to have departed from this biblical practice through accomodation to unilateral state control since its imposition by the fourth century emperor Constantine, with nominal church membership compulsory for all subjects of the state independently of personal choice or commitment as disciples of Jesus, and so lacking the communal relation such commitment would engender. Consistently, on their part they also limited themselves only to "witness," not act, to bring reform to the nation.

The externally visible sign of the radical reformation, the one that gave the originally derisive name "anabaptist" (*Wiedertaufer*, rebaptizer) to the movement, was "believer's baptism"—the requirement that a person make an individual, intentional commitment to discipleship before being baptized. This rule voided the routine baptism of all infants as practiced in European states. Both Judaism and Christianity traditionally have had a two step initiation, respectively celebrating community membership and responsible exercise of that membership, learned interactively by community participation between the two steps.

The sixteenth-century anabaptists were systematically put to death throughout German-speaking Europe—the life expectancy of those receiving believer's baptism was on the order of a year. Correspondingly, anabaptists emphasized following Jesus without regard for material and social consequences. Comforted by the implication to be found at the sect pole of the remnant strand in first-century apocalyptic (above, page 151) passive waiting for God to bring in the new age, the powerless anabaptists advocated following Jesus' example without expecting in this world to see a relation between such action and the coming of God's kingdom. But the New Testament itself (as we saw in chapter 3, above), although necessarily written in literalistic Greek, intended a first-century apocalyptic message to be taken metonymically (as in Semitic culture) as a prophetic call to the faithful to a continuously active role in building the new age.

Although the early anabaptists' conception of their fellowship as disciples of Jesus had corporate elements, two of their doctrines, believer's baptism and discipleship without regard for consequences, are logical derivatives of generic elements common to all European sixteenth century Christianity. Believer's baptism derives from the view that commitment to Jesus is generic and, thus, logically prior to membership in the body of his disciples; and the sectarian stance derives from the view that individual salvation is independent of the fate of those outside the body of saved ones. The recent more communal radical baptist renewal, as we will see, attempts to overcome both these generic tendencies.

The recent radical baptist movement offers its new insights to the whole Christian community, not just to baptists. Yoder writes, "I therefore describe the radical reformation model as a paradigm of value for all ages and communions, rather than as an apology for a denomination claiming the last—or the best—word."[20] James McClendon puts it politely: "There is indeed this 'free church' or 'believer's church' or *baptist* style of Christian thought that is widely displayed but only haltingly voiced. Not until it has sounded its own note can there be full and fair conversation in our times between it and other voices, other styles in the one kingdom of Christ."[21] Stanley Hauerwas described himself in 1981 as "a (Southern) Methodist . . . who teaches and worships with . . . Roman Catholics; who believes that the most nearly faithful form of Christian witness is best exemplified by . . . anabaptists or Mennonites."[22]

---

20. Yoder, *The Priestly Kingdom*, 4–5.
21. McClendon, Jr., *Ethics*, 8.
22. Hauerwas, *A Community of Character*, 6.

Thus, the recent baptist renewal movement explicitly denies a sectarian stance over against the Christian movement as a whole.

It also denies to the Christian movement as a whole, understood in these baptist terms, any sectarian stance over against the world; but this denial is qualified by the necessity of finding the right balance between mission to the world and "anti-Constantinian" freedom from influence by secular social structures, or as Yoder puts it in *The Priestly Kingdom*, how "to be separated from the world once again in order to be appropriately in mission to the world."[23] The prophetic tradition in Scripture itself reveals such a balance, from the separation of the leadership functions of prophet and king in David's time to the opposition between the followers of Jesus and the colonial rulers in the first-century.

Just how separated from the world should the church be? The recent baptist renewal seeks to move the church away from a separation so extensive as to be plainly sectarian. At the same time Latin-American liberation theology sought to move the church away from an equally obvious Constantinian identification with a ruling class controlled by exploitive elite interests. The sectarian and Constantinian extremes both forego the church's call to act creatively and redemptively as a community within and in complementary corporate relation with the whole civil society—the sectarian by withdrawing from such a relation and the Constantinian by changing the relation into unilateral control of the community from above. Both positions preclude the church from being a redemptive agent in the community. The two renewal programs each seek to move their part of the church toward a common corporate position that is neither Constantinian nor sectarian. Each group tends to see the other as not having yet moved far enough—baptist theology finding a lingering Constantinian tolerance for violence in liberation theology and liberation theology finding vestiges of sectarian withdrawal in baptist renewal theology.

Stanley Hauerwas tries to bring the two sides together but in fact combines sectarian elements from early anabaptism and unilateral relations from Reformation Protestantism. His position is summarized here as a contrast to the more corporate view reached by Yoder.

In *The Peaceable Kingdom* Hauerwas analyzes the church's internal structure as an organic, visible community, agent of God, and built on a transmitted tradition that forms the character of its members so that

---

23. Yoder, *The Priestly Kingdom* 85.

they are predisposed to act according to God's will. Much of this analysis openly coincides with Alasdair MacIntyre's ethics of virtue (above, chapter 1), including Macintyre's development of tradition and social imputation of individual identity as components of an organic but not corporate community interaction. Hauerwas proposes for the church a unilateral servant ministry to the world, one that influences the world while being insulated against any reverse influence from the world by the church's avoiding of any *controlling* position in society or any *calculation of means*. He says, "the isolation of 'consequences' as the determining factor in our decisions invites a sense of control and omnipotence that is not easily justified" (p. 128). He says concern with the consequences of one's actions too easily implies acceptance of the sinful worldly context within which one's actions occur. Instead, the church is to concentrate on receiving and transmitting a Christian character within the Christian community. "Christians therefore cannot be content with a morality that accepts sin as a given. It is our task to call ourselves and others to be true to ourselves as God's creatures" (p. 128). The church's servant role toward the world is only to be an unstained example. "The first social task of the church . . . is to be the church and thus help the world understand itself as . . . . God's world" (p. 100). He disagrees explicitly with political theology. "The proponents of 'political theology' are . . . wrong . . . to associate 'politics' only with questions of social change. Rather the 'political' question crucial to the church is what kind of community the church must be to be faithful to the narratives central to Christian convictions."[24]

For Hauerwas, the church should not only protect itself from the world but should not even help the world. "It cannot be our task to transform the violence of this world into God's peace, for in fact that has been done through the cross and resurrection of Jesus. Our joy is the simple willingness to live with the assurance of God's redemption" (p. 147). The required passivity is consistent with perennial, modern, and existentialist orientations. It prohibits stopping violence, even that indirectly caused by oneself. "The peace Christians embody and seek is . . . just the opposite of order, as its institutionalization necessarily creates disorder and even threatens anarchy. In effect the peace of God, rather than making the world more safe, only increases the dangers we have to negotiate. All social orders and institutions to a greater and lesser extent

---

24. Hauerwas, *A Community of Character*, 2.

are built on the lie that we, not God, are the masters of our existence" (p. 142). The prohibition against exercising control is absolute. "We are not called upon to be the initiators of the kingdom, we are not called upon to be God's anointed. We are called upon to be *like* Jesus, not to *be* Jesus .... It involves seeing in his cross the summary of his whole life" (p. 76). God does not want help.

In contrast, Scripture sees the summary of Jesus' whole life not in his crucifixion but in his resurrection, articulated in John 29:21 "as the Father sent me so I send you," as call to the disciples actively to continue his mission, to participate in and interactively spread the community's delegated responsibility, "dominion" (Gen 1:28), to build multilaterally internal community interaction. Human beings cannot build a multilaterally interacting community without both offering initiatives to others and accepting some initiatives from others. But Hauerwas chooses unilateral divine control, "the simple willingness to live with the assurance of God's redemption," over unilateral human action, "the lie that we, not God, are the masters of our existence," never recognizing the scripturally claimed call from God to accept humanity's part in a *joint* creation of the social world. We saw Assmann (above, page 365) claiming that Christian avoidance rather than redemption of controlling roles allows a Christology with crucifixion separated from resurrection. Missing from Hauerwas are the resurrection and the church as the continuing body of Christ.

Although attracted by the baptist renewal movement, Hauerwas has not recognized its corporate basis, and has used MacIntyre's organic ethics of virtue derived from Homer and Aristotle, along with Reformation neo-Platonism, to support a virulent sectarianism.

John Howard Yoder carries the baptist renewal movement far toward the corporate ideal balance, at once non-sectarian and non-Constantinian.

In *The Politics of Jesus* (1972) Yoder introduces the Christian *radical subordination frame* through the "household precept" passages of the New Testament:

> Wives, be subject to your husbands ...
> Husbands, love your wives ...
> Children, obey your parents ...
> Fathers, do not provoke your children ...

> Slaves, obey your earthly masters . . .
> Masters, treat your slaves justly and fairly

(Col 3:18—4:1 = Eph 5:21—6:9 = 1 Peter 2:13—3:7). These three relations (wife-husband, children-parent, and worker-supervisor) are those of the first-century rural family of perhaps fifty, with husband as chief executive officer and also head of the food production department with twenty workers, and wife as head of two departments: a nursery for fifteen grand-children and a restaurant for all fifty. This biblical passage, so shocking to the modern Western world, *does not* legislate this structure, rather it urges responsible exercise of the roles in the existing community structure created by the community over centuries to meet prevailing physical economic conditions under its delegated authority or "dominion" (Gen. 1:26). The modern industrial society's nuclear family of four or less no longer manages production, nursing and schooling of the young, and feeding of fifty. Wife and husband now work, or are managers, for a salary. They purchase food, clothing, shelter, nursery care, schooling, and entertainment from outside the home through non-internal arms-length relations. It appears that community through corporate creative internal interaction needs even more prophetic encouragement today than it did in the biblical times that produced the above displayed passage.

How does Yoder use this passage? He says it asks the participants in these relations to redeem the social roles they already have by exercizing them as servant ministry to one another. The persons in the subordinate roles are addressed first: "The subordinate person in the social order is addressed as a moral agent. . . . The center of the imperative is a call to willing subordination to one's fellow man" (pp. 174–75). This is a call to fulfill one's social role as an active ministry to the family rather than out of fear or resignation. The subordinate role becomes an opportunity rather than an indignity (p. 185). Next, the holder of the dominant role is equally called to subordination (p. 180). A presiding role also should be exercised as a ministry to the community. The husband helped produce the lamb; the wife helped cook it. The subordination required is *mutual:* "Be subject to one another out of reverence for Christ" (Eph 5:21). Yoder calls the partners to *symmetrical* subordination to one another within a *non-symmetrical* complementary civil order all of whose members, including those with presiding responsibilities, are equally needed. Working within the civil order does not make the church a tool of the civil society (p. 181) but incarnates the power of God in the civil order to transform it.

Yoder contrasts this subordination from that of Stoic ethics. "Stoicism addresses man in his dignity and calls upon him to live up to the highest vision of himself.... The free man should avoid coming into bondage to a woman or to his subordinates" (pp. 173–74). Yoder sees, rather, the civilly subordinate partner as in a more strategic position to influence the other to a mutual subordination: 1 Peter 3:1 "Wives, ... accept the authority of your husbands, so that, even if some do not obey the word, they may be won over without a word by their wives' conduct"— won over to the word and so also to subordination, something that wives cannot do by manipulation or by rejecting the obligations of the work relation. Again, here is another reform from below. The wife in that culture ranked *lower* in management, *equal* in responsibility for improving the relation, and *higher* in potential redeeming power. The same held for employer-employee relations, the second can enable the first to have the second "no longer as a slave [δουλος, servant] but more than a slave, a beloved brother ... both in the flesh and in the Lord" (Philemon 16; Yoder p. 181 n. 32).

The subordination Yoder advocates is active, not passive. It is "revolutionary" (pp. 163–92); it changes things. It is not Greek or modern but an application of early Christian teaching on the power of Christ's cross and resurrection: "whoever wishes to be first among you must be slave [δουλος, servant] of all" (Mark 10:44), "God's weakness is stronger than human strength" (1 Cor 1:25, 27). The seven deacons, servants, were appointed to better facilitate corporate interaction "from below" (Acts 6:1–6). Subordination of the parties to one another redeems the *community they form*, not just its individual members.

Subordination redeems small scale leadership roles—husband, parent, employer. But can it also redeem the leadership role in the state? Yoder's subordination is active, revolutionary, efficacious, but it is not violent. Yoder excludes the "sword" function of government (control by unilateral force) as a Christian alternative. He says, "the function exercised by government is not the function to be exercised by Christians. However able an infinite God may be to work at the same time through the sufferings of his believing disciples who return good for evil and through the wrathful violence of the authorities who punish evil with evil, such behavior is for men not complementary but in disjunction" (p.

199). In his work *The Priestly Kingdom* (1984), to which page numbers refer from this point on, Yoder extends the redeemable leadership roles beyond the household scale to some modern governmental roles. "The interlocking of society is far more than civil government.... When modern societies institutionalize opposition and the separation of powers, it is not evident that all 'involvement' in public office need be swordlike" (pp. 164–65).

Nevertheless, Yoder says, civil order has a fundamental coercive character prior to any attempt to justify it by a social contract or any other theory: "It remains the nature of civil order itself that its coercive control is prior to any justifications or qualifications thereof" (p. 159). Thus, civil order is still unredeemable. There is an unyielding difference between the worldly and church ethical frames. In the worldly frame, leaders "lord it over" their subjects, whereas in the church frame, the leader is servant to the group (Luke 22:24–27; Yoder, pp. 156–57). The worldly frame emphasizes filling all the roles in society so that the society runs well, while the church frame emphasizes the distinct charisma-based contribution available from each member. The worldly frame perceives a society to run well when the establishment successfully maintains order, whereas the church frame perceives the church to run well when the distinct gifts of the members work together to form the body of Christ (pp. 160–63).

The church has often reached the world by collaborating with, and thus adopting, the world's coercive ethical frame. According to Yoder, in such a collaboration the church's distinctive ethic is lost. For church-world relations, Yoder instead proposes precisely the subordination ethical frame prescribed above for household relations, a frame within which the church can interact in mission to the civil society without adopting its worldly ethical frame. Whereas the world starts from a collection of social roles that need to be filled, and the church starts from the particular gifts of its several members, the subordination frame places church members strategically in those worldly roles where they can best witness to the Kingdom of God, and accordingly, "their preference will not be for dominion roles but for servant roles" (p. 162). In the worldly frame things go well if they go well for the establishment and in the church frame they go well if they go well for cooperation of brother and sister in Christ. And the subordination frame tests to see whether things go well for the victims (the oppressed) within the worldly frame (pp. 160–65). The subordination frame puts the church in a bilateral, corporate relation with the world, rather than the unilateral relation entertained by Hauerwas (above, page 369). But, as noted, it does not redeem civil society completely.

Latin-American liberation theology shares many insights with baptist renewal theology. For liberation theology, the people of God are also called to a different behavior from the world, and the difference also consists in prosecuting relationships within society as a ministry to others rather than as mere means of survival of the self or the church. Gutiérrez says, "The freedom to which we are called presupposes the going out of oneself, the breaking down of our selfishness and of all the structures that support our selfishness; the foundation of this freedom is openness to others."[25] The Brazilian Leonardo Boff says, "We today live in a situation of captivity. To believe and hope and work for liberation in such a situation, when we are fairly sure that we will not live to see the fruits of our work, is to incarnate in our own day the cross of Christ.... The suffering implied in hope can generate awesome and unexpected forces for liberation.... Like the seed falling into the ground, our bodies must prepare the way for the future."[26] Liberation theology depends on the strategic advantage of the oppressed as agents for the conversion of the oppressors (above, page 357). The survival tactic of the church allying itself in classical Constantinian fashion with the dominating class is resoundingly condemned. And Liberation theology explicitly rejects the Zealot solution of armed revolt and seeks to reduce the total amount of violence in the world.[27]

Both Yoder and liberation theologians follow the long scriptural tradition of a smaller group called to serve as redemptive agency for a larger group: Israel among the nations, the classical prophets and disciples of Jesus within Israel, the Christian movement in the world, the wife within the extended family. But Yoder emphasizes the redemptive role of the smaller group, while the Latin-Americans focus on redemption of the larger group. Yoder tends to read the undoubtedly uncompromising reform ethic of Jesus as an ethic for a minority in Israel. But Jesus belonged to a prophetic tradition whose very program was the extension

---

25. Gutiérrez, *A Theology of Liberation*, 36.

26. Boff, "Christ's Liberation via Oppression," 130.

27. Segundo, *Liberation of Theology*, 162; Galilea, "Liberation Theology and New Tasks," 174–78.

to a civil monarchy (with its powerful political and economic leaders), of an ethic for all, an ethic that was developed in a less complex pre-monarchic setting (above, page 357). The all-pervading continuity of the New Testament with the Old (chapters 2 and 3, above) implies that Jesus' reform program was for Israel as a whole, including its leadership, so that it could better follow its call to "servanthood" to the other nations as wholes, including their governments. The New Testament remnant doctrine especially upheld this prophetic tradition against any minority or sectarian one (above, pages 144, 147, 149).

It would be unscriptural to bypass this called-for inclusion of leadership in the state by placing it safely in a world-to-come on the other side of an eschatological discontinuity, or by hiding from it inside the borders of a sectarian church—two possible locations, "the age to come" or "the free church," suggested by Yoder for the "Kingdom" (p. 160). Both these solutions are rejected by the New Testament—they are the first and fifth of the five methods used by modern theology to genericize the New Testament (above, page 151). The prophets sought the reform of the Israelite monarchy, and Jesus of the rulers of Israel in his day. The majority of figurative uses of "good shepherd" in the two Testaments refer not to God or Jesus but to *human leaders*. When the Pharisees recognized that Jesus was implicitly criticizing them (John 9:40), Jesus replied, "The one who enters by the gate is the shepherd of the sheep" (John 10:2). Even Yoder lets Baptist Roger Williams and Quaker William Penn govern as founders of the colonies of Rhode Island and Pennsylvania with disestablished church (p. 187).

The problem is the *a priori* presence of coercion that Yoder recognizes in civil society. The difference between Yoder and the Latin-Americans comes down to whether a Christian servant ministry can engage at all in civil leadership with its *a priori* coercion, whether a *presiding* role in community can be redeemed. The question remains: Is there a fundamental difference between the presiding roles in government and in the family?

Juan Luis Segundo offers a solution. He claims the inevitable *a priori* force Yoder has found (and perennialist Luther, page 202, above, has indirectly avoided by claiming a perennial-based appointment from God as teacher) is an intrinsic element in *all* social relations, and is to be redeemed by redistributing it so that every member has a share of it in relations, as in our definition of *corporate community* as community with *distributed anthropological control*. In his *Liberation of Theology* Segundo explores this issue for the church by distinguishing its special social calling by its *ends* rather than its *means*.

The terms "violence," "coercion," "control," "force" have too wide a range of meanings to use in differentiating good and bad relations among members of a corporate community, where by definition an *intrinsic* relation applies a force to those in the relation that changes all their essences. Segundo says distinguishing between violence and non-violence must be distinguishing between ends rather than means. "Conscious and unconscious mental tendencies can constitute a weapon more effective in killing millions of people than any weapon that is traditionally viewed as armament. So why focus the whole problem of violence around the picture of a person bearing arms?" (p. 157). In responsible behavior, the total results of an action must count as its end. A telling example comes from the political theologian Dorothee Sölle. "The civil war in Biafra . . . . broke out when the oil companies, which had prospected in the Nigerian delta, switched their payment of royalties from Gowon to Ojukwu. . . . Half a nation starved for the sake of their business interests."[28] Different means may serve the same end.

Conversely, the same means may serve different ends. In particular, the ends of love and of egoism both employ the same means. There is only one means and that is interaction with others. In the communal perspective presupposed by both Yoder and the liberation theologians, interaction with others is intrinsic. Anything of significance done by one person changes the context within which others can act, that is, applies a partially controlling force to the others. Segundo says, "Our love must place in its service the very same instruments that can and usually do serve egotism: e.g., sex in its direct and sublimated forms, aggressivity, and the fundamental tendencies which Freud called Eros and Thanatos. There is no other energy available for effective love" (p. 157). Hence, both love and egoism are coercive or "violent." "Any phenomenological analysis will readily show that violence is part and parcel of both of these opposed tendencies. . . . Egotism is no more violent than love; love is no less violent than egotism" (p. 157). This argument makes immediate sense in a culture built around human interaction, human solidarity, thus where love and hate are *impacting* relations between persons, that is, they are "violent." It is less obvious in utilitarian cultures where "love"

---

28. Sölle, *Political Theology*, 80.

is a desire only internal to the lover—a feeling distinct from any impact the lover makes on the loved.

The problem with the coercion of egoism lies not with it as means but with the end for which it is used. If interaction with others is eliminated as a means because it is often used for egoistic ends, then the means for loving is also removed. "Love for one's mother . . . clearly has the same psychic roots as patriotism, prejudice, racism, and war. Does this mean we must uproot the facility for maternal love in order to free ourselves for peace?" (p. 158). This is not just a rhetorical question: Daly, for example, answers this question precisely "yes" (above, page 326). She does so consistently with the *self-as-such* orientation, for which non-interference is preferable to entanglement in responsible love of another.

Added to the conflict between love and egoism is the conflict between competing loves, the key Levinas used to begin the escape from Heidegger's egocentric phenomenological standpoint toward community (chapter 7, above). Segundo says (in the previous section) human beings have limited resources for relating with others and it is necessary to choose: effective love cannot be universal. "Love can only be effective and therefore real when it possesses motives and instruments for being feasible. Such is the case with our neighbor" (p. 158). Selectivity in relationships, an essential aspect of interacting with others, is therefore a necessary aspect of loving, but it is equally useful in egoism. Jesus' ministry was primarily limited to Israel: Matt 10:5–6 "These twelve Jesus sent out with the following instructions: 'Go nowhere among the Gentiles, and enter no town of the Samaritans, but go rather to the lost sheep of the house of Israel.'" Segundo asks, "What distinguishes this brand of 'love' in Jesus from the worst forms of racial segregation in South Africa? . . . The difference certainly does not lie in the means. We cannot decide whether love or egotism is at work by examining the means employed. Both use the same means because at bottom both make use of the same energy, the same canalizations of instinct and reason" (p. 164). The difference, rather, is a difference in ends. Jesus, of course, worked on whole Israel to make it a light to whole nations, not to single individuals in those nations.

Every act of relating among people applies force. What is needed is a force that calls on all sides in a relation to act not out of egoistic interests but for the well-being of their community, thus giving all members opportunity to participate effectively in creative mutual interaction. The liberation in such a relational structure is not freedom from all force but from a unilateral, non-complementary application of force for self-serving purposes that preempts creative mutual interaction. The appropriate amount of force on individuals will be that which optimizes their chances of contributing freely to *liberation for the whole*. For example, leaders are called to apply a communally regulating force commensurate with the power implicit in their community-delegated authority, and at the same time may need closer supervision than others through an institutionalized system of checks and balances. And the same is true for spouses, parents, and work supervisors as for heads of state.

To one whose ethics is a discrimination among means, the communal position's discriminating only among the ends (all consequences) of acts appears as a species of Constantinianism. But Segundo's position, treating force neutrally as intrinsic relating element of human community, and like both Testaments accepting its use in corporate relations and rejecting its use in exploitive ones, does not reject force as such and so can work for a church both non-sectarian and non-Constantinian.

*4 Language Philosophy in Theology: Louis-Marie Chauvet*

In *Symbol and Sacrament: A sacramental reinterpretation of Christian existence* (1987) the sacramental theologian Louis-Marie Chauvet opposes the prevailing Western theology (based on causal, instrumental, arms-length relations, both within the human community and with God) in favor of a theology based on essence-exchanging relations by *language*, *sacraments*, and *service*, without manipulation (outside the market, "for nothing") that respects the participants as subjects—relations in which subjects exchange *themselves*.

Whereas Gadamer reaches a corporate perspective by extending early Heidegger's internally relating *fore-structure* (above, page 42, Chauvet completes later Heidegger's language as path (above, page 41) from self to Being by identifying Heidegger's unidentified "Being" as *human community*, so that language mediates internally between self and community and, thus, is a means by which a *self* becomes a human *individual*.

Chauvet illustrates the prevailing Western view of relation as instrumental cause with Plato's *Philebus* 53c–55a, which explains the relation of lover to beloved by analogy with the relation of shipbuilder to ship, both moving from *genesis*, becoming, to rest in *ousia*, a fixed existence. Not so for Chauvet:

> Shipbuilding aims at making boats; it builds them, that is all there is to it. [But] the lover ... does not produce the beloved. He only causes the other to exist *as a beloved*, and thus as capable of making a response in return ... and ... of not making a response in return. The boat is a finished product; but the beloved is precisely ... *not finished* ... not a *"product"* at all. *Because the beloved is a "subject," this person can never be simply reduced to an "achievement" but is always process* (p. 24).

Chauvet says, "reality is never present to us except in a mediated way, which is to say, constructed out of the symbolic network of the culture which fashions us" (p. 84). "Between sensation and perception there is a margin.... What is perceived by humans is not only the physical reality that affects the senses but the 'semiological layer' in which this event is embedded by the culture." Water is not perceived as in a chemical analysis but "inevitably apprehended to some degree as expressing my culture and desire" (p. 85). Water is a feature not merely of the individual's world of sensations but of the language, the symbolic network, the culture, to which all individuals belong. "There is no emergence of [human] subjects without the *subjugation* of each of them to this ... cultural agreement which is the symbolic order." Language mediates this cultural agreement in such a way that members of the community both learn from it and contribute to it. "It is in the symbolic order that subjects 'build' themselves, but they do this only by building the world, something that is possible for them insofar as they have inherited from birth a world already culturally inhabited and socially arranged—in short, a world already spoken" (p. 86). "Language is not an instrument but a *mediation;* it is in language that humans as subjects come to be .... language does not arise to translate after the fact a human experience that preceded it; it is *constitutive* of any truly *human* experience" (p. 87).

Chauvet argues linguistically that there can only be a linguistic *I* if there is also a *You* who can in turn be an *I* when responding as the two discuss something beyond the two, an *It*. In the relation, the two are both *different* and *similar*, and mediated with a world greater than the two, unlike the metaphysical perspective in which another person may be merely a projection of "myself," and God is "wholly other" (pp.

94–95). And he argues the same point psychologically, saying that death is a prerequisite to life. "To become someone, someone 'among others' . . . we must renounce to be everything, to have everything . . . . *To reject this death is to forfeit one's life.* . . . This is a scheme of regeneration through a symbolic death which is at work in all rites of initiation . . . The treasure is never separable from the very process of killing our primary narcissism . . . our imaginary omnipotence and right-to-enjoy-everything" (pp. 97–98). Chauvet summarizes: "Thus, it is only through a *breach* that a subject comes to birth . . . . To consent to this presence of the absence is to consent to never being able to leave mediation behind—mediation of the symbolic order that always-already precedes human beings and allows them to become human because they start from a world already humanized before them and passed on to them as a universe of meaning." (p. 98). One only becomes a human being through internal, essence-changing relations with others by symbolic exchange using the community's cultural structure.

One who becomes human through symbolic internal relation with human community can only come to relation with God through that relation; one can only have the same kind of relation with God. "One does not affirm God at the expense of the human person; the wholeness of grace is never so well attested as when one takes into account the freedom of the human return-gift it solicits" (p. 109). The God-humanity relation mediated by symbol, like relations between humans, is not a unidirectional "instrumental" cause-and-effect relation, but a two-way creative corporate one. Chauvet says, "like the *manna* in the desert . . . grace is of an entirely different order from that of value or empirical verifiability. Its very name is a question: *Man hu?*. . . 'What is this?'" It has the consistency of something, the traits of nothing. They gather it, some more, some less, but there is no excess, no shortage. When they try to hoard it, it breeds worms and becomes foul (Exod 16:9–21). It is love; it is of the order of grace (p. 45).

Chauvet asks, "How does one become a believer?" He answers by recounting the Emmaus story (Luke 24:13–35). "In the first section of the story . . . the disciples have in effect abandoned their mission; in turning away from Jerusalem, they are also in effect turning their backs on their previous experience with Jesus. They talk between themselves, . . . a definitive postmortem on the failed mission of their Master. Consequently, their eyes are 'kept from recognizing him': their spirits, like their eyes, are shut.... Their past is dead....'They stood still, looking sad.'" In the second section of the story:

> [T]hey open themselves to this stranger who has joined them. They break out of their closed conversation to address someone who listens to them.... their desire awakens anew as they relate to this third person how their hopes have been dashed. Then, however, "reality" intrudes again ... they know all there is to know about Jesus of Nazareth. But their understanding is a misunderstanding.... However, .... in allowing Jesus to open the Scriptures for them, the two disciples begin to enter into an understanding .... Suppose the scriptures disclosed a reality about God which they had never suspected because it directly contradicted the most authoritative doctrines. ... Could God still be God, our God, the God of our ancestors, if he raised up *someone who had been justly condemned* to death for having blasphemed against the Law of God given to Moses, that is, against God himself?.... One gets an inkling of the depth of the necessary conversion; for the two disciples it is a question of accepting the possibility that the word of God, according to the Scriptures, *has come to "deconstruct" their best established evidence* concerning the "reality" of God.... But now, their eyes begin to "open" when the Risen One, appealing to their memories, "opens" the Scriptures to them.... "Were not our hearts burning within us?" they will say to each other when remembering in retrospect.... they begin to see the Risen One while *hearing* him "raise himself up" from the Scriptures: *he lives there where his word is heard,* there where people witness to him "according to the Scriptures." "There," that is to say, in the *Church* .... [They say] "Stay with us" [but] the Stranger is not yet recognized in his radical strangeness. It is not outside, on the road, but *inside*, around the table, that the two disciples have the decisive experience of their encounter ... the Risen One brings to completion the initiative he has taken: his "word" becomes flesh in the shared bread. At this point, their eyes are opened; what they see allows them to understand ... the Eucharist *of the Church* .... Their eyes open on an *emptiness*— "he vanished from their sight"—but an emptiness full of a presence.... Jesus the Christ is absent as "the same"; he is no longer present except as "the other." From now on, it is impossible to touch his real body; we can touch it only as the *body symbolized* through the ... Scriptures reread as his own word, the sacraments performed as his own gestures, the ethical witness of the communication between brothers and sisters lived as the expression of his own "service" (*diaconia*) for humankind. From now

> on, it is in the witness of the Church that he takes flesh . . . "That same hour" [they] rise up and return to Jerusalem. . . . Their return to Jerusalem is the symbolic analogue of the transformation that has taken place in them . . . . the dispersion of the group [has been turned around] into a renewed communion. For it is the entire group of disciples that, having passed through death, is now reborn as the Church. It burst forth from the Easter words, "he is risen (pp. 167–70).

Thus, the disciples, no longer able to touch the sensible body of Jesus, continue their relation with him as church, as *body*, through the symbolic mediation of the *Scriptures*, the *sacraments*, and the ethical witness of *diaconia*, three internally related components in the symbolic "structure of Christian identity" (p. 160).

These three components are not new; they have been symbolic mediators between God and his people from the beginning. The *Scriptures* interpreting Jesus in the Emmaus story are the Old Testament. The eucharistic *sacrament* continues Israel's communal meal as God's people, the *diaconia* continues the work for justice proclaimed by the Old Testament prophets. The tradition, both of Israel in the Old Testament and its Christian continuation in the New Testament, developed through mutual historical interaction among these three components—writing the history of the community under God, celebrating it liturgically, and acting it out in diaconia (pp. 190–265).

Because the church is for human beings, "our structure Scripture-Sacrament-Service thus appears as homologous to a more fundamental *anthropological structure*: cognition-recognition-praxis. . . . Every human subject is born [i.e. formed] from the possibility of conceiving a world, of celebrating it, of acting in it" (pp. 179–80). Correspondingly, the structure of Christian identity is communal, is the church as historical and cultural body. "The question 'Who is God?' . . . takes flesh for us not by descending from the theologies of the hypostatic union but rather by rising from the languages of the New Testament witnesses, which are historically and culturally situated" (p. 69). "Alliance with [Jesus] can be lived only in the mediation of alliance with others, and not in an imaginary direct contact with him that presupposes his 'full' presence" (p. 188). "The Gospel is *by nature communal*" (p. 183). "The true scandal is ultimately this, the path to our relation with God passes through our relation with human beings" (p. 187).

Chauvet treats Christian identity as "a viewpoint of identity and not one of salvation. It does not mean 'outside the Church, there is no salvation,' but rather 'outside the Church, there is no *recognized* salvation'" (p. 180). Rahner's "pre-apprehension of absolute being" (above, page 313) is rejected by the quotations in the previous paragraph, and made both useless and unnecessary in accounting for "anonymous Christians" in this one. Although Chauvet does not rescue the technical term "typology" from its neo-Platonic meanings, he does characterize the use of Scripture by Scripture within each Testament and between them, and the proper use of Scripture by the church, as typology in the sense defined in chapter 2 of this study. Following Paul Beauchamp[29] Chauvet says, "the Spirit is discovered only if the Letter is not avoided. . . . Each time, it is singular historical destinies that mediate God's revelation: this person (Abraham), this people (Israel), this particular Jew (Jesus) . . . the letter is the socio-historically conditioned deposit of this revelation . . . . in an empirical 'scriptural body'" (p. 215). The letter resists the avoidance of the otherness that it makes present, exactly as in the fourth-century Antiochian theologians' claim that spiritual understanding of Scripture must not oppose the narrative base, the letter (above page 174). Chauvet defines *idol* as something used in the attempt to place God at our disposal, while an *icon* by contrast both conceals and discloses what it mediates; it preserves the *otherness* in the presence of the absence of God:

> If the Scriptures are sacramental in the concreteness of their letter, they are so from an iconic perspective. The letter, in effect, can be the mediation of the revelation of God only to the extent that, as Beauchamp emphasizes, it forms figures. . . . [thus] splitting itself in two: a witness to the "has been" of the creation, the Exodus, or the manna, it is at the same time a witness to the "must be" of a new creation, a new exodus, a new manna . . . . [The letter] is Word in the present only insofar as it is a letter stretched between the past it recounts and future it announces. Consequently it resists any gnostic claim to a full presence (pp. 218–19).

It rejects the removal of the historical distance either by a critical-historical attempt to interpret past events as though they were immediately present in the current culture, or by a literalistic or metaphysical attempt to fit them into a timeless abstract truth immediately present in every age. Chauvet's use of the literal historical body of a past text

---

29. Beauchamp, *le Récit, la lettre et la corps*, (narrative, letter, and body).

figuratively to incite a change in future history, typology as it is called in this study, is in agreement with the Antiochian school, Newman, Dodd, and von Rad, all treated above. In fact, Chauvet quotes from von Rad's *Old Testament Theology*: "each generation finds itself before a task that is always the same and always new—to understand itself as Israel."[30] The New Testament cross and resurrection are such a "new," typologically based on the old. Within the New Testament tradition, they are in turn the basic type for a continuing "new": for each generation the task is to be the Body of Christ, the people of God. Chauvet sees such a changed emphasis in tradition under changed circumstances as similar to the de-emphasis of the conquest by the Deuteronomic and Priestly editors after the loss of the northern kingdom in 721 as compared with earlier creeds with climaxes Deut 26:5-9 "a land flowing with milk and honey" and Josh 24:2-13 "a land on which you had not labored" (pp. 201–2).

Chauvet analyzes the eucharistic prayer as symbolically mediating God's offering the church his relation with it in history, Scripture, and historical Christ—and the church receiving this gift as the sacramental body of Christ in the way Israel received the manna, not as something graspable, but only "in dispossessing themselves of it through the oblation of giving thanks," which is a return gift of being the church, the body of Christ, active in justice and mercy in the world (pp. 278–79). This liturgy is a continuation of Israel's symbolically mediated relation with God—for example, in the equally liturgical offering of firstfruits (Deut 20:1–11), including God's offer to Israel of deliverance from slavery and land on which to produce life-sustaining food, and Israel's offer back to God of Israel's undertaking that Exodus and that sustained life represented by the firstfruits (p. 283).

Chauvet asks, "in view of all this, where is the Christian difference? It does not appear in the process of symbolic exchange, which functions in both cases according to the same fundamental mechanism" (p. 286). The difference, he says, is eschatological: it is between *oldness* and *newness*. Oldness and newness are not to be identified with the Old and New Testaments, "for newness already cut across the Old Testament: let us recall especially the prophets, the summary of the Law that the scribe gives Jesus, the followers of the Baptist, many Pharisaic rabbis, . . . . did

---

30. Von Rad, *Théologie de l'Ancien Testament*, 1:109 [*Old Testament Theology*, 1.119]; Chauvet, *Symbol and Sacrament*, 201.

not the Spirit 'speak through the prophets'?" (p. 286). The difference is whether Israel and the Church are doing their job:

> [T]he hinge that both links and distinguishes one from the other [newness from oldness] in our biblical canon represents, *from the viewpoint of the Bible itself*, the task enjoined on *all humanity* taken collectively, as on each one taken personally. According to the Bible, what is at work for Israel is representative of what must be at work for all the nations: the blessing of Abraham is concluded with the blessing of the nations ("in you the families of the earth shall be blessed") according to the promise of Genesis 12:3, repeated in Genesis 18:18 and 22:18, renewed to Isaac (26:4), then to Jacob (28:14), and declared accomplished in Galatians 3:8 and Acts 3.23.... In the priestly tradition ... the blessing of humankind, created "male and female" in the image of God in Genesis 1:27–28, is repeated to Noah and his sons (9:1–7) and is accompanied by a covenant with all of humanity through Noah (9:9–17). Still, it is always through Abraham's descendants that this divine blessing reaches the peoples. The Psalms insist on this: ... (Ps 96:10) ... (Ps 127). So that, if "yes, it is in Philistia, in Tyre, or in Nubia that a person was born," then one can say of Zion, "in her, every person is born" (see Ps 87:4–5) .... Election is a particular choice, but it is not the exclusion of others. It is simply the condition of every love, for there is no love without a choice.... In the symbolic order, there is no universality except in the concrete mediation of the particular (pp. 288–89).

For Chauvet symbol is metonymic, not allegorical.

Chauvet uses later Heidegger and his followers in French philosophy to support his rejection of classical metaphysics. He quotes Heidegger: "where the word is lacking, there is no thing. Only the available word confers being on the thing."[31] Later Heidegger's significant innovation is placing language above the individual as mediator of Being rather than below it as expression of thought (above, page 41). But this Being is still abstract, a Platonic ghost. Chauvet says, "the German philosopher does not remain any less, through his very act of climbing back toward the origin—even if this origin is impossible to name as such—a prisoner of metaphysics" (p. 142, n.). But Chauvet *does* name this origin, does specify the unspecified. His communal orientation frees him to replace Heidegger's abstract *Being* with *human community*, Heidegger's language-

---

31. Heidegger, *Acheminement vers la parole*, 207. [*On the Way to Language*, 141], Chauvet, *Symbol and Sacrament*, 55.

as-mediation-of-Being with language-as-mediation-of-community, to replace Heidegger's claimed pre-Socratic internal relation of the self with abstract Being with biblical internal relation of the individual with community. Symbol and language are at the heart of human community, as in Wittgenstein's "The *speaking* of language is part of an activity, or of a form of life" (above, page 47). And Chauvet says, "The communication of grace is to be understood, not according to the 'metaphysical' scheme of cause and effect, but according to the symbolic scheme of communication through language, a communication supremely effective because it is through language that the subject comes forth in its relations to other subjects within a common 'world' of meaning" (pp. 139–40)—that communal world unreachable by phenomenalist early Heidegger (above, page 37).

A *transcendent* God does not violate the *immanent* humanity he endowed with community, diversity, creativity, and authority (Gen 1:27–28), and encouraged to create language (Gen 2:19). Rather, he relates with it by *immanent* incarnate anthropological means through the historical human community as *body*, particularly through the called community body common to the two Testaments through symbolic mediation of its *Scriptures, sacraments*, and witness of *diaconia*, three internally relating components in the symbolic structure of this and any other anonymous or potential community internally related with this God.

# Bibliography

Adams, Doug. *Meeting House to Camp Meeting*. Austin: The Sharing Company, 1981.
Adams, Doug, and Alexander Blair. "Changing Biblical Imagery and American Identity in Seventeenth and Eighteenth Century Sermons and Arts." In *Papers of the Annual Meeting, Academy of Homiletics*, 1–10. Atlanta: American Academy of Homiletics, 1982.
Ames, William. *The Substance of Christian Religion, or a plain and easie Draught of the Christian Catechisme, in LII Lectures, on chosen Texts of Scripture, for each Lord's Day of the Year, Learnedly and Perspicuously Illustrated with Doctrines, Reasons, and Uses*. London: Thomas Davies, 1659.
Amsler, Samuel. *L'Ancien Testament dans l'Église: Essai d'herméneutique chrétienne*. Neuchâtel: Delachaux et Niestlé, 1960.
Anderson, Bernhard W. "Exodus Typology in Second Isaiah." In *Israel's Prophetic Heritage: Essays in honor of James Muilenburg*. New York: Harper & Bros., 1962.
Andrewes, Lancelot. "A Sermon Preached before the King's Majesty at Whitehall, on the Thirteenth of April, A.D. MCCXXIII., being Easter-Day." In *Works*, 3:60–79. Oxford: Parker, 1854.
———. "Upon the Third Commandment, Preached in the Parish Church of St. Giles, Cripplegate, on the Eleventh of June, A.D. MDXCII." In *Works*, 5:71–81. Oxford: Parker, 1854.
Antoncich, Ricardo. "Hermeneutical Problems of the Social Documents of the Church: Private Property." In *Resource Service II*, 5. Chicago: Jesuit Project for Third World Awareness, 1975. Lectures on the Latin American Hermeneutic of Christian Faith, at the Jesuit schools of theology in Chicago and Berkeley.
Apel, Karl-Otto. "Wissenschaft als Emanzipation? Eine Kritische Würdigung der Wissenschaftskonzeption der 'Kritischen Theorie.'" In *Zeitschrift für allgemeine Wissenschaftstheorie* 1 (1970): 173–95.
*The Apocrypha and Pseudepigrapha of the Old Testament in English*. Edited by R. H. Charles. 2 vols. Oxford: Clarendon, 1913.
Aristotle. *De anima*. Oxford: Clarendon, 1993.
———. *De interpretatione*. Oxford: Clarendon, 1908–1952.
———. *Nicomachean Ethics*. Oxford: Clarendon, 1908–1952.
Assmann, Hugo. "The Power of Christ in History: Conflicting Christologies and Discernment." In *Frontiers of Theology in Latin America*, edited by Rosino Gibellini. Maryknoll: Orbis, 1979. [*La nuova frontiera della teologia in America Latina*. Brescia: Queriniana, 1975.]
Augustine. *The City of God*. [*De civitate Dei*.] New York: Modern Library, 1950.
———. *Confessions*. [*Confessiones*.] Harmondsworth: Penguin, 1961.
———. *De gratia Christi, et de peccato originali, contra Pelagium*. In *NPNF* 5.
———. *De gratia et libero arbitrio*. In *FOTC* 59.

———. *De nuptiis et concupiscientia.* In *NPNF* 5.
———. *De peccatorum meritis et remissione, et de baptismo parvulorum.* In *NPNF* 5.
———. *De praedestinatione sanctorum.* In *FOTC* 86.
———. *De spiritu et littera.* In *NPNF* 5.
———. *De utilitate credendi.* In *Augustine: Earlier Writings*, 291–323. Philadelphia: Westminster, 1953.
———. *Epistola* 145. In *FOTC* 20.
———. *In Ioannis evangelium tractatus.* In *FOTC* 78, 79, 88, 90, 92.
———. *On Christian Doctrine.* [*De doctrina Christiana.*] Indianapolis: Bobbs-Merrill, 1958.
Austin, John L. *How to Do Things with Words.* The William James Lectures, 1955. Cambridge: Harvard University Press, 1962. 2nd ed. 1975.
Barr, James. *Old and New in Interpretation: A Study of the Two Testaments.* London: SCM, 1966.
Barrett, C. K. "The Interpretation of the Old Testament in the New." In *Cambridge History of the Bible I: From the Beginnings to Jerome.* Cambridge: Cambridge University Press, 1970.
Barth, Karl. *Church Dogmatics.* Edinburgh: T. & T. Clark, 1936–1977. [*Die Kirchliche Dogmatik.* Zollikon: Evangelischer Verlag, 1939–1967.]
———. *The Epistle to the Romans.* London: Oxford University Press, 1933. [*Der Römerbrief.* 1st ed., Bern: G. A. Bäschlin, 1919; Zurich: Theologischer Verlag, 1985. 2nd ed., Munich: Kaiser, 1922. 6th ed., 1928.]
———. "Evangelium und Socializmus." In *Vorträge und kleinere arbeiten 1909–1914*, 732. Zurich: Theologische Verlag, 1993. Lecture at the worker's union Küngolingen February 1, 1914.
———. "Jesus Christ and the Movement for Social Justice." In *Karl Barth and Radical Politics*, edited by George Hunsinger, 19–45. Philadelphia: Westminster, 1976. ["Jesus Christus und die soziale Bewegung." In *Vorträge und kleinere arbeiten 1909–1914*, 386–409. Zurich: Theologische Verlag, 1993.]
———. "Rudolf Bultmann—An Attempt to Understand Him." In *Kerygma and Myth: A Theological Debate* 2. London: SPCK, 1962. [*Rudolf Bultmann: ein Versuch, ihn zu verstehen.* Zollikon: Evangelischer Verlag, 1952.]
———. *The Word of God and the Word of Man.* Gloucester: Smith, 1978. ["Die neue Welt in der Bibel." *Das Wort Gottes und die Theologie.* Munich: Kaiser, 1924.]
Baumgärtel, Friedrich. "The Hermeneutical Problem of the Old Testament." In *Essays on Old Testament Hermeneutics*, edited by Claus Westermann, 2nd ed., 134–59. Richmond: John Knox, 1964. [*Probleme Alttestamentlicher Hermeneutik.* Munich: Chr. Kaiser, 1960.]
———. *Verheissung: Zur Frage des evangelischen Verständnisses des Alten Testaments.* Gütersloh: Bertelsmann, 1952.
Baur, Ferdinand C. "Über Zweck und Veranlassung des Römerbriefs und die damit zusammenhängenden Verhältnisse der römischen Gemeinde." *Tübinger Zeitschrift für Theologie* 3 (1836): 59–178.
Baxandall, Michael. *Patterns of Intention: On the Historical Explanation of Pictures.* New Haven: Yale University Press, 1985.
Beauchamp, Paul. *le Récit, la lettre et la corps.* Paris: Cerf, 1982.
Beker, J. Christiaan. *Paul the Apostle: The Triumph of God in Life and Thought.* Philadelphia: Fortress, 1980.

Betz, Hans Dieter. "The Concept of Apocalyptic in the Theology of the Pannenberg Group." In *Apocalypticism*, 192-207. *Journal for Theology and the Church* 6. New York: Herder & Herder, 1969.
The Bible. *The Holy Bible: New Revised Standard Version*. New York: American Bible Society, 1989.
Biehl, Peter. "Zur Frage nach dem historischen Jesus." *Theologische Rundschau, N.F.* 24 (1957-1958): 54-76.
Blenkinsopp, Joseph. *Prophecy and Canon: A Contribution to the Study of Jewish Origins.* Notre Dame: University of Notre Dame Press, 1977.
Boff, Leonardo. "Christ's Liberation via Oppression: An Attempt at Theological Construction from the Standpoint of Latin America." In *Frontiers of Theology in Latin America*, edited by Rosino Gibellini, 100-32. Maryknoll: Orbis, 1979. [*La nuova frontiera della teologia in America Latina*. Brescia: Queriniana, 1975.]
Böhler, Dietrich. "Zum problem des emanzipatorischen Interesses und seiner gesellschaftlichen Wahrnehmung." *Man and World* 3.2 (May 1970): 26-53.
Bousset, Wilhelm. *Die Religion des Judentum im neutestamentlichen Zeitalter*. Berlin: Reuther und Reichard, 1902.
Brown, Peter. *Augustine of Hippo*. Berkeley: University of California Press, 1967.
Brown, Raymond E. *The Gospel According to John*. The Anchor Bible. Garden City: Doubleday, 1966-1970.
Brown, Raymond E. and John P. Meier. *Antioch and Rome*. New York: Paulist, 1983.
Brueggemann, Walter. "A Convergence in Recent Old Testament Theologies." *JSOT* 18 (1980): 2-18.
Buber, Martin. "The Baal-Shem-Tov's Instruction on Intercourse with God." In *Hasidism and Modern Man*. New York: Horizon, 1958. [*Das Baal-Schem-Tow Unterweisung im Umgang mit Gott*. Hellerau: Hegner, 1927.]
———. *Daniel: Dialogues on Realization*. New York: Holt, Rinehart & Winston, 1964. *Daniel: Gespräche von der Verwirklichung*. Leipzig: Insel, 1913.
———. "Dialogue." In *Between Man and Man*. London: Kegan Paul, 1947. [*Zwiesprache*. Berlin: Schocken, 1932.]
———. *Die Schrift*. Translation of the Hebrew Bible by Martin Buber assisted by Franz Rosenzweig. Cologne: Jakob Hegner, 1954-1961.
———. "Ekstase und Bekenntnis." Introduction to *Ekstatische Konfessionen*. New edition, Leipzig: Insel Verlag, 1921. Original edition, Jena: Eugen Diedrichs, 1909.
———. *I and Thou*. Edinburgh: T. & T. Clark, 1937. [*Ich und Du*. Leipzig: Insel-Verlag, 1923.]
———. *Kingship of God*. New York: Harper & Row, 1967. [*Königtum Gottes*. Berlin: Schocken, 1932.]
———. *The Legend of the Baal-Shem*. New York: Harper & Row, 1955. [*Die Legende des Baalschem*. Frankfurt: Rütten & Loening, 1908.]
———. *Moses*. Oxford: East West Library, 1946. [*Moses*. Heidelberg: Lambert Schneider, 1952.]
———. "My Way to Hasidism." In *Hasidism and Modern Man*. New York: Horizon, 1958. [*Mein Weg zum Chassidismus: Erinnerungen*. Frankfurt: Rütten & Loening, 1918.]
———. *Paths in Utopia*. London: Routledge & Kegan Paul, 1949. [*Pfade in Utopie*. Heidelberg: Lambert Schneider, 1950.]

———. "Postscript." In *I and Thou*, 2nd ed. New York: Scribner's, 1958. ["Nachwort." In Nachlese. Heidelberg: Schneider, 1965.]

———. *The Prophetic Faith*. Translated from the Hebrew. New York: Macmillan, 1949.

———. "The Question to the Single One." In *Between Man and Man*. New York: MacMillan, 1965. ["Die Frage an den Einzelnen." In *Werke I, Schriften zur Philosophie*. Munich: Kösel, 1962.] 1936 elaboration of address at three German-Swiss universities in 1933.

———. "Über Jakob Boehme." *Weiner Rundschau* 5 (1901): 251–53.

———. "What is Man?" In *Between Man and Man*. New York: MacMillan, 1965.

———. "The Word that is Spoken." In *The Knowledge of Man*. New York: Harper & Row, 1965. ["Das Wort, das gesprochen wird" (1960). In *Beiträge zu einer philosophischen Anthropologie*. Werke I. Munich: Kösel, 1962.]

Bultmann, Rudolf. *The History of the Synoptic Tradition*. Rev. ed. New York: Harper & Row, 1963. [*Die Geschichte der synoptischen Tradition*. Göttingen: Vandenhoeck & Ruprecht, 1921, 3rd. ed. with Ergänzungsheft, 1957–1958.]

———. *Jesus Christ and Mythology*. New York: Charles Scribner's Sons, 1958. Schaffer Lectures, Yale Divinity School, and Cole Lectures, Vanderbilt University, 1951.

———. "Karl Barth's *Epistle to the Romans* in its second edition." In *The Beginnings of Dialectic Theology*, edited by James M. Robinson, 1:100–20. Richmond: John Knox, 1968. ["Karl Barths *Römerbrief* in Zweiter Auflage." In *Anfänge der dialektischen Theologie*, 1:119–42. Munich: Chr. Kaiser, 1962–1963. From *Christliche Welt* 36 (1922): 320–23, 330–34, 358–61, 369–73.]

———. "Liberal Theology and the Newest Theological Movement." In *Faith and Understanding*. New York: Harper & Row, 1969. ["Die liberale Theologie und die jüngste theologische Bewegung." *Theologische Blätter* 3 (1924) 73–86. Reprinted in *Glauben und Verstehen: Gesammelte Aufsätze*, 1:1–25. Tübingen: J. C. B. Mohr, 1933.]

———. "New Testament and Mythology." In *Kerygma and Myth*, edited by Hans Werner Bartsch, 1–44. New York: Harper & Row, 1961. ["Neues Testament und Mythologie." In *Kerygma und Mythos*, 1:15–48. Hamburg-Volksdorf: Herbert Reich, 1948.]

———. "Prophecy and Fulfillment." In *Essays Philosophical and Theological*, 182–208. London: SCM; New York: Macmillan, 1955. Also in *Essays on Old Testament Hermeneutics*, edited by Claus Westermann, 2nd ed., 50–75. Richmond: John Knox, 1964. ["Weissagung und Erfüllung." In *Glauben Und Verstehen: Gesammelte Aufsätze* 2. Tübingen: J. C. B. Mohr, 1952.]

———. "The Significance of the Old Testament for the Christian Faith." In *The Old Testament and Christian Faith: A Theological Discussion*, edited by Bernhard W. Anderson, 8–35. New York: Harper & Row, 1963. ["Die Bedeutung des Alten Testaments für den christlichen Glauben." In *Glauben und Verstehen: gesammelte Aufsätze* 1. Tübingen: J. C. B. Mohr, 1933.]

———. *Theology of the New Testament*. New York: Charles Scribner's Sons, 1951–1955. [*Theologie des Neuen Testaments*. Tübingen: J. C. B. Mohr, 1948–1951.]

———. "Ursprung und Sinn der Typologie als hermeneutischer Methode." *Theologische Literaturzeitung* 75 (1950), cols. 205–12.

Cahill, P. Joseph. "Hermeneutical Implications of Typology." *CBQ* 44 (1982): 266–281.

Cartwright, Thomas. *A Commentary vpon the Epistle of Saint Paule written to the Colossians. Preached by Thomas Cartwright, and now Published for the further vse of the Church of God*. London: Nicholas Okes, 1612.

Chauvet, Louis-Marie. *Symbol and Sacrament: A sacramental reinterpretation of Christian existence*. Collegeville: Liturgical, 1995. [*Symbole et sacrement: Un relecture sacramentelle de l'existence chrétienne*. Paris: Cerf, 1987.]
Childs, Brevard S. *Biblical Theology in Crisis*. Philadelphia: Westminster, 1970.
Chomsky, Noam. *Reflections on Language*. New York: Pantheon, 1975.
Clement of Alexandria. *Stromata*. Book 3 in *Alexandrian Christianity: Selected Translations of Clement and Origen*. The Library of Christian Classics, vol. 2, 40–92. London: SCM, 1954.
Clement of Rome. *The First Epistle of Clement to the Corinthians*. In *The Apostolic Fathers I*. Loeb Classical Library. Cambridge: Harvard University Press, 1952.
Collins, John J. "The 'Historical Character' of the Old Testament in Recent Biblical Theology." *CBQ* 41 (1979): 185–204.
———. "Introduction: Towards the Morphology of a Genre." In *Apocalypse: The Morphology of a Genre*, Semeia 14, 1–20. Missoula: SBL, 1979.
Cone, James. *A Black Theology of Liberation*. Philadelphia: Lippincott, 1970.
Conzelmann, Hans. "Jesus Christus." In *Die Religion in Geschichte und Gegenwart: Handwörterbuch für Theologie und Religionswissenschaft*, 3rd ed., vol. 3, (*RGG³*), cols 619–53. Tübingen: J. C. B. Mohr, 1957–1965.
———. *Jesus: The classic article from RGG³ expanded and updated*. Philadelphia: Fortress, 1973.
Cotton, John. Exchange of letters with Richard Saltonstall. In *A Collection of Original Papers Relative to the History of the Colony of Massachusets-Bay*, edited by Thomas Hutchinson, 2:127–34. Boston: T. & J. Fleet, 1769; reprinted Albany, 1865.
———. *God's Promise to his Plantations*. London: John Bellamy, 1630.
———. "The Life of Faith." In *The Way of Life*, 255–481. London: L. Fawne & S. Gellibrand, 1641.
Cox, Harvey. *The Secular City*. New York: Macmillan, 1966.
Cross, Frank Moore. *Canaanite Myth and Hebrew Epic: Essays in the History of the Religion of Israel*. Cambridge: Harvard University Press, 1973.
Crossan, John Dominic. *In Parables: The Challenge of the Historical Jesus*. New York: Harper & Row, 1973.
Cullmann, Oscar. *Christ and Time: The Primitive Christian Conception of Time and History*. Rev. ed. Philadelphia: Westminster, 1964. [*Christus und die Zeit*. Zollikon: Evangelischer Verlag, 1946.]
Daly, Mary. *Beyond God the Father: Toward a Philosophy of Women's Liberation*. Boston: Beacon, 1973.
———. *Gyn/Ecology: The Metaethics of Radical Feminism*. Boston: Beacon, 1978.
Daniélou, Jean. *Origen*. London: Sheed & Ward, 1955. [*Origène*. Paris: La Table Ronde, 1948.]
*The Dead Sea Scrolls in English*. Translated by Géza Vermès. Harmondsworth: Penguin, 1962.
Descartes, René. *Discourse on Method*. Chicago: Open Court, 1907. In *The Rationalists*. Garden City: Anchor Books, 1974. [*Discours de la methode pour bien conduite sa raison, et chercher la verité dans les sciences*. Leyden: Ian Maire, 1637.]
———. *Meditations*. Chicago: Open Court, 1901. In *The Rationalists*. Garden City: Anchor Books, 1974. [*Meditationes de prima philosophia in qua Dei existentia et animae immortalitas demonstratur*. Paris: Michael Soly, 1641.]

Devreesse, Robert. *Essai sur Théodore de Mopsueste*. Studi e Testi no. 141. Vatican: Biblioteca Apostolica Vaticana, 1948.

Dilthey, Wilhelm. *Der Aufbau der Geschichtlichen Welt in den Geisteswissenschaften*. In *Diltheys Gesammelte Schriften* 7. Leipzig: B. G. Teubner, 1927.

Diodore of Tarsus. *In Psalmum*. The preface and the prologue to Psalm 118 in "Extraits du Commentaire de Diodore de Tarse sur les Psaumes," edited by Louis Marès. *Recherches de Science Religieuse* 9 (1919): 79–101.

Dodd, C. H. *According to the Scriptures: The Sub-Structure of New Testament Theology*. London: Nisbet; New York: Charles Scribner's Sons, 1953.

———. *The Parables of the Kingdom*. Welwyn: Nisbet, 1935.

Dussel, Enrique. *History and the Theology of Liberation: A Latin American Perspective*. Maryknoll: Orbis, 1976. [*Caminos de liberación latinoamericana I: Interpretación histórica de nuestro continente latinoamericano*. Buenos Aires: Latinoamerica Libros, 1972. Presented at archdiocesan conference of Religious, Buenos Aires, 1971.]

Edwards, Jonathan. *Christ the great Example of Gospel Ministers. A Sermon Preach'd at Portsmouth, At the Ordination of the Reverend Mr. Job Strong, To the Pastoral Office over the South Church in that Place, June 28, 1749*. Boston: T. Fleet, 1750.

Eichrodt, Walther. "Is Typological Exegesis an Appropriate Method?" In *Essays on Old Testament Hermeneutics*, edited by Claus Westermann, 2nd ed., 224–45. Richmond: John Knox, 1964. ["Ist die typologische Exegese sachgemässe Exegese?" *Vetus Testamentum*, Supplement 4 (1957): 161–80. In *Probleme Alttestamentlicher Hermeneutik*. Munich: Chr. Kaiser, 1960.]

———. *Theology of the Old Testament*. Philadelphia: Westminster, 1961–1967. [*Theologie des Alten Testaments*. 6th, 5th ed. Stuttgart: Ehrenfried Klotz, 1959–1964.]

Ellis, E. Earle. *Paul's Use of the Old Testament*. Edinburgh: Oliver & Boyd, 1957.

Enoch. *The Ethiopic Book of Enoch*. 2 volumes. Vol. 2 Introduction, Translation, and Commentary by Michael A. Knibb. Oxford: Clarendon, Oxford University Press, 1978.

*The Fathers of the Church*. (FOTC). New York and Washington: Catholic University of America Press, 1947–.

Feuerbach, Ludwig. *The Essence of Christianity*. New York: Calvin Blanchard, 1855.

Frege, Gottlob. *Begriffsschrift: eine der arithmetischen nachgebildete Formelsprache des reinen Denkens*. Halle: L. Nebert, 1879. §§1–12 in *Translations from the Philosophical Writings of Gottlob Frege*, 1–20. Oxford: Basil Blackwell, 1952.

———. "Boole's Logical Calculus and the Concept-script." In *Posthumous Writings*, 9–46. Chicago: University of Chicago Press, 1979. [*Nachgelassene Schriften und wissenschaftlicher Briefwechsel* 1. Hamburg: Felix Meiner, 1969.]

———. "Logic." In *Posthumous Writings*, 1–8. Chicago: University of Chicago Press, 1979. [*Nachgelassene Schriften und wissenschaftlicher Briefwechsel* 1. Hamburg: Felix Meiner, 1969.]

———. "On Sense and Reference." In *Translations from the Philosophical Writings of Gottlob Frege*, 56–78. Oxford: Basil Blackwell, 1952. ["Über Sinn und Bedeutung." *Zeitschrift für Philosophie und philosophische Kritik* 100 (1892): 25–50.]

———. "The Thought: A Logical Inquiry." *Mind* 65 (1956): 289–311. Reprinted in *Philosophical Logic*, edited by P. F. Strawson, 17–38. Oxford: Oxford University Press, 1967. ["Der Gedanke. Eine logische Untersuchung." *Beitrage zur Philosophie des deutschen Idealismus* 1 (1918–1919): 58–77.]

Frye, Northrop. *Creation and Recreation*. Toronto: University of Toronto Press, 1980.

Gadamer, Hans-Georg. *Hegel's Dialectic*. New Haven: Yale University Press, 1976. [*Hegels Dialektik*. Tübingen: J. C. B. Mohr, 1971.]

———. "On the Scope and Function of Hermeneutical Reflection." *Continuum* 8 (1970): 77–95. Also in Gadamer, *Philosophical Hermeneutics*, edited by David E. Linge, 18–43. Berkeley: University of California, 1976. ["Rhetorik, Hermeneutik und Ideologie-kritik: Metakritische Erörterungen zu *Wahrheit und Methode*." In *Kleine Schriften*, 1:113–30. Tübingen: J. C. B. Mohr, 1967.]

———. *Truth and Method*. New York: Continuum, 1999. [*Wahrheit und Methode*. Tübingen: J. C. B. Mohr, 1960; 5th ed. (*Gesammelte Werke* I), 1986.]

Galilea, Segundo. "Liberation Theology and New Tasks Facing Christians." In *Frontiers of Theology in Latin America*, 163–83. Maryknoll: Orbis, 1979. [*La nuova frontiera della teologia in America Latina*. Brescia: Queriniana, 1975.]

Goppelt, Leonhard. *Typos: The Typological Interpretation of the Old Testament in the New*. Grand Rapids: William B. Eerdmans, 1982. [*Typos: Die Typologische Deutung des Alten Testaments im Neuen*. Gütersloh: Gerd Mohn, 1939. Reprint, Darmstadt: Wissenschaftliche Buchgesellschaft, 1966. Chapters 1–9 PhD diss., Erlangen; Chapter 10 "Apokalyptik und Typologie bei Paulus." *ThLZ* 89 (1964), cols. 321–44.]

Gottwald, Norman K. *The Tribes of Yahweh: A Sociology of the Religion of Liberated Israel, 1250–1050 BCE* Maryknoll: Orbis, 1979.

Grant, R. M. *The Letter and the Spirit*. London: SPCK, 1957.

Gunkel, Hermann, and J. Begrich. *Einleitung in die Psalmen*. Göttingen: Vandenhoeck & Ruprecht, 1933.

Gutiérrez, Gustavo. "Hacia una teología de la liberación." A paper presented at the Encuentro Nacional del Movimiento Sacerdotal ONIS, July 1968, Chimbote, Peru. Montevideo: Centro de Documentación MIEC-JEIC, 1969.

———. *A Theology of Liberation*. Maryknoll: Orbis, 1973. [*Teología de la liberación: Perspectivas*. Lima: CEP, 1971.]

Habermas, Jürgen. *Knowledge and Human Interests*. Boston: Beacon, 1971. [*Erkenntnis und Interesse*. Frankfurt: Suhrkamp, 1968.]

———. "A Postscript to *Knowledge and Human Interests*." *Philosophy of the Social Sciences* 3 (1975) 157–189. [The postscript to the paperback edition, *Erkenntnis und Interesse: Mit einem neuen Nachwort*, 367–417. Frankfurt: Suhrkamp, 1973.]

———. "A Review of Gadamer's *Truth and Method*." In *Understanding and Social Inquiry*, edited by Fred R. Dallmayr and Thomas A. McCarthy, 335–63. Notre Dame: University of Notre Dame Press, 1977. [*Zur Logik der Sozialwissenschaften*, *Philosophische Rundschau* 14, Beiheft 5 (1967): 149–80.]

———. "Summation and Response" [to Gadamer's "On the Scope and Function of Hermeneutical Reflection"]. *Continuum* 8 (1970): 123–33.

———. *Theory and Practice*. Boston: Beacon, 1973. [Author's abridgment of *Theorie und Praxis*. 4th ed. Frankfurt: Suhrkamp, 1971.]

———. "What is Universal Pragmatics?" In *Communication and the Evolution of Society*, 1–68. Boston: Beacon, 1979. ["Was heisst Universalpragmatik." In *Sprachpragmatik und Philosophie*, edited by Karl-Otto Apel. Frankfurt: Suhrkamp, 1976.]

Haevernick, H. A. C. *Vorlesungen über die Theologie des Alten Testaments*. Edited by H. A. Hahn. Erlangen: Heyder & Zimmer, 1848.

Hanson, Paul D. "Apocalypticism." In *Interpreters Dictionary of the Bible, Supplementary Volume*, 28–34. Nashville: Abingdon, 1976.

———. *The Dawn of Apocalyptic: The Historical and Sociological Roots of Jewish Apocalyptic Eschatology*. Philadelphia: Fortress, 1975; rev. ed. 1979.

———. *Dynamic Transcendence: The Correlation of Confessional Heritage and Contemporary Experience in a Biblical Model of Divine Activity*. Philadelphia: Fortress, 1978.

———. "The Theological Significance of Contradiction within the Book of the Covenant." In *Canon and Authority*, edited by George Coats and Burke Long, 110–31. Philadelphia: Fortress, 1977.

Hanson, R. P. C. *Allegory and Event: A Study of the Sources and Significance of Origen's Interpretation of Scripture*. London: SCM, 1959.

———. "Biblical Exegesis in the Early Church." In *CHB* 1:412–53. Cambridge: Cambridge University Press, 1970.

Harnack, Adolf von. *The History of Dogma*. New York: Dover, 1961. *Lehrbuch der Dogmengeschichte*. 3rd ed. Freiburg I. B.: J. C. B. Mohr, 1894. 1st. ed. 1885.

———. *Marcion: Das Evangelium vom Fremden Gott*. Leipzig: Hinrichs, 1921.

———. *What is Christianity?* New York: Harper & Bros., 1957. [*Das Wesen des Christentums*. Leipzig: Hinrichs, 1900.]

Hasel, Gerhard F. "A Decade of Old Testament Theology: Retrospect and Prospect." *Zeitschrift für die Alttestamentliche Wissenschaft* 93 (1981): 165–83.

———. *Old Testament Theology: Basic Issues in the Current Debate*. Rev. ed. Grand Rapids: Eerdmans, 1975.

———. *The Remnant: The History and Theology of the Remnant Idea from Genesis to Isaiah*. Berrian Springs: Andrews University, 1972. A revision of "The Origin and Early History of the Remnant Motif in Ancient Israel," dissertation, Vanderbilt University, 1970.

Hauerwas, Stanley. *A Community of Character: Toward a Constructive Christian Social Ethic*. Notre Dame: University of Notre Dame Press, 1981.

———. *The Peaceable Kingdom*. Notre Dame: University of Notre Dame Press, 1983.

Hebert, A. G. "Introduction." In *The Root of the Vine: Essays in Biblical Theology*, by Anton Fridrichsen et al. New York: Philosophical Library, 1953.

Hegel, Georg W. F. *Logic*. Part I of *Encyclopaedia of the Philosophical Sciences*. Oxford: Clarendon, 1975. [*Encyclopädie der philosophischen Wissenschaften in Grundrisse I, Die Logik*, 3rd ed. Heidelberg: Osswald, 1830.]

———. *Phenomenology of Spirit*. Oxford: Clarendon, 1977. [*Phänomenologie des Geistes*. Hamburg: Felix Meiner, 1952.]

Heidegger, Martin. *Being and Time*. New York: Harper and Row, 1962. [*Sein und Zeit*. 7th ed. Tübingen: Neomarius, 1953.]

———. *Hegel's Phenomenology of Spirit*. Bloomington: Indiana University Press, 1988. [*Hegels Phänomenologie des Geistes*. Frankfurt: Klostermann, 1980. Lectures at University of Freiburg, 1930–1931.]

———. *Identity and Difference*. Bilingual edition. New York: Harper & Row, 1969. [*Identität und Differenz*. Pfullingen: Neske, 1957.]

———. *An Introduction to Metaphysics*. New Haven: Yale University Press, 1959. [*Einführung in die Metaphysik*. Tübingen: Max Niemeyer, 1953. Lectures at University of Freiburg, 1935.]

———. "Language." In *Poetry, Language, Thought*. New York: Harper & Row, 1971. [Lecture at Bühlerhöhe, 1950. Part of *Unterwegs zur Sprache*. Pfullingen: Neske, 1959.]

———. "Letter on Humanism." In *Martin Heidegger, Basic Writings*. New York: Harper & Row, 1977. ["Brief über den Humanismus." In *Wegmarken*. Frankfurt: Klostermann, 1967. *Brief über den "Humanismus."* Bern: Francke, 1947.]

———. "Nachwort zu: 'Was ist Metaphysik?'" In *Wegmarken*. Frankfurt: Klostermann, 1967. In *Existence and Being*. Chicago: Regnery, 1949.

———. *On the Way to Language*. NewYork, Harper & Row, 1971. [*Unterwegs zur Sprache*. Pfullingen: Neske, 1959.] [*Acheminement vers la parole*. Paris: Gallimard, 1976.]

———. "What is Metaphysics?" In *Martin Heidegger, Basic Writings*. New York: Harper & Row: 1977. ["Was ist Metaphysik?" In *Wegmarken*. Frankfurt: Klostermann, 1967.]

Hengel, Martin. *Judaism and Hellenism: Studies in their Encounter in Palestine during the Early Hellenistic Period*. Philadelphia: Fortress, 1974. [*Judentum und Hellenismus: Studien zu ihrer Begegnung unter besonderer Berücksichtigung Palästinas bis zur Mitte des 2 Jh.s v. Chr.* 2nd ed. Tübingen: J. C. B. Mohr, 1973. A revision of the author's Habilitationsschrift at Tübingen, 1966.]

Hobbes, Thomas. *Leviathan*. London: Andrew Crooke, 1651. Reprint with 1651 pagination indicated, Harmondsworth: Penguin, 1981.

Hobbs, Edward. "Norman Perrin on Methodology in the Interpretation of Mark." In *Christology and a Modern Pilgrimage*, edited by Hans Dieter Betz, 79–91. Missoula: SBL, 1971.

Hooker, Richard. *A Remedy against Sorrow and Fear: Delivered in a Funeral Sermon*. Oxford: Jos. Barnes, 1612. Reprinted in *Works*, edited by John Keble, 7th ed., 3:643–53. Oxford: Clarendon, 1888.

Howard, Roy J. *Three Faces of Hermeneutics: An Introduction to Current Theories of Understanding*. Berkeley: University of California Press, 1982.

Hume, David. *Enquiry into the Human Understanding*, 1748. Reprinted as "An Enquiry Concerning Human Understanding." In *Essays and Treatises on Several Subjects*, vol. 2. London: T. Cadell, 1777.

Irenaeus. *Contra Haereses*. In *Ante-Nicene Christian Library* 5. Edinburgh: T. & T. Clark, 1874.

Jakobson, Roman. "Two Aspects of Language and Two Types of Aphasic Disturbances." In *Fundamentals of Language*, by Roman Jakobson and Morris Halle. The Hague: Mouton, 1956.

Jeremias, Joachim. "Paulus als Hillelit." In *Neotestamentica et Semitica: Studies in Honour of Matthew Black*, edited by E. Earle Ellis and Max Wilcox, 88–94. Edinburgh: T. & T. Clark, 1969.

Johnson, Roger A. *The Origins of Demythologizing: Philosophy and Historiography in the Theology of Rudolf Bultmann*. Leiden: E. J. Brill, 1974.

Jonas, Hans. *Gnosis und spätantiker Geist*. Göttingen: Vandenhoeck & Ruprecht, 1934–1954.

———. *The Gnostic Religion*. 2nd ed. Boston: Beacon, 1963.

Kant, Immanuel. *Critique of Practical Reason*. Indianapolis: Bobs-Merrill, 1956. [*Kritik der praktischen Vernunft*. Riga: Johann Friedrich Hartknoch, 1788.]

———. *Critique of Pure Reason.* Cambridge: Cambridge University Press, 1997. [*Critik der reinen Vernunft.* Riga: Johann Friedrich Hartknoch, 1781, and 2nd ed. 1787.]

———. "What is Enlightenment?" In *Critique of Practical Reason and other writings in Moral Philosophy*, 286–92. Chicago: University of Chicago Press, 1949. ["Zur Beantwortung der Frage: Was ist Aufklärung?" *Berlinische Monatsschrift*, December, 1784.]

Käsemann, Ernst. "The Beginnings of Christian Theology." In *New Testament Questions of Today*, 82–107. London: SCM, 1969; Philadelphia: Fortress, 1969. [A part of *Exegetische Versuche und Besinnungen* 2, 2nd ed. Göttingen: Vandenhoeck & Ruprecht, 1965.]

———. *Essays on New Testament Themes.* London: SCM, 1964; Philadelphia: Fortress, 1982. [A part of *Exegetische Versuche und Besinnungen* 1, 2nd ed. Göttingen: Vandenhoeck & Ruprecht, 1960.]

———. *New Testament Questions of Today.* London: SCM, 1969; Philadelphia: Fortress, 1969. [A part of *Exegetische Versuche und Besinnungen* 2, 2nd ed. Göttingen: Vandenhoeck & Ruprecht, 1965.]

———. "On the Subject of Primitive Christian Apocalyptic." In *New Testament Questions of Today*, 108–37. London: SCM, 1969; Philadelphia: Fortress, 1969. [A part of *Exegetische Versuche und Besinnungen* 2, 2nd ed. Göttingen: Vandenhoeck & Ruprecht, 1965.]

———. *Perspectives on Paul.* London: SCM, 1971; Philadelphia: Fortress, 1971. [*Paulinische Perspectiven.* Tübingen: J. C. B. Mohr, 1969.]

———. "The Problem of the Historical Jesus." In *Essays on New Testament Themes*, 15–47. London: SCM, 1964; Philadelphia: Fortress, 1982. [A part of *Exegetische Versuche und Besinnungen* 1. 2nd ed. Göttingen: Vandenhoeck & Ruprecht, 1960.]

Kee, Howard Clark. *Community of the New Age: Studies in Mark's Gospel.* Philadelphia: Westminster, 1977.

———. "The Function of Scriptural Quotations and Allusions in Mark 11–16." In *Jesus und Paulus: Festschrift für Werner Georg Kümmel zum 70. Geburtstag*, edited by E. Earle Ellis and Erich Grasser, 165–88. Göttingen: Vandenhoeck & Ruprecht, 1975.

Kelly, J. N. D. *Early Christian Doctrines.* London: Adam & Charles Black, 1958.

Kenny, Anthony. *Wittgenstein.* Cambridge: Harvard University Press, 1973.

Kierkegaard, Søren. *Concluding Unscientific Postscript to the Philosophical Fragments. By Johannes Climacus.* Princeton: Princeton University Press, 1941. [*Afsluttende unvidenskabelig efterskrift til de philosophiske smuler.* Copenhagen: C. A. Reitzel, 1846.]

———. "'The Individual': Two 'Notes' Concerning My Work as an Author." Appended to *The Point of View for my Work as an Author.* New York: Harper & Row, 1962. [*Synspunktet for min Forfatter-Virksomhed.* In *Samlede Vaerker* 18:79–169. Copenhagen: Gyldendal, 1962–1964.]

Koch, Klaus. *The Rediscovery of Apocalyptic.* Naperville: Alec R. Allenson, n.d. [*Ratlos vor der Apokalyptik.* Gütersloh: Gerd Mohn, 1970.]

Köhler, Ludwig Hugo. *Old Testament Theology.* London: Lutterworth, 1957. [*Theologie des Alten Testaments.* Tübingen: J. C. B. Mohr, 1935.]

Küng, Hans. *Justification: The Doctrine of Karl Barth and a Catholic Reflection.* New York: Nelson, 1964. [*Rechtfertigung: Die Lehre Karl Barths und eine katholische Besinnung.* Einsiedeln: Johannes, 1957.]

Lakatos, Imre. *The Methodology of Scientific Research Programmes*. Cambridge: Cambridge University Press, 1978.
Lampe, G. W. H. "The Reasonableness of Typology." In *Essays on Typology*, by G. W. H. Lampe and K. J. Woollcombe, 9–38. Naperville: Alec R. Allenson, 1957.
———. "Typological Exegesis." *Theology* 56 (1953): 201–8.
Lampe, G. W. H. and K. J. Woollcombe. *Essays on Typology*. Naperville: Alec R. Allenson, 1957.
Laud, William. *A Sermon Preached before His Maiesty, on Tvesday the Nineteenth of Iune, at Wansted. Anno Dom. 1621*. London: Matthew Lownes, 1621. Reprinted in *Works*, 1:1–29. Oxford: John Henry Parker, 1847.
Lenin, V.I. *Philosophical Notebooks*. In *Collected Words*, 38. Moscow, 1961.
Levinas, Emmanuel. *Alterity and Transcendence*. New York: Columbia University Press, 1999. [*Alterité et Transcendence*. St Clement: Fata Morgana, 1995.]
———. "Beyond Dialogue." In *Alterity and Transcendence*, 79–89. New York: Columbia University Press, 1999.
———. *Ethics and Infinity*. Pittsburgh: Duquesne University Press, 1985.
———. "Martin Buber's Thought and Contemporary Judaism." In *Outside the Subject*, 4–19. Stanford: Stanford University Press, 1987. [*Hors Sujet*. St Clement: Fata Morgana, 1987.]
———. "Meaning and Sense." In *Basic Philosophical Writings*, edited by Adriaan T. Peperzak et al., 34–64. Bloomington: Indiana University Press, 1996. ["La signification et le sens." *Revue de Métaphysique et de Morale* 69 (1964): 125–56.]
———. *Otherwise than Being*. Pittsburgh: Duquesne University Press, 1998. [*Autrement qu'être*. Dordrecht: Nijhoff, 1974.]
———. "Peace and Proximity." In *Basic Philosophical Writings*, edited by Adriaan T. Peperzak et al., 161–69. Bloomington: Indiana University Press, 1996. ["Paix et proximité." In *Les Cahiers de la Nuit Surveillée 3: Emmanuel Levinas*, edited by J. Rolland, 339–46. Lagrasse: Verdier, 1984.]
———. "The Proximity of the Other." In *Alterity and Transcendence*, 97–109. New York: Columbia University Press, 1999.
———. *Totality and Infinity*. Pittsburgh: Duquesne University Press, 1961. [*Totalité et infini: Essai sur l'exteriorité*. The Hague: Martinus Nijhoff, 1961.]
———. "Violence of the Face." In *Alterity and Transcendence*, 169–82. New York: Columbia University Press, 1999.
Lindars, Barnabas. *New Testament Apologetic: The Doctrinal Significance of the Old Testament Quotations*. London: SCM, 1961.
Lindbeck, George A. *The Nature of Doctrine: Religion and Theology in a Postliberal Age*. Philadelphia: Westminster, 1974.
Loisy, Alfred. *The Gospel and the Church*. London: Isbister, 1903; reprinted Philadelphia: Fortress, 1976. [*L'Évangile et l'église*. Paris: Picard, 1902.]
Luther, Martin. *The Babylonian Captivity of the Church. Luther's Works* 36:11–126. St. Louis: Concordia, Philadelphia: Muhlenberg, 1958–1967. [*De captivitate Babylonica ecclesiae*. 1520. In *WA* 6.]
———. "Concerning the Ministry." In *Luther's Works*, 40. St. Louis: Concordia, Philadelphia: Muhlenberg, 1958–1967. ["De instituendis ministris ecclesiae, ad clarissimum senatum Pragensem Bohemiae." In *WA* 12.]
———. *D. Martin Luthers Werke. Kritische Gesammtausgabe*. (*WA*). Weimar: Hermann Bohlau, 1883–1948.

———. *Lectures on Romans*. Philadelphia: Westminster, 1961. Lecture notes for a three semester course at Wittenberg on Romans in 1515–1516. [Provisionally published in 1908 and critically edited by Johannes Ficker as *Römerbriefvorlesung*. WA 56, 1938.]

———. Letter to Georg Spalatin, July 9, 1520. No. 309. *WA Briefe* 2.

———. Letter to Jodocus Trutvetter, May 9, 1518. No. 74. *WA Briefe* 1.

———. Letter to Johann Lang, May 18, 1517. No. 41. *WA Briefe* 1.

———. "The Papacy in Rome: Against the Most Celebrated Romanist in Leipzig." In *Luther's Works*, 39. St. Louis: Concordia, Philadelphia: Muhlenberg, 1958–1967. ["Von dem Bapstum zu Rome widder den hochberumpten Romanisten zu Leiptzck." In *WA* 6.]

———. Preface to the 1518 edition of anonymous *Theologia Deutsch*. In *WA* 1.

MacIntyre, Alasdair. *After Virtue: A Study in Moral Theory*. London: Gerald Duckworth, 1981; Notre Dame: University of Notre Dame Press, 1981.

———. *Whose Justice? Which Rationality?* Notre Dame: University of Notre Dame Press, 1988.

Marx, Karl. *A Contribution to the Critique of Political Economy*, Introduction. Chicago: Kerr, 1904.

———. *The Economic and Philosophic Manuscripts of 1844*. New York: International, 1964. [From *Karl Marx: Friedrich Engels: Historisch-kritische Gesamtausgabe*, part 1, vol. 3. Berlin, 1932.]

———. *The German Ideology*. Part 1 in *The Marx-Engels Reader*, edited by Robert C. Tucker, 110–64. New York: W. W. Norton, 1972. [*Die Deutsche Ideologie*. Berlin: Dietz, 1969.]

———. "Theses on Feuerbach." In *Karl Marx: Frederick Engels: Collected Works*, 5:3–5. London: Lawrence & Wishart, 1976. In *The Marx-Engels Reader*, edited by Robert C. Tucker, 108–9. New York: W. W. Norton, 1972. ["Marx über Feuerbach." In *Karl Marx: Friedrich Engels: Historisch-kritische Gesamtausgabe*, part 1, vol. 5, 533–35. Glashütten im Taunus: Detlev Auvermann, 1932.]

Mather, Increase. "A Plain Discourse Concerning every Man's Birth Sin." In *Five Sermons on Several Subjects*, 1–27. Boston: Daniel Henchman, 1719.

McCarthy, Thomas. *The Critical Theory of Jürgen Habermas*. Cambridge: MIT Press, 1978.

McClendon, Jr., James William. *Ethics: Systematic Theology, Volume I*. Nashville: Abingdon, 1986.

Metz, Johannes B. *Faith in History and Society: Toward a Practical Fundamental Theology*. New York: Crossroad, Seabury, 1980. [*Glaube in Geschichte und Gesellschaft: Studien zu einer praktischen Fundamentaltheologie*. Mainz: Grünewald, 1977.]

———. *Theology of the World*. New York: Herder & Herder, 1969. English Chapter V from *The Word in History*, edited by T. Patrick Burke. New York: Sheed & Ward, 1966. [*Zur Theologie der Welt*. Mainz: Matthias-Grünewald; Munich: Chr. Kaiser, 1968.]

Meyer, Ben F. *The Aims of Jesus*. London: SCM, 1979.

Meyers, Carol. "The Roots of Restriction: Women in Early Israel." *BA* 41 (1978): 91–103.

Migne, J. P. *Patrologiae Cursus Completus, Series Graeca*. (*PG*). Paris: Migne, 1857–1866.

Milbank, John. *Theology and Social Theory: Beyond secular reason*. Oxford: Blackwell, 1990.
———. *The Word Made Strange*. Oxford: Blackwell, 1997.
Miranda, Jose. *Marx and the Bible*. Maryknoll: Orbis, 1974. [*Marx y la biblia: Crítica a la filosofía de la opresión*. Salamanca: Sigueme, 1971.]
*The Mishnah*. Translated by Herbert Danby. Oxford: Clarendon, 1933.
Möhler, Johann Adam. *Symbolism: Exposition of the Doctrinal Differences Between Catholics and Protestants as Evidenced by Their Symbolical Writings*. 5th ed. New York: Crossroad, 1997. [*Symbolik, oder Darstellung der dogmatischen Gegensätze der Katholiken und Protestanten nach ihren öffentlichen Bekenntnissschriften*. 5th ed. Mainz: Florian Kupferberg; Vienna: Karl Gerold, 1838. 1st ed. 1832.]
———. *Unity in the Church or the Principle of Catholicism Presented in the Spirit of the Church Fathers of the First Three Centuries*. Washington: Catholic University of America Press, 1996. [*Die Einheit in der Kirche oder das prinzip des Katholizismus dargestellt im Geist der Kirchenväter der drei ersten Jahrhunderte*. Köln: Jakob Hegner, 1957.]
Moltmann, Jürgen. *The Crucified God: The Cross of Christ as the Foundation and Criticism of Christian Theology*. London: SCM, l974. [*Der gekreuzigte Gott: das Kreuz Cristi als Grund und Kritik christlicher Theologie*. 2nd ed. Munich: Chr. Kaiser, 1973. 1st ed. 1972.]
———. *Theology of Hope: On the Ground and the Implications of a Christian Eschatology*. New York: Harper & Row, 1967. [*Theologie der Hoffnung*. 5th ed. Munich: Chr. Kaiser, 1965. 1st ed. 1964.]
Müller, Werner E. *Die Vorstellung vom Rest im Alten Testament*. Edited by Horst Dietrich Preuss. Neukirchen-Vluyn: Neukirchener Verlag, 1973. Edited from a private printing of his inaugural dissertation at Leipzig, 1939.
Muñoz, Ronaldo. "The Historical Vocation of the Church." In *Frontiers of Theology in Latin America*, 151–62. Maryknoll: Orbis, 1979. [*La nuova frontiera della teologia in America Latina*. Brescia: Queriniana, 1975.]
Newman, John Henry. *An Essay on the Development of Christian Doctrine*. 1st ed. London: J. Toovey, 1845. Harmondsworth: Pelican, 1974. "New edition." London: Longmans, Green, 1885.
*Novum Testamentum Graece*. 26th ed. Edited by Eberhard Nestle et al. Stuttgart: Deutsche Bibelstiftung, 1979.
Nygren, Anders. *Agape and Eros*. London: SPCK, 1932–1953. [*Den kristna kärlekstanken genom tiderna. Eros och Agape*. Stockholm: Svenska Kyrkans Diakonistyrelses Bokförlag, 1930–1936.]
Ollman, Bertell. *Alienation: Marx's Conception of Man in Capitalist Society*. 2nd ed. Cambridge: Cambridge University Press, 1976.
Origen. *Commentaria in epistolam ad Romanos*. In *FOTC* 103–4.
———. *Commentaria in Ioannem*. In *FOTC* 80.
———. *Commentaria in Matthaeum*. In *Ante-Nicene Fathers* 9. New York: Scribner, 1899.
———. *In Genesim homiliae*. In *Homilies on Genesis and Exodus*. Washington: Catholic University of America Press, 1982.
———. *Homiliae in Exodus*. In *Homilies on Genesis and Exodus*. Washington: Catholic University of America Press, 1982.

———. *Homilia in Numeros. Homilies on Numbers.* Downers Grove, Ill.: IVP Academic, 2009.
———. *Homilia prima in Psalmum.* In *PG* 12.
———. *On First Principles.* [*De principiis.*] London: SPCK, 1936; reprint, Gloucester: Peter Smith, 1973.
Ovid. *Ovid's Fasti.* Translated by Sir James George Frazer. Cambridge: Harvard University Press; London: William Heinemann, 1951.
Pannenberg, Wolfhart. "Redemptive Event and History." In *Basic Questions in Theology: Collected Essays*, 3 vols. 1:15–80. Philadelphia: Fortress, 1970-1973. In shortened form in *Essays on Old Testament Hermeneutics*, edited by Claus Westermann, 2nd ed., 314-35. Richmond: John Knox, 1964. [*Probleme Alttestamentlicher Hermeneutik.* Munich: Chr. Kaiser, 1960.]
Peirce, Charles Sanders. *The Collected Papers of Charles Sanders Peirce.* Cambridge: Harvard University Press, 1931-1958.
Perkins, William. *A Discourse of Conscience Wherein Is Set Down The nature, properties, and differences thereof: as also the way to get and keep good Conscience.* Cambridge: J. Legate, 1596. Reprinted in *William Perkins, 1558-1602, English Puritanist: His Pioneer Works on Casuistry.* Nieuwkoop: B. de Graaf, 1966.
Perrin, Norman. *Rediscovering the Teaching of Jesus.* New York: Harper & Row, 1967.
Pfeiffer, Robert H. *Introduction to the Old Testament.* New York: Harper & Brothers, 1941.
Philo. *De cherubim.* In Philo 2. Loeb Classical Library. Cambridge: Harvard University Press, 1929-1952.
———. *De migratione Abrahae.* In Philo 4. Loeb Classical Library. Cambridge: Harvard University Press, 1929-1952.
———. *Legum Allegoriae.* In Philo 3. Loeb Classical Library. Cambridge: Harvard University Press, 1929-1952.
———. *Quod deterius potiori insidiari soleat.* In Philo 2. Loeb Classical Library. Cambridge: Harvard University Press, 1929-1952.
Plato. *Cratylus.* In *Cratylus, Parmenides, Greater Hippias, Lesser Hippias.* Cambridge: Harvard University Press, 1977.
———. *The Republic.* London: Oxford University Press, 1941.
Powell, Walter and Paul DiMaggio. *The New Institutionalism in Organizational Analysis.* Chicago: University of Chicago Press, 1991.
Rad, Gerhard von. *Old Testament Theology.* Edinburgh: Oliver & Boyd; New York: Harper & Row, 1962-1965. [*Theologie des Alten Testaments.* Munich: Chr. Kaiser, 1957-1960.] [*Theologie de l'Ancien Testament.* 3rd ed. Geneva: Labor et Fides, 1971.]
———. "Typological Interpretation of the Old Testament." In *Essays on Old Testament Hermeneutics*, edited by Claus Westermann, 2nd ed., 17–39. Richmond: John Knox, 1964. [*Probleme Alttestamentlicher Hermeneutik.* Munich: Chr. Kaiser, 1960.]
Rahner, Karl. "Anonymous Christians." In *Theological Investigations*, 6:390-92. London: Darton, Longman & Todd, 1961–. [From *Schriften zur Theologie.* Einsiedeln: Benziger, 1954–.]
———. "Christianity and the Non-Christian Religions." In *Theological Investigations*, 5:115–34. London: Darton, Longman & Todd, 1961–. [From *Schriften zur Theologie.* Einsiedeln: Benziger, 1954–.]

———. "Christology within an Evolutionary View of the World." In *Theological Investigations*, 5:157–92. London: Darton, Longman & Todd, 1961–. [From *Schriften zur Theologie*. Einsiedeln: Benziger, 1954–.]

———. *The Church and the Sacraments*. Freiburg: Herder, 1963. Also in *Inquiries* 189–299. New York: Herder & Herder, 1964. [*Kirche und Sakramente*. Freiburg: Herder, 1960.]

———. "The Development of Dogma." In *Theological Investigations*, 1:39–77. London: Darton, Longman & Todd, 1961–. [*Schriften zur Theologie*. Einsiedeln: Benziger, 1954–.]

———. *Hearer of the Word*. New York: Continuum, 1994. [*Hörer des Wortes. Zur Grundlegung einer Religionsphilosophie*. Munich: Kösel-Pustet, 1941. Based on lectures, Salzburg, 1937.]

———. *Spirit in the World*. New York: Continuum, 1994. [*Geist in Welt*. 2nd ed., edited by Johannes Metz. Munich: Kösel, 1957.]

———. "Theology and Anthropology." In *Theological Investigations*, 9:28–45. London: Darton, Longman & Todd, 1961–. [From *Schriften zur Theologie*. Einsiedeln: Benziger, 1954–.]

———. "The Theology of the Symbol." In *Theological Investigations*, 4:221–52. London: Darton, Longman & Todd, 1961–. [From *Schriften zur Theologie*. Einsiedeln: Benziger, 1954–.]

Rendall, Robert. "Quotation in Scripture as an Index of Wider Reference." *Evangelical Quarterly* 36 (1934): 214–21.

Rendtorff, Rolf. "Hermeneutik des Alten Testaments als Frage nach der Geschichte." *ZThK* 57 (1960): 27–40.

Richardson, Alan. *History, Sacred and Profane*. The Bampton Lectures, 1962. Philadelphia: Westminster, 1964.

———. *An Introduction to the Theology of the New Testament*. London: SCM, 1958.

Robinson, James M. *A New Quest of the Historical Jesus*. London: SCM, 1959.

Rorty, Richard. *Philosophy and the Mirror of Nature*. Princeton: Princeton University Press, 1979.

Rousseau, Jean-Jacques. *The Social Contract*. Harmondsworth: Penguin, 1968. [*Du contrat social ou Principes du droit politique*. Amsterdam: Marc Michel Rey, 1762.]

Sahlin, Harald. "The New Exodus of Salvation according to St. Paul." In *The Root of the Vine: Essays in Biblical Theology*, by Anton Fridrichsen et al., 81–95. New York: Philosophical Library, 1953.

Sanders, E. P. "The Genre of Palestinian Jewish Apocalypses." In *Apocalypticism in the Mediterranean World and the Near East*, edited by David Hellholm, 447–59. Proceedings of the International Colloquium on Apocalypticism, Uppsala, August 12–17, 1979. Tübingen: J. C. B. Mohr, 1983.

———. *Paul and Palestinian Judaism: A Comparison of Patterns of Religion*. London: SCM, 1977; Philadelphia: Fortress, 1977.

Sartre, Jean-Paul. *Existentialism*. New York: Philosophical Library, 1947. [*L'Existentialisme est un humanisme*. Paris: Nagel, 1946.]

Schaff, Philip. *The Nicene and Post-Nicene Fathers*. (*NPNF*). Grand Rapids: Wm. B. Eerdmans, 1971.

Schleiermacher, Friedrich. *The Christian Faith*. Edinburgh: T. & T. Clark, 1928. [*Der christliche Glaube nach den Grundsätzen der evangelischen Kirche im Zusammenhange dargestellt*. 2nd ed. Berlin: G. Reimer, 1830.]

———. *On Religion: Speeches to its Cultured Despisers*. London: K. Paul, Trench, Trubner, 1893; reprint, New York: Harper & Row, 1958. [*Über die Religion: Reden an die Gebildeten unter ihren Verächtern*. Berlin: Johann Friedrich Unger, 1799.]

Schweitzer, Albert. *The Mysticism of Paul the Apostle*. London: Adam & Charles Black, 1931. [*Die Mystik des Apostels Paulus*. Tübingen: J. C. B. Mohr, 1929.]

———. *The Quest of the Historical Jesus: A Critical Study of Its Progress from Reimarus to Wrede*. London: Adam & Charles Black, 1910. [*Von Reimarus zu Wrede: eine Geschichte der Leben-Jesu-Forschung*, 1906. Reprinted in *Gesammelte Werke* 3. Munich: C. H. Beck, 1973.]

Searle, John. "Chomsky's Revolution in Linguistics." *New York Review of Books* (June 29, 1972): 16–24.

———. "A Classification of Illocutionary Acts." In *Minnesota Studies in Philosophy of Science* 6. Minneapolis: University of Minnesota Press, 1975.

———. "Meaning, Communication, and Representation." Typescript of paper delivered at the University of Hamburg (1974) and the American Philosophical Association Western Division meeting (1976).

———. *Speech Acts*. London: Cambridge University Press, 1969.

Segundo, Juan Luis. "Capitalism Versus Socialism: Crux Theologica." *Frontiers of Theology in Latin America*, edited by Rosino Gibellini, 240–59. Maryknoll: Orbis, 1979. [*La nuova frontiera della teologia in America Latina*. Brescia: Queriniana, 1975.]

———. *Liberation of Theology*. Maryknoll: Orbis, 1976. [*Liberación de la teología*. Buenos Aires: Carlos Lohlé, 1975.]

Sellin, Ernst. *Theologie des Alten Testaments*. Leipzig: Quelle & Meyer, 1933.

Sölle, Dorothee. *Political Theology*. Philadelphia: Fortress, 1974. [*Politische Theologie, Auseinandersetzung mit Rudolf Bultmann*. Stuttgart: Kreuz, 1971.]

———. "'Thou Shalt Have No Other Jeans Before Me' (Levi's Advertizement, Early Seventies): The Need for Liberation in a Consumerist Society." In *The Challenge of Liberation Theology: A First World Response*, edited by Brian Mahan and L. Dale Richesin, 4–16. Maryknoll: Orbis, 1981.

Stendahl, Krister. "The Apostle Paul and the Introspective Conscience of the West." *HTR* 56 (1963): 199–215. Reprinted in *Ecumenical Dialogue at Harvard*, edited by Samuel H. Miller and G. Ernest Wright. Cambridge: Harvard University Press, 1964.

Steudel, Johann Christian Friedrich. *Vorlesungen über die Theologie des Alten Testaments*. Edited by G. F. Oehler. Berlin: G. A. Reimer, 1840.

Stone, M. "Lists of Revealed Things in the Apocalyptic Literature." In *Magnalia Dei*, edited by Frank M. Cross et al., 414–52. Garden City: Doubleday, 1976.

Sundberg, Albert C., Jr. "On Testimonies." *Novum Testamentum* 3 (1959): 268–81.

The Talmud. *The Babilonian Talmud*. 34 vols. Edited by Isodore Epstein. London: Soncino, 1935–1948.

Terrien, Samuel. "Amos and Wisdom." In *Israel's Prophetic Heritage: Essays in Honor of James Muilenburg*, edited by Bernhard W. Anderson and Walter Harrelson, 108–15. New York: Harper & Brothers, 1962. Reprinted in *Studies in Ancient Israelite Wisdom*, edited by James L. Crenshaw, 448–55. New York: Ktav, 1976.

———. *The Elusive Presence: Toward a New Biblical Theology*. San Francisco: Harper & Row, 1978.

Tertullian. *Adversus Marcionem*. In *The Ante-Nicene Fathers* 3:271–474. Buffalo: Christian Literature, 1885.

Theodore of Mopsuestia. *Commentarius in Ionam prophetam*. In *FOTC* 108. Washington: Catholic University of America Press, 2004.

———. *Commentarius in Michaem prophetam*. In *FOTC* 108. Washington: Catholic University of America Press, 2004.

———. *In Amosum prophetam commentarius*. In *FOTC* 108. Washington: Catholic University of America Press, 2004.

Theodoret. *In loca dificilia scripturae sacrae quaestiones in Numeros*. In *The Questions On The Octateuch* 2. Washington: Catholic University of America Press, 2007.

Thomas Aquinas. *Summa Theologiae*. Blackfriars edition. 61 vols. New York and London: McGraw-Hill and Eyre & Spottiswoode, 1964–1980.

Tillich, Paul. *Biblical Religion and the Search for Ultimate Reality*. Chicago: University of Chicago Press, 1955.

———. *Dynamics of Faith*. New York: Harper & Row, 1957.

———. *Systematic Theology*. Chicago: University of Chicago Press, 1951–63.

*The Tosephta*. Translated by Jacob Neusner. New York: Ktav, 1981.

Trible, Phyllis. "Depatriarchalizing in Biblical Interpretation." *JAAR* 41 (1973): 30–48.

Troeltsch, Ernst. *Der Historismus und seine Probleme I: Das logische Problem der Geschichtsphilosophie*. Gesammelte Schriften, vol. 3. Tübingen: J. C. B. Mohr, 1922.

———. "The Dogmatics of the 'Religionsgeschichtliche Schule.'" *AJT* 17 (1913): 1–21.

Tyconius. *Tyconius: The Book of Rules*. Translation by William S. Babcock. Atlanta: Scholars, 1989

Vincent of Lérins. *Commonitorium Primum*. In *FOTC* 7. New York: Catholic University of America Press, 1949.

Voegelin, Eric. "History and Gnosis." In *The Old Testament and Christian Faith: A Theological Discussion*, edited by Bernhard W. Anderson, 64–89. New York: Harper & Row, 1963.

———. *Science, Politics, and Gnosticism*. Chicago: Henry Regnery, 1968.

Weber, Max. *The Protestant Ethic and the Spirit of Capitalism*. New York: Scribner's, 1958. *Die protestantische Ethik und der Geist des Kapitalismus*. Archiv für Sozialwissenschaft und Sozialpolitik, 20–21 (1904–1905). Revised in *Gesammelte Aufsätze zur Wissenschaftslehre* I. Tübingen: J. C. B. Mohr, 1920.

———. "R. Stammlers 'Überwindung' der materialistischen Geschichtsauffassung." In *Gesammelte Aufsätze zur Wissenschaftslehre*. Tübingen: J. C. B. Mohr, 1922.

Weiss, Johannes. *Jesus' Proclamation of the Kingdom of God*. Philadelphia: Fortress, 1971. [*Die Predigt Jesu vom Reiche Gottes*. Göttingen: Vandenhoeck & Ruprecht, 1892.]

Westcott, Brooke Foss. *The Epistle to the Hebrews*. London: Macmillan, 1889.

Westermann, Claus. *Elements of Old Testament Theology*. Atlanta: John Knox, 1982. [*Theologie des Alten Testaments in Grundzügen*. Göttingen: Vandenhoeck & Ruprecht, 1978.]

Wieman, Henry N. "Intellectual Autobiography." In *The Empirical Theology of Henry Nelson Wieman*, edited by Robert W. Bretall, 1–18. Carbondale: Southern Illinois University Press, 1963.

———. "Reply to Bernhardt." In *The Empirical Theology of Henry Nelson Wieman*, edited by Robert W. Bretall, 209–10. Carbondale: Southern Illinois University Press, 1963.

———. "Reply to Smith." In *The Empirical Theology of Henry Nelson Wieman*, edited by Robert W. Bretall, 257–64. Carbondale: Southern Illinois University Press, 1963.

———. "Reply to Weigel." In *The Empirical Theology of Henry Nelson Wieman*, edited by Robert W. Bretall, 354–77. Carbondale: Southern Illinois University Press, 1963.

———. *The Source of Human Good*. Carbondale: Southern Illinois University Press, 1946.

Wilckens, Ulrich. "The Understanding of Revelation within the History of Primitive Christianity." In *Revelation as History*, edited by Wolfhart Pannenberg, 55–121. New York: Macmillan, 1968. [*Offenbarung als Geschichte*. Göttingen: Vandenhoeck & Ruprecht, 1961.]

Willard, Samuel. *The Duty of a People that have Renewed their Covenant with God. Opened and Urged in a Sermon Preached to the second Church in Boston in New-England, March 17, 1679/80, after that church had explicitly and most solemnly renewed the Ingagement of themselves to God, and one to another*. Boston: John Foster, 1680.

———. *A Sermon Preached upon Ezek 22.30,31. Occasioned by the Death of the much honoured John Leveret Esq; Governour of the Colony of the Mattachusets*. N-E. Boston: John Foster, 1679.

Winch, Peter. *Ethics and Action*. London: Routledge and Kegan Paul, 1972.

———. *The Idea of a Social Science and its Relation to Philosophy*. New York: Humanities, 1958.

Winthrop, John. "A Modell of Christian Charity," aboard the Arbella, 1630. In *Winthrop Papers*, 2.295. Boston: Massachusetts Historical Society, 1865.

Wittgenstein, Ludwig. *Philosophische untersuchungen; Philosophical Investigations*. Translated by G. E. M. Anscombe. New York: Macmillan, 1953.

Wolff, Hans Walter. "The Understanding of History in the O. T. Prophets." In *Essays on Old Testament Hermeneutics*, edited by Claus Westermann, 2nd ed., 336–55. Richmond: John Knox, 1964. [*Probleme Alttestamentlicher Hermeneutik*. Munich: Chr. Kaiser, 1960.]

Woollcombe, K. J. "The Biblical Origins and Patristic Development of Typology." In *Essays on Typology*, 39–75. By G. W. H. Lampe and K. J. Woollcombe. Naperville: Alec R. Allenson, 1957.

Wrede, William. *Paul*. Boston: American Unitarian Association, 1908; reprint, Lexington: American Theological Library Association, 1962. [*Paulus*. Halle: Gebauer-Schwetschke, 1904.]

Wright, G. Ernest. *God Who Acts: Biblical Theology as Recital*. London: SCM, 1952.

Yoder, John Howard. *The Original Revolution*. Scottsdale: Herald, 1977

———. *The Politics of Jesus*. Grand Rapids: Eerdmans, 1972.

———. *The Priestly Kingdom: Social Ethics as Gospel*. Notre Dame: Notre Dame University Press, 1984.

Zimmerli, Walther. *The Old Testament and the World*. Atlanta: John Knox, 1976. [*Die Weltlichkeit des Alten Testaments*. Göttingen: Vandenhoeck & Ruprecht, 1971.]

———. "Promise and Fulfillment." In *Essays on Old Testament Hermeneutics*, edited by Claus Westermann, 2nd ed., 89–122. Richmond: John Knox, 1964. [*Probleme Alttestamentlicher Hermeneutik*. Munich: Chr. Kaiser, 1960.]

www.ingramcontent.com/pod-product-compliance
Lightning Source LLC
Chambersburg PA
CBHW071228290426
44108CB00013B/1327